A GIANT COW-TIPPING BY SAVAGES

A GIANT

THE BOOM, BUST, AND BOOM CULTURE OF M&A

COW-TIPPING
BY SAVAGES

JOHN WEIR CLOSE

palgrave
macmillan

A GIANT COW-TIPPING BY SAVAGES
Copyright © John Weir Close, 2013.
All rights reserved.

First published in 2013 by PALGRAVE MACMILLAN® in the United
States—a division of St. Martin's Press LLC, 175 Fifth Avenue, New York, NY
10010.

Where this book is distributed in the UK, Europe and the rest of the world,
this is by Palgrave Macmillan, a division of Macmillan Publishers Limited,
registered in England, company number 785998, of Houndmills, Basingstoke,
Hampshire RG21 6XS.

Palgrave Macmillan is the global academic imprint of the above companies and
has companies and representatives throughout the world.

Palgrave® and Macmillan® are registered trademarks in the United States,
the United Kingdom, Europe and other countries.

ISBN 978–0–230–34181–4

Library of Congress Cataloging-in-Publication Data

Close, John Weir.
  A giant cow-tipping by savages : the boom, bust, and boom culture of M&A
/ John Weir Close.
      pages   cm
   ISBN 978–0–230–34181–4 (alk. paper)
   1. Consolidation and merger of corporations—United States—History. 2.
Big business—United States—History. I. Title.
HG4028.M4C56   2013
338.8'30973—dc23

                                                                    2013014658

A catalogue record of the book is available from the British Library.

Design by Letra Libre, Inc.

First edition: October 2013

10 9 8 7 6 5 4 3 2 1

Printed in the United States of America.

To my father,
Raymond Hooper Close,
a river to his people

CONTENTS

Eight pages of photographs appear between pages 152 and 153.

CHAPTER ONE
THE TEMPLE OF DENDUR

All of First Boston knows. His lawyers at Cravath, Swaine & Moore are well aware of it. New York society, which he thought he was impressing, is in on the secret. So is his actual audience. But Robert Campeau has no clue. He is the mergers and acquisitions (M&A) raider writ large: driven, volatile, charming, seductive, grounded in poverty, a collector of assets and houses, companion to beautiful women, desperate for respect. "When I was growing up, I thought every house with indoor plumbing was a palace, and I hated the people who lived there," he once said.[1] On this night, he has immersed himself among those he has envied and despised for so long.

A vast assemblage has gathered at the Temple of Dendur, a gift from the government of Egypt in the 1960s in thanks for the $16 million the United States contributed to the rescue of Nubian antiquities from the lake created by the Aswan High Dam. Thomas Hoving, then director of the Metropolitan Museum of New York, won what became known as the Dendur Derby among American cities by offering to build the temple a glass palace all its own. There it now sits on Fifth Avenue, as forlorn as a reluctant takeover target, a favorite place for New York parties for decades. At the Campeau coming-out party in the 1980s, the guest of honor oddly replicates the temple's own deracination and godlessness.

On Halloween 1986, a few months earlier, Bob had pulled off the unlikeliest of deals and taken over Allied Stores, which included Brooks Brothers, Ann Taylor, Jordan Marsh, Garfinckel's, and Bonwit Teller, for $3.6 billion in borrowed money. Later, on April Fool's Day 1988, he would conquer Federated for another $6.5 billion in loaned cash, mostly because he wanted to be king of Bloomingdale's. Knowing no one on Wall Street, he was "a guy over at the Waldorf Hotel who thinks he's going to buy Allied

Stores,"[2] as Joe Perella put it to his First Boston colleague Mike Rothfeld at the start of the whole fiasco. Eighteen months and over $10 billion later, this real estate developer, who made his first fortune on postwar tract houses that were once called an excuse for a nuclear bombardment, with no experience in retail whatsoever, owned virtually every department store of note across the United States except Macy's. He learned fast. He had arrived in New York just as Ron Perelman was conquering Revlon and had watched as an unknown from a perennially overlooked city, dismissed as little more than a traveling salesman with a rich wife, took over one of the greatest houses of glamour in the world. If a Jew from Philadelphia could do it, why not a French Canadian from the provinces who had pulled himself up from nothing, stiff-armed by English Canada but now feeling wholly at home in New York?

The Anglo moguls of Toronto looked on Campeau (pronounced: Compoh) with contempt, and he built a massive tower, Scotia Plaza, in the heart of Toronto that functioned as his own middle finger to the establishment. Resentful, driven to prove himself, eager for adulation, he could also win bankers, employees, and women to his side. He had two families and two sets of children, each long unknown to the other, with the strain of such a double life, if not the truth, all too obvious for decades. He would alternate between states of depression that resembled mammalian hibernation and periods of febrile activity inflamed by a sense of his own invincibility and perceived genius. Sam Butler of Cravath, who gave Campeau his first taste of acceptance in Manhattan when Sam agreed to take him on as a client, puts it simply: "Campeau was a nut case."[3]

Everything about Bob Campeau was more extreme, and disturbed, than it appeared. He was a great chest thumper and screamer, but layered, with prejudices and bitterness; he was a frightened man, prone to sudden and rather cringe-making admissions of doubt. He was vain, but it was only a symptom of his fear of aging and death. He should have been in treatment, but instead, during his many absences at the climaxes of his deals, he sought the help of cosmeticians, nutritionists, tanning salons, and plastic surgeons, as well as "a toupee and then hair transplants; capped teeth; face lifts . . . Rolfing rituals; health-food diets; the daily swim in his specially purified pool; all of which produced a vigorous and dashing figure, slim and deeply tanned, with bright, prominent uppers and a healthy crop of medically harvested gray hair."[4] He called it all "physical rejuvenation." Bob was reportedly also enamored of a rather unusual anti-aging treatment: injections of fetal lamb brain cells. For this he got a secret nickname. Rob Kindler, then a partner at Cravath who came to know his client well, rechristened him "*B-a-a-a-b* Campeau."[5]

At the Temple of Dendur, B-a-a-a-b is feeling expansive after his triumph over Allied, this foreigner born to poverty and ostracism, still an alien in both the United States and his own land. He feels he is at last getting the respect he has worked so inexhaustibly to attract. But he is fooling no one but himself. He stands at the podium and, at first, lectures the audience "unintelligibly," according to one guest, about currency rates, and then in orotund phrases of oleaginous sycophancy, he tells the black-tied and ball-gowned ensemble in front of him how gratified he is to be among them in the heart of Manhattan, what a feeling it is to be a Canadian taking over US companies instead of watching it happen to Canadian targets, how much it has meant to him and his wife to be so welcome in the greatest city in North America, how he plans to make New York his home, how he feels that he is among friends.

But the truth, as always for Bob, is impenetrably camouflaged. Aside from the cardinal of Toronto and Pierre Trudeau, the former prime minister of Canada, what Bob sees is New York's aristocracy at his feet. But many of those applauding are not even from New York, nor are most of them particularly elite, although all of them are rich. History is blessed to have the recollections of one of Bob's advisers, the irrepressible Kim Fennebresque, then of First Boston, to pull back the curtain. "Basically, it was every teenager's worst dream about their party," says Fennebresque. "No one wanted to come. We got reject after reject." Something had to be done. There was a big place to fill, what Fennebresque calls "the artistic equivalent of the Astrodome which could hold hundreds and hundreds and hundreds of [Campeau's] newfound fans," and a big ego to satisfy. Bruce Wasserstein, the rising M&A sorcerer at First Boston, solved the crisis. He simply ordered his colleagues from New York and regional offices such as Dallas and Houston to come to the temple. That was an invitation no one could refuse. "It was either that," says Fennebresque, "or call Central Casting for people who looked like investment bankers to fill up the room."[6]

That night in Manhattan, Robert Campeau was euphoric. Yet in a matter of months, he would lead no fewer than 250 formerly profitable and iconic department stores in a death march to the abattoir of bankruptcy. Thousands of people would lose their jobs, and millions of dollars would remain forever unpaid to a stunning list of financial houses around the globe. With the disaster still in the future and his history of mental breakdowns, secret wives, and hidden children still relatively unknown, dressed in his immaculate dinner jacket, beaming from the podium in sublime ignorance at his new best friends, he appeared to have come such a long way. And, in his own way, he had.

So, too, had M&A itself.

CHAPTER TWO
WASPS, JEWS, AND M&A

I t was an odd coincidence that Bob Campeau got his first job at International Nickel Company, the mining giant that launched the modern takeover era. He was in the eighth grade, an urchin with a single mother and seven siblings in the blighted town of Sudbury, Ontario. He swept floors for 50 cents an hour. Later, he graduated to truck mechanic, helping to maintain the fleet that carried the asteroid-sized blocks of ore from the steam-shoveled pits to the crushing mill and finally to the smelter. It was a life of noise, of 300 polluted lakes in a blasted lunar landscape surrounded by blackened hills, inhabited by a poisoned, downtrodden people.

Contemporary mergers and acquisitions (M&A) is often said to have sprung forth in 1974, when Morgan Stanley became the first established financial house to represent a hostile bidder, International Nickel, in its successful takeover of Philadelphia's old-line ESB Inc. There was a stunned silence, followed by a collective lupine grin, as Morgan Stanley's Robert Greenhill and his team hauled in a cool $14 million from that one deal. Greenhill had passed over his bank's longtime counsel at Davis, Polk & Wardwell in favor of Joe Flom at Skadden, Arps, Slate, Meagher & Flom. "I hired Joe," Greenhill said, "because I wanted to build an M&A business here, and I knew he could help me do it."[1] A fever began to spread with the realization that corporations, many of which were conglomerates with abnormally low stock prices, were possessed of virtually undefended riches. If they could be taken over, they could then be broken up, their various divisions sold separately for far more than the sum of all the parts, or subsumed by a rival on the hunt for more market share, more assets, and fewer competitors.

M&A has a deceptively mundane definition. It means taking control of a company, with or without the consent of the executives running it. Since it is expensive to build a business from nothing, it is often seen as more profitable to take over what has already been built by others. In one stroke, you expand your business and eliminate a competitor. If you're purely an investor, you can keep the company or sell it off for profit. To gain control of a corporation in the modern era, you either offer to buy the stock from the existing shareholders or ask them to vote their shares in favor of your nominees for the board of directors, who, if elected, turn over the company to you. That's basically it. It sounds simple, and it is, but variations proliferate as fast as the human mind can invent them, and M&A has grown rampantly in power and complexity. It has revolutionized corporate Earth and enriched the members of the guild as perhaps none of them ever imagined.

Fights for control of corporations are not new. In fact, in earlier times, they could come close to actual war—for example, the nineteenth-century fight between Cornelius Vanderbilt and the Erie Gang (also known as Jay Gould, Daniel Drew, and James Fisk) for control of the New York & Erie Railroad. This takeover three years after the Civil War, as Professor Steven M. Davidoff writes in his *Gods at War,* roiled the country with the raising of rival militias, the secret escapes across rivers, as well as bribed police and corrupt lawmakers.[2] At one point the target was even abruptly reincorporated as a New Jersey company, to the shocked horror of New Yorkers who were forced to see their beloved railroad metamorphose into "a denizen of the kingdom of Camden and Amboy," as Charles Francis Adams Jr. put it in his classic contemporaneous account, published under the title *Chapters of Erie* with his brother Henry's essay on the New York gold conspiracy. This early takeover is the story of "a knot of adventurers, men of broken fortune, without character and without fortune who come to control an essential artery of commerce," Charles Adams writes, that touches "very nearly the foundations of common truth and honesty without which that healthy public opinion cannot exist which is the life's breath of our whole political system."[3] Words that hold true today.

The Erie Gang had long been busily plundering the railroad and stealing its profits until the company was anorexic and no longer strong enough to pay its debts. Vanderbilt wanted it badly. If he could get his hands on it, his rails would run from the center of Manhattan to the Erie Canal and ensure him virtually complete control of all rail traffic in and out of New York City. In 1867, Vanderbilt tried to gain control of a majority of the stock. The Erie Gang quickly issued bonds convertible into stock to water down Vanderbilt's holdings while soaking up his funds as he bought their fake stock with alacrity. When Vanderbilt realized he was being duped, he had one of his pet judges issue an injunction banning the threesome from continuing their chicanery. They responded with their own judge, who issued an injunction banning Vanderbilt's machinations. The commodore then had arrest warrants issued for the Erie Gang. The gang's allies fled.

"[A]stonished police saw a throng of panic-striken railway directors—looking more like a frightened gang of thieves, disturbed in the division of their plunder—than like the wealthy representatives of a great corporation—rush headlong from the doors of the Erie office, and dash off in the direction of the Jersey ferry," Charles Francis Adams writes. Other members of the Erie Gang later crossed "in open boats concealed by the darkness and a March fog." One member of the board "bore away with him in a hackney-coach bales containing six millions of dollars in greenbacks." They took a total of fully $7 million of Erie's money.[4] Vanderbilt dispatched an armed posse to attack the Erie Gang, whose own henchmen fought back, repelling the advance. Cannons were installed on the ramparts of Erie's redoubt in New Jersey. The gang then bought the votes of legislators in Albany to side with them and approve their moves. Vanderbilt, uncharacteristically, backed down and left them to it, nursing the loss of a fortune said to be as much as $1 million.[5]

Modern M&A has not been driven by Scottish immigrants in Pittsburgh or French Huguenots in the Hudson Valley capturing entire swaths of the nation's resources in the absence of any government regulation whatsoever. In the late twentieth century, it was driven by two Jews with a simultaneous epiphany about how to take advantage of new government regulation, how to turn the rules into an instruction manual for transforming the buying and selling of companies into a profession in itself. Rather than seek to buy, sell, or keep anything themselves, they became the Sherpas, interpreting regulatory maps and making up new law as they went along.

Jews and all others not of the white Anglo-Saxon Protestant (WASP) ascendancy were at the time excluded from any position of real power at the bar, on the bench, at banks, and in boardrooms. America was still an agglomeration of ghettos: Italians knew Italians, Jews knew Jews, Poles knew Poles, Irish knew Irish, WASPs barely knew any of them existed at all, and the Cabots spoke only to God. "When I came to New York in the seventies, the WASP aristocracy still reigned," recalls former Skadden partner Stu Shapiro. "You didn't see an Asian face above Canal Street. You didn't see a black face in a law firm unless it was the mailroom. You certainly didn't see a Hispanic face. Swarthy Italians and Jews? They were not people you dealt with."[6]

Yet again, as happened so often in their history, the Jews somehow found their own methods to carry them past such barriers. They became expert in taking over companies against the will of their existing executives. The white-shoe law firms and elite investment banks found this simultaneously distasteful and tantalizing as medieval burghers viewed the lending of money at interest. Both groups were barred from joining in one of the most profitable enterprises of their day, the former by the establishment's social codes of behavior and the latter by an ecclesiastical ban on the practice of usury. Again, the Jews found themselves in control of a monopoly that perpetuated their own stereotype, that of the omnipotent, conniving Machiavellian with hands sullied by the unsavory. But the business of takeovers paid the rent. And then some.

Until the cusp of the 1980s, Joe Flom and his archrival Marty Lipton were largely unknown to the country. Then in 1976, Steve Brill, a young writer fresh out of Yale Law School, wrote an article for *New York* magazine about "two tough lawyers in the tender offer game," as the headline announced. "It was absolutely the first time that Joe and Marty were written about," Steve says. "I showed two lawyers whom no one had ever heard of and predicted that they would have two of the most successful law firms of all time. All of which turned out to be true."[7] Here is the first information the public ever read about the Lipton and Flom phenomenon:

> At eight o'clock Tuesday morning, November 18, of last year [1975], a black limousine rolled down Fifth Avenue. . . . So squat that he looked lost in the limousine's back seat, the 52-year-old [Joseph] Flom wore scuffed shoes, a dull tie on a dark-colored shirt, and a rumpled suit. He was everything it takes to be the opposite of flamboyant. Still, that morning he was directing a major corporate war. Within eight days, his client, Colt Industries, would successfully fight and take over Garlock Inc., a $151-million gasket-maker.
>
> On Park Avenue the same morning, another limousine carried another lawyer from another plush apartment to another law office a few blocks from Flom's. In this back seat sat Martin Lipton—eight years Flom's junior, huskier and slightly better tailored, in his habitual white shirt and black suit, and wearing bottle-thick glasses. . . . Two hours later Lipton would be called by Garlock and asked to defend the corporation against Colt's attempt to buy control out from under them through this "tender offer." It would be a tough fight. . . . Lipton welcomed the challenge, not just for the money it would bring his growing law firm [Wachtell, Lipton, Rosen & Katz], but also because it was another time he'd be up against Joe Flom, the only lawyer who might be better at the game than he was.[8]

Steve's article was the first to show the world that the names Flom and Lipton were to become as inseparable as Federer and Nadal or Frazier and Ali. They proved the adage about the town with one lawyer in which the lawyer starves and the town with two lawyers in which each gets rich. Theirs was a symbiosis the likes of which has rarely been seen in law and business. At times, the two men seemed interchangeable. "One time, Joe's niece was getting married. Her father was dead, and Joe was going to give her away," says James Freund, a retired Skadden partner. "The wedding was being held up in Westchester someplace, outdoors on a beautiful summer day. As the time of the thing neared, Joe was nowhere to be found. Everybody started looking around—what are we going to do if Joe doesn't show up? Then a shout went up from somebody: 'Get Marty!'"[9]

In his *New York* magazine piece, Steve also revealed just how small a village it was, the New York world of finance, its Jewish community, and the social events among the growing ranks of M&A specialists that drove much of its professional and personal life. He described a competition between Flom and Lipton that did not center on a takeover. It was at a dinner for Lester Pollack, a vice-president of Loews Corporation, who would later become a renowned investment banker as well as chairman of the Conference of Presidents of Major American Jewish Organizations:

> "It was terrible," recalls one guest. "Every time there was a toast Joe would butt in with some crack. And then if Joe said something, Marty felt obliged to top him, and vice versa. These guys were hysterically competitive. It ruined [the] party. Not only that, they kept jockeying with each other to get Bob or Larry's [the Tisch brothers, who own Loews] ear about a deal."[10]

Neither Marty nor Joe was born rich. Marty's father was a manager at a factory. Joe's father, Isadore, was a union organizer who worked sewing shoulder pads on dresses. Joe's mother did piecework at home. The Floms were especially poor. The UJA-Federation delivered food baskets to their house. Most of Joe's neighborhood friends ended up as either cops or convicts. Marty's law-firm partners came with identical histories, as Malcolm Gladwell describes in his book *Outliers*.[11] Herb Wachtell's father worked at a ladies' undergarment business. Leonard Rosen's father worked in the garment district as a presser. George Katz's father sold insurance, and "his grandfather, who lived a few blocks away, was a sewer in the garment trade, doing piecework out of his house."

All of these men, however, were lucky, according to Gladwell. Each was born at a time ideally suited to a career as a New York Jewish lawyer. It made each a member of a "blessedly small generation," as Gladwell puts it, that would hit 40 in 1970, "when the revolution in the legal world first began" and "the white-shoe lawyers lingered, oblivious, over their two-martini lunches."[12] With competitors thus anesthetized, Marty and Joe turned their law firms into places that never shut down. When Skadden built a massive kitchen at its new premises on Third Avenue, it was cause for derision. A kitchen at a law firm! But it was a new species of law firm. Both Skadden and Wachtell soon had 24-hour word-processing, round-the-clock reception staff, showers, and changing rooms. They were creatures with mouths perpetually agape as they swam through the seas ingesting nutrients without cease. Word spread. The business changed.

Yes, they were making money. And yes, that got the attention of the rest of Wall Street. But the takeover gang was also having fun. When he sent one of his more buttoned-down young corporate associates, Mike Mitchell, into a takeover courtroom battle, Mitchell expressed with some surprise that it turned out to be "quite interesting." Joe Flom replied, "Of course it's interesting! It's show business!"[13] They were running through the streets wielding megaphones and announcing the revolution. They were the instant, and only, experts to whom judges and fellow lawyers would come on bended knee for explication of the techniques and doctrines that they were creating on the backs of menus at the hottest celebrity-stuffed restaurants and clubs in town. They were gleefully throwing rocks at the stained-glass windows of the great and the good, the disapproving and the entitled. "In the early sixties," Joe Flom once said, "we were supposed to do an underwriting for a client but when the client called his investment banker, he was told there were only seven firms—all old Wall Street firms—qualified to do underwritings for the bank. So I figured, shit, we gotta do something about that. We've got to show the bastards that you don't have to be born into it."[14] And that's just what they all did.

In *Butch Cassidy and the Sundance Kid,* Robert Redford and Paul Newman regularly peer over the cliff at the posse in pursuit, which is raising a small cloud of dust far across the flat scrubland, never breaking formation, never hungry, never stopping. They ask themselves, "Who *are* those guys?" M&A is made of two separate but equally important gangs: the corporate acquirers who do the buying and the M&A advisers who show them how it's done.

Among the former club we find the Anglo-French, half-Jewish billionaire with a phobic aversion to rubber bands; the Princeton graduate from the Queens of the 1950s who plays with an elaborate customized toy airport before buying TWA; the German immigrant with a penchant for predator pits who arrived in America as a toddler with a single mother and became the richest man in the country. These men are the collectors. They collect compulsively: houses, wives, antique carriages, acres, books, furniture, pheasant, airplanes, companies. They are human versions of male bower birds, who attract female mates with the beauty and splendor of the colorful trinkets they have gathered around the forest to decorate their nests. "The evolutionary thinking goes that only a high-quality male could spend all of his time searching around for otherwise meaningless decorations," says Berkeley professor Justin Brashares. "It is not unknown for human males also to signal their quality using objects—gold watches, sports cars, and the like."[15]

The second group consists of the lawyers and bankers who actually do the work, create the law, run the trials, negotiate the deals, and at times manipulate their putative masters into waging the long campaigns that generate the massive fees and intellectual stimulation that become so addictive. These are the troops of vervet monkeys. Somewhat more highly evolved than bower birds, they are clever, quick, highly social mammals. They live in groups of around 70, strictly organized under a clear order of dominance. As infants, they demonstrate an innate knowledge of the different alarm calls to make for each predator, whether leopard or snake or eagle.

The adults join in the call when it is correct, and the mothers punish the young when it is not. Adult males have bright blue testicles and a red penis, thought to be signals to other males as much as to females, says Professor Brashares. "Males hide their blue balls when around a more dominant male or when threatened by a predator—you don't want to be so easy to see when your life is on the line."

Some of M&A's bower birds have become public figures, notorious or otherwise; some of the vervet monkeys have achieved more fame than their clients. Many of both contingents have never become known to the laity and have been left largely in undeserved obscurity. Neither could have flourished without the other. Together they changed everything. Like West Indian slave revolts in the 1800s that disrupted the fortunes and the society of the likes of Jane Austen's Sir Thomas Bertram, the new M&A transformed public corporations, the establishment's repositories of power and wealth, into very public, very visible, very vulnerable sugar plantations open to all with the will, the intelligence, and sometimes the personality disorders needed to gain entry.

Soon after his article broke open the new M&A, Steve Brill founded the *American Lawyer* magazine, the first publication of its kind, banking on the wild buzz his story about Marty and Joe had provoked. Over the next 20 years, his magazines and his Court TV would be his own hot-air balloon, permanently afloat above the savanna as he watched the predators and their prey turn red in tooth and claw. He had a battalion of underpaid and over-worked young neophytes who have since fanned out across global media—people like Jill Abramson, now executive editor of the *New York Times;* Jim Kramer, host of NBC's *Mad Money;* Connie Bruck, author of *The Predators' Ball* and a *New Yorker* writer; James Stewart, author of *The Den of Thieves* and a writer at the *New York Times;* Terry Moran, coanchor of ABC's *Nightline* with fellow Court TV graduate Cynthia McFadden; Robert Safian, editor in chief of *Fast Company;* Ellen Pollock, executive editor at *Bloomberg Businessweek;* Stephen Adler, president and editor in chief of Reuters; Alison Frankel, also at Reuters; as well as Roger Parloff and Nicholas Varchaver, both editors at *Fortune.*

James Stewart recalled the early days of the *American Lawyer* in an article at its tenth anniversary in 1989: "Work was exhilarating. Steve Brill was imbued with what seemed boundless enthusiasm, and idealism, and that infected all of us. The legal profession at that time was insular, privileged, affluent, powerful—and unscrutinized. For a reporter, being unleashed on such a subject was like being an anthropologist who discovers an as-yet-untouched civilization. We had a mission to better society through our reporting and writing, and however flawed our efforts sometimes were, our motives were pure. And what stories we produced [!] ... We weren't afraid of controversy, and we wanted to attract attention. We also wanted to survive."[16]

Anthropologists speak of the changes in behavior they can catalyze simply by observing their subjects in the field. Before Steve found the hidden urban tribes of merger men, tucked into the canyons of Manhattan, they were communicating, if at all, with tom-toms and fire towers. Steve brought them cell phones and video cameras and tied them to satellites orbiting the earth itself. For young firebrands entering the business of M&A, and for clients and analysts and the knowledgeable reading public, Steve was the god of revelations, although not a particularly revered deity. "There was total outrage," he remembers, "because we dared to treat them like businesses that deserved to be covered by the media."[17]

Steve himself, perhaps also like an anthropologist, quickly began to emulate his subjects in a kind of reverse observer effect. He became an M&A hostile raider in all but name. He wore the uniform every day, and he sported the cigar. "We all did," Stu Shapiro remembers. "We all had these $2,500 suits from Billy Fiorvanti over at 45 West 57th Street, and we all wore suspenders, or 'braces,' from Calvin Curtis, and we all smoked the best cigars from Havana." Steve worked his staff like the head of an investment bank, granting and withdrawing and reallocating bonuses to his writers at will, offering a prize to anyone still in the office after hours until one of the few still there was a staff member he didn't like, and firing an art director who had argued against combining blue with orange on a cover with the memorable bark, "Make it fucking blue and you're fired."

Steve also stoked competition at work and play. Gay Jervey, a former senior writer at *American Lawyer* and *Brill's Content,* says with a laugh, "It was the era of Gordon Gekko and Wall Street's glorification of being a shithead—a sort of well-heeled Don Corleone—all in the interests of mega bucks and power. No doubt about it, Steve is a maverick and a visionary—and his particular brand of free-wheeling bravado and flamboyant success captured the zeitgeist of the time." Brill has been described as having bitten a staffer, Jim Cramer, during a feverish water polo game at his Westchester country house. Brill has denied this ever happened, but it still became part of *American Lawyer* lore. "The pool he had was coated in quite a rough material," one staff member says. "Many of us would emerge with cuts and abrasions from those games."

He was a "slightly mad tub-thumper and muckraker," as Jeff Goodell put it in his 1993 profile of redoubtable Brill.[18] "*Wired,* huh," Steve said at the beginning of their interview. "Great magazine. Too bad it's unreadable. Whoever designed that thing should be taken out and shot." He often displayed this kind of pugnacity, so typical of the M&A revolutionaries he wrote about. Toward the end of the *American Lawyer*'s tenth anniversary party he threw at the Rainbow Room, for example, Steve wandered into a performance by the German chanteuse Ute Lemper. Then 25 years old, she was making her debut at Rainbow & Stars, the Rainbow Room's adjoining cabaret, and had been quoted as saying that the prospect frightened her. "What if nobody comes to hear me? And in a room like that, you have to be able to do this American joking, which I can't do very well," Lemper told *People* magazine just before her opening night.[19] As Brill settled into a sofa a few feet from the singer, his cigar smoke curling into the rays of Lemper's spotlight, he said to no one in particular, "Who hired this fucking Nazi?" and promptly fell asleep.

CHAPTER THREE

THE HELLFIRE CLUB

I n the 1980s, the meatpacking district was still true to its name. The boutiques and cafés had yet to colonize the territory, and it remained Manhattan's center for the killing, evisceration, and processing of large mammals—mainly sheep, cattle, and pigs. Racks of swinging skinned and headless carcasses still pushed through the plastic strips that covered the openings to the slaughterhouses, releasing short blasts of cold, fetid air before rattling down the cobblestone streets in a Gahan Wilson caricature of Seventh Avenue. Just a few blocks to the south, Wall Street, in that long-ago time, also still evoked its past. With the apartments and strollers yet to come, the financial district maintained its grip as an as-yet-unbreached ghetto that walled out all but lawyers, traders, brokers, and bankers. For New Yorkers, a weekend bike ride through the quiet alleyways of the Old City was still a secret pleasure, unknown to tourists. Like alimentary canals, the two arrondissements ingested their human fodder at first light and evacuated the transformed and somewhat diminished remains at dusk, returning to somnolence until the cycle began again at dawn.

In the meatpacking district, however, a nocturnal life-form had begun to reverse this process, pulling in the targets of its appetite late at night from the cubicles and corner offices of the downtown canyons and ejecting them, exhausted and sated, at sunrise. The creature was difficult to find in the dark and seedy neighborhood. Only the mouth was visible in the gloaming, an unmarked and easily overlooked opening to an esophagus of dark steps that led to an unseen intestinal labyrinth below. There, in the subterranean darkness, it writhed nightly in peristaltic ecstasies, coiled in the catacombs beneath the warren of narrow lanes surrounding the abattoirs at river's edge. It was called the Hellfire Club, the name taken from the establishments that proliferated across the British Empire for gentlemen of a certain kind of leisure.

On a mucilaginous summer night in the Manhattan of the 1980s, two women in their early 20s agreed to help a group of their fellow Merrill Lynch bankers and traders entertain a visiting M&A raider and his entourage. Elizabeth and her immediate boss were the only two women in their division other than secretaries. The bachelor herd of young men did not mention that they were off for a night on the prowl. Their M&A clients had already seen the Statue of Liberty. Like *Mad Men* clients looking for bars, boobs, and Broadway tickets, they were ready for something a bit more stimulating. They found it—the Hellfire Club—at 675 Hudson Street, at 13th Street, in what is known as the Little Flatiron Building. In its past lives, the place was known as the Catacombs and before that the Sewer. It was the first club in New York to bring together the gay, straight, and bisexual demimondes, where Bridget Fonda follows Jennifer Jason Leigh through the wind-machine-driven street garbage into the world of *Single White Female*.

As our party descended the concrete stairs into the darkness, the first sensation was olfactory. But it was not merely a smell. It was a halitosis born of putrefaction, an admixture of ancient meatpacking offal, cigarettes, beer, whiskey, vomit, urine, feces, sweat, and semen, all simmering in a bacteria-laden, suppurating soup of sealed, rebreathed air that swirled up at them from the blackness. Kathy was dressed in her favorite pink-and-white-striped Laura Ashley number with leg-o'-mutton sleeves, puffed at the shoulders and biceps and tight at the forearms. She had on her blue espadrilles. Elizabeth was wearing what she called her Roman slave dress, an off-the-shoulder sleeveless shift. Both women had decided not to put in their contacts or wear their glasses, and as a result, they looked like "little mole people," their arms linked to steady themselves, peering into the darkness that thumped with music and other as-yet-unexplained sounds. The floor was sticky.

There was a large central room, the main bar and dance floor, and a warren of smaller caves off a U-shaped hall. They fought their way through the bodies to get to the bartender, a strapping young lad, shirtless, wearing a large straw cowboy hat and leather chaps. The two friends giggled when he turned around to reveal that the chaps opened in the back to reveal his naked buttocks. It was then that they noticed the large Lazy Susan on the bar, where staff members would dance as the dish turned. A man waved at them from across the central room, smiling and gesturing to them to come over. They thought they must know him. As they approached, "like two little old ladies holding on to each other in the park," they saw that he was standing in front of a raised stage where a naked woman was bent over in a stockade.

"Michelle doesn't want to do this," the man said sadly.

"Doesn't she?" Kathy asked.

"No," the man said. "No. But Michelle is very *very* ashamed."

"She is?" Elizabeth asked.

"Yes. Michelle is very *very* ashamed. And so she *must* do this."

"Must she?" Elizabeth asked, looking at Kathy.[1]

At that moment, a man in a leather mask cracked a whip and brought it down across Michelle's backside. Michelle was silent. Kathy and Elizabeth looked at their new friend with wide eyes. He smiled pleasantly, and it was only then that they realized he had no trousers on and that his right hand was stroking his erect penis. They squealed. Each room they passed on their frightened flight to the ladies room, which had its own hygienic issues and doubled as a cocaine lounge, enclosed a different scene. In one cave, they saw a man sitting in a leather swing, his feet in holsters slightly above his head. Four other men stood behind him, rocking him back and forth slowly as a woman stood to one side, belting on a large black dildo. Rose-lipt maidens and light-foot lads danced in cages, barely clad. One young girl reached out to stroke Elizabeth's hair, startling her and smiling sadly as Elizabeth recoiled. Beneath the high laughter, the music, and the screams was the constant hum of groans, a bass line like an off-key, oddly arrhythmic Gregorian chant. They were lucky to find a cab, two women standing in the predawn lightlessness in the silent meatpacking district, haunted by only the dispossessed and the depraved. The next morning, the stink in invisible shimmers still rose from the evening clothes each had piled in a far corner of Elizabeth's apartment.[2] They had three hours to sleep before work.

Life during the day in the high-rises of early M&A was not far short of nocturnal underground Wall Street. All across the financial district on that day, or any day, you would have found similar hellfire microcosms: men risking $100,000 on whether one of them could throw a football across a vast low-ceilinged trading floor; a naked woman stepping out of a gorilla suit onto an executive's desk to the INXS hit "Original Sin"; a Japanese manager in a conference room getting his lunch-hour lap dance from his assistant; young 20-somethings talking about nothing but sex while they played riotously with other people's money; and everywhere cocaine, cocaine in the bathrooms, cocaine at the desks, cocaine in little brown glass snorters, cocaine on the backs of hands, cocaine to kill the hangover in time for the meeting with the client about the loss of a hundred grand on margin with a second hundred now due, cocaine to get through it all until the first bottle of Dom Perignon, cocaine for cocaine's sake.

The morning visit of Coffee Man enabled the clubbing crowd to revive themselves. The elevator doors would open, and he would push his steel cart to one side of the hall and ring his bell. He sold coffee, tea, doughnuts, and grams of cocaine in little rectangles of folded, shiny white paper. When Elizabeth arrived early on that Monday after Hellfire, the

guys already had their centerfolds open. There were the usual catcalls—
"Hubba hubba, who's got the rubba!"—but today a new game was in
progress.

Each man was being asked to calculate the cost of having sex with his
wife, a number reached by dividing the monthly carrying cost of the house
by the number of uxorious couplings in that same period. One banker said
that it cost him $25,000 per session, as the house was expensive and the
sexual encounters few in number. "I think you should count yourself lucky,
Hal. I don't know anybody who'd fuck you for 25 grand." Elizabeth wondered if she had gone too far, but the boys threw back their heads and emit-
ted loud primate barks of laughter. They began cheering and hooting and
throwing paper cups and food wrappers at Hal, who was laughing louder
than anyone.

It was the peak of Don Regan's reign at Merrill Lynch, the era of the
Irish American ex-Marine, of green cupcakes and green lemonade on offer
throughout the offices on St. Patrick's Day, of tough-talking, buzz-cut, big
swinging dicks. Elizabeth was raised an agnostic Episcopalian in a high-
WASP enclave of Connecticut and knew little of this ecosystem. On one
Ash Wednesday, she heard herself helpfully pointing out to a colleague that
he had something on his forehead, no doubt a smudge from that cheap *New
York Times* ink that just gets all over you before you know it. It happened to
her all the time. She totally understood.

Today was the boss's birthday. Jeffrey Chandor was the unlikely head
of the Department of International Institutional Sales, given the fact that
he took pride in having little knowledge of anything international and that
only twice had he abandoned American shores, once to serve as a Marine
in 'Nam, which he pronounced to rhyme with "ma'am," and then to take a
brief family vacation in Jamaica. Each time, he would say, he could barely
contain his desire to get back to "the good old Yooessuvay." Jeff would also
tell the story of how his wife got him through college. "She was in the top
10 percent of our class! Ha! I was in the bottom 10 percent! Ha! Ha!" He
seemed to be at least six-feet-seven-inches tall. Japanese clients called him
"Jaws" behind his back. He would sardonically call them "the little yellow
people" behind theirs.

Jeff's first appointment that morning was an interview with a young
woman applying for the position of sales assistant. She duly arrived precisely on time and knocked on the door of his glass office. She was carrying
a briefcase and was dressed in the uniform of the day for women who were
not part of the secretarial pool: a dark boxy jacket, a matching dark skirt, a
blouse with a clownishly large floppy bow tie at the neck, stockings, and low
heels. Never trousers, never any clothes that hinted at female sexuality; the
costume was designed to signal that she was not a working girl from Staten
Island, with big hair and a clinging dress and a sliver of an ankle bracelet,

and to convey simultaneously that her junior version of the male suit and tie meant that she was not deviating from established sexual dimorphism.

Instead of taking a seat, Job Applicant took off her glasses and let her hair fall to her shoulders. She took out a boom box, which she placed on Chandor's desk, and pressed play: "Last dance, last chance for love / Yes, it's my last chance / For romance tonight / I need you by me, beside me, to guide me / To hold me, to scold me / 'Cause when I'm bad, I'm so so bad / So let's dance." The men surrounded the glass box, as if at a hockey game. Jeff tapped on his desk. Job Applicant climbed onto it quickly, naked now, and presented him with two lighted candles attached to her nipples on little pasties. He blew them out to the roar of the crowd. She got off her knees and danced inches from his face. She cost $300. Everyone was obliged to chip in to these regular diversions, and among more than 100 men, there was at least a birthday a week. Other strip-o-gram favorites included Construction Woman and French Maid, but none drew louder ovations or higher hilarity with her wiggling arias than Fat Soprano, a grotesquely obese singer with a G-string barely visible in the skin folds.

Elizabeth was neither shocked at all this nor particularly disapproving. That would come later in life. For now, for her, in her early 20s, it was just what happened at the office. She would often find herself gazing out at the Statue of Liberty and the vast view of New York harbor, which one gets from the forty-ninth floor of One Liberty Plaza.[3]

Unscathed by any scandal and a survivor of many employee pogroms, Jeff Chandor would spend roughly 30 more birthdays at Merrill Lynch. From Rhode Island, where he would later day-trade to keep himself busy, he has said, "Everything I've got, with the exception of my family, was due to Merrill Lynch, so I've got no complaints." His son, J. C. Chandor, shot to fame with his first independent movie released to critical accolades and an Academy Award nomination in 2012 for his screenplay. With an ensemble cast that includes Kevin Spacey, Demi Moore, Jeremy Irons, and Zachary Quinto, the film covers 24 hours in the life and death of a Wall Street investment bank and is, in part, an effort to reveal the human frailty of those in finance so often demonized after the crash of 2008. The work is widely understood to be a film à clef: the story of the house of Lehman in extremis. J. C. Chandor was recently asked if his father had given him any insights into the financial world: "He did not." The title of the movie is *Margin Call*.

Brian Campbell was not one of the men cheering at Chandor Senior's glass box. He was an earnest, eager-to-please twentysomething, still a bit gawky, still the blond kid from the provinces come to the Big Apple to seek his fortune. He had, however, quickly picked up the mannerisms of Wall Street, adding a slight swagger to his walk, sporting striped shirts with white collars and flamboyant suspenders, and referring to clients in Europe or England as "our friends across the pond." At his high school in Michigan, his date for his junior prom had been Louise Ciccone, now known as Madonna. That was his first brush with fame. His second began with his flirtation with Elizabeth. He was giving her tips on companies about to be taken over or about to acquire a target, the stock prices of which would leap when the news became public. He was a soldier in the great insider-trading family of the 1980s.

Brian sat two desks behind Elizabeth. She had noticed that Brian had a new habit of talking to a particular client in the Bahamas in a low tone. At times, he bent over so far that it looked as if he were searching for a lost item under his desk, holding the phone and whispering intently. It was Bernie this and Bernie that, and "How ya doing, Bernie? How's the weather out there? Wish I could be there with ya, Bernie," and then it all went into whispers. Brian had recently developed another habit. After a conversation with the mysterious Bernie, Brian would pass by Elizabeth's desk and, barely pausing, punch in a few symbols on her Quotron. The next morning, she would invariably see the companies in the headlines. He would always fix her with an impish smile as he sauntered back to his own nearby perch. "That one may smile, and smile, and be a villain."

Another young M&A player, isolated from the wild 1980s in his law-firm tower and utterly unaware of such haunts as the Hellfire Club, had long since abandoned the same insider-trading ring with which he, too, had been entangled. Neither he nor Brian would escape his fate for long.

CHAPTER FOUR
THE LAND OF THE SCREAMERS

"The traditional problem has always been alcohol: The aging senior partner who keeps a fifth in his desk drawer; the rainmaker whose two-martini business lunches have turned into five-martini afternoons; the down-and-out solo lawyer whose periodic binges have decimated his practice," Robert Safian wrote in the *American Lawyer*. "But behind closed doors, America's lawyers are also dabbling in illegal drugs. And, for a handful, occasional use has grown into addiction. Although far less prevalent than alcoholism, illegal substance abuse is pervasive. Even in the most profitable and prestigious white-shoe firms, lawyers have been enticed and then entrapped by white powder, colored pills, and needles."[1] It was no wonder.

Kim Fennebresque, then at First Boston, remembers another aspect of the ferocity of the assault on body and mind of those febrile times. "I have often likened these transactions to that scene in *The Godfather* after Don Corleone gets peppered by the newsstand, he gets Swiss-cheesed, and there's that big fat Italian stirring spaghetti back at the house saying, 'We're going to the mattresses,' which is I guess when everybody moves into their mother-in-law's house and they all stay there until the siege passes. There's a little bit of going to the mattresses on these transactions. Everybody stays at the office. It's around the clock. You're eating pizza and smoking cigars. Sometimes you get confused and you're smoking pizzas and eating cigars, and it goes on and on and on, and you've got Rolaids by the case."[2]

Safian recounts the stories of four associates who were buying other kinds of relief. One young associate at two of the largest firms in New York, whom Safian renames "Steve," came to the city in the early 1980s and started on cocaine in law school with friends, but it was only when he joined his first firm in Manhattan that he used it alone, often shooting up in conference rooms. For a long time, his colleagues knew nothing. "It was the last thing on people's minds," Safian quotes Steve as saying. "Absolutely the last reason they would think I had a bloody nose. Or the last reason why I wore a long-sleeved shirt at the firm outing."

A second addict, whom Safian calls "Peter," recalls watching television with a friend one night when an antidrug commercial compared taking drugs to frying one's brain like an egg on a skillet. "I had a straw up my nose, and I turned to my friend and said, 'Think we have a problem?' And we both laughed at the set." Peter began taking cocaine "to stay up and work longer."[3]

Ilan Reich, who joined the firm of Wachtell, Lipton, Rosen & Katz just as the 1980s were revving up, says he and his fellow laborers would often joke that five years of work at Wachtell in the early days of modern M&A were equivalent to a hundred years in a dog's life. Under a typical law firm system, not every hour on the job can be billed to a client, so the actual hours at work exceed even the high number listed on a client's tab. Ilan racked up several years of 3,000 billable hours, which he now calls "insane." Often, he would put in 400 hours a month, or 100 hours a week, which means not a single normal night's sleep. "It's not that hard to stay up all night," he says, "especially if you get a 20-minute to 40-minute nap like around six in the morning, and then a shot of coffee or orange juice. But by two in the afternoon, boy, the eyelids get heavy. It's very hard to stay up at that point."[4]

For Ilan, there was never any need for artificial stimulation. He was driven by the love of his work and his ambition to succeed. A few years before Brian's phone calls to Bernie, Ilan did not yet know it, but his future as a young M&A lawyer at Wachtell, Lipton, Rosen & Katz would depend on his ability to forego sleep. His first major M&A deal was the first to exceed a billion dollars and it would become the incubator for Marty Lipton's greatest inspiration.

On Easter Sunday, April 6, 1981, Edgar Bronfman was sitting in his library on his farm in Albemarle County, Virginia. Georgetown Farm is not a distinguished house, resembling so many much smaller but equally derivative colonial tract houses that began their colonization of the landscape after the Second World War. Built around 1975, it sits along the Moormans River and is about 30 minutes from Jefferson's Monticello. Eventually, with what Bronfman estimates turned out to be $5.5 million in improvements and the addition of several adjacent properties, Georgetown Farm would encompass 636 acres staring across to the Blue Ridge Mountains and expand to nearly 8,000 square feet, with a swimming pool, a tennis court, a gazebo, a two-bedroom guesthouse, a farm manager's house, and two barns. Bronfman would become famous in the county for his herd of bison and for building his own abattoir nearby. The meat was sold at an outlet at a shopping mall in the town of Charlottesville, including such delicacies as bison cheek. Items made from the hides were also available. Pencil holders made from bison bull scrotums achieved a certain renown.

In 1981, the library at Georgetown Farm was one of the Seagram chairman's favorite rooms, one where he would write several books and, in this instance, receive word that the Sun Oil Company was willing to pay $2.1 billion for his Texas Pacific Oil Company, a business he had been eager to abandon for some time. Bronfman sent back word that the price was not good enough, although privately he was elated. Texas Pacific was sitting on his books for $566 million. With the help of the late Steve Banner of Simpson Thacher & Bartlett, Seagram, built by patriarch Samuel Bronfman into the largest liquor company in the world, got $2.3 billion for its unwanted oil company. "Sons of strong and wealthy fathers sometimes have difficulty building worthwhile careers, but the Bronfmans overcame that, establishing identities of their own," Irving Shapiro, the former chief executive of DuPont and Skadden partner, was quoted as saying at the time. (The Shapiros, incidentally, did the same.)[5]

What to do with all that money? While Seagram pondered the question for the next year, the cash pile grew to $3.7 billion. Bronfman asked Averill Harriman about buying the Union Pacific Railroad but backed away when Harriman explained that he would be happy to sell but management would not. Then, Bronfman spotted St. Joe Minerals, a company rich in gold, lead, copper, zinc, coal, oil, and gas.[6] St. Joe would quickly become knee deep in advisers, a group that was not yet as famous as it would become, including a Wachtell second-year associate named Ilan Reich.

Edgar Bronfman christened the deal with the code name "Mary," since the target was St. Joe. On March 11, Joseph E. Seagram & Sons announced an offer for the stock of St. Joe Minerals at $48 per share, for a total of $2.1 billion in cash. Wachtell lawyers went on high alert. Marty Lipton saw that as few as 20 large institutions owned more than half of St. Joe. Why not get them to agree to collective actions since together they owned enough stock to block anyone from owning the company? What if they agreed to hold on to their shares, to keep it out of the hands of Edgar Bronfman, if St. Joe, in turn, would commit itself to selling the company if the stock did not improve substantially within 18 months? "We were singularly unsuccessful," Marty said later. Not a single institutional shareholder agreed to go along with his plan. He was determined to find a way to give more power to boards of directors in the merger feeding frenzy, not least because he worried about an anti-Semitic backlash, as so many of the hostile raiders of the day were Jews. It would not be long before Marty's obsession would spawn one of the most powerful takeover defenses ever invented.

With the shareholders refusing to cooperate, Marty Lipton had another idea for St. Joe. He wrote a one-page memo to his tax partner, Peter Canellos. "Peter," the cover note read, "I'm thinking of doing this. Does it make any sense from a tax standpoint?" At 6:00 p.m. on a Thursday evening, young Ilan Reich stopped by Peter's office. Peter showed him the note. "Here's this great idea Marty has. He's going to talk to the management tomorrow about it." Ilan was intrigued and asked to make a copy. "Sure," Ilan recalls Peter Canellos saying. "You're on the deal." By this time, the firm was virtually empty. Back at his office, Ilan immediately called down to ask for three Vydec people to work with him all night. No one had computers on their own desks in those distant days. Vydec was the word-processing company that produced all firm paperwork. Then, Ilan settled in for the night.[7]

He realized that no one had ever tried this defense before, a simultaneous self-tender for cash and for notes that was designed to entice the shareholders away from the Seagram bid and to sell their stock to the company instead. The company would stay independent, and the shareholders would get value for their stock. It was the board negotiating in public, Ilan says, telling the acquirer, "We don't want your offer because we can do it better ourselves. We're not just going to sit here hoping there is some antitrust thing we can pull out of the sky." In an exchange offer, you're buying people's stock for paper, either with other stock, preferred stock, notes, or debt. This requires registration with the SEC. If you're buying stock for cash, you just offer to do so with no review by securities regulators. The structure Marty designed was an attempt to satisfy the shareholders, a very high percentage of whom wanted cash, and to win over the rest who might be more interested in securities instead. It required a massive amount of documentation and hard thinking. Ilan prepared all the contracts and letters, including the exchange offer, an indenture for the bonds, a joint tender offer/exchange offer, and a no-action letter request to the SEC seeking an unprecedented exemption to be allowed to proceed.

At five in the morning, 11 straight hours after reading Marty's one-page memo, Ilan placed a two-inch-thick pile of paper on the desks of George Katz and Peter Canellos and went home for a short sleep of less than an hour and then a hot shower. That Friday morning, the firm was deposing Edgar Bronfman himself. Ilan wanted to get in early to pick up what he calls the equivalent of a free ticket to a Broadway show. He went to George Katz's office first. "I didn't want to go to Lipton's office. It was like a dangerous place to go. You could get your head bitten off sometimes in the morning. I didn't know whether he had seen it yet. I didn't want to bother him. You tread lightly. You didn't go to Marty's office to shoot the breeze. Usually. And certainly not early in the morning. So I went to George's office, and George said, 'Ilan, this is great. He loves it. This is great. Let's go talk to Marty.'"

They ran the 180 degrees to the opposite side of the floor at 299 Park Avenue, where they found a very rushed Marty Lipton. "Let's go."[8]

In a deal with so many firsts, actually accompanying Marty to a meeting was yet another. "Lipton had no patience for me. Had no patience for anybody internally. He basically did his own thing. He wasn't one of these guys who relied on other people. So if he had to go to a meeting and you weren't ready, he went without you. So here the client was three blocks down the street, on Park Avenue, and half the time he'd go for a daily meeting, and I wasn't there because he'd leave and he wouldn't tell me he was going. He'd just be gone."

At the conference room at St. Joe Minerals, Ilan saw Sam Butler from Cravath, the burly midwestern powerhouse who would become Cravath's presiding partner, and Bruce Wasserstein and Joe Perella from First Boston. The *American Lawyer*'s Stephen Adler tells the story of how Bruce Wasserstein and Joe Perella came together. Back in 1976, Bruce was a quiet drone at Cravath, working as one of Butler's protégés, inching his way toward what he hoped would be the ultimate reward of a partnership. He was not known as "the assertive type," as one of his former colleagues put it to Adler. Joseph Perella, then 35, was, at least at first glance, Wasserstein's opposite: tall, thin, lean, given to flashes of wit, insight, and temper. Bruce was "shorter, plumper, and decidedly calmer." Perella was a star and he knew it and showed it. As head of the embryonic M&A group at First Boston, he was in charge of First Boston client Combustion Engineering's purchase of Gray Tool for $66 million. Bruce was a junior member of the deal team as an associate at Cravath, counsel to First Boston.[9]

As was the case in those days with so many bromances, the M&A hunting pairs that sprung up during the long slogging hours, this one blossomed at the financial printer, where Bruce and Joe worked all night to get the deal documents assembled. Bruce "seemed to pick up the nuances of various proposals, and [was] steady under pressure," Adler wrote. Perella, more impulsive, suddenly left at two in the morning for an appointment with his acupuncturist but not before he knew what he wanted. He wanted Bruce. "Twenty minutes into the meeting, Bruce made a couple of points," Perella told Stephen Adler, "and I nudged the guy next to me and said, 'I don't know who this son of a bitch is, but we've really got to get to know him because he is a piece of work.'"

Perella tried to make a deal with Butler: Cravath would get a major chunk of First Boston's nascent M&A work as long as Bruce was the first port of call. Bruce was willing, but the partnership was about to rotate Bruce into project finance, in keeping with the Cravath system of associate training, and they let it be known to Bruce that he would do well to follow the established path toward seniority. "There was some deprecation of M&A as a specialty for a full-fledged Cravath partner," Bruce told Adler in 1983. "But Perella insisted. 'I'm the kind of person who, when I smell an opportunity, I don't let it rest,'" Adler quotes him as saying. "Even as Wasserstein was immersing himself in the intricacies of financing a nuclear utility," Adler wrote, "Perella had him advising on a First Boston deal. On a plane ride back from a deal-making session, Perella struck: 'I turned to him and said, "Why don't we cut through this bullshit? If Cravath can't see that it's an important enough piece of business for them to maybe bend their system a little, why don't you just come work for us?"' He offered Wasserstein twice his Cravath salary of $50,000 and the title of vice-president. After some hesitation, Wasserstein jumped ship." The two would later launch their own firm together in time to advise Campeau on his Federated deal as Wasserstein Perella & Co.[10]

St. Joe had traditionally used a bank other than First Boston, but Bruce and Joe had muscled their way in, Ilan remembers. "They basically called up the company and wedged their way into the deal by sheer force of personality and aggressiveness. They just said, 'How could you possibly do a defense without the smartest people in the world on your side?' So it was a roomful of very heavyweight bankers and lawyers, and the company executives were no slouch either. Marty wasn't yet famous. I mean, he was well known, and in his own mind, of course, he was the best thing since sliced bread—which was true—but he was up against very, very substantial egos. Given the people around the table, the CEO probably deferred more to Wasserstein, just because of Bruce's personality and his reputation, but Marty put on a masterful performance."

The meeting went on for six hours. Marty gently pointed out the flaws in all the alternatives, Ilan recalls. "Wasserstein was a genius and full of ideas, floated a lot of balloons. And Lipton very artfully poked each balloon. But he didn't do it in a defensive way. He did it in the smoothest, most generous, least abrasive, most collegial way that you could have a debate with people. Finally they all said, 'Well, Marty, what do *you* think?' Then it was like the door was open, and he said, 'Well, I think we should do this'—and then he explains his own idea." The group was intrigued and asked how fast they could move. "Marty pulls a two-inch-thick pile of papers out of the briefcase and says, 'Ilan's already drafted the papers. We'll be ready on Monday morning.' As Ilan and Marty walked back to Wachtell, Marty said, 'Take anybody in the firm to help you.'"

Ilan "worked like a dog all weekend." The financial printer, luckily for the exhausted associate, was at 111 Eighth Avenue, now the Google building, which was close to where Ilan lived. "It was Chelsea, a crappy neighborhood back then. But we had bought a loft there in the early eighties on Seventh Avenue and Fifteenth Street. So it was really easy for me to spend the night at the printer, go back home, take a nap for 20 minutes, and then go back to the printer. We had to deal with the projections, with the accountants and the company's financial department, had to deal with the SEC, had to deal with a distribution list on the deal. It was probably 20 people, and everybody had their comments on everything. It was really a massive thing." It was ready on Monday morning. Then the battle moved into court.

The case was before US District Judge Milton Pollack, who often viewed powerful lawyers before his bench as potential hunting trophies, and will go down in history as having presided over the later failure of Drexel. In St. Joe's, Judge Pollack began to get the sense that Wachtell was throwing several kitchen sinks at Seagram. The buyback, which was to launch on March 26, 1981, the day of the court hearing, was designed to sweep into St. Joe's coffers 2 million shares of its stock at $60 each and swap a new issue of convertible preferred stock for an additional 5 million shares. The company said it might buy as many as 18 million shares if it could raise more money through the sale of CanDel Oil Ltd., its Canadian oil and gas company. What's more, it announced that if all else were to fail, it would commit suicide by liquidating itself rather than be taken over. Seagram's lawyers from Simpson Thacher then told the court that St. Joe had just hurriedly awarded top executives a series of benefits said to be worth $13.5 million.

And just what was this all about, the judge wanted to know. Marty took over from George Katz to defend the move as "proper," that the benefits were designed to "assure that no matter what happens, they won't be at the mercy" of a takeover. This was not going well. Marty then conferred with John Duncan, the chairman of St. Joe, who was present in the courtroom, and hurriedly said to Judge Pollack, "Your Honor, if you think there is a problem with that, then the board will just rescind it." The judge was not impressed. "Mr. Lipton," he said, "as an old Tennessee lawyer once told me, 'You can take the skunk out of the jury box, but the smell lingers on.'" Recalls one lawyer who watched the scene, "The whole courtroom erupted."[11]

For Ilan, just two years out of Columbia Law School, St. Joe was a triumph. He had done it all on his own. Never once had he even been tempted to pick up his office phone and call the magic three-digit number, 201, that would ring the telephone in Marty Lipton's Park Avenue apartment. There were, of course, no cell phones and no pagers, no e-mails and no personal computers. With this special extension, Marty granted access to his brain at any time, day or night, to any colleague who wanted it. It was often an invaluable help, but it was always a risk. Ilan had let the giant sleep rather than arouse him and fill him with a terrible resolve.

Ilan's work on St. Joe made his name at Wachtell and cemented his symbiotic relationship with Marty Lipton. "When I got done with that deal," Ilan says, "I never worked for anybody else again in my whole career there. Everybody trusted me. They would say, 'Here's the deal. Go take care of it. Come back if you have any questions.' There were no opinion committees in those days. If you had an issue with a legal opinion, you'd go talk to somebody, but it was not yet the deep structured world it evolved into. And billing? Essentially I'd just go back after the deal was done and tell whoever the partner was, I'd say, 'Oh, by the way, I decided to bill a million dollars. You think that's a good number?' Sure Ilan, whatever you want."

Ilan is a boy living his dream. He is reading about his own deals in the *Wall Street Journal* and *Fortune,* both of which he had devoured earlier in his life, brought home from the office of his eye-doctor father. Here is Ilan walking past a conference room on the thirty-fifth floor of 299 Park. Through the open door, he watches Rupert Murdoch, in the midst of losing his bid for St. Regis to a white knight, excoriating his pharaonic attendants, yelling into the phone over a tiny detail of a deal provision, terrorizing dozens of people at once. On another day, Ilan meets Hank Paulson, a young banker from Goldman Sachs, and watches him roar around a conference room blurting out orders in all directions. Ilan is becoming a full citizen in the land of the screamers.

Marty Lipton is known to have described Ilan to Joe Flom as a great and rare discovery, a lawyer barely out of his 20s who was already masterminding transactions virtually alone. He was possessed of an intellectual brilliance so renowned that he was often rumored to have created the shareholder rights plan himself. It is not known whether Lipton used the term "prodigy" to describe his protégé, but if he did, the etymology of the word would not have been inapt, derived as it is from the Latin *prodigium,* something outside the natural order of things that would eventually anger one of the gods.

Yet all was not perfect. Even with his own partners, Ilan was sometimes more than assertive, complaining to them with dangerous daring when he found himself stuck with some of the deeply boring work that can so often blanket M&A. If he had wanted to do financings, he was known to say directly to his bosses, he would have taken a job at a place like Sullivan & Cromwell. Clients were not spared his impatience with drudgery, and there are tales of Ilan burrowing into a newspaper in a client's office until the negotiations crawled closer to where his mind had already catapulted the deal.

This behavior did not go unnoticed. For three years in a row, Ilan got bad reviews and was told that his chances at partnership were growing slim; this at a firm that prided itself on hiring a handful of associates each year with the assumption that they were expected to make partner. Ilan thought seriously of leaving the firm. "On a late-afternoon flight back from Chicago," Wachtell partner Larry Lederman would later write, "he spent the entire trip discussing the situation with me. I felt that it was a moment of decision and told him that I wanted him to stay, that as the practice grew he would share it."[12] How right Larry would turn out to be. At the end of 1986, the *American Lawyer* would report that Wachtell, Lipton, Rosen & Katz had hauled in gross revenues of $59.5 million, with just 83 partners and 42 associates. In fiscal 2012, revenue per lawyer would hit $2.465 million for the firm's 249 lawyers, and profits per partner for the 79 equity partners came in at $4.975 million. Both numbers were the highest of the 100 law firms in *American Lawyer*'s annual survey of April 2013. "[Ilan] tucked in his chin," Larry writes, "and became less assertive in the firm. For the next year his relations with the partners were untroubled. Freed from his confrontations, they could enjoy tilting with their adversaries, and recognize his brilliance."[13] Ilan made partner effective January 1, 1985, the first day of the greatest year in modern M&A.

Ilan, as intelligent as he was, as charming as he could be, with an unusual perception and intuition when confronted with legal issues, always had trouble reading people. It would be a talent forced on him later. Still, he and his then wife, Diane, did make an effort while he was a Wachtell associate, and the response was gratifying. "When we had an open house when we moved to a loft in Chelsea, I invited all the people I worked with, partners and associates. Marty didn't come, but he made a point of saying to me, 'Sorry I didn't come, but you should invite me on another time and we'll be happy to come.' I never picked up on that social cue." For the bris of his second son, Ilan remembers, "They all came. They all did come for that." For the bris of his third son, 18 months later in 1987, the only partner who would show up would be Larry Lederman.

Meanwhile, Ilan was young and moving fast, perhaps faster than even he realized. "[Wachtell] was like the Marine Corps. It was very, very selective and it only took five associates in my year. It was really just tiny. Just tiny. I knew I would get a lot of responsibility early. I was looking for a place that would really be a live wire. That's what I wanted. That's what I got."[14]

In the end, St. Joe still slipped from Seagram's grasp. Judge Pollack issued a temporary restraining order banning St. Joe from taking on Marty's defenses. Fluor Corporation came in as a white knight with an offer that Edgar Bronfman did not want to top. Having lost St. Joe, Seagram still had its $3.7 billion burning holes in its pockets. Bronfman spotted the perfect target, Conoco, and the perfect, if perhaps unintentional, plan: win by losing. In the complex, multibidder battle, Bronfman ended up losing Conoco to DuPont, advised by Bruce Wasserstein, but Bronfman walked away as one of DuPont's largest shareholders with a 20 percent stake.

For this and his battle for St. Joe Minerals, Edgar Bronfman won a spot in *People* magazine's list of "The 25 Most Intriguing People in 1981" in one of the first M&A stories to cross over into pop culture. At the time, Bronfman was president of the World Jewish Congress, a man who ran 1.5 miles to work every day, who had married his third wife (after Ann Loeb and

Lady Caroline Townsend) and had two new children in addition to his five adult offspring. His profile in the magazine stood alongside such luminaries as Diana, Princess of Wales, Ronald Reagan, Lech Walesa, Bryant Gumbel, and Ted Turner. The headline was "A Liquor Baron Enlivens a Year of Corporate Merger Mania."[15]

CHAPTER FIVE

THE SIZE OF THEIR TOYS

n its "Separated at Birth" section in the December 1987 edition, *Spy* magazine paired, among others, Mick Jagger with Don Knotts, Tama Janowitz with Grampa Munster, corporate raider wife Gayfryd Steinberg with Marie Osmond, and Carl Icahn with Mel Brooks.[1] *Spy* may have had more than looks in mind when it twinned the last pair, for Carl Icahn is an actor who talks to himself. "He is like a smart person playing a slightly psychotic person," says Ilan Reich.[2]

It is as if Icahn channels "Jimmy the Chin" Gigante, the head of one of the greatest of Mafia families, who would walk along Bedford Street outside the Italian Social Club in his pajamas mumbling into his unshaven beard, playing insane to avoid arrest and prosecution. Icahn's tactic is similarly designed to convince his opponents to dismiss him as a crackpot but also to drive those opponents to distraction from one hour to the next, no matter how many in sequence it might take, until they cede one negotiating point after another. Everything is wrapped in clouds of words that he can always later claim he never said. He shuts his eyes and paces the floor, muttering various tactics he might pursue, offers he could propose, concessions he could grant, dismissing one with a snarl, another with a long pause and a contemplative "Hmmmmmmm," and still another with "Fuck 'em."

Growing up in the 1940s in Bayswater, Queens, Carl was the only son of intense intellectual liberals who saw wealth and consumption as anathema. Bella was a pianist manqué, who became a teacher to satisfy her mother's insistence on job security and who, in turn, did her best to turn her son, her life's obsession, into a doctor. Michael Icahn was a Jew who became an atheist, a frustrated singer who became a cantor, a grim and argumentative nonpracticing lawyer who would rail against what he called the "robber barons" of American capitalism, including his wife's brother with the rich wife. Carl's uncle, Elliot Schnall, remembered the disparity between his brother-in-law and nephew as follows: "When Carl used to visit me in Scarsdale, he'd get a look at the affluent life. It was Carl's first exposure to living on the high scale, and he was taken immediately by the gracious living, the beautiful home, and cars and servants. But Carl's father never liked the way I lived. He looked askance at it. His attitude was: 'How can you have all of this—the pool, the maids—when there are children starving.'"[3]

At Princeton, where he was one of very few Jews granted admission in the 1950s, and where, like John Kluge at Columbia, he reportedly paid for half his tuition from poker winnings, Carl majored in philosophy and worried about what he should do with his life. He thought of becoming a chess master but dismissed that idea when he considered that it would be nearly impossible to make a living, let alone a fortune. His senior thesis is titled "The Problem of Formulating an Adequate Explication of the Empiricist Criterion of Meaning." Here is a sample passage, which may hold clues to his unorthodox conversations with himself:

> Another failing of the verifiability criterion is that sentences containing mean-
> ingless disjuncts will still be found meaningful providing that one of the dis-
> juncts is meaningful. For example, let N designate the sentence, "The absolute
> is perfect." There is no finite class of observation sentences conceivable from
> which this sentence might logically be inferred, and this sentence is not ana-
> lytic. Therefore, the verifiability criterion finds this sentence both cognitively
> and empirically meaningless.[4]

And a life in M&A was born. "Empiricism says knowledge is based on observation and experience, not feelings. In a funny way, studying twentieth-century philosophy trains your mind for takeovers," Carl has said. "There's a strategy behind everything. Everything fits. Thinking this way taught me to compete in many things, not only takeovers but chess and arbitrage."[5]

And greenmail. Indeed, Carl can be said to have invented the technique. The term is a 1980s neologism that describes the practice of buying a large block of stock in a company and then threatening the management with some kind of rebellion or takeover unless the corporation agrees to buy back the stock at an acceptably high price. Carl got very rich as a result of his innovation and has long been famous as its most skilled and frequent practitioner. He is less well known for a disarmingly frank description of himself: "I'm not a Robin Hood." In 1980, Carl wrote a confidential memo to prospective partners unsealed from court records at the request of the *American Lawyer.* It is the M&A equivalent of an early cuneiform tablet describing Darius's plans to invade Athens and Eretria.

> It is our opinion that the elements in today's economic environment have
> combined in a unique way to create large profit-making opportunities with

relatively little risk.... It is our contention that sizable profits can be earned by taking large positions in "undervalued" stocks and then attempting to control the destinies of the companies in question by:

a. trying to convince management to liquidate or sell the company to a "white knight";
b. waging a proxy contest, or
c. making a tender offer; and/or
d. selling back our position to the company.

      Icahn & Co., Inc. has already utilized these maneuvers successfully three times during the past two years [each of which, the memo noted, yielded returns of between 100 and 250 percent].[6]

Option "d" became known as greenmail. By the mid-1980s, Carl had 14 framed annual reports in the reception area of his office on Sixth Avenue. It's a kind of murderers' row of companies in which he has successfully bought a tranche of stock and walked away with millions in profits after each couldn't wait to get rid of his voting power, his threats of a proxy fight for the board, a full-throated takeover offer for the rest of the stock, his looming presence at shareholder meetings, or all of the above. Like the severed heads of large mammals, his hunting trophies included Gulf + Western, Dan River, Hammermill Paper, ACF, Phillips, Marshall Field, Chesebrough-Ponds, Baird & Warner, and Owens Illinois. His encounter with Uniroyal would be slightly different if even more enriching than many of his other skirmishes to date.

In April 1985, the Middlebury, Connecticut, tire and chemical company turned to Wachtell to fend off a takeover offer that had just surfaced from the dreaded Icahn & Co. Carl offered to pay $18 per share in cash until enough people sold him their stock to put him over 50 percent and then pay anyone else who wanted to sell an equivalent amount in debt securities. Soon, he owned 10 percent of the company. He demanded as part of his offer that the shareholders vote down two takeover defenses that Uniroyal management was asking they install to block Carl's bid. First, Carl wanted the shareholders to defeat a proposal that all shareholders would have to be paid the same amount in any takeover attempt. Next, he wanted the shareholders to refuse management's proposal to set up what is known as a staggered board. At the time, all of the company's directors were elected at the same time. Management wanted to change the company's election procedures for their board of directors so that different groups of directors would come up for election in different, or staggered, years. This prevents any takeover bidder from replacing the entire bench of directors at a single annual shareholder meeting.

Uniroyal's executives and board members were relieved when the shareholders agreed to both proposals. But Carl was not ready to give in.

He claimed that 500,000 of his votes had been thrown out on a technicality, and he asked Judge Robert E. Tarleton of State Superior Court in Jersey City to reinstate the votes, which Carl maintained would have killed both takeover protection measures proposed by Uniroyal executives. The company had had enough of all this and urgently looked for a white knight, some other buyer to come in and shove Carl to one side. They found their savior in the private investment firm of Clayton & Dubilier, who was willing to pay $750 million to buy all the shares and take the company off the public stock markets.

But what to do with Carl? He would not join in the deal unless it were made to be worth his while to do so. Enter Ilan Reich, by now one of the youngest partners at Wachtell and Marty Lipton's anointed acolyte. Representing Uniroyal, Ilan was simultaneously negotiating the merger agreement with Clayton & Dubilier and orchestrating the greenmail deal with Carl. The board meeting was on Friday, May 3. All night on Thursday, Ilan hopped from one negotiating table to another.

Ilan was in the midst of a sleepless mattress marathon when dealing with Carl on Uniroyal. He had been up for days on a series of deals. He was in no mood for tolerance, and he was known for his moody impatience in any case. Just after dawn, it looked as though an agreement with Carl had at last coalesced. Ilan took off for the Uniroyal board meeting at nine in the morning, leaving the junior people to finish up the final details of the greenmail agreement. When Ilan came back at two in the afternoon, still without sleep, he found a virtually completed deal utterly unraveled. Carl Icahn's people were still coming back with more and more points.

"Nothing had remained nailed down. Everything was now, like, loose as could be. This guy was the ultimate rug merchant," says Ilan. "He had a way of hondling and hondling and chipping and chipping. He figured, 'Okay, these guys are eventually going to have to announce their deal with Clayton & Dubilier, and they're up against the wire.' He was right. He was a master negotiator. He was going to keep dragging it out until he got what he wanted. It was like giving crack to a drug addict who says he's going to stop. At some point you've just got to say no. This is a guy from Queens! This is a nobody! The idea that he would play the same game over and over again and got away with it!"

Ilan turned to the lead banker, also on Uniroyal's team, Michael "Zimmy" Zimmerman of Salomon Brothers. "I said, 'Michael, please do me a favor. Don't take Icahn's calls.'" Ilan picked up one of the phones in the conference room and dialed Carl's direct number. "Carl. It's Ilan. If your signature isn't on the page in half an hour, *fuck you*. You're not going to get your deal, and this is the biggest payout you've ever gotten. I don't care what the board says. I'm just not going to do the deal with you. You can just go *fuck* yourself." Well within the half hour, Carl Icahn's signature page began sputtering through the fax machine.

Carl agreed to end his hostile $18-per-share tender offer for 53 percent of Uniroyal and to support the leveraged buyout or any proposal that guaranteed Uniroyal shareholders at least $22 per share in cash. He promised not to increase his own 10 percent stake for six months and gave Uniroyal a right of first refusal on those shares if he ever decided to sell them during that time. He agreed to withdraw his lawsuit challenging the results of the shareholder vote on the antitakeover defenses agreed at Uniroyal's annual meeting on April 16. In return, Uniroyal agreed to pay Carl $5.9 million. He was entitled to sell his stock to the LBO group for $22 per share.[7]

The company maintained that this agreement was not technically greenmail, as the $5.9 million was to reimburse Carl for expenses and for his carrying charges on the Uniroyal stock. Some experts argued that this was a distinction without a difference. But Arthur Fleischer Jr. of Fried, Frank, Harris, Schriver & Jacobson took the approach of a realist. When a company makes a relatively small payment to a bidder that makes a good deal possible for shareholders, Fleischer said at the time, "your level of cynicism has to be different."[8] For Carl Icahn, the debate mattered not. He made a profit of $17.6 million on his 3.2 million shares of stock in Uniroyal.

It would not be long before Ilan and Carl came together again. This time, it was Carl's attack on ACF, a railcar leasing company. Carl's right-hand man was Alfred Kingsley. The two of them became a renowned duo, Carl shouting expletives, Al quietly producing the numbers. "I'm sure behind closed doors the two of them had a good guy/bad guy routine all figured out," says Ilan. They also had another shtick, rarely witnessed and still in some way inexplicable.

It is three in the morning. Carl and Al have drifted away from the negotiating fray to a roundtable in the corner of Carl's office. Ilan begins to realize that the two of them are playing some kind of game. On the table is a Lionel train set, a custom-made set, with small train cars rolling through the miniature landscape, all with perfectly reproduced ACF logos on their sides. They play together in silence. "They sat with that train set half the night, while we were trying to negotiate," Ilan says. "Obviously, he had this figured out as a way of telling us that he was serious about taking over the company."

It was not only trains that night. On another table was a miniature custom-made airport. The two men donned hats and began to play airline pilots. Looking more closely, Ilan could see that on all the planes, all the trucks, all the miniature buses and staircases and uniforms was the logo for TWA. "I ran into a bunch of Skadden guys, and I said, 'You know, Carl is serious about TWA.' They said, 'How do you know?' 'I just know.'"

CHAPTER SIX
THE VISIT OF THE BRITISH COMPANY MAN

The year 1985 began with Ronald Reagan's second inauguration on January 20 and Mikhail Gorbachev's ascension as general secretary of the Soviet Communist Party two months later. It was the year of New Coke, of Sally Field, who didn't feel it the first time but who couldn't deny the fact that this time they liked her. It was the year of the discovery of the grave of the *Titanic* and of a mob shooting in the center of Manhattan outside Sparks Steak House. Madonna released "Like a Virgin." Broadway staged *The Search for Intelligent Life in the Universe*. The San Francisco 49ers triumphed over the Miami Dolphins, 38–16. Boris Becker and Martina Navratilova won Wimbledon. Natalie Wood drowned. Anwar Sadat was mowed down. Moshe Dayan and Omar Bradley died. And, ironically enough, Franco Modigliani won the Nobel Prize in economics in part for his "capital structure irrelevance principle," which posits that the value of a corporation is unrelated to whether it is financed by debt or equity. In M&A, it was the year of deal after deal and court ruling after court ruling that turned mergers and acquisitions into an engine of commerce, a driver of culture, politics, and finance.

In addition to the king on horseback with a chuckling face on the throne of America and the king with male-pattern baldness and a large birthmark on the throne of Russia, there was also a king with a toupee and an X-shaped throne at Wilshire and Rodeo. His name was Michael Milken. He lived simply in a blue-shingled cottage that had once served as a guest house for Clark Gable and Carole Lombard. He worked at Drexel. He sold bonds to buyers eager to loan money at high interest payments to companies that other lenders shunned as too unstable to bet on. By 1985, a mere letter from Milken saying that he was "highly confident" that he could raise money for a given company had become the equivalent of a billion-dollar bill. Milken was close to running the financial affairs of the country on this simple premise, a one-man second Wall Street.

In his book *Frozen Desire: The Meaning of Money,* James Buchan describes Milken as "the most visionary U.S. financier":

> [D]uring his tenure as head of the Beverly Hills office of Drexel Burnham Lambert in the middle years of the 1980s, from a sleepless eyrie at the intersection of Wilshire and Rodeo boulevards, he saw that a corporation need have no book-keeper's value. Indeed, it could have an immense *negative* net worth—that its debts could vastly exceed its book assets—provided its income—his conception of profit was perhaps the broadest ever promulgated—could pay the interest on its immediate obligations. With the greatest brutality, he ripped the equity capital out of corporations as one might roe from a sturgeon, and tossed the body back into the predatory waters of American business. A large portion of the cash freed passed to Milken himself as a fee: he himself had little or no future interest in the entities he'd crippled. Not surprisingly, he made many enemies, and though the ninety-eight charges brought against him were technical in the extreme, he was obliged to serve a prison sentence in a minimum-security federal penitentiary. . . . In 1986, according to the indictment filed against him on March 30, 1989, he received a salary of $550 million. Capitalised at twenty times on Sir William Petty's model, those wages gave Milken a theoretical worth of $11 thousand million, more than anybody else at that era, and unexampled for a mere employee.[1]

Every spring, Drexel gave a party, a big party. Some 2,000 bondholders, CEOs, M&A raiders, and assorted camp followers would gather at the Beverly Hills Hotel for four days at an extravaganza that became known as the Predators' Ball. For Kevin O'Keeffe, a British executive, and his wife, Claudette, it was an introduction to the good old US of A. "It was mind boggling," this executive says.

> I don't remember how many delegates there were, but it seemed like thousands upon thousands. Lorimar Telepictures gave a swinging barbecue inside a vast sound studio. There were side shows, swings, and even a big wheel. Down on the floor of the studio, casts of the various Lorimar productions were on show, including the *Dallas* actors. Most of the *Dallas* team were not making any effort to be sociable, but Howard Keel was really friendly and had a chat with us. The next night, there was an enormous banquet with Dolly Parton singing. One curious by-product business was the fleet of high-class call girls that followed the band wagon. My wife got a call from some woman wanting to know if Mr. O'Keeffe wanted to have some fun. She was not at all bothered when Claudette said she was Mrs. O'Keeffe and *she* looked after the fun. At the airport on our way home, a hopeful woman approached me. I think she was desperate for one

last bit of business and I was carrying a Drexel shoulder bag. An interesting economic lesson on how one successful business can provide spin-off opportunities for employment in other fields.[2]

At the Predators' Ball of 1985, Connie Bruck recounts that Marty Lipton's partner, George Katz, known for his kindness and lack of suspicion, turned to a companion and said, "I've got to hand it to these guys—I've never seen so many beautiful wives!"[3] That year, Diana Ross sang for free in return for a chance to join one of Milken's investment partnerships, like so many others on the same pilgrimage. "This little guy created this huge business, pretty much out of his own head," says Stu Shapiro. "That takes a particular kind of brain and drive. You can be there and not create it, fail to recognize it, blind to the moment. But there are these outliers, these people who do see it, who do create it, and they do all this for some reason that no one knows or can explain."[4]

As the leader of the Supremes obviously realized, Drexel was more than one big, rather unorthodox, party. That all happened, of course, says a former senior Drexel executive, who worked closely with Mike Milken at the adjacent X-desk and still sees Milken regularly. "You mix guys and alcohol and money, and very predictable things happen, but that was not all that happened. I called it the University of LBOs. Every day you woke up and you were involved with something that made the front page of the *Wall Street Journal*." Many of the people who sat at this executive's "X," as the communal desks were known, have gone on to start what have become massive businesses around the world: Tony Ressler, a founding partner of Ares Management LLC, which has approximately $50 billion in assets; Bob Beyer, who is head of the Trust Company of the West; Mark Antanasio, who owns the Milwaukee Brewers; among many others. "You didn't realize how talented people around you were, until 20 years later, when you saw what they did,"[5] he says.

Even the receptionists were unlike others in their line of work. They were typically as beautiful as any young aspiring starlet in Los Angeles, but they were also extremely intelligent. "You're out in L.A.," says the former Drexel executive, "so if you're going to hire attractive girls to answer the phone, you might as well make them really attractive. But Mike paid them $75,000 a year, at a time when they would have made $25,000 anywhere else. It was peanuts for Mike to pay them so well, but because he did, he could hire people who were not only beautiful but competent. And not only competent but very, very bright. They held their own with all these guys who have done so well."[6]

For the guy in the short-sleeved nerdy shirt and the toupee, whose friends wouldn't allow him to drive because he was always so distracted in his silence and was asleep by 7:00 p.m. and awake by 3:00 a.m., there was little time for the outside world. He was all business. "I wouldn't necessarily describe the guy as friendly. He's super-smart; he's super-intense; he's super-demanding. There's very little chitchat. I don't remember ever really having any sort of small talk with him to speak of," the former Drexel banker says. "I knew he was a Lakers fan, and I said to him once, 'Hey, Mike, great Lakers game, huh?' He sort of looked at me funny. So I vowed I wouldn't do that again."[7]

Instead of basketball games or any shard of popular culture, Milken had an uncanny vision for what was unseen by those around him. He was often to be found at the Gelson supermarket staring into the shopping carts for clues to the state of the economy and the stock market. "He was always working on big stuff and big ideas, many of which you would think were crazy," the Drexel alumnus recalls. "I remember sitting in a room with Steve Wynn, who I thought was just insane. No one had ever financed a big casino in Las Vegas before. Steve owned this tiny little dump, but here he sat with his carpet swatches talking about volcanoes and white tigers, and I was like, 'This is nuts, right?' Mike jumped out of his seat and said, 'This is amazing. We're going to do it!' So we raised $800 million for the guy to build the Mirage. It's a city now. And none of it made sense to anyone but Steve Wynn and Mike Milken. They now have houses near each other at Tahoe. Who knew?"[8]

People thought big. "You're sitting in a room, and they're going, 'Okay, how do we buy a country? Can we do an LBO on a whole country? Can we buy Pennzoil or Texaco or whatever? Can we take over the school system of California? It was crazy, but every once in a while they're able to sort of execute on one of these things." Milken's former colleague remembers his sight of the first cell phone, for example. Says Milken, "Don't worry guys, these things are going to get smaller. This is going to be great. Run a model. Let me know what this thing is worth if 2 percent of the country use cell phones." Ridiculous, the executive remembers thinking to himself. Who can even lift this "cell phone" thing? It was the size of a shoe box and the weight of a brick.

It was also hard work, and it only got harder. "It was never easy," he remembers, "because with every deal, people got more and more aggressive, and everything got more and more challenging. When we did RJR Nabisco, I remember a meeting where Peter Ackerman, Mike's number two, went around the room and said, 'Okay, if everybody buys the maximum amount of bonds they've ever bought, what does that add up to?' It added up to 3 billion, and we had to commit to 5 billion. So Peter said, 'Okay, we're just going to expand the market. We're going to get all the people who've never bought bonds before.' Very aggressive stuff, all of this. Normal people don't take those sorts of risks, and we were tiny. Drexel only had maybe $13 billion in capital. There were deals that went well: the guys buying

Duracell—okay in hindsight, they made a fortune. It made sense. But at the time, who knew anything about batteries? It was a much simpler world back then. If you bought batteries once or twice a year, that was sort of it. But they could see electronics exploding into the future. It was the democratization of capital. People who would never have had access to capital were suddenly equal to those who always could. It changed the world."[9]

The world of Drexel ended abruptly. "No one really had any idea how bad it was. For one thing, you didn't have the 24-hour news cycle like you do now. Plus, people didn't talk about any of the investigations. It was all sort of in the background. Everyone kept their mouths shut. And then one day, Fred Joseph's voice came over the loudspeakers and said, 'Except for a handful of people that we're going to need to wind it down, we're terminating everybody effective immediately.' And that was that. About 10,000 people. Done. It was the first time we knew just how bad it was."[10]

The Predators' Ball in 1985 had our stars in attendance. Proving the point that the Drexel phenomenon was not just about money and prostitutes, they came to do business that would reverberate across the economy, which, beyond Milken's heaven and earth, would not have been dreamt of in other philosophies. Carl Icahn listened to a speech by the chief financial officer of TWA, Robert Peiser. Carl went up to him afterward and peppered him with questions. John Kluge's Metromedia company gave a big presentation about itself before the 2,000-member audience of potential lenders, spotlighting all its many assets, from the Ice Capades to the Harlem Globetrotters, from the Ponderosa Steakhouse chain to television stations. Sir James Goldsmith was there, reveling in the vulgarity he so often proclaimed was a sign of American vitality.

Jimmy's friend Ezra Zilkha, the scion of a Baghdadi-Jewish banking dynasty and a member of the board of Revlon, was more reticent than most about the cult of Mike. "I met Milken early one morning in Los Angeles. We talked for about half an hour, and he seemed like an intelligent man. He invited me to several of the affairs he used to host for clients and investors, but I never went. Although many honorable people attended them, I had heard that they were often followed by scandalous parties where I would not have wanted to be seen."

Sir James had no such qualms. He wanted junk bonds to finance his bid for Crown Zellerbach.

CHAPTER SEVEN
RUBBER PHOBIA

Jimmy Goldsmith and Lady Annabel Birley gradually realized that each was staring at the same thing. An inoffensive rubber band had formed a lopsided curlicue on the floor of the center aisle of the airplane. She turned away first, hoping that her lover had somehow missed it and that their holiday in Rio for Carnival would therefore remain unaffected. It was not to be.

Jimmy was in his 40s in the 1970s when he and his then mistress, Lady Annabel, boarded their plane for Brazil. He had been a global celebrity since the early 1950s. For half a century, he was a star in the worlds of finance, politics, and hedonism until his death in 1997. He was a feared serial acquirer of corporations in Europe and the Americas, a driven politician in both Brussels and Whitehall, and, perhaps most notoriously, a collector and mate of famously beautiful and well-born women. He would become Sir James, at Her Majesty's pleasure; "Goldenballs," by the pen of Richard Ingrams; and Sir Larry Wildman, courtesy of Oliver Stone.

At 20, Jimmy had eloped with 18-year-old Isabel Patino, the daughter of the Duchess of Durcal and Antenor Patino, the tin mogul of Bolivia, who pursued the couple across France, North Africa, England, and Scotland but failed to block the marriage. Jimmy's young wife died of a cerebral hemorrhage and on her deathbed was delivered of a daughter, the first of Jimmy's eight children by four women. The story entranced the British and European newspaper-reading public for months and was never forgotten as long as he lived.

By the late seventies, he was without subterfuge dividing his time among three women and three cities. In Paris, it was Ginette Lery, who was first his secretary and eventually his second wife. In Richmond, it was Lady Annabel, his mistress and then his third wife. In New York, it was

French journalist Laure Boulay de la Meurthe. They were an interesting group. Laure was the great niece of the Comte de Paris, a pretender to the French throne. Lady Annabel came from one of the grandest families in the land, the daughter of the eighth Marquis of Londonderry, the sister of one of the queen's maids of honor at the coronation, the wife of Mark Birley, who founded the eponymous Annabel's Club in Berkeley Square, and the mother of Jemima Khan.

Jimmy also collected houses. Perhaps the most splendid were his Mexican estates: a main house at Cuixmala, a 60,000-square-foot fever dream of Agra and Cordoba, which relies for its effect not on endless interior fussiness but on its own open spaces and the surrounding pre-Columbian wilderness of cliffs and jungle along the Virgin Coast; La Loma, a blue-and-gold-domed aerie; and, 300 miles away, a 4,500-acre hacienda with a pink palace known as Jabali, which had belonged to his first father-in-law and was built at an altitude of 5,000 feet under the violent, perpetually steaming Colima volcano.

It was his own private Jurassic Park—25,000 acres of lagoons and swamps and wild jungle, of crocodiles elsewhere extinct, pumas and jaguars no longer seen in other parts of Mexico, migratory whales, giant turtles, seabirds, all in a vast human-less landscape. Guests would fly to Puerto Vallarta on Jimmy's 757, itself a winged Taj Mahal, and then take a smaller plane for the trip 100 miles to the south. As the plane touched down into Edenic wilderness, egrets, herons, pelicans, zebras, and elands would fan out before it as an honor guard into the primeval. It was often likened to house-party weekends with Dr. No, complete with what the *Economist* called a "spooky private army."[1]

Yet Jimmy was ever a son of the ghetto. His paternal Jewish ancestors had lived in Frankfurt's Judengasse at least since 1521, when the first "Goldschmidt" made his appearance in the records. "Although the confident, worldly billionaire Jimmy Goldsmith, with his fine house, his private jets, yachts and his women may seem a million miles away," Ivan Fallon writes in his biography *Billionaire*, "he is in fact only a generation away from Frankfurt. His father was born in that same tight Frankfurt Jewish community (although by that stage they had moved out of the ghetto to live in some style outside), his great-uncle married the last of the Frankfurt Rothschilds (and changed his name to Goldschmidt-Rothschild), and Jimmy Goldsmith himself learned early in life some of the pride and bitterness of that inheritance."[2] From the same city within a city came other ghetto families that metamorphosed into the great banking dynasties of the world: the Salomons, the Oppenheimers, the Wertheims, and, above all, the Rothschilds. Even after his grandparents left Germany in 1895 and established themselves in London and at their country seat in Surrey, it was never forgotten that they were "different." His father, assimilated to the point of caricature, suffered undeserved disgrace at the outset of the Great War. Like Lord Mountbatten's father, who was famously forced to resign as First Sea Lord under anti-German pressure, Frank Goldsmith relinquished his seat in Parliament when his loyalty to England was brutally challenged. His son saw that foreignness is forever secretly suspect in tribal England.

As if in some reaction to the centuries of sequestration his family endured, the erudite and sophisticated, multilingual, and supremely confident young Jimmy could not have been more of a nomad or more the quintessence of a global citizen, with his French mother and his Anglicized German-Jewish father, his childhood spent in a kind of royal progress among the hotels of southern France managed by his father, his adolescence as an upper middle-class English schoolboy at Eton.

Jimmy was dyslexic. His brother Teddy once asked him, when Jimmy was seven years old, why he had no interest in learning to read. Jimmy answered, "Because when I grow up I'm going to be a millionaire and hire someone to read for me."[3] He was also precocious in the extreme. At the age of nine, in boarding school in Toronto, he started a business. He would set nightly traps for small animals, mostly skunk and rabbit and mink, and sell their skins. At 16, now at Eton, he bet ten pounds on three horses at the Lewes races—Bartisan, Your Fancy, and Merry Dance—in what is known as an accumulator, under which the winnings of the first move on to the second and thence to the third. All three won, and his tenner turned into 8,000 pounds, a fortune for a teenager in the early decades of the twentieth century. Before leaving Eton with his racing riches, he bought his hated housemaster the Beethoven symphonies. When the surprised man, deeply affected, began to thank him, Jimmy took the package back, pulled out each record in turn, and broke them over the housemaster's desk.[4]

Jimmy was hypochondriacal: "The slightest sign of a cold would be seen as the onset of a dreadful flu and a headache translated into a brain tumor," Lady Annabel writes in her autobiography. He was obsessive and jealous. His temper could erupt with the magma of the dyslexic's frustration. At Jabali, the pink hacienda under the volcano, high in the western Mexican mountains, Lady Annabel once came upon a clutch of pink-clad maids weeping. Jimmy had been unable to sleep because of a noisy boiler and had thrown a television set and video recorder out over the mountainside and announced that he was closing the house and would never return. After some time and a good dinner, all was forgotten.[5]

Back in the late 1950s, desperate to make a living, Jimmy was given a crucial leg up by a banking family, the Zilkha clan, who opened a small branch office in Paris at 23 Rue de la Paix, where Jimmy also leased space. Unlike the Goldsmiths of the Frankfurt ghetto, the Zilkhas were proud members of the free Jewish community that thrived in Iraq for centuries. "There was no ghetto," says the present patriarch of the family, Ezra Zilkha, "except the one that rich Jews imposed on themselves because they lived in the best part of town, by the Tigris River. At one time one-quarter of Baghdad's population was Jewish, and they were totally integrated. There were Jewish landowners, Jewish banks, Jewish stevedores, Jewish *everything*."[6]

Jimmy entranced Selim Zilkha, Ezra's younger brother. "Selim would call me every day, and it was always, 'Jimmy this,' and 'Jimmy that.' My brother, you see, like so many, was obsessed with Jimmy. Jimmy was a cult leader," Ezra says. Jimmy and Selim became business partners. Calling himself a capitalist without capital, Jimmy would come to Selim with an incessant stream of ideas. "And Selim would always say yes," Ezra recalls.[7] Not all Jimmy's ventures were as successful or salubrious as they might have been. One was a skin cream designed to turn dark skin to white. "Have you tested it?" a Zilkha uncle asked him. Jimmy answered that it had undergone trials. "Is it dangerous?" the older man asked. Jimmy answered, "Well, it doesn't really matter if a Brazilian or two dies, does it?"[8] Such was his penchant for saying the shocking.

Jimmy would become known for several aphorisms. His most famous described his own life: "If you marry your mistress, you create a vacancy." It is an amusing, if flippant, statement, but it also conceals the true nature of the life he created. Lady Annabel acknowledges the complexity and the pain of it when she writes, "I can hardly pretend that any of the three women in his life was entirely happy with the arrangements. . . . But he was the only man I can think of who could get away with such behaviour because when he was with each of us, he was totally protective and kind to us. Just because he had found another woman to love did not mean he changed his behaviour towards or feelings for her predecessor. Jimmy's private life may have shocked and puzzled people but he never made a secret of it. One of the things I most admired about him was his remarkable lack of hypocrisy, as he could not have cared less what people thought of him or may have whispered behind his back. He got away with having three separate families because he compartmentalized his life so effectively."[9]

Yet it could not have been easy, even for him.

"His morality was certainly different from mine, but that didn't make him any less of a friend," says Ezra Zilkha. "He was also more of a gambler than I could ever be. . . . Jimmy had a brilliant yet utterly impulsive mind. He accumulated his immense fortune by taking very long chances that worked out against all the odds. To put it succinctly, he gambled well. Gambling is hard on the nerves, however, and always keeping just one step ahead of bankruptcy took its toll on Jimmy. I remember a dinner at Selim's home in London when Jimmy looked like a tortured man. He clutched a long-stemmed wine glass so tightly that it shattered in his hand."[10]

Despite, or perhaps because of, the force that gave the twists to the spiral of his life, Jimmy had a much-loved laugh, a languor that intrigued, a capacity to seduce. "One of the most lovable things about him was his cosi-ness," Lady Annabel writes. "His favorite sort of evening was dinner in bed, preferably scrambled eggs and bacon, which I would make for him, with a cup of tea and sometimes yoghurt and apple puree. . . . It was impossible to be bored by him."[11]

Just before their plane could begin to taxi down the runway toward their holiday in the Rio of the 1970s, Jimmy quietly called for a stewardess and asked her to remove the offending rubber band he and Lady Annabel had discovered in the aisle of the plane. "He could be physically sick if he saw one," writes Lady Annabel. "If anyone brought in his post bound by a rubber band there would be a shriek of horror, and you had to remove and dispose of it immediately, while you went to wash your hands."

We have to get off, he said. If there is *one,* there will be *another,* he said, as if he knew that little latex creatures had been breeding furiously and would soon burst from their nests and swarm the plane. It is nowhere re-vealed what Jimmy did next. But the flight crew evidently saw that the best course was to acquiesce. The plane returned to the terminal, where they, and the rest of the passengers, waited for their "vast quantity" of luggage to be unloaded from the hold. "We never made it to Rio."[12]

CHAPTER EIGHT
THE GUNS OF AQABA

There was one compulsion propelling Jimmy Goldsmith that remained largely unknown. In the early years of the nineteenth century, the Goldsmiths and the Rothschilds were of equal rank, although the latter were acknowledged to be the leading family of Frankfurt's *vicus Judaeorum*. By 1815, however, Nathan Rothschild had become the British government's main banker, financing Wellington's armies at the Battle of Waterloo, and transforming his family of successful financiers into one of the greatest commercial dynasties in history. Jimmy worked assiduously to redress the imbalance and recover his family's ancient position relative to his famous cousins-in-law.[1]

One wonders what it might have meant to him that two of his sons, Ben and Zac, were married for a time to Rothschild sisters, Kate and Alice, respectively. How fitting he must have found his friendship and his alliance with Jacob Rothschild as the two "modern scions of those same Frankfurt ghetto forebears" ignited one of the largest takeovers the world had ever seen—their offer to buy British-American Tobacco for 13 billion pounds, or roughly $21 billion. In the end, Jimmy and his partners, including Gianni Agnelli and Lord Weinstock, were forced into defeat by the labyrinthine regulatory procedures he decried so eloquently.[2] It was estimated that the takeover attempt cost both sides a total of at least $150 million.[3] It was a difficult defeat. One adviser to the Goldsmith/Rothschild alliance said, "We lost by the length of a bee's dick."

Although he failed to pull off one of the largest takeovers in history, Jimmy had already triumphed in America and won his place in M&A history four years before the B.A.T debacle. In 1985, Jimmy blithely obliterated an early form of the most famous takeover defense ever invented. It was Marty Lipton's poison pill.

Like early cars, the first pills were creaky creatures, sputtering and sparking and stalling even as they changed human existence forever. Now they have an elegant simplicity. If a buyer purchases more than a certain percentage of a company's stock, the other shareholders instantly get the right to buy stock in either their own company or the buyer's corporation at a steep discount. Because this turns the buyer's stake into a much smaller percentage of the total number of shares, modern pills are virtually never triggered. The device is meant to give boards of directors some time and force a hostile buyer to the negotiating table. The board can put in or remove a pill at its pleasure. The Crown Zellerbach pill in 1984, one of the early Model Ts, however, was set off not by the level of a buyer's purchases but by an actual merger. Jimmy saw the flaw and made his move accordingly.

For several years since the Seagram hostile bid for St. Joe Minerals, Marty had been working in his secret laboratory in Midtown Manhattan with Ilan Reich, exploring everything from insurance law to Delaware court rulings in search of some kind of Bondian death ray to protect corporate America from the invasion of the body snatchers. In September 1982, Marty at last sent around a secret memo to his partners and to a few trusted investment banks. It was a magna carta for M&A. In it, Marty described what he called the warrant dividend plan as a device that would deter takeovers but could not prevent them entirely. His readers were intrigued. Now the time was right to get a corporation to install the death ray on its ramparts.

On a rainy night in July 1982, Marty arrived at Houston's Warwick Hotel. The directors of El Paso Natural Gas were to meet the next day to discuss a front-end-loaded, partial offer for their company from Burlington Northern Railroad. It was an aggressive offer for less than a majority of the stock, with no promise of a back end. Known as two-tiered bids, such offers promised to pay a certain percentage of stockholders in cash and anyone past that percentage in stock or paper. They were criticized as high-pressure catalysts for a stampede, as the stockholders would rush to sell their stock so they could be part of the percentage to be paid in cash. The railroad had announced the bid Christmas Eve and given the target very little time to attempt an escape. El Paso was thrashing around like a gaffed fish, trying to find someone else to bid and take the company off the hook. No competitors were interested. The price was high. Time was short.

Marty had just come from Dallas, where he had been advising another client, General American Oil, facing a similar coercive offer from T. Boone Pickens. For vulnerable General American, which did not even have a staggered board, Marty had thought of a way to protect back-end shareholders. The company had some authorized blank-check preferred stock that a board could custom tailor and issue without shareholder approval. Marty's idea was to insert a fair-price provision in this preferred stock to protect shareholders from a low-ball second step. But Marty had no luck in Dallas.

The foundation that controlled General American decided against using the preferred stock. Rather than take its chances against Pickens with an unorthodox and a somewhat suspect takeover defense, the foundation decided to throw in its lot with a second bidder offering a higher price. "This security," Marty recalled, "became academic."[4]

Near midnight in the Houston hotel, Marty and his partner, the late James Fogelson, mulled over the El Paso board meeting the next day. "Look, there's nothing. Absolutely nothing," Fogelson told Marty, bemoaning El Paso's lack of a staggered board or defensive charter provisions. "They're just dead." "Well," Marty asked, "do they have blank-check preferred stock?" Yes, Fogelson said, they did. That was all Marty needed to know. El Paso, on the other hand, was desperate. The company was "rocking on the lip of bankruptcy," so the objective was not to preserve its autonomy but to get it a capital infusion and protect the 49 percent of shares not targeted in the tender offer from a second-step squeeze out. The two Wachtell partners devised a blank-check preferred that would keep 40 percent of the stock in the hands of back-end shareholders.[5]

Marty placed a call to Stephen Fraidin, then of Fried, Frank, who would advise Ted Forstmann in the battle for RJR Nabisco seven years later. Fraidin was representing Burlington Northern with his partner Arthur Fleischer Jr. Marty told Fraidin that unless they could come to some arrangement for improving the bid, he would advise El Paso to issue the blank-check preferred and possibly his newly minted warrant dividend plan as well.

Fraidin was not impressed. He was convinced the Delaware courts would view the new stock as a meaningless fabrication, and as fast as possible, he sought a temporary restraining order from the chancery court. The court denied Fraidin's motion. The nascent pill, the preferred stock, had achieved what it was designed to do. The target won some desperately needed time and gained some much-needed negotiating leverage. Burlington Northern did not raise its offer of $24 per share, but it did agree to offer it to more shareholders and to grant El Paso a capital infusion for a fair-priced second step.

The denial of a restraining order does not amount to court approval. It is not an actual precedent, but it did encourage the firm to offer the new device elsewhere. After El Paso, a handful of companies, including Bell & Howell and Enstar, made similar use of blank-check preferred. "It proved to be useful in each case," Marty told the Tulane conference in March 1995.[6]

Marty has long maintained that the El Paso stock was the first poison pill. Soon after El Paso, it got its name. In 1983, Wachtell was defending Lenox Inc. against a bid by Brown-Forman Distillers Corp. Lenox had no blank-check preferred, so the company used a convertible debenture instead. The Lenox pill included a flip-over provision, the first to give the target company power over the capital structure of a hostile bidder. This pill also for the first time gave the board of directors the explicit right to lift the pill if it wanted to go ahead with a friendly deal. In New Orleans, Marty said the use of a different security freed his firm conceptually from thinking of the device strictly in terms of preferred stock. Acceptance of this new device was still grudging at best. So far, it had never been tested in battle. It had always been erected as a permanent defense in peacetime. Was it a worthy weapon, or was it merely a Maginot line?

The world would find out in the summer of 1984. On July 19, Crown Zellerbach became the first company to adopt it in the absence of a specific threat. This pill was yet another creature of Marty's restless mind: the warrant dividend plan. Preferred stock could turn into a messy blot on an otherwise lucid balance sheet. Warrants, on the other hand, could be issued to shareholders as a dividend and not appear on the balance sheet. The bulk of the new plan was its flip-over provision. If an unwanted buyer amassed 20 percent or more of Crown Zellerbach stock and squeezed out shareholders in a second-step merger, then those Crown Zellerbach stockholders would have the right to buy at a discount one-quarter of the market value of the acquirer's stock, seriously diluting the predator.

Jimmy Goldsmith was determined to take over Crown Zellerbach. He had no intention of setting off the pill. Armed with an opinion from his advisers at Skadden, he had discerned that it would fire only if he decided to go through with an actual merger. If he took control of the company by buying 51 percent of its shares, he could simply carry on as the new owner, utterly unaffected by the defense set up by Marty Lipton. The pill would be the guns of Aqaba immovably aimed at the sea, in Sir David Lean's version of the battle, and Jimmy would be T. E. Lawrence, who, in the film, took the city by approaching from the Great Nefud desert that no one thought could ever be crossed.

Moira Johnston describes in her book *Takeover* the triumphant progress of Jimmy Goldsmith on his way to the closing of his deal for Crown Zellerbach. It is July 25, 1985, less than a month before the TWA board will vote to give TWA to Carl Icahn. Jimmy arrives at JFK by Concorde and moves in resolutely for the kill:

> Sir James was whisked by limousine to a brick town house on East Eightieth Street marked only by a discreet number, buzzer, and locks. Inside, moving past marble busts of two powerful Florentines, Cardinal Soderini and his brother, for whom Machiavelli had worked as secretary of the influential governing committee Dieci di Balia, he crossed a three-story atrium carved from the bowels of the staid Victorian town house, ... and climbed a splendid curved stairway to the drawing room where Goldsmith's team waited, watched by a

haughty bust of a Medici. There, . . . [he] and his team refined the terms of surrender that would be negotiated with Crown Zellerbach that afternoon.

The denouement came at Wachtell's offices. Marty and his colleagues had represented Crown Zellerbach, and its CEO, Bill Creson, [and] senior executive George James were at the closing, along with outside Crown director Warren Hellman. The CEO, Bill Creson, who had raced over four years to revive the company, did not respond to Jimmy's agenda.

The lead-off response came [from] Warren Hellman, grandson of the founder of Wells Fargo Bank, and now a San Francisco investment banker with Jewish establishment credentials to match those of old James D. Zellerbach, grandson of the founder, who died in 1963. An attractive, lean ultra-marathoner who had raced to the presidency of Lehman Brothers in New York at twenty-nine, he spoke Goldsmith's language much more comfortably than did Creson. It was as if, intuitively, a voice more like that of the founding entrepreneur, not a professional manager's, needed to be heard at the gallows. The principals left the meeting in the late afternoon, with the fine-tuning in the hands of the team that had lived and breathed the deal since December 1984. At 9:00 p.m., Creson and Goldsmith signed the agreement. With a signature, Crown Zellerbach ceased to exist as an independent company. . . . Sir James caught the Concorde back to Paris.[7]

For Marty, there was no conveyance faster than the speed of sound that could carry him to a better place. "It was the worst disappointment of my professional life," he said at the time. His pill was a joke.

CHAPTER NINE
ERECTILE DYSFUNCTION

"This isn't giving me an erection," Joe Flom said, tossing the brief back across his desk with a scowl at young associate Stuart Shapiro. "I'm not surprised, at your age," Stu said without missing a beat. Joe used the erection remark often to shock, intimidate, and galvanize, but no one had ever answered him in quite the same way. "We got along well after that, because all the partners were afraid of him, and I just figured if the guy's going to be a bully, I can do it back. And he actually respected that. I was a second-year associate, and he was about 50 at the time." Stu laughs now. "I look back on it now, at my age, and I'm a lot older than he was then!"[1]

Malcolm Gladwell in *Outliers,* written not long before Joe's death in February 2011, describes him as follows: "He is short and slightly hunched. His head is large, framed by long prominent ears, and his narrow blue eyes are hidden by oversize aviator-style glasses. He is slender now, but during his heyday, Flom was extremely overweight. He waddles when he walks. He doodles when he thinks. He mumbles when he talks, and when he makes his way down the halls of Skadden, Arps, conversations drop to a hush."[2]

Flom was well aware of his unconventional appearance and often made an entrance that blotted out potential mockery or criticism and established him as the alpha male in an instant. His partner Jim Freund recalls a story often told at Skadden. It is 1969. Saul Steinberg, "then a little fly-by-night," has launched a hostile bid for Chemical Bank, one of the country's largest financial institutions. All the millionaire advisers and all the vice presidents and senior vice presidents and partners from eminent firms like Cravath are assembled at the bank for the first strategy meeting. All but Joe Flom. "Well, shall we get started?" someone says. Ten o'clock has come and gone. The minutes hasten like waves toward the pebbled shore. People grow ever more restless. Watches are checked. Harrumphs are heard. Joe appears, shuffling in, mouthing a cigar. Everyone stares at him. Joe growls. "Have you checked this room for bugs?" "Bugs? *Bugs?* At Chemical Bank?" Joe turns to the number-two guy: "You check this place for bugs?" The number-two guy turns to the number-three guy: "Have you checked this room for bugs?" Joe says, "No? Then I suggest we adjourn this meeting and move to another room that has been so checked." Jim Freund points out the strategy behind it all. "Joe took over. With that little gesture, he just took over the whole thing. It was his show from then on. Nobody else opened his mouth after that. Flom was a cocky guy. He walked into the room with a big cigar, and he was not awed by the presence of all these hitters. Just took it over."[3]

Joe was lucky in his first wife, Claire. They met in the late 1950s when Joe asked her to decorate an apartment he had just rented on the Upper East Side. It was the first time he had "two nickels to rub together" and could leave his downtown roommates behind. She found Joe "arbitrary and capricious," according to Lincoln Kaplan's account in his book *Skadden*, "and exasperating to work for." He was impressed by her credentials as an interior designer. She had done work for senior partners at Cahill Gordon. "I discovered just before the job was finished," she told Kaplan, "that Joe was color-blind, and that was a big part of the problem."[4]

Tall, glamorous, with green eyes and "a dusky voice," as Kaplan describes her, Claire was not to be trifled with. "We're all sitting in Joe's office," Stu Shapiro remembers, "back when we were in the French building when I first joined the firm. It's Christmas Eve, and she walks in. A bunch of us are having a meeting, and she grabs Joe by the ear and says, 'It's Christmas Eve, and you're coming home.' Drags him out. She says over her shoulder, 'The only time I'll let him get away with this is if Roy Cohn is on the other side. Then he can take whatever time it takes to beat that son of a bitch.' These were real people. They weren't polished. They weren't spinners. They were real, interesting, complex people. You don't meet a lot of people like that anymore."[5]

At the top of his class at Harvard Law School and an editor of the law review, where he dazzled his professors when he would all but take over a lecture, Joe was not showered with job offers after graduation. Ostracism causes deep pain, and Joe was not immune. He could voice disdain for those who shunned him, but there was also a profound longing to be included, to be welcomed, to be liked, to belong.

Stu saw this often-hidden need during the great blackout in New York in the summer of 1977. The two men were trying to get down to Washington to see Stanley Sporkin, then head of the division of enforcement at the SEC, but the airports were closed, and they came back to Manhattan. "There was one swath in the midtown area that had electricity. We went to Le Perigord because they were serving lunch, and Joe said to me, 'You go in and see if we can get served. If I go in, they won't give us a table.'"[6]

His joy at inclusion could be poignant. Stu and Joe were guests of Stu's father at the Alfalfa Club's annual dinner. "It's a club that has no purpose other than one dinner a year," Stu says. "The president comes, most of the Supreme Court justices, the vice president, all the leaders of Congress, CEOs of all the major corporations. Being a member of the Alfalfa Club is a big thing for people. It means you're really connected. There were lots of military there, generals with four stars, three stars, all wearing their medals, and a grinning Joe looks around and says, 'Man, I haven't ever seen so much salad in my whole life.' Here's a guy who's arguably the most important business lawyer in twentieth-century America. But he'd been in the army as a private. He's with generals now."[7]

Stu, whose grandparents were equally hardworking with no bequeathed advantages, came from a similar but profoundly different world and time. Born in the mid-1940s, he grew up an all-American kid in a suburb on the edge of downtown Wilmington, Delaware, called Fairfield Manor. Patches of asparagus still sprung up in the backyard every spring from the days when the area had been open farmland. It was a boyhood of sandlot baseball, basketball in driveways, public high school.

For a while, life was a series of responses to random stimuli. He went to Carleton College because a cousin from Minneapolis had gone there. He went to law school because the Vietnam War loomed over him, and all those in his generation said he had to stay in school somehow, particularly as he was from Wilmington with its large population of children of PhDs who worked for the chemical companies, all of whom went to college. "There was not a huge pool of poor kids who could be sucked into the war while the rich kids went off to college," Stu recalled. The war disrupted life for those Stu's age. "We were all tremendously at loose ends. Everybody was focused on what has always been the most important thing—girls. The second most important priority was avoiding the war. I had no desire to be a lawyer at all. My father was a lawyer. I didn't want to be a lawyer. I mean, it just never occurred to me that that was something I'd want to do." His father convinced him that law school would be a gateway to a world of possibilities, so he entered Georgetown.

On October 21, 1967, an estimated 100,000 people marched on the Pentagon, demanding an end to the war. Organized by the National Mobilization Committee to End the War in Vietnam, affectionately known as the Mob, a loose coalition of 150 groups, it would become the prototype for the demonstrations at the 1968 Democratic Convention in Chicago. Crowds gathered at the Lincoln Memorial to listen to speeches and to welcome the peace torch, set alight at Hiroshima, flown to San Francisco, and carried across the United States. Flowers were placed in the barrels of guns, and Abbie Hoffman tried to levitate the Pentagon and turn it orange as a rite of exorcism. Stu was in the thick of it, this seminal event of the decade, as a volunteer for Legal Aid, a task that involved taking possession of the protesters' drugs so that the police would have less of an excuse to arrest them. He met David Dellinger, Jerry Rubin, Mark Rudd, and Bernardine Dohrn, a leader of the domestic activist group Weather Underground, now married to Bill Ayers, formerly a tenured professor at the University of Illinois at Chicago. "I actually hit on Bernardine," Stu says. "Unsuccessfully."

Meanwhile, back at law school, Stu says he made law review after, according to Stu, the people who'd made it on merit got drafted. It, too, was not for him. "I could not figure out why arguing over whether a period in a footnote should be italicized was meaningful. I got thrown off law review because I didn't do anything, but I got a clerkship." It was not just any clerkship but a chance to sit at the feet of one of the greatest judges in the country, Collins J. Seitz of the US Court of Appeals for the Third Circuit, former chancellor of the Delaware Court of Chancery, where he presided over the *Gerhard v. Belton* case, later combined with other cases into the US Supreme Court's decision in *Brown v. Board of Education,* affirming Chancellor Seitz's ruling in chancery.

Then came Skadden. "Out of the blue, I got a call from Barry Garfinkel from Skadden, Arps," Stu remembers. "I had no idea who Barry Garfinkel was, and I'd never heard of Skadden, Arps. He asked me to come up for an interview, if I didn't have a job already." Stu also had no idea how Garfinkel had heard of him. One of his professors had recommended him virtually at random, never having taught Stu in law school but knowing of his clerkship with Judge Seitz. "Joe Flom is one of the best securities lawyers in the country," Stu's professor told him, "and you're working for one of the greatest judges in the country, so you must be good."

It was dark and cold and snowing in New York when Stu showed up at Skadden just before Christmas. The firm had offices in the Fred F. French building at the time, at 551 Fifth Avenue at the northeast corner of 45th Street. The premises were not luxurious, but the partners were welcoming. Stu asked all of those who interviewed him what it was they disliked most about their work. "I got one consistent answer," Stu says. "They all said, 'I enjoy what I'm doing so much that I'm shortchanging my family.'" Only one partner made a comment that did not turn out to be true. John Feerick said, "The one thing you can count on here is that we're going to stay small and intimate." Skadden now has 23 offices around the world, from Brussels to Wilmington, with 40 practice areas and no fewer than 1,832 lawyers, including 414 equity partners. "Whenever I see John," Stu says, "I remind him that he misled me."

Skadden made Stu an offer. It was the only one he got. He took it. When Stu joined the firm in 1970, there were 44 lawyers, 4 of whom left soon after he arrived. Cravath had just stunned the law world the year before by raising first-year salaries to $15,500. Stu was making the princely sum of $15,000 a year, roughly 50 percent more than he would have made had he started in 1969. Partners got roughly $60,000. In 1985, when Cravath next startled its competitors in the same way, first-year associate salaries hit $65,000. In fiscal 2012, according to the *American Lawyer*'s annual ranking chart, Skadden was the fourth-highest-grossing law firm in the country. Its gross revenue was $2.210 billion. Revenue per lawyer was $1.275 million, net operation income hit $1.026 billion, and profits per partner were $2.615 million.[8]

When Skadden hired Stu, it had no office for him for the first few months, as the firm was about to move to its new headquarters at 919 Third Avenue, and Stu spent much of his time, of which he had quite a bit on his hands at first, in the library. He once made the mistake of leaving a book open on the table in the library while he took a break. Thomas J. Schwarz, also a first-year associate but with seniority over Stu since he had been a summer associate at Skadden, growled a command: "Put that book back. Don't just leave it on the table!" "Tom became a friend. He's now president of Purchase College. He was a New York kid just establishing the pecking order."

Stu has long since left Skadden, and for many years he has had his own firm: Shapiro Forman Allen & Sava in the heart of Midtown Manhattan. His former team just got too big. In what he calls semiretirement now, Stu often wears shorts and T-shirts at work. One day in the summer of 2012, his shirt from the legendary Gleason's Gym in Brooklyn had a quote from Virgil in the original Latin. He translates the aphorism as follows: "Now, whoever has courage and a strong and collected spirit in his breast, let him come forward, lace on the gloves and put up his hands." Preparing to lay down the gloves he has worn for so long, he could not have known all those years ago just how many bouts he would end up doing in the ring, more of the most important M&A cases than perhaps any other lawyer of his generation.

Stu's father was Irving Shapiro, later chairman and CEO of DuPont; a former senior Justice Department official and a lawyer at the Office of Price Administration (where he shared a desk with two colleagues—Henry Putzel, who later became the Supreme Court reporter, and a man who would later become a congressman from California, Richard M. Nixon); an international advocate for peace, particularly between the Israelis and the Arabs; a chairman of the Business Roundtable; a leading candidate for secretary of the treasury, withdrawing his name from consideration and paving the way for Michael Blumenthal's appointment to the position; a renowned litigator; and a famed public figure. When Stu told his father that he was moving to New York to take up his new job, Irving Shapiro was unimpressed.

"Skadden, Arps?" he asked his son. "What's Skadden, Arps?"

CHAPTER TEN
A BONDIAN DEATH RAY

I was an odd scene to watch. The object of ridicule was the absent John Whitehead, a man who was then in his early 70s. A Haverford College graduate with an MBA from Harvard, Whitehead became the chairman of Goldman Sachs, retiring from the bank after 38 years in 1984 as co-chairman and co-senior partner. He was deputy secretary of state under George Schultz from 1985 to 1989. Over the course of his luminous career, he has been chairman of the board of the Federal Reserve Bank of New York, chairman of the Andrew Mellon Foundation, a director of the New York Stock Exchange, and chairman of the Brookings Institution. In 1987, he was awarded the International Rescue Committee's Freedom Award along with Elie Wiesel. He is a longtime friend of the Rockefeller family and has held high positions at organizations founded by the family. He was married to the late television pioneer Nancy Dickerson until her death. Most recently, Whitehead served on the World Trade Center Memorial Foundation.

In front of some 300 people at Tulane's M&A conference in 1995, Marty Lipton in mock high dudgeon did an impression of a pompous John Whitehead, one of two members of the board of directors of Household International who, in 1984, refused to vote to implant Marty's new invention, the poison pill, in the company: "Well, I think it's most inappropriate for a big prominent company like Household to enact something like this," Marty mimicked. "I'm shocked that we would consider anything like this. I believe that it works, and I believe that it creates these benefits, but I certainly don't want to be associated with anything like this."

Did Whitehead really assert that he knew how it worked, that his adviser had explained it clearly enough for Whitehead to understand its benefits, a helpful statement for the adviser accused precisely of having failed to do just that? Had uber-WASP John Whitehead treated Marty's genius like trickery? Had Marty been offended at what he felt to be an ancient species of disdain? If you prick us, do we not bleed?

On August 17, 1984, John Moran, another Household board member and Whitehead's only other ally against the newfangled device, sued Household in the Delaware Court of Chancery, asking the judge to invalidate the poison pill. Marty's invention and his career were now at stake. Wachtell and the Wilmington, Delaware, firm of Richards, Layton & Finger prepared for the fight of their lives. No one at Skadden, the firm representing Moran, knew what the pill actually was, including Joe Flom, Stu remembers. "Flom kept giving us his ideas, but he basically didn't know what to make of it. I don't know of any idea in the law that is anywhere near the pill's level of sophistication," he says. "I took the depositions, and not one of the directors could explain to me what the poison pill actually was."

Just before the trial began, Stu was drinking wine and puzzling over the issues. He discovered what he thought was a fatal weakness in the Household pill. "I got up very excited. I got on the phone and started calling people, saying, 'Look at this. The pill's triggered if you have a proxy contest. The one thing the Delaware courts will never allow is an interference with the shareholders' right to vote. We win.'" At the trial, Stu asked, as casually as he could, a question of one of the directors: "So, if somebody solicits proxies and gets more than 20 percent of those proxies, that will trigger your pill. Is that correct?" Instantly, Charlie Richards, of Richards, Layton & Finger, saw the knife about to be drawn across his client's jugular. "He leapt to his full height of six feet ten inches, waving his arms," Stu says. "'That's not how we interpret it, Your Honor. That's not how it's meant to be. If it says that, we'll change it. If it literally says [that], that's wrong. We would never enforce it that way. It's not an issue, judge.' To his credit, Charlie just obliterated my point." That was the essence of Skadden's dilemma. Whatever flaws in execution or drafting the lawyers might unearth could be made to disappear in an instant. "They could just amend the contract," Stu explains. "We had to deal with the substance, the fundamental substance of it. None of us had a clue. None of us understood it."[1]

In its "Pre-Trial Memorandum of Points and Authorities," Skadden was on the attack from the first sentence. The pill is referred to as a "Poison Pill Rights device," which has an antique feel to it, much as older episodes of *Law & Order* have the characters planning "a search on the World Wide Web." Stu and his colleagues wrote the following section:

> The device is unnatural. It does not result from arm's-length negotiations with a third party or from a stockholder vote. It is purely a paper creation. It is created by a "dividend" which confers no value on the stockholders and thus is not really a dividend. The fraction of a preferred share a Right holder can buy is as far "out-of-the-money" as to make it illusory. The Right itself only exists as a

springboard for the Poison Pill. The Delaware General Assembly, however, has not authorized rights convertible into some other corporation's stock. Thus, there is a non-dividend dividend of an illusory right to buy preferred stock, all in order to force an unidentified (and presumably unwilling) company in the future to sell its shares at half price.[2]

Household's lawyers at Richards, Layton & Finger and Wachtell, Lipton fired right back. They argued that the pill did nothing to prevent takeovers or restrict shareholder power. Companies have a right to make sure that nobody bullies their shareholders into an unfair price for their stock. "There is no legal or moral right to stampede shareholders in the first step of a two-step takeover and then freeze them out in the second step," they maintained. "It defies law and logic to argue, as plaintiffs do, that a corporation has no right to protect against these tactics."[3] On January 29, 1985, Vice Chancellor Joseph Walsh announced that the shareholder rights plan, or poison pill, was valid. He did nothing to help define the device. He ruled merely that it did no harm, that it had been put in place fairly, and that it was helpful to targets.

Skadden wasted no time in filing an appeal to the Delaware Supreme Court, but who should argue it? Mike Mitchell and Rod Ward were eager to lead the charge, but Joe Flom had another idea. "Let's have Irv argue it," Joe Flom said. Irv it would be. "Irv" was Irving Shapiro, who had not argued a case in court since the 1940s as a criminal lawyer for the Justice Department in the Truman administration. What he had done more recently after retiring as the head of DuPont was to join Skadden as a partner, at Joe Flom's invitation, the law firm he had barely heard of 15 years earlier. Stu got a note from Mike Schwartz of Wachtell, saying that Bella Katz would be arguing their case. When Stu asked, "Who's Bella Katz?," Schwartz replied facetiously, in a reference to the fact that Shapiro's father was leading the argument for Stu's side, "George Katz's mother."

The oral argument was slated for May 20 in Dover. It was Irving Shapiro against Charlie Richards. Anyone in the takeover world who could get there did so. "Every limousine in Delaware had been rented," Stu remembered. He was worried. His father had been anything but a volunteer for the job, and Stu had secretly lobbied for him with Joe Flom.

When Irv got the call, it was not a request he could refuse the head of the firm, although he told his son he felt that Stu had "blindsided" him. He wondered whether he still had it in him. As an 11-year-old, he had testified before a grand jury in Minneapolis against a man accused of shaking down his father, Sam Shapiro, in the family's dry-cleaning shop; he had argued before the US Supreme Court before turning 30; he had been a star litigator at the Justice Department; he knew the dynamics of boardrooms intimately and was known as a corporate statesman. But he had not been before the bench since the 1940s.

Now Irv stood before three members of the Delaware Supreme Court, most ominously the redoubtable Justice Andrew G. T. Moore II. Moira Johnston describes Irv Shapiro that day as "a man of compact build and average height in a navy pinstripe suit, with an air of both warmth and toughness and the same deep rich voice that made Stuart so effective in court," who knew that the court could relegate him to "the rather quaint picture of a retired CEO making a case for the shareholders." He made the case for the shareholders. But quaint he was not. He reminded the judges that Delaware shareholders should have the power over their corporation's future, and he shrewdly warned that if the pill were allowed to stand, Delaware might be invaded by regulators from Washington, always the state's nightmare:

> We can't find any statutory provision that says a board acting on its own has the freedom to deny the vote to the shareholders . . . and that's what this plan does . . . and one has to keep asking, and I'm going to keep asking all morning: Why did this board choose not to go to the stockholders? That's what corporate democracy is about. . . . This plan says that if there is a merger that the board hasn't approved, and if the rights haven't been redeemed, then the acquiring company not only pays for the corporation at its value, but it pays a penalty of a hundred dollars a share in addition. Someone buying Household would have to pay somewhere in the range of $2 billion and then an additional $6 billion to manage this flipover. The penalty is so enormous that there could be no merger. What it's designed to do is say, "The risk over here is an atom bomb, so if you want to talk about a merger, you better do it on terms that this board finds acceptable, otherwise go away." . . .
>
> What are the values that are important here? In our society we expect corporations to be held accountable. The stockholder has been assigned the function of performing that job, and so far the system has worked pretty well. I would make the argument that corporate management . . . would recognize that keeping the shareholders in an active role in the corporation is absolutely vital to the health of corporate America. . . .
>
> When you deny the shareholders an active participation, what the corporation is doing is inviting the Ralph Naders and Senator Metzenbaums . . . to opt for government regulation of corporations as the best way to hold managements accountable. Accountability is the ball game.[4]

It was a fine moment for father and son, one that even the final result could not mar.

* * *

TUESDAY, NOVEMBER 19, 1985, WAS AN ORDINARY DAY FOR MOST PEOPLE BUT NOT FOR Marty Lipton. The stories in the *New York Times* had no disasters to display.

Donald Trump was seeking permission to build the world's tallest building, a 150-story tower, designed as the centerpiece of what the paper called "a massive complex of apartments, shopping centers and television studios" on a 13-block-long site along the Upper West Side waterfront that was once the Penn Central railyards. Robert Bork, a federal appellate judge and "a possible Supreme Court nominee," had issued a ruling saying that judges may not add new rights to those specified by the framers of the Constitution. A second summit meeting on how to stop the nuclear arms race was seen as likely between President Reagan and Mikhail Gorbachev after their two days of talks in Geneva. A deluded woman, as the *Times* put it, fatally shot a receptionist and the chairman of the Deak-Perera foreign exchange company. Apparently homeless and convinced she was part owner of the company, she had been asked to leave the executive office on lower Broadway but had returned two hours later to kill Nicholas Deak, the 80-year-old founder, and Frances Lauder, the 58-year-old receptionist.

Ilan Reich had spent a grueling and boring weekend at the office, constructing a deal for a "third-rate company" as a favor to Marty's friend, the Chicago power broker Ira Harris, head of the Chicago office of Salomon Brothers. He walked into Marty's office and launched into a series of comradely complaints about having had to miss one of his kid's birthdays and what "a shitty weekend" he had just endured. Marty, for the first time in Ilan's memory, erupted. "He yelled at me, 'Get out of my office! I don't need to hear this!' I just cowered out. I didn't know what was wrong."[5]

A verdict had come down from Texas that morning. The 12 jurors decided that Texaco had wrongly broken up a deal between Pennzoil and Getty Oil. They handed Texaco a bill for one of the largest damages awards in US history: $10.53 billion. Marty had taken the stand to testify for Texaco. He had tried to explain that the "agreement in principle," the handshake between Getty and Pennzoil, was not yet a binding contract. But Joe Jamail's bullying questions kept coming, as Stephen J. Adler described in his classic account of the trial in the *American Lawyer:* "Are you saying that two people cannot agree unless they hire a bunch of lawyers to tell them they've agreed? Are you saying that you have some distinction between just us ordinary people making contracts with each other and whether or not it's a ten-billion-dollar deal? It's a different standard in your mind?"[6]

Few of the jurors had a clue that Marty was one of the eminent experts in takeover law in the world. What's more, it was obvious that Jamail was trying to present Marty, with his massive black glasses and city-slickerish expensive suit, as not one of "us ordinary people" but a conniving New York lawyer with horns growing out of the sides of his head. Here is how Adler revealed what the jurors saw during the 18-week trial and why they handed Texaco the $10.53 billion bill, the largest verdict of its kind to date, after only 11 hours of debate:

Texaco lead counsel Richard Miller of Houston's Miller, Keeton, Bristow & Brown kept asking the jurors why they had decided against his client and why they had assessed such a gargantuan penalty. "Did I blow the case?" he asked. And the jurors kept pointing to the same Texaco witness—Martin Lipton of New York's Wachtell, Lipton, Rosen & Katz—who, they claimed, had severely damaged Texaco's defense.

"Texaco should have left him at home," jury foreman Richard Lawler, a forklift salesman, later said in an interview. "He didn't come across as very credible." Juror James Shannon ... put it more strongly, calling Lipton "a fast-talking double dealer." Juror Theresa Ladig ... said she thought Lipton was "just in it for the money."[7]

This was just the morning of Marty's day. The Delaware Supreme Court had told the main lawyers in the case that it would release its opinion in *Moran v. Household* at four that afternoon. Jimmy Goldsmith had already handed Marty the ultimate insult when, with aristocratic insouciance, he had simply ignored the shareholder rights plan and conquered Crown Zellerbach as if the pill did not exist. Marty had staked everything he had on the poison pill: his own reputation, his standing with his partners, the future of the firm, his very identity as an officer of the court.

Once, or only once that history knows of, did Marty actually reveal in words the depth of his concern. Marty and Gershon Kekst, whom Bruce Wasserstein described as "the dean of the financial public relations community," were standing in a corner outside a boardroom during a deal, talking quietly together. Ilan stood next to Marty. "Gershon, boy if this thing doesn't work," Marty said, his voice betraying uncharacteristic emotional vehemence, "it's really going to blow up in my face." It was, says Ilan, "a moment when a person of immense stature essentially admits his own vulnerability and fear."[8] Has any lawyer had such devastating news in a morning and faced a court opinion more ominous on the same afternoon as Marty Lipton on November 19, 1985?

Skadden was also on edge, waiting for word from Delaware. As the hour approached, a small group gathered in the office of Mike Mitchell at Skadden's headquarters in New York. Stu Shapiro saw the speakerphone light up. The opinion was telecopied to the firm as they listened to a colleague in the Wilmington office give them the news. They had lost. The state's highest court ruled that the pill was legal. M&A would never be the same again.

The pill did not halt takeovers. Indeed, it passed muster in Delaware in part because its creators insisted it was not designed to do so. What the pill did was just what Marty predicted: it gave boards power. No longer would a well-heeled bidder simply declare plans to take over a company and then do so without a fight. The pill was also a boon for Delaware. It became an umbilical cord between M&A and the courts of the state. It funneled money into the major New York law firms that set themselves up rapidly as expert pharmacologists in the chemistry and dosages that the pill required. Had the pill never been invented, federal courts would have seen far more take-over litigation; lawyers would have seen far less business in the boardrooms of the world and would most probably have been confined to issues of what information to file with the SEC and how to get deals closed and ownership officially transferred. The endless battle between shareholders and directors would have been fought in the halls of state legislatures and on Capitol Hill rather than corporate law's own Vatican City—Wilmington, Delaware.

Skadden moved on quickly. Within three weeks, it sent a fat, three-ring binder to its clients all about the pill. By the end of 1986, Skadden was tied with Wachtell at 79 pills each. Hundreds and ultimately thousands of companies adopted pills, and within a year, there wasn't a law firm in the country that did not consider itself qualified to set one up at any corporation that asked.

Years later, at a dinner in Key Biscayne, with Jim Freund playing a hotel piano brought out into the warm spring night for the occasion, Joe Flom agreed to look back at the battle over the poison pill. "I had been taught that a security had certain characteristics," he said. "This had none of those characteristics. You had a so-called security, which has no dividend rights and no equity rights. So you know, I mean, you gotta ask what the hell is it? And you know what it was pure and simple? A takeover defense. That's it. And you know why the courts upheld it? Because it was the popular wave at the time: The sky is falling with these takeovers, so do something."

Did Flom feel that the loss of Household was a moral defeat, that the law of takeovers would now suffer an endless wrong? He scoffed at this. "A 'moral defeat'? What are you talking about? There's no moral question involved. You try. You lose. The court said that this is okay, then it's the law. Then you live with it, and you make it better. We did that. We modified it for the good of the client. That's it. A moral defeat!"[9]

Marty Lipton has said privately, "It's just become boilerplate." Boilerplate, however, while it may sound like death, is actually where fixtures in the law go to enjoy eternal life.

CHAPTER ELEVEN
UP, UP, AND AWAY!

When the rotting severed head of an elk is thrown through the front window of the home of a pilot who has broken with his union to return to work, when striking employees spit and scream at former colleagues and replacement pilots, and when police in San Antonio, Texas, arrest two strikers carrying pipe bombs and a map to the houses of strike breakers, it can safely be said that the owner of that airline has a public relations problem, one that can make even Carl Icahn look good.[1]

Like Icahn, Frank Lorenzo was a middle-class kid from Queens, the third son of Basque immigrants, his father a beauty salon owner. He grew up within sight of the runways of LaGuardia, got himself an Ivy League degree, as did Icahn (in Lorenzo's case from Columbia), and followed it with a Harvard MBA. Lorenzo then worked as a financial analyst at TWA and Eastern and turned himself into an expert at restructuring flailing airlines. In 1972, he and a partner took control of Texas International Airlines from its creditors and set about getting the company back in the air. He hollowed out the workforce, ordered ground personnel to do a third of their jobs as part-time employees, and gritted his way through a four-month strike by all the company's unions.[2]

Six years later, he made the first takeover bid by an airline executive for a competitor, and although he lost when mammoth Pan Am captured National Airlines, he quickly sought other targets. In 1980, he turned his gimlet gaze to Continental Airlines. After a year of fighting, he got it, having promised California officials the usual: the headquarters in Los Angeles would not be moved, no jobs would be eliminated, and no assets would be sold.

Along the way, on August 9, 1981, the CEO of Continental Airlines, Alvin Lindbergh Feldman, fired a bullet into his head and killed himself at the age of 53 in his office at the Los Angeles airport. In letters to his three children, found with his body by a security guard, Feldman wrote that the recent loss of his wife, Rosemily, had sent him into a depression. "Apparently after his wife died, he threw himself heart and soul into the company and then the bottom fell out," a company spokesman said at the time. It wasn't long before Frank Lorenzo, after only ten years in the business and without using any money of his own, had himself the country's ninth-largest airline.[3]

Continental was an airline in serious trouble, suffering strikes by machinists and flight attendants, a threatened walkout by its pilots, and losses the previous year of $27 million, so Lorenzo wasted no time. He turned to Harvey Miller, the renowned bankruptcy lawyer at Weil, Gotshal & Manges, and took the airline into Chapter 11 in 1983. This allowed the company to suspend its debt payments, abrogate its union contracts, and decimate wages. The unions were outraged. Lorenzo basically had them thrown off the property.[4]

Lorenzo had been eyeing TWA for years. Toward the end of the 1970s, he made a brief run at his competitor, but the board and management brushed him away. He got his second chance in early June 1985 when Salomon Brothers called him, seeking a white knight willing to ride into the fray at TWA and save the airline from Carl Icahn. "We must have called a hundred airlines," Salomon's Michael Zimmerman said at the time. "No one wanted TWA because of the labor problems. Only Lorenzo didn't care."[5]

Lorenzo had his own way of dealing with labor, and he was fully aware of just what he saw before him. If he could capture the ailing company and whip it into health, he could combine it with Continental and New York Air, which he also owned, and turn himself into the owner of the largest transatlantic airline in the world, with flights from Tokyo to Bombay and total domestic market share second only to that of United Airlines. He had some vote-getting to do, however. His main asset, Continental, was still in bankruptcy, rapidly racking up record fees, some $60 million in the end, to become one of the most expensive restructurings of the day, not to mention that he was loathed by airline boards and unions in equal measure.

Icahn, meanwhile, was still the only bidder, with an $18-per-share offer worth $600 million. But what was he bidding for? Greenmail and another massive payday from a company eager to rid itself of his presence as a large stockholder? Or did he want to run an airline? Carl and his genius-in-residence, Alfred Kingsley, had been studying TWA for more than a year and had established a foothold in the stock in September 1984. The two men had long acted as an M&A hunting pair ever since Carl had hired Al as a summer intern in 1965 while Al was at Wharton. It was a powerful partnership, but a partnership in all but name, as Carl never actually made Al a business partner, which may explain why the latter finally moved on in the 1990s. Neither had much reticence when dealing with the establishment, both sounded like only native New Yorkers can, and each was as rapaciously intelligent as the other. Moira Johnston, in her book *Takeover,* rescues for history a glimpse of Al's infamous "library" at 1370 Avenue of the Americas in the early 1980s:

> Behind his desk, Kingsley is barely visible above a two-foot-high mountain of paper. He appears to have kept every business journal, proxy statement, legal brief, dog-eared letter, annual report, computer printout, and telephone memo that has touched his fingers since the day he started with Icahn in 1965. It's a corner room. But the light level has been substantially reduced by the drifts of paper piled on the counters behind his desk. . . . Here it is, a monument to takeover, a paper graveyard of deals that have been profitably put to bed.

At one point, Johnston describes Al's father, Herman, drinking coffee and watching his son work. "Whadda ya watching, Al?" he asks. "Everything," is his son's reply.[6] Did they see "everything" they were walking into when they began their attack on TWA? Were Carl and Al drawn so far into a labyrinth that their only exit turned out to be ownership of a very troubled airline that crashed and burned around them? To await the board's vote after his audition before the directors on August 20, 1985, Icahn and his team gathered at his offices. It had been quite a day. "The board meeting was as dramatic as any board meeting I've ever been to," says Jim Freund, the Skadden partner who was the chief lawyer for the defense of TWA.[7] He called Icahn with the result of the vote: TWA was his, but, as always with Carl, there was a final, tense, deal-breakingly agonizing series of demands, which Freund negotiated like the mediator he prefers to be. But Carl had won. Al mimicked Tonto: "Okay, Kemo Sabe, we do good in this town. We go on to next town now."

The head of the pilots' union took off his captain's jacket and handed it to Icahn. Dancing around the room, Carl chanted, "We've got ourselves an airline!" Word of this moved quickly through the ranks of the pilots, machinists, and flight attendants, some of whom still resent it to this day. This ebullient buyer, this newly triumphant airline owner, was not the same Carl who had held a celebratory breakfast just over two months earlier, soon after dawn on June 13, 1985.

On the evening of Sunday, June 10, Skadden's Jim Freund and his wife, Barbara Fox, the noted real estate maven, were in New Jersey at a party. A call came in for Freund from Stephen Jacobs, the Weil, Gotshal partner advising Icahn. Freund took the call while dinner was held in abeyance. If Icahn could sell his stock without being tripped up by the SEC rules against short-swing profits, if a deal with Lorenzo could be reached that was fair, then he would consider not opposing a purchase of the company by Texas Air. It was a signal, Freund remembers, a weak signal to be sure but a signal nevertheless that Icahn might be willing to leave TWA to its white knight. Freund and his wife returned to New York as soon as they could.

On Monday, Freund's team abandoned Resorts International, the third bidder circling TWA, and began continuous talks with Lorenzo's lieutenants. On the night of June 12, as so many takeover specialists like to put it, the Lorenzo, Icahn, and TWA armies went to the mattresses at the offices of Wachtell, Lipton, Rosen & Katz. Icahn was nowhere to be found. Lorenzo spent most of his time talking to a group of senior TWA people about golden passes, the tradition that gave the directors the right to a first-class TWA seat on any flight to anywhere in the world. This was extraordinarily important to the board. Lorenzo agreed to continue the practice and then slipped out into the night at 9:00 p.m., remaining incommunicado for the rest of the meeting.

Icahn had yet to show up and didn't appear until two o'clock in the morning. For Carl, this late-night-appearance thing was a negotiating tactic, recalls one Icahn veteran. Carl would go home, have a nap and a shower, and then make his entrance. The negotiators would be a bedraggled, exhausted bunch, eyes red from the cigar smoke, mouths rancid from cold pizza, heads aching with fatigue and stress. Carl would walk in, looking like a million bucks. In this instance, he went on a night cruise around Manhattan, according to Connie Bruck in the *American Lawyer.* "But at least he showed up," Freund says. "Lorenzo liked to withdraw from the fray and stay behind a curtain, manipulating things. He liked to operate through proxies. That night, we were all there past midnight and he wasn't around. We couldn't reach him. Couldn't believe it. A tough guy. Very complex guy." Lorenzo's vanishing act was his way to remain at a distance, retaining his veto power until the very end.

That night, as usual, Icahn was in his element as the hours crawled on. He insisted he did not want greenmail, but he did want a higher price from Lorenzo for all the stockholders. He demanded that any agreement protect him from the rigors of section 16(b), which would force him to return any profits he might make on his stock. He wanted to be paid for his expenses. All this, he couched in his inimitable negotiating style: questions to the group, questions to himself, muttering, mumbling, demanding, arguing, charging and retreating, pondering and expostulating to himself and his audience through a universe of possibilities.

Icahn told the *American Lawyer*'s Connie Bruck in December 1985 about the night soon after the war was finally over: "Freund kept saying, 'We can bring Resorts back with the two-tier bid. We know you can fight it, but it won't be pleasant for you.' And Leon [Black of Drexel] worked on me all night, saying, 'We've been friends with you. You're friends with us. Step out. You've already made over sixty million dollars.' I said, 'Leon, your man is making a billion dollars. He's getting synergy with his airline. I'm giving him a billion dollar gift, and you're arguing over a few million dollars?'"[8]

Finally, an agreement began to coalesce. Texas Air would raise its offering price to $23.50 per share, up from $23. There would be price supports for Icahn's preferred stock. To save him from the snares of 16(b), he would not have to vote for the merger, and the closing would be delayed for six months. Icahn and Lorenzo had a deal. As dawn broke, Icahn and assorted advisers, including Jim Freund, repaired to New York's 24-hour restaurant Brasserie. "It was now six a.m.," says Freund. "We were all dragging, but Carl was ebullient, feeling terrific. He won't get the airline. He's a seller. But he's perfectly satisfied."

As well he should have been. Icahn had just won himself a package that would give him $16 million in expenses and price supports for his preferred stock. Now that the offer from Texas Air was $23.50 per share for a total bid of $9.25 million, he would be selling his block of shares for $79 million. His grand total therefore came to $95 million. This would be the largest profit he had ever made on a deal. It was no wonder that he felt he could play the stand-up comic, imitating former takeover foes and telling war stories to his admiring advisers.

And yet . . . and yet . . .

Freund was worried. He raced back to Wachtell to get the word from Lorenzo's advisers. On the way, he bought a new shirt and a razor, changed in a Wachtell men's room, and awaited word from Drexel's Leon Black and Wachtell's Richard Katcher as to whether Lorenzo would accept the work his advisers had created. They looked grim when Freund saw them. Leon Black had called Lorenzo and told him the details. He assured Lorenzo that Drexel had the financing for him to pay Icahn the $9 million in fees.

"Fuck him," Lorenzo said into the phone. "He's a pig." He then hung up the phone.

Leon Black called him back. He told Lorenzo that he understood that paying Icahn fees for peace was difficult to accept, but he stressed that Icahn was a gorilla holding a club made of one-third of TWA's stock, with which he could bludgeon Lorenzo's future with TWA.

"Carl will never take over the airline."

The deal was off. This was the first of Lorenzo's two blown chances to neutralize Icahn and win the airline he coveted.

The takeover of TWA is at first the tale of a corporate raider going about his work, a renowned greenmailer buying chunks of companies and threatening trouble unless the board agrees to buy him off. Here, the target is not only sputtering and losing altitude over many years of bad luck and financial mismanagement. It is also naked, devoid of any of the defenses that M&A was still in the midst of developing as standard shields for those in the line of takeover fire. It becomes a story of how an emblematic M&A robber baron decided to abandon his usual tactic of either disappearing with a bag of money or moving in to break up the business and sell it for parts. Instead, it turns into a saga of seduction, how a man who considered himself a financial wizard thought he could also manage what had once been one of the most glamorous companies in the world, a red-white-and-blue symbol of America itself.

The child of the 1930 union of Transcontinental Air Transport and Western Air Express, TWA was known in its infancy as Lindbergh's Line. Charles Lindbergh himself had flown TWA's first transcontinental flight and associated himself closely with the company. In 1939, Howard Hughes bought the company, and as a celebrity, an aviator, and a renowned playboy, he was welcomed at first as a source of money and fame for TWA. Hughes would own it for the next 27 years. What he refused to own, for far too long, was a fleet of jets for the airline. In an eerie precursor of his eventual madness and isolation, Hughes finally ordered eight short-range Boeing 707s through his Hughes Tool Co., but TWA did not own the planes, and they were not nearly enough to combat the likes of United and Pan Am with their ever-growing fleets. Hughes famously kept one TWA plane on the ground for his own use on demand.[9]

By the late 1950s, the obsessive-compulsive recluse was taking the company into his own darkness. Both TWA and Hughes himself were running out of money. By 1960, in a prefiguring of the madness of the Icahn era, TWA faced bankruptcy. Hughes gave up control and would finally sell the last of his stock in 1966. TWA filed two lawsuits against Hughes, again foreshadowing Icahn, and the litigation would rattle on for a quarter of a century. TWA would finally lose one case and win the other, recovering damages of $50 million.

Meanwhile, the American economy, and TWA with it, enjoyed some lift. In 1962, the airline opened its new terminal only eight months after its designer, architectural star Eero Saarinen, died from a brain tumor at 51. Renovated in recent years by the firm of Beyer Blinder Belle, the landmarked building combines *The Jetsons* and *Mad Men* with its wide, white, double-winged exterior, its ethereally lighted white and red "flight tubes" that once led to the waiting planes, its geometry of circles and curves and wide lines of sight. It was a gateway to the world and a place to watch the world go by from the Lisbon Lounge, the Paris Café, and the Constellation Club. One can almost hear TWA's one-time theme song, the Fifth Dimension's "Up, Up and Away," which still sends former TWA staffers into tears.

Beneath all the glamour of the day, however, there was much that was somewhat less salubrious. In an era when the fear of flying was the new phobia, stewardesses were sex symbols deliberately dressed and trained as Bond girls, taking anxious minds away from the altitude to fixate on something more earthy. Braniff, in one of the more extreme examples of the syndrome, turned to Emilio Pucci to design its in-flight uniforms, and the flight attendants quickly became known as "Pucci Galores," after the character of a similar name in *Goldfinger*. The television commercial, blatantly

titled "The Air Strip," starred a blonde hostess, unzippping to reveal different uniforms for different stages of the flight: the first layer for the passengers' arrival, another for the bringing of the evening meal. "After dinner, on
those long flights, she'll slip into something a little more comfortable," says
the suggestively sultry, deep male voice-over, as the star first arches her
arms over her head and then cups her blonde flip. "The Air Strip is brought
to you by Braniff International, who believes that even an airline hostess
should look like a girl." The term "girl" was what Icahn would later use
when faced with a protesting crowd of flight attendants at the wrought-iron
gates of his Bedford estate.

In the mid-1960s, TWA stood at its peak with a fleet of transatlantic
jets and war-trained, crisply uniformed pilots held in awe by the larger
culture, along with cowboys, quarterbacks, and astronauts. But trouble yet
again lay ahead. Still lifting heavy debt, TWA was bought by an investor
group that took on new assets, including Hilton International and Century
21, and marginalized the airline itself. President Jimmy Carter signed the
Airline Deregulation Act in 1978 and set the industry aflame.[10]

In 1984, TWA's parent company kicked the airline out of the nest,
and it fluttered to the ground, "a broken-winged bird helpless before the
ultimate corporate predator, Carl Icahn."[11] The airline had nothing in
place to protect it from a hostile bidder when Icahn began his investment the next year. "This was a defenseless company," says Jim Freund.
"Nobody conceived of it as a takeover opportunity. Who would want this
crazy airline?"

Not only was it assumed that no bidders would be interested, but also
many of the shields against hostile raiders that were soon to become standard defenses were still being developed by lawyers and bankers and the
Delaware courts. Much was happening at speed, but little was in final form
in 1985. "It was quite a year," Jim Freund remembers. "Revlon was coming
up through the courts. Unocal came down in the middle of the fight. The
Household case was still in the lower court in Delaware. The court rulings
were hitting us every day. We had to make quick decisions: If you go one
way, this happens; if you go the other way, that happens. You weigh 'this'
against 'that' and try to do right by the stockholders. It was a very exciting
time, and a risky and unpredictable one. Amazing."

The airline lacked a crucial, well-established defense: the classified
board, the same mechanism that Uniroyal tried to install to fend off Icahn.
This defense is one of the oldest available, with a simple, effective mechanism. The members of a board of directors are elected at different times
and serve overlapping terms of office. This means that the entire board
can never be replaced in one election, with only portions of the board running for office in any given year. Companies can also decree that the shareholders can vote on corporate business only once a year, at the company's

annual meeting. Without such a rule, the shareholders can vote at any time during the year in the privacy of their homes and offices simply by filling out a ballot and sending it in to the company.

TWA also lacked a ban on shareholder votes by written consent. A raider could therefore throw out the entire board in one fell swoop, without even calling a shareholders' meeting. Freund explains, "This is exactly the threat that Carl Icahn was to use throughout the whole affair, and it affected our strategy at all points along the way." Icahn also had another weapon, charged and ready to fire at any moment. He could continue to buy stock. He could cross the 50 percent threshold at will and control the airline, much like Howard Hughes before him.

Icahn had waited until hours before a crucial SEC deadline to call Stephen Jacobs on May 7, 1985, at Weil, Gotshal and tell him about his mass of TWA stock. After wondering why on earth Icahn wanted to invest in TWA, Jacobs then asked just how much TWA stock Carl owned. "Twenty percent," he said. Jacobs gulped. And when did he cross over 5 percent? "Eight days ago," Carl answered.

"16(b)," Jacobs said.

"I know," said Carl. "Draft up a 13D."[12]

Schedule 13D is designed to disclose to the world the identities and intentions of major stockholders of public companies. The most important part of the filing, required of anyone who buys 5 percent or more of a public company, is the section that asks the investor why he or she has bought the stock and what he or she intends for the future. Icahn's lawyers had 48 hours to file the 13D.

"We said, 'What!'" Weil's Dennis Block, Icahn's main litigation chief at Weil, Gotshal, recalled to the *American Lawyer*'s Gay Jervey in 1986 when he and his colleagues heard that Icahn told them he now wanted to own and manage the airline. Block also knew that they faced a serious problem. It was obvious to all that TWA would immediately take Icahn to court and argue that his SEC filings were full of lies about his intentions. "We had a smoking gun in our own hands," Block said.[13]

Icahn had commissioned several months earlier from Sanford "Sandy" Rederer, an expert in the airline business, a series of reports on TWA. At a meeting with TWA executives and Jim Freund, Icahn and Rederer had recommended that TWA close down or sell the domestic routes and run only the profitable overseas routes. Icahn talked of selling off facilities and leasing out planes. "He behaved himself at the first two meetings," Jim Freund says. "He was very low key. But we disliked his game plan because it would bust up the airline."

The Rederer reports would quickly rise again like a specter, pointing an accusing finger at Icahn in federal court. By the time the 13D was filed, his lawyers argued that Icahn no longer intended to pursue the Rederer plan. But they would have to convince a judge that Icahn was sincere and that he had changed his mind in early May after meetings with TWA executives. "We had all these documents [pertaining to Rederer's advice] that painted Carl as a liquidator, and we knew we would be facing massive attacks," Block said.[14]

TWA had already rushed to the courthouses, filing suit in New York on May 15 and also in state court in Missouri. "What could we do?" Jim Freund asks rhetorically. "We did what any target does in that situation. We sued. We brought two lawsuits, one on federal issues in the Southern District of New York and one on state issues in the state court of Missouri. The principal issue in the federal lawsuit was TWA's allegation that Icahn failed to disclose his plan to dismantle the airline, sell off the choice routes, close down major facilities, and lay off people. Icahn, who had received early advice from Rederer along those lines, claimed that he had been persuaded that this was not good strategy and, in fact, had no such plans." On May 16, TWA also filed an appeal to the Department of Transportation, seeking an investigation into Icahn's fitness as an owner of an airline, the first time the DOT had ever received such a request.

On May 17, just four days before Carl's formal bid for TWA, the famous Unocal decision roiled the M&A establishment, written by the omnipresent and omniscient Justice Andrew G. T. Moore II of the Delaware Supreme Court. Icahn had to craft his offer with that opinion in mind, and the TWA board had to respond, also subject to the new M&A law handed down by the redoubtable Moore.

In that case, T. Boone Pickens had made a run at Unocal; he bought 13 percent of the company's stock and then launched a tender offer of somewhat dubious value to Unocal's remaining stockholders. To fend him off, Unocal told its shareholders that it would buy back their shares at a big price to protect them from the low-ball bid from Pickens and his Mesa Petroleum. Unocal specifically excluded Pickens from its offer. The company would not buy back his stock since "every Mesa share accepted by Unocal would displace one held by another stockholder," as Justice Moore recounted. What's more, the justice wrote, "if Mesa were permitted to tender to Unocal, the latter would in effect be financing Mesa's own inadequate proposal." Mesa challenged the Unocal plan as unfair to both the corporation and all the stockholders.[15]

Justice Moore first stressed that whenever a board fights back against an outsider trying to take over the company, there is what he called, in now immortal words, "an omnipresent specter that a board may be acting primarily in its own interests, rather than those of the corporation and its shareholders." Because of this danger, the courts must look especially closely at any defenses mounted against the attacker. The defense must be "reasonable in relation to the threat posed," and the directors must not have leveled its defense "solely or primarily out of a desire to perpetuate themselves in office." Unocal passed both these tests. Justice Moore also noted pointedly that in this instance, Mesa's tender offer was coercive, too low, and designed to induce a stampede of stockholders eager to get the higher part of the two-part offer. Then came the zinger. "Wholly beyond the coercive aspect of an inadequate two-tier offer, the threat was posed by a corporate raider with a national reputation as a 'greenmailer.'"[16]

Weil's Stephen Jacobs was helping Icahn put together his bid for TWA when Justice Moore delivered his Unocal decision. Jacobs read sections of the opinion to his client. "Wait a minute," Carl said to him. "A court might think Boone Pickens is a greenmailer, but if they reviewed my record, they wouldn't think I was one, would they?" Jacobs had to choose his words carefully in response. "That conversation really occurred!" the Weil partner recalled. With some wry circumlocution, Jacobs went on: "It was fairly easy to conclude that Carl was within the universe of people whose prior activities might give rise to some inference that he was seeking greenmail from TWA, thus justifying all sorts of nefarious responses. . . . So, we had to assess where we were and what we could do."[17]

Icahn faced the possibility of a definitive and humiliating defeat in the Southern District court of Judge John Cannella. TWA was asking the judge to block Icahn from buying any more stock and from voting the stock he already owned, and to ban him from launching a tender offer to buy more shares from the existing stockholders or from launching a proxy fight to get their votes for a new board of directors. The judge could easily kill any hope of winning TWA, sticking Icahn with a mass of company shares that was very likely too large for TWA to neutralize with greenmail and unlikely to find buyers in the stock markets for anything close to the millions he had paid. Such a crash and burn would be Icahn's own fault because he was going into court holding his own smoking gun, as Weil's Dennis Block put it, with the evidence of his guilt curling forth from its barrel for all to see.

The night before Carl was to face Judge John Cannella at the courthouse in Lower Manhattan, Icahn had dinner with his top advisers, led by Block, at Christ Cella's, a steakhouse on 46th Street between Second and Third Avenues. It was a fitting place to meet: It was one of Carl's favorite restaurants. It was where he and Al Kingsley had repaired to analyze TWA and where so many of his assignations during the ensuing battle would unfold.

The neighborhood has changed over the years, with most of the steakhouses built in the early years of the 1900s now gone. In the mid-1980s, however, Christ Cella was an institution, although no longer in its prime. It was, in the tradition, a gruff and plain place, women unwelcome for years, drink and red meat and martinis and cigars in full spate. It was not unusual at Christ Cella to see famous athletes and sports figures such as

Muhammad Ali, Howard Cosell, or boxing promoter Don King enjoying a martini or two with a slab of red meat. Icahn was a frequent patron. In the summer of 1985, Bryan Miller of the *New York Times* paid a visit and delivered his verdict. He called it a pillar in the pantheon of New York steakhouses, but his enthusiasm dissipated after that: "Everything about Christ Cella has a faded, almost sad, patina. Groups of two-fisted ex-linemen still frequent the wood-paneled bar before hunkering down to a meal that likely rekindles memories of the pre-game steak dinner. The remaining patrons appear to be older New Yorkers who made a habit of going there in its heyday and continue. The dowdy downstairs dining rooms would probably be described as 'homey' if the food were better. The front room upstairs, the largest of all, at least benefits from sunlight and a street view. . . . [M]enus are superfluous. Steaks, chops and several fish entrees were rattled off so quickly in a rote manner by our waiter that we had to ask him to repeat them twice. The veteran service team—our waiter had been there nearly 30 years—has its routine down pat, but don't expect any fine touches."[18]

Christ Cella closed in the mid-1990s, but not far from where it once stood is a place that still carries on more than one tradition of the old vanished Steak Row. It is called Sparks Steak House, founded in 1966 by brothers Pat and Mike Cetta. On December 16, 1985, just a few months after Icahn took over TWA, Salvatore Gravano, a Mafia underboss and self-described backup shooter, was—as he later told a federal jury—sitting with John Gotti in a Lincoln Town Car with darkened windows at the northwest corner of Third Avenue and 46th Street. A car pulled up beside them and stopped at the red light. It was Paul Castellano, often called "the Howard Hughes of the Mob," and the alleged head of the Gambino family, sitting in another Lincoln driven by his associate, Tommy Bilotti. When the light turned green, Castellano and Bilotti crossed Third Avenue and parked in front of Sparks Steak House. Four gunmen wearing white trench coats and black Russian hats shot them both to death. Gotti drove slowly past the scene and continued on to Brooklyn. Ever since, the waitstaff has had to find the strength to smile yet again when new patrons ask for the no-shooting section.[19]

A few months before the mob hit at Sparks, Christ Cella had its own war council under way: Icahn and his three closest advisers—in-house lawyer Gary Duberstein, Dennis Block, and his partner Irwin Warren from Weil, Gotshal—were having dinner to discuss strategy. Block had decided that Icahn should put himself out there and make his case. He should tell the world that as a man who acted on his instinct, he had simply changed his mind. Now he saw a great future for the airline. He was not a destroyer; he was a builder. This was an opportunity to create a great airline, a mission at which management had failed. He saw ways to cut costs. He was sure that labor was coming around. He would restore TWA to its old glory.

Block recalled his own words in an interview soon after the dinner: "I told [Icahn] that tomorrow he would be on his own, that it would be up to him to convince the judge that despite the litany of other evidence, he did not want to liquidate. My favorite line from that night, I told him: 'Carl, it's time to grovel.'"[20]

And that turned out to be just what Carl did, masterfully, before all subsequent opponents, and with success on all fronts. First, Icahn won the confidence of the judge.

TWA's 19 members of the board of directors gathered on May 28 at the airline's headquarters at 605 Third Avenue to await word from Judge Cannella's court. It was a distinguished group, some of whom were well known around the world: Andrall Pearson, a professor at Harvard Business School; Lester Crown, the largest shareholder in General Dynamics; Jack Valenti, president of the Motion Picture Association of America; Brock Adams, former secretary of transportation; Robert McNamara, former secretary of defense and president of the World Bank; Arjay Miller, dean emeritus of Stanford University's business school; and, making one of his first appearances in the board room, Peter Ueberroth, commissioner of baseball and head of the Los Angeles Olympics.

The wait was agonizing. Skadden's Robert Zimet, who had handled the litigation, was standing by at the courtroom, ready to relay the judge's decision directly to Jim Freund in the TWA boardroom. As an example of what a small village M&A was, and to some extent continues to be, Zimet had worked on the Skadden team when Texas International made its first aggressive moves on TWA in 1979. At the time, Zimet's wife, Barbara, was an in-house lawyer at TWA, helping to defend the company against Frank Lorenzo.[21] Six years later, Zimet found himself defending TWA with his Skadden colleagues.

Zimet got the bad news. Judge Cannella had sided with Icahn. The judge said he dismissed TWA's claims that Icahn had misled the public in his SEC filings about his plans for TWA. He found "credible" Icahn's argument that he had at one time contemplated a bust-up but was now committed to piloting the airline to profits. "It is not unreasonable for him," Judge Cannella declared, "to have changed his mind after having his consultants' report heavily criticized by the people who had been running TWA."[22]

The court could not "infer from his past conduct that Icahn has a particular pattern or game plan that necessarily or even most likely implicates the sale of major assets or a 'greenmail' attempt. Evidence that Icahn may have sold substantial assets or divisions of previously acquired companies on two occasions is some evidence of his current intent. It does not overcome, however, the explicit and public statements made repeatedly by Icahn. . . . The [c]ourt finds it unlikely that such a skilled businessman would make such public announcements concerning a corporation with such a visible profile if he did not intend to carry out his stated plans."[23]

The judge's decision brought euphoria to the Icahn army. Stephen Jacobs called it absolutely crucial. "At that point," he remembered in late 1985, "the Department of Transportation was involved. Congress was being whipped into a frenzy. Everyone was being subjected to TWA publicity that Carl was going to loot the airline. If Cannella had said he didn't believe him, we would have been almost dead in the water."[24] Block was similarly overjoyed and, perhaps unintentionally, evoked Shakespeare's Mark Antony in his oration to the Roman crowds after Caesar's assassination: "Another hurdle had been jumped. We were then able to flag and wave the Cannella decision, saying, 'Look! A federal judge is saying Carl is an honorable man.'"[25]

In his appearance on Capitol Hill in early June, Icahn struck a pose of wounded honor. "I haven't appreciated the efforts by TWA's management to impugn my personal integrity and misstate the terms of my offer. As you have heard this morning, TWA's management continues to claim that I would seriously damage or even destroy the airline. This would make me both a liar and a fool, and I am neither. I am in a business where my word is my bond. I buy and sell increments of hundreds of thousands of shares, solely by oral agreement. My reputation as a man of my word is something that I would not risk for any transaction."[26]

Emblematic of his public relations triumph was the crowd of TWA pilots, still wearing their "Stop Icahn" buttons after Carl's testimony at the congressional hearings, swarming around their erstwhile enemy and his team, offering to exchange business cards, the rough equivalent of primates taking turns with personal-grooming rituals. Henry Hoglander, head of the pilots' union, watched Icahn testify and recalled at the time, "His answers were straightforward and deliberate. He said that it was his money, that he didn't intend to break up the airline. He'd said it before a federal judge, and he said it now before a congressional committee: he intended to run it as an airline. Despite all the propaganda, my impression was that he was a very shrewd and intelligent individual." Hoglander, one of those still with his "Stop Icahn" button, went up to Carl during a break in testimony and said, "Carl Icahn, I'm Harry Hoglander. I think that you and I, at some point, should have a talk." They would soon be immersed in negotiations, brutal but successful.[27]

Carl won yet another victory at the DOT, which rebuffed TWA's request for an investigation into his fitness to run the airline. He continued his winning streak in federal court in Jefferson City, Missouri. Block and his fellow litigators dismantled what could have been a heat-seeking missile that could have atomized the bid.

Irwin Warren, a securities law partner at Weil, told the story to the *American Lawyer*'s Gay Jervey a year later: "Melanie [Dennis Block's secretary] had gotten an urgent call from our Jefferson City counsel and, because Dennis was not there, transferred it to me. Basically they told me that both houses of the Missouri state legislature had waived their normal rules, met in a special session, and rammed through a bill to prevent Icahn from buying more stock. I quickly called Dennis, who was at Carl's office. Since it was already early afternoon, my question was, 'What can we do fast enough? We're in New York, they're in Missouri. It was obvious that we were going to have to sue, but what would we do fast enough?' His exact words were, 'Get a complaint out today!' I said, 'Today?' He then said, 'I don't care if you have to write the complaint on a [expletive deleted] napkin and telecopy the napkin to local counsel, but get it out today, because we have to sue today in federal court.' After I stopped laughing and decided a napkin would not telecopy well, I went to my office and dictated a four-page complaint which we filed in Jefferson City federal court at 5:20 p.m., only minutes after the governor signed the amended bill." On June 3, Judge Brook Bartlett issued a temporary restraining order, nullifying the new law until he could determine whether it violated the Commerce Clause of the Constitution.[28]

Thus had Carl Icahn, the awkward six-foot-three-inch gruff, tough raider, won over virtually all of his volatile and numerous public foes: Senator John Danforth of Missouri, who had been attacking Icahn on behalf of TWA's hub in his state; the crowd at the congressional hearings as well as the legislators themselves, the former having hoped to watch a public hanging and the latter planning on tying the rope around his neck; Judge Cannella of the Southern District of New York; and now Judge Bartlett of the Show-Me State.

His first defeat hit the team on the same day, June 3. It was a pivotal victory for TWA. Missouri state court judge B. C. Drumm Jr. issued a temporary restraining order that did exactly what the blocked statute would have accomplished. The court order stopped Icahn from buying any more TWA stock so that his target could organize its case before the judge with the status quo intact. For the time being, Icahn was idling in neutral. Jim Freund knew only too well that Carl would soon be on the move once again and at full throttle.

Jim Freund and his team knew that the board had to take a stand and respond to Icahn's offer, which Freund called Icahn's "I'll take the high road, but I may take the low road" approach. "We were convinced that if we did nothing and were unable to stop Carl in the courts—where we had already lost—or Congress or the DOT, he would get the company at the $18 price. If we put his offer to the shareholders, we believed that in the absence of any alternative, they would accept the offer, since it was higher than the market price, and there were plenty of arbitrageurs in the stock. If we did not submit the merger to the shareholders, we believed he could succeed on his threat to solicit consents and remove the board. The fear throughout was that if the TWA board were removed, Carl could come in, drop that $18 offer to something less, get the company, and dismantle the airline. The board wanted to stay in place until the deal was done, not for entrenchment reasons, but to make certain that the shareholders got a good deal."

After the verdict from Judge Cannella, Freund bluntly confronted the TWA directors, who were awaiting advice as to what they should do now that a federal court had blessed Icahn's motives and set him free to go on the attack. "Zimmy [Michael Zimmerman of Salomon] and I made major presentations to the board. We told them straight. In the absence of doing something, the company's lost. We must actively look for a better deal than Carl's. Then we'll submit the best deal we get to the shareholders."

In the meantime, Freund knew that the company had to keep Carl from simply buying more stock and getting written votes from the shareholders to throw out the board and give him the company. Freund, his partner Rich Easton, and Salomon's Michael Zimmerman suggested a gesture to Icahn, but with a twist. The board would agree to submit Carl's offer to its shareholders if nothing better could be rounded up within 60 days. To stop Carl from canvassing for shareholder votes for a new set of directors, they would say in a press release that they expected Icahn not to ask the shareholders for votes until the end of those 60 days. The board voted unanimously for the Freund plan.

"After we sent out the press release, we held our breaths," Freund remembers. "Icahn didn't reply directly. He sputtered to the *New York Times* about level playing fields and 'I don't know if I'll be here in 60 days' and all that crap. He did buy some more shares, until he was restrained by the Missouri court a few days later. But he never did the consent thing. That strategy is one of the things I'm proudest of in the whole deal."

Carl's agreement to stand fast for 60 days, as TWA requested as part of its counteroffer, and now the restraining order from Missouri, gave TWA what it needed most—time. Enter the white knights. First came Resorts International, not an airline and not subject to federal regulation, not Icahn, and not Lorenzo. Designed by their lawyer, Stuart Katz of Fried, Frank, the company presented a carefully planned, ingenious structure designed to be Icahn's straitjacket, as Katz put it.[29]

Resorts would offer $22 for each TWA share, with 60 percent of that in cash—later reduced to 50 percent—and the rest in debentures. They would proceed in either of two ways. Everyone would get the $22 in cash and securities, or they would do a front-end-loaded tender offer. The first stockholders who tendered their shares would get cash, and all those who sold after Resorts had 50 percent of the stock in hand would get securities worth less than the $22. Carl would not be able to join in the front end, the

cash offer, because of his potential liability under section 16(b). After signing this double-barreled contract, they would then approach Carl and tell
him he had one hour to decide what to do. If he agreed not to oppose the
deal, Resorts would choose their first option and offer all stockholders the
$22 in cash and stock. If he refused to agree, they would do the front-end-
loaded merger, and he would be stuck taking the back end, the securities
worth less than the cash portion of the two-tiered bid.[30]

Freund was dubious. "In our view, this was very risky. We felt that Carl
would have said no on principle. He would challenge it in the courts and
buy TWA stock in the market underneath the tender, presumably sweeping
the Street to get 51 percent. Then he would provide the TWA shareholders
with a lower than $18 back end. At the time, it was the best deal around.
We had talked to Texas Air, but they had indicated an interest at $20, not
higher."

Then came Frank Lorenzo, who officially topped Icahn's $18 bid and
offered $20. At the end of the nightlong haggle on June 12, Texas Air had a
deal to buy TWA at $23, and Icahn was salivating at the prospect of his $95
million in profits, but in the dawn debacle, Lorenzo killed the arrangement
with Icahn, calling him a pig and ruining hours and hours of painstaking
construction work by his own advisers.

TWA and Texas Air announced their merger agreement anyway. But it
was a fragile creature. Icahn was not bound by a standstill, now that Lorenzo
had rejected the pact. Carl owned 32.77 percent of TWA. Since the Missouri
judge had lifted his restraining order against further stock buys, Icahn was
free to buy as much TWA stock as he wanted. He had said that he wasn't
going to be a spoiler, that he would not stand in the way of the best deal for
stockholders, but it was hard to tell what that meant. Carl remained what
Leon Black continued to emphasize to Lorenzo, the 10,000-pound gorilla.

Still, precarious as it might be, a deal with the board for the sale of
TWA was now in the hands of Frank Lorenzo. Aghast at the thought of
Lorenzo taking over TWA and angry at what the pilots' union chief, Harry
Hoglander, saw as a betrayal, the unions marched forth to do a deal with
Icahn. The pilots were in the vanguard, advised by Davis, Polk & Wardwell
and Lazard Frères. It was the usual Carl Icahn show: endless nights, brutally long talks, temper tantrums, disappearing acts, threats, manipulations,
advances, and retreats. Fierce fights broke out between Davis, Polk, a conservative white-shoe firm on Wall Street, and lawyers from Weil, Gotshal
& Manges, the midtown pugilists whose firm's nickname was "While I Got-
cha, I'll Mangle Ya."

Brian Freeman remembers one night when Icahn himself lost control. "It was very late at night," says Freeman, an adviser to the machinists,
"maybe two a.m., and I was grabbing a nap on an office couch. Then suddenly, I was awakened by this yelling and screaming, and as I sat up I saw

Icahn putting on his suit jacket and storming out of the room. He was mut-tering something like 'I don't need this crap. I don't have to take it.' When I told Carl to calm down, he told me to bug off. Just like that, Carl was gone. And he stayed away for at least a half hour. We were worried that he'd gone off to Lorenzo. Leon Black and Lorenzo had been putting pressure on him to return to their side, and we thought maybe he did. But then Carl finally returned. It seemed he'd gone for a long walk and that had taken the steam out of him. He said, 'We're here to do a deal. Let's get on with it.'"[31] And get on with it they did.

Lorenzo and his team soon got word toward the end of June that Icahn was about to put together an alliance with the unions. Texas Air's deal with TWA was in mortal jeopardy. Leon Black, meanwhile, had not given up and continued to urge Lorenzo to pay Icahn's fees and get his rival at long last to agree to stand down and let Lorenzo into the cockpit. Icahn was not interested. But then Black heard that Carl was headed for a dinner at Christ Cella once again.

That early summer night, Black got a table across the dining room and waited for Carl's guest to leave. He rushed over to a bemused Icahn, who had already seen Black oddly dining alone, and urged Carl to restart talks with Lorenzo. Carl refused to deal with Lorenzo except face-to-face, thinking that would be the end of it, at least for the time being. Black ran from the table and out into the night. He did not keep Carl waiting long. He returned with Lorenzo himself at his side. Black was pleased with his sleight of hand. Not so either Carl or Frank Lorenzo. It would prove to be a long night.

Carl abruptly got up to leave. Lorenzo and Black followed him out the door, and along the streets, until they got to the entrance to Carl's build-ing. Black begged Carl to take them to his apartment and continue talking. Once inside, Black and Lorenzo retreated to a bedroom for a not-so-private shouting match, with a bewildered Icahn left alone in his own living room, until he felt the need to ask the two men to lower their voices in deference to the neighbors. Finally—by this time, it was close to midnight—Lorenzo came out and made his offer.[32] Memories differ as to what Lorenzo offered and precisely when, but what is not in dispute is that Lorenzo first offered Carl the same $16 million as the price for peace as had been negotiated on the night of June 12. Icahn refused and demanded $25 million. Lorenzo agreed, and the trio parted company.

The next day, once again, Lorenzo changed the deal. It would not be fair, he argued, simply to pay Icahn to vote for the Texas Air merger. What if, Lorenzo asked, another bidder came along and made a higher offer? Icahn could sell his stock to the new bidder, with $25 million in his pocket from Lorenzo, for nothing. Now, Lorenzo said, he wanted an option to buy Icahn's shares. If Icahn refused, Lorenzo said he would cut the offer from the agreed $25 million to $20 million. Icahn, advised by his lawyers that granting an option might trigger his liability under section 16(b), would have none of it. For the second time, Lorenzo had his hands on his prize and then threw it away.

When Icahn announced his agreement with the pilots' union, Lorenzo seemed to sink into desperation, begging TWA to give him some kind of leg up: redeem its convertible securities, which would dilute the size of Icahn's stake; sell him preferred stock; grant him an option to buy its transatlantic routes. But Freund was adamant and advised the TWA directors to stand firm. Skadden had long feared that Icahn would simply buy up more stock, cross the 50 percent ownership mark, vote out the board, throw out the Lorenzo agreement, and take control of the company. He could also just sit contentedly with his one-third stake and wait for the stock to drop before moving ahead with a full merger at a much lower price per share. For TWA to grant any special treatment to Lorenzo would be what Freund called waving a red flag in front of a bull. What's more, the bull had given his word not to buy more stock as long as his offer was not the best bid on the table. Icahn had issued a public statement promising that he would not use his TWA stock to prevent the other shareholders from getting the benefit of the best available offer. He would keep his word, he told Jim Freund, as long as "Lorenzo isn't buying stock and there are no shenanigans between you and Texas Air."

There were no shenanigans between TWA and Lorenzo, but Lorenzo waved a red flag in front of the bull that Freund had been trying so desperately to restrain. Lorenzo was banned from buying stock under a letter agreement he signed with TWA in return for confidential information about the company, which he needed in order to make his offer. In June, he asked to be released from his bond. TWA refused. Faced with the unions shifting their weight to Icahn, Lorenzo begged again. Freund agreed to relay his request to Stephen Jacobs, Icahn's lead lawyer. Lorenzo needed a voting trust to be the actual buyer under DOT rules that require its approval for one airline to own more than 10 percent of another. Icahn agreed that he would do nothing to stop this. Once. The next day, Lorenzo wanted to buy more. Freund emphasized that he would allow Lorenzo to do so only if Icahn approved. This time, Icahn folded his arms and refused. Freund called Lorenzo to tell him the bad news. Lorenzo admitted that he had just bought 500,000 shares of TWA without authorization. Even that was not true, as Lorenzo actually bought 973,800 more shares for $20 million. He said he had misunderstood.

Icahn came close to charging into the ring, horns lowered for the kill, when he heard what had happened in a call from Salomon's Michael Zimmerman. "That son of a bitch. I'm going to buy two for every one he bought," was the response.[33] Icahn bought 200,000 more shares. Lorenzo blinked. He said he would buy no more and would give TWA any profits from the eventual sale of what he had just added to his portfolio. Icahn said later, "I was tempted to go to fifty-one percent. It was clear to me that any obligation I had was over and I could have used it as an excuse to do it, as I was advised to do. But I decided basically to keep the status quo, so no one on the other side could even remotely hint that I had in any way broken my word."[34]

On August 5, Icahn announced that he had a final deal with two out of the three unions. With this pact, the airline instantly jumped from barely breaking even to $300 million in profits. The machinists and the pilots had agreed to deep wage cuts and benefits. Only the flight attendants held out. This would haunt Icahn for years to come. In the meantime, Icahn moved in for the kill. He raised his bid from $18 to $24 per share. He reserved the right to withdraw his offer if the board failed to approve it by August 8. Over the next two days, he bought 1.688 million shares for $38.2 million, raising his stake from 32.77 percent to 45.5 percent. "That was the moment of truth," he said at the time.[35]

Lorenzo made one last stab at victory. He raised his bid to $26 per share on August 9. With Icahn holding fast at $24, this meant Texas Air had the highest offer on the table. Freund and Icahn then had their worst confrontation of the whole battle. Freund demanded that Icahn either match the offer or step aside. This was Freund, later a specialist in mediation, the negotiated-deal guy. "It went on and on for hours, trying and trying and trying to get more dollars out of him. I've never worked over anybody like that in my life."

Carl Icahn likes to think he is unpredictable, Jim Freund says. "Well, he is predictable. The predictability is that he is not giving an inch on anything. There are no gimmes, as they say in golf. Carl also likes to take postures. He'd say, 'I'm a man of my word.' That was his thing: 'I'm a man of my word. You might not like me, but I'm a man of my word.' One of the things he said in the TWA thing was, 'I won't steal this company. If I don't have the best offer on the table, you can do the deal with somebody else. I'll go away.'"

Lorenzo now had the highest offer on the table. "So we're in talking to Icahn, Zimmy and I. And I said, 'You've got to top Lorenzo.' He says, 'I'm not going to top it. My offer's my offer.' I said, 'Wait a second. That offer's better than yours. You said that you would always let TWA go to somebody who made a higher offer.' He said, 'Oh, that's not a real offer. That's a phony offer. It's spurious.' I said, 'Wait a second; it is a real offer. What are you talking about?' I said, 'Carl, you said you're a man of your word, and you said that you would never stand in the way of the highest price. Isn't that right?' He says, 'Well, I'm 75 percent a man of my word.' We cracked up. The tension was terrible, and then he would say something like that. 'I'm 75 percent a man of my word.' Nobody like him."

The climax of it all was approaching: the August 20 board meeting when the directors would vote on the deals before them. On that day, Icahn could begin buying as much stock as he wanted. He could cross into a majority stake in TWA stock within hours. On that day, TWA could award

Lorenzo the lockups he had been begging to get for so long. Skadden's Freund and Salomon's Zimmerman hammered away at Icahn to raise his bid. Lorenzo was refusing to release TWA from its merger agreement with Texas Air. Carl seemed relaxed, having flown back from a break in Sun Valley, sure that his bid would triumph, with the unions on his side. The showdown was within days.

After making his case at the board meeting, Carl and his team repaired to his office to await the results of the vote of the directors. The phone rang. It was Jim Freund with good news. "We left the board meeting, Zimmy and I, and we call Icahn. I said, 'Carl, they're going to go for you! They're about to vote. Just one item—I want you to clarify and then this board will go with you. I want to be sure the directors will still have their passes.'"

Back when Carl and Al Kingsley were studying TWA and discussing over dinner at Christ Cella whether, when, and how to make a move on the airline, Carl had developed a hatred for the "golden passes," the free airline seats for directors and their families, which the directors could bequeath to their heirs. TWA even paid the necessary tax on this benefit. Lorenzo, at the infamous June 12 all-nighter, had offhandedly agreed to preserve the golden passes. Not Carl Icahn.

"'Fuck 'em!' he said to Jim Freund. 'Carl,' I said, 'Wait. These are the guys that are going to vote for your deal now. You can't tell them "Fuck 'em."' He said, 'Fuck 'em. They don't deserve it.' I said, 'Carl, it costs nothing. It's immaterial. The guys are ready to close the deal.' He says, 'I ain't giving them the fucking passes.' We're on the phone and the board is sitting in the other room. Zimmy and I are on that phone with Carl for half an hour. We finally worked out a deal where they kept the passes, but only if nobody else wanted the seat and you couldn't take your wife with you, and on and on, a whole convoluted thing. He finally said, 'Okay, I can go along with this. But no more. Not a penny more.' The board was shocked. And they blamed me. They said, 'You couldn't get Icahn to give us this, of all things? After all that time?' I couldn't get the extra. So. They were ready to make a deal. Zimmy and I still meet every year and we rehash these scenes."

Carl Icahn, at last installed in the cockpit, celebrating in his office dressed in a pilot's jacket and hat, was 49 years old. He was now CEO of an illustrious American corporation. At his fiftieth birthday party in February 1986, six months after his triumph, the cake was a massive replica of a TWA jet. As the cake was cut, the airline's death spiral was already accelerating to its inevitable end.

* * *

IN THE MIDST OF THE TAKEOVER, JIM FREUND, WHILE ON A TWA FLIGHT, STRUCK UP A conversation with a stewardess. "Her last name began with a 'Z.' Let's say it was 'Zim.' It turns out her father and I were at Princeton together, and we got to talking, and in the midst of it I said I was representing TWA in the Icahn thing. She says, 'Oh, we're so worried about this. All the girls are so worried about this. There's rumors that he's going to lay off flight attendants, and it's terrible. We'd lose our jobs and everything.' So I don't know if I said, 'I'll see what I can do'—I don't know. But the next time I saw Carl, I said, 'Hey, Carl, there's a stewardess named Elaine Zim, who's the daughter of a friend of mine, and she's worried that if you get control of this airline, you're going to lay off stewardesses and she's going to lose her job. Is there anything I can tell her that would make her feel better?' He says, 'Tell her if I lay them off, I'm going to start with the As.' And that's why, although he was a tough adversary, he was never dull to do business with. We had so many laughs."

The flight attendants' union was not laughing. A regular gathering became something of a tradition in the spring of 1986. It was reminiscent of the Mothers of the Plaza de Mayo demonstrating silently for the disappeared, except that these women looked like American soccer moms; they weren't wearing white scarves embroidered with the names of their missing; they were not silent, they were protesting lost jobs rather than children or husbands, they were not standing in the central square of Buenos Aires, and the target of their protests was not an invisible government but a six-foot-three-inch-tall man who would wander out regularly with his mug of coffee and chat with them as they shouted their slogans, standing next to their minivans and station wagons outside the gates of his estate. But they were just as determined as their Argentine sisters to be taken seriously. These women were TWA flight attendants, and they went on strike on March 7, 1986.[36]

The one union that spurned Carl Icahn was the Independent Federation of Flight Attendants, 85 percent of whom were women. The one woman of prominence in the TWA battle was the head of that union, 38-year-old Victoria Frankovich. She refused to accept a 22 percent wage cut on behalf of her constituents. The strike lasted through the spring and dissipated, but Frankovich's union then took Carl to court in November 1986, seeking back pay that looked set to total more than $400 million, or four times TWA's 1987 net income, for the 5,000 unsuccessful strikers. The charge was bad-faith bargaining. "Six days after the strike began," Tony Kaye and Miriam Rozen noted in an article in the *American Lawyer,* "Icahn appeared on CNN's 'Larry King Live' show and compared the flight attendants' behavior to that of a spoiled daughter who complains that her father spends more money on necessities instead of on her."[37] During the negotiations, Icahn said it would not be difficult for him to find other untrained women to be stewardesses for less than he was paying the machinists. "A janitor is a breadwinner, probably has got a family at home to support, you girls are second incomes and don't need the money."[38]

Icahn denied this; then he said he might have said it. US District Judge Howard Sachs in Missouri, in his opinion after two years at trial, ruled in favor of TWA. He found Icahn's remarks about breadwinners to be "foolish and offensive" but not a "persuasive showing that sex stereotyping governed or influenced Icahn's economic demands, only his rationalizations." The flight attendants lost a long and contentious fight, but, as so often happened with Icahnic battles, some ended up viewing him with a sort of shoulder-shrugging, eye-rolling amusement. After his many impromptu chats with the flight attendants at his gates in Bedford, Merry Keller was one such adversary. "He would come out with his cup of coffee and his attack dogs," she recalled later in her deposition. "We started to feel he is not so bad."[39]

It was not long after his victory that disgust with his new toy began to permeate this guy who was "not so bad." The first quarterly report after the deal showed a drastic loss. Carl demanded to see the TWA executives responsible. "Carl was furious," Freund remembers. "He said, 'Get those guys over here.' He says, 'I'm coming over to your office, and I'm going to give them hell.' So we arranged a meeting, and Carl came in waving this thing about the quarterly earnings down. And then one guy turns to Carl and he says, 'Hey, Carl. Welcome to the airline business.' It was such a great remark. Welcome to the airline business."

In 1988, Icahn took the company private and gained $469 million from that transaction. In 1991, he sold TWA's London routes, which decapitated the airline. In January 1992, TWA went into bankruptcy, emerging from Chapter 11 in 1993 with creditors owning 55 percent of the company, one of whom was Icahn himself, who was owed $190 million. In 1993, he resigned as chairman. Two years later, TWA was back in bankruptcy court. Then came the explosion of Flight 800 off Long Island on July 17, 1996. Finally, in 2001, TWA went bankrupt yet again and was about to be bought by American Airlines, a deal that collapsed after the attacks of 9/11.[40] At one point, Carl Icahn also managed to stare down the Pension Benefit Guaranty Corporation. On the hook for $1 billion for the airline's underfunded pensions, he got off that hook for about $200 million. Icahn made a $1.1 billion offer for TWA yet again, but the bankruptcy judge treated his offer as a joke. This time the company never rose again.

For the victor, it was the winner's curse. "Carl never showed weakness," says Freund. "That wasn't his style. Everything about him had to be tough. But there was one personal thing that happened. It must've been a year after the deal. He was up at our office; some hangover issue was still around. I have a picture of us in my mind walking down the hall together, and him saying, 'Jim—I was really a schmuck to do this deal.' He says, 'I attribute it to loyalty to the pilots. I let loyalty, which is not my usual thing'—you know, Carl was the guy that said, 'If you want love, buy a dog'—'I let my loyalty get the better of my judgment, and I was a schmuck to do this deal.'

It was the one human moment I ever had in all my dealings with him. Of course, it was at a time removed from the deal, so he wasn't losing anything by it. Still, it was nice to have one honest-to-goodness moment with the guy."

In 1985, Carl Icahn revealed his secret reliance on an omniscient anonymous telephone caller. "I have no idea who the hell it is," Icahn testified at a deposition unrelated to TWA. "He has my private phone number. I don't know how the hell he got it. And he called me once in January when I went down to Palm Beach. He seemed to know where the hell I was and everything." The mystery caller had been dialing in since the early years of the decade, Icahn said, with intriguing information, encouragement, coy promises of ultimate success. "I said, 'Who the hell are you?' He said, 'When the time comes, you will know. . . .' Normally, I wouldn't talk to people like this, but there is something about it that makes me stay with it."[41] Perhaps it was this mystery muse that convinced Icahn to "stay with it" until he got himself an airline.

As for TWA, its epitaph was written by Elaine Grant in the magazine of the airline's hometown:

> *TWA was the Marilyn Monroe of the airlines:*
> *an American icon done in by powerful men*
> *who wanted a piece of its magic.*
> *Glamorous, tragic, gone before its time.*[42]

CHAPTER TWELVE
THE BEGGAR'S PURSE

The beggar's purse was an innocuous but a seductive little crêpe confection. Pulled into swirling symmetrical creases by a drawstring of chives and topped with a gold leaf, it bulged with beluga and crème fraîche. Consumed in a bite, its uncanny flavors would explode as if Glumptious Globgobblers or Scarlet Scorchdroppers had come to life. Barry and Susan Wine adapted their little icon from Vielle Fontaine, a restaurant on the outskirts of Paris, where they were known as *aumonières*. At the Quilted Giraffe, which the aptly named Wines opened at an auspicious moment in Manhattan on the site of the old Bonanza Coffee Shop on Second Avenue, the beggar's purse became the Proustian madeleine of the 1980s.

A collection of them would typically arrive at your table on top of five little saucers perched on what looked like a silver toast holder. The gold plaster version of a human hand that came as part of the presentation appeared to be either offering the beggar's purses with a flourish, palm open and fingers curved up, or asking for spare change. If you liked, and if you were a beautiful woman, you could agree to let Mr. Wine handcuff you to the dining room railings, after which he would ask you to "close your eyes and take the whole thing in your mouth," and you would find a single beggar's purse resting on your tongue. Each rich little morsel was at first a $30 addition to the $75 prix fixe, ultimately jumping to $50. "Investment guys would order them by the dozen, just as a way to spend money," Morgen Jacobsen of the senior kitchen staff remembered years after the Quilted Giraffe had ended its run.[1]

With sex in the bathroom and cocaine in the lost and found, the restaurant happened to track the same arc as early contemporary M&A from 1979 to early 1990, and, at Second Avenue and 50th Street, it also happened to be just six blocks from the offices of Skadden, Arps, Slate, Meagher & Flom on

Third Avenue. "The Quilted Giraffe was our clubhouse," says Stu Shapiro, who started his career at Skadden. And the name of their club? "We called it the Lucky Sperm Club."[2]

Its members were Joe Flom's boys, young Skadden partners lucky enough to sit at the feet of the guru of a generation who rewarded talent and a lack of groveling. A gruff, small man, with both pitiable social insecurities and serene confidence in his prodigious intellect, who often described himself as a hunchback, Joe and his archrival and co-conspirator, Marty Lipton, invented modern M&A, which, because of these two men, became both a craft with a name all its own and a phenomenon that has ruled commerce ever since. At Marty's firm—Wachtell, Lipton, Rosen & Katz—a similar if unnamed group of youngish men also rose rapidly to top positions and grew ever richer, working directly and often virtually single-handedly with powerful clients, while always able to draw on the genius of Marty. In all but name, the Lucky Sperm Club gradually spawned new chapters at other firms and banks around the city and beyond, as the emerging specialty gathered shape.

Let's join three members of Skadden's Lucky Sperm Club—Stu Shapiro, Morris Kramer, and Don Drapkin—as well as their president, Joe Flom, at their table at the Quilted Giraffe. They are enjoying Havana's finest, smuggled in from Geneva in special nondescript white plastic boxes, each with its tell-tale gold-foil ring removed. They have just ordered another plate of beggar's purses and another bottle of Montrachet. It is just after Columbus Day in October 1985. By this time, our hitherto-ostracized takeover lawyers have taken their rightful place at these expensive tables. They are just as integral to the scene as the rest of the patrons of the Quilted Giraffe, the clout merchants, financiers, celebrity artists, dancers, Hollywood stars, New York stage actors, network news correspondents, arms dealers, media emperors, rock icons, diplomats, and junk bond hawkers.

The members of the Lucky Sperm Club are not without their own ambitions. And they are succeeding. Stu Shapiro, when we meet him now at the age of 39, is at work on a number of the greatest deals and court rulings of the era. With catholic tastes, he's an epicurean open to all of life, from a certain retsina from the Peloponnesus, front-row seats at the Olympic boxing finals in London, to a New York production of *Uncle Vanya*, interrupted by a cell phone call from his Manhattanite son at a loss when faced with a flat tire. A handsome man with a surprisingly loud laugh, he has a manner that fits well with the formalities of the courtroom, yet he is anything but conventional. One also gets the sense from his resonant voice and coiled calm that he would not hesitate to execute the emperor's two favorite concubines for insubordination.

Morris Kramer, originally a lawyer at Cahill Gordon & Reindel for several years, is the only one of these three who will stay at Skadden until retirement. He is ruthless and deliberately eccentric, renowned at one point for his ponytail and bell bottoms and jewelry, then for his intense exercise obsession, and always for his fetishistic work ethic. "Kramer is the wild man of Skadden's corporate team," Jill Abramson, now the executive editor of the *New York Times,* wrote in the *American Lawyer* in 1984. "The lawyer who is still happiest in the frenzy of a takeover fight, going without sleep for days, as he did on the Getty-Texaco deal. 'Without crisis to crisis,' he says, 'I'm not happy.'"[3]

In the first edition of the *American Lawyer,* Steven Brill asks Kramer to name the stars in the firm other than Joe Flom himself. What does Morris say without hesitation? "I'd say I'm one of them. And I bet you that every other partner would say he's one of them. That's the kind of people we are." They were also the kind of people known for bragging about missing their children's birthdays as proof of their dedication. "'Sure, this can be tough on your family life, if you let it,' he says, [having] just married for the second time, this time 'a woman who also has a career.' 'But I'll bet you our divorce rate is no higher than that of other lawyers,' he adds. To prove it, Kramer flips through the Skadden, Arps directory and finds that 'our divorce rate is maybe 30 or 35 percent. Nothing special.'"[4] At his death in April 2013, Kramer had been married and divorced three times.[5]

The third club member on hand that night at the Quilted Giraffe, Don Drapkin, is a consummate strategist. Don looks like the Cat in the Hat, as if separated at birth from Wilbur Ross. He will have his sadness when a son dies too young and his closest friendship and business relationship publicly unravels, but he will metamorphose into one of the great shareholder investors of the early twenty-first century. On our October night, he is a hero among his fellow Lucky Sperms for developing a tactic that has infuriated and frustrated the rulers of Revlon. After the victory, he becomes Ron Perelman's vice chairman and one of the richest of his generation of lawyers. He and Ronnie will soon have their own table at the Quilted Giraffe: number 11.

We can see Mick Jagger and Jerry Hall at table 8, which is near the door. Ivan Boesky and Mike Milken have just left. Henry Kissinger has lumbered into his limo after a long drinking session. Woody Allen has dibs on table 7, as on other nights do Mia Farrow, Diane Keaton, and Adnan Khashoggi. Warren Beatty is, as usual, at table 6. Gianni Agnelli is holding court at table 5, which is also a favorite of both William Paley and Ann Getty. Table 3 has Sid and Anne Bass; later it will seat Heather Watts and Peter Martins. Table 2 is assigned to Mr. and Mrs. Andy Rooney, to be followed by Don and Marilyn Hewitt, and then Mr. and Mrs. Walter Cronkite in turn. There is Jacqueline Kennedy in her blue Chanel suit with Jayne Wrightsman. We can see Donald Sutherland, Annette Reed, and Brooke Astor. You never see Bernie Madoff, who always orders in and always at lunch.[6]

Here is Billy Guilfoyle, the sommelier, at a table hosted by one of the Bass brothers, leading his party in celebration of the closing of a lucrative deal. Mr. Guilfoyle pretends not to hear one of the guests bragging about buying a new Ferrari that day with his proceeds. He waits for the man to turn to the question of the wine.

"What should we drink?" the man finally asks.

Mr. Guilfoyle points out several of the cellar's greatest prizes.

"No. More."

"I'm sorry sir? More?"

"More. We want to *spend* more."

They end up with a double magnum of '62 Lafite Rothschild. For $3,000.[7]

As we approach the Skadden stars, there is a certain schadenfreude at work among their circle this evening. Although history does not record, nor will the surviving participants reveal on the record, the details of their discussions, much can be unearthed about what this war council is masterminding at that midpoint of the 1980s, that apex of contemporary mergers and acquisitions. They are embroiled in their campaign to conquer Revlon for Ron Perelman, then an unknown adventurer and a serial acquirer. It is 1985, the year of years for M&A, when the business could be said to reach its full powers in the courts and boardrooms in a sudden explosion into maturity. The Revlon war most epitomizes this sudden transformation of both commerce and culture. Few American corporations in 1985 more thoroughly and with more fanfare epitomized glamour and power than Revlon, a global brand brought to full flower by its former leader, the terrifying, womanizing, self-aggrandizing, painfully conflicted, and self-tortured Charles Revson. But this was not the typical confrontation between a Jewish outsider and a WASP aristocrat. Revlon was long known as a Jewish company. Eli Tarplin, a member of Revson's inner coterie, once said, "Even those of us who weren't Jewish were alike. The New York Telephone Company is Irish-Catholic. Marriott Corporation is Mormon. The Mafia is Sicilian. Morgan Guaranty is blue-blood. Revlon was tough, unpolished Jewish."[8]

If it was not the typical clash between the entitled and the iconoclast, the Revlon takeover battle was still a confrontation between the upstart and the ensconced, for by the time Revson handed over much of his empire to his regent, and later his handpicked successor, Michel Bergerac, the company had become the cultural and commercial lodestar of the establishment. Bergerac was the erudite, witty, imperious Frenchman from International Telephone & Telegraph (ITT). In an *American Lawyer* excerpt from her classic account of Drexel and M&A in *The Predators' Ball*, Connie Bruck says this about Bergerac:

Bergerac had long inhabited the corporate stratosphere. In the 1960s, when Harold Geneen was building International Telephone & Telegraph into the world's biggest conglomerate, Bergerac helped negotiate about 100 acquisitions of companies for ITT in Europe; and in 1971, at the age of 39, he was promoted to the job of running all ITT European operations. During the next three years, he doubled European sales to $5 billion. But in 1974, Bergerac, considered the most likely candidate to succeed Geneen as head of ITT, was wooed away by Charles Revson, the legendary founder of Revlon. Bergerac received what was then an unprecedented bonus: $1.5 million. For a time, the financial press referred to Bergerac as "Catfish," after Yankee pitcher Catfish Hunter, who also won a seven-figure contract at that time.

In 1978 Bergerac was the subject of a fawning cover story in *Time* magazine, which noted that the company had survived Revson's death "triumphantly," and that in the four years since Bergerac had taken over the helm, sales and profits had multiplied about two-and-a-half times, twice as fast as the industry average.

In the last several years, however, Bergerac had lost some of his star quality. The company's earnings peaked at $192 million in 1980, dropped to $111 million in 1982, and stayed at that level through 1984, though in the first half of 1985—just as Perelman was approaching—they rose by about 10 percent. The weakness was in the cosmetics business; when demand slackened in the early 1980s and competition intensified. Revlon lost market share and profits. Meanwhile, however, Bergerac had expanded Revlon's health-care business vastly, making 11 acquisitions and increasing revenues tenfold in the previous decade.[9]

Michel Bergerac created his own splendid court at Revlon's headquarters in the General Motors building, one of the most prestigious office addresses in the city. The white marble tower, set back from Fifth Avenue, faces the Plaza and looks down on the southeastern quadrant of Central Park. On the forty-ninth floor, the Revlon rooms are done *à l'Afrique* and very Big-Five-y: vast murals with stylized versions of prides of lions in the Ngong Hills, a crash of rhinos at a watering hole in the Aberdare, a herd of Cape buffaloes in the Masai Mara, leopards in the Okavango, parades of elephants in Chobe. The walls are hung with the heads of greater kudu and steenbok and the masks of the Urhobo, Bozo, and Yoruba. The floors are covered with zebra and impala skins and dotted with elephant's-foot stools. It is a palace of the masters of all living things, the lords of all creation.

"There was this sense that we are the nobility. 'And who is this— (you should excuse the expression)—*Jew* from Philadelphia who is being financed by Drexel Burnham? How dare he? Who is he to interrupt our garden party in our Fourth-Floor-of-Abercrombie-&-Fitch-decorated headquarters in the city's fanciest building with the best views of Central Park in New York?'" says Skadden's Stu Shapiro.

"This Jew" is Ronald Owen Perelman, salivating on his cigar, blurting out his ungrammatical sentence fragments, daring to attack august Revlon, with its $2.3 billion in assets, from his perch atop a small, recently bankrupt Florida food chain with assets of barely $400 million. Perhaps most galling of all was the silly name of the upstart's company: Pantry Pride. The Revlon grandees called it "Pant-*y* Pride"; Ronnie was "Peril-man," pointedly pronounced in the French way by CEO Michel Bergerac so that it sounded like the name of a comic-book supervillain.

Revlon certainly has reason to feel impregnable not only because of its size but also because it has hired an army of the best New York M&A specialists who feel the same way: Arthur Liman leading a platoon from Paul, Weiss, Rifkind, Wharton & Garrison; Marty Lipton of Wachtell; Felix Rohatyn in charge of a team from Lazard Frères. A worried Ezra Zilkha, a Revlon director, called Bill Loomis at Lazard, Revlon's investment adviser, only to be assured that there was no cause for worry, that Lazard would never allow a conquest of Revlon. Marty Lipton has just told a young Dennis Levine, a Drexel banker and catalyst of future scandal who joined Perelman's team, not to bother to do so. "Don't waste your time," he said. "Pantry Pride will *never* get Revlon."[10]

That night at the Quilted Giraffe, the Lucky Sperms are enjoying themselves shamelessly. Revlon has tripped over itself and grievously offended the Delaware judge who is to decide its future. "He had steam coming out of his ears," says one member of the Skadden team.[11]

The Skadden boys order another bottle of Montrachet and, of course, a plateful of beggar's purses. They can feel that their triumph is at hand. They are enjoying themselves shamelessly. The establishment is growing increasingly appalled. Peril-man charges on brazenly, Drexel-fueled, Skadden-led, adrenalin-stoked.

*   *   *

RON PERELMAN COULDN'T LET IT GO, EVEN IN VICTORY. HE HAD TO KNOW WHY EZRA Zilkha, a member of the illustrious board of directors of Revlon, had fought his takeover with such ferocity. Ezra, an early mentor of Jimmy Goldsmith, had been the first member of the board to see Perelman as the serious threat he would soon become. In the early days of the fight only two other directors heeded his warnings: Lewis Glucksman, the head of Lehman Brothers, and Aileen Mehle, the society columnist known as "Suzie." The rest soon saw that he was right. Indeed, Ezra became in effect the lead director on Revlon's board. "I do not want the title," he says today, "but it seems they did listen to me in that way."

For Ezra, the conquest of Revlon was the destruction of the temple. For Ron Perelman afterward, it was as if he sought an audience with one of the old priests in search of absolution or at least for some kind of benediction. At first, Ezra would have nothing to do with Perelman and repeatedly declined the offer of lunch. At last, he relented slightly. So Ron Perelman came to 30 Rockefeller Center.

Ezra Zilkha is the scion of an ancient Baghdadi-Jewish banking family that traces its lineage to pre-Christian Mesopotamia. He is one of the last people alive who knew, loved, and inhabited the greatest cosmopolitan cities in history: Baghdad, Istanbul, Smyrna, Beirut, Damascus, Cairo, Alexandria; the names are like fugues, captivatingly contrapuntal but so often since Ezra's day violently etch-a-sketched of all their multiplexity. He was born in 1925 into the free Jewish community that Nebuchadnezzar II established in Baghdad almost six centuries before Christ. Ezra got his name from the hope of his parents for another son. Khedouri Zilkha and his wife, Louise Bashi, made a pilgrimage from Baghdad to the tomb of Ezra the Scribe near Basra at the southern tip of Iraq. They promised, if their wish were granted, to name the child they expected after the prophet. In 1899, his father, Khedouri, then only 15 years old, established the bank that marked the beginning of what Ezra calls "the family's good fortune," K. A. Zilkha, Maison de Banque. The business and the family moved around the world, propelled at times by persecution or war and at all times by mercantile genius.

Ezra, a graduate of Wesleyan University in Middletown, Connecticut, is a global citizen, a devoted Francophile, an Arab, a Jew, an American, and a New Yorker. It is a cliché to say that a person knows everyone who is anybody, but it is true of Ezra. He appears at private lunches at Kykuit with Nelson and Happy Rockefeller and Henry Kissinger. He stays with the Kluges at Albemarle House in Virginia. He is a guest of the Annenbergs at Sunnylands. He gives advice to Paul Volker. He hosts small dinners for the Saudi ambassador. His rank in the Légion d'honneur is elevated by the French ambassador at a ceremony where he debates the relative merits of Cardinal Richelieu. He is the lead director in all but name on the board of Revlon during one of the most critical takeovers in history. He is never rude, if he can avoid it, but he never forgets an infraction or an insult, and he finds a way to make that known and to redress the imbalance, even if it takes 30 years.

Ezra's connection to Revlon went back to 1968. That year, France and global finance were in trouble. The infamous student and worker strikes, *les événements de mai,* had shut down the country. Finally, a settlement was reached, but it included massive wage increases that fueled inflation and rampant speculation against the franc, turmoil that threatened to bring down the international monetary system, as NBC's Chet Huntley put it in a newscast on November 22. Finance ministers from the Group of Ten had just met in Bonn, and devaluation of the French franc seemed definite. "The franc," Huntley intoned, "will be devalued but by how much is not yet known." It was rumored that de Gaulle was considering a devaluation by as much as 20 percent, which NBC News said could "bring the whole temple of free world finance crashing down."

Panic was beginning to spread. There was talk of a run on France's reserves and on the franc itself. De Gaulle dispatched squads of police to help customs men enforce orders that limited the amount of francs that could be taken out of the country. The French were buying anything, furs and jewelry and gold and stamps, to convert their paper money into something tangible "that could withstand the ravages of monetary chaos," as the newsmen put it. The year 1968 is seen as one of the most tumultuous years on foreign exchanges since 1931.

One of the many international businesses that faced serious disruption was Revlon. The mercurial Charles Revson was cruising the Mediterranean on his yacht, the *Ultima II*. Revson had just bought the yacht in the summer of 1967 from D. K. Ludwig, the mysterious billionaire shipbuilder, and its extensive renovation was at last complete. It was as long as a full New York City block. It slept 15 guests. There was a full-time staff of 31, with 9 officers and 22 crew members. It was powered by the equivalent of ten Cadillacs and a Toyota.

A typical shopping list telexed from Puerto Rico to New York, according to Andrew Tobias in *Fire and Ice,* his 1975 biography of Charles Revson, would include 60 pounds of chateaubriand, 20 pounds of corned beef, 20 pounds of brisket, 48 pounds of hamburger, 168 chickens, and 60 ducks. It cost $3.5 million in late 1960s dollars to buy and rebuild. "The maintenance and crew," Tobias recounts, "the transoceanic phone bills, the Gucci Bingo prizes, the fuel ($20,000 for a tank of gas), the steaks, the buckets of golf balls whacked off the bridge—by 1975 expenses were averaging $1,800 a day. Add in the cost of tying up $3.5 million, plus depreciation, and the ship cost Revson, personally, better than $3,000 a day. Four days out of five no one used it."[12]

The owner of this floating palace was well known as an idiosyncratic man. What was not well known were his profound insecurities, the yearning for acceptance, the fear of strangers, the need to project power, the odd mirrored toilet seat strategically aimed to enhance the size of what it reflected. "No one who grows up in a tenement," Tobias writes, "starts a business in the middle of the Depression, and ultimately builds a half-billion-dollar global corporation, is ordinary, or even 'normal.' Charles Revson least of all." He was abrasive, eccentric, and volcanic in temper and affection.[13]

This man phoned Ezra one day in the autumn of 1968 from the deck of the *Ultima II*. "I knew him socially in the world"—a phrase only Ezra could use—"and one day he called me. I think it was on a Friday. He called me from his boat. He had been told that the franc would be devalued that weekend, and he wanted to know what I thought. I just said to him, 'I don't think de Gaulle, as long as he's in power, will let the franc devaluate. He'll do *anything* in his power to stop that. Monetary stability is one of the general's most treasured achievements, and he has little talent for eating his words. The franc will only be devalued if de Gaulle resigns.'"[14] On November 25, sure enough, de Gaulle announced that he had no intention of devaluing the franc. After de Gaulle left office in April 1969, and only after that, was the franc devalued by 12 percent. It all happened as Ezra said it would.

Revson was impressed. He called Ezra once again. "He said to me, 'I want to hire you as an adviser.' I said, 'I don't really do that.' He said, 'Name your price.' You know, he was like that—very tough. I said, 'I don't do that.' He said, 'Just name your price. I want you to come to the company once a month, if you can, just to talk to my financial people.' And I said, 'Okay, fifty thousand.' Just like this was, you know, a simple little thing for him. So I used to go there. And eventually, Michel Bergerac asked me to come on the board when he took over, and I went on the board, because I like Michel. So, I was on the board."[15]

Ezra found a meeting with Perelman with the guillotines still in the town square a distasteful thought, but he at last agreed to grant an audience. "Look, I really don't think we should have lunch. If you want to see me, come to my office and we'll talk." Ron's first question was, as always, direct: "Why were you so opposed to my buying Revlon?" Ezra began with the standard response about low bids and directorial duties to shareholders: "I didn't want you to get it because your offer was too cheap. I wanted to work for the benefit of the shareholders and I strongly believe—"

"What do you have against me?" Perelman interrupted.

"If you want to discuss this on a personal level, I'll tell you what I have against you. I've met you three times in my life. The first time was with your stepfather-in-law [Clement Hakim, a friend of Ezra's, who had married the widowed mother of Faith Golding, Perelman's first wife]. We had lunch when you wanted your daughters to go to Spence School and I was a trustee. I wrote a letter, and I never heard a word from you. It doesn't matter to me whether they went or not, but it might have been nice if I had heard whether they got in. The second time we met, you wanted to buy Handy & Harman [a precious metals broker with Ezra on its board]. You came to see me and I sent you down to Goldman Sachs. The third time I saw you was at Hermès, with a lady who was not your wife. Out of discretion, I just nodded to you, didn't shake your hand, and moved on. It was none of my business. What did I get for this? I never got a thank you, but I don't care about thank yous. What I got was deposed at your law firm in a room that smelled of deli by a rude lawyer wearing a golf shirt who asked stupid questions."

"Do you know who the father of that lawyer is?" Perelman asked, referring to Skadden's Stu Shapiro. "Yes," Ezra said immediately. "He was the chairman of DuPont. Do you know who Prince Charles's mother is? The Queen of England. Is Prince Charles rude? No. There is no excuse for being rude."[16]

In Ezra's eyes, there was also no excuse for the use of junk bonds, but Revlon would be the first target captured by a hostile bidder funded by Drexel, in this instance, some $750 million worth of borrowed cash in Perelman's pockets ready for the spending. Perelman's attack on Revlon also had some other firsts to its credit. Eric Gleacher, who had recently left Lehman Brothers to become head of M&A at Morgan Stanley, one of the old-line banks that had held itself aloof from takeovers, had convinced his colleagues after an intense debate that he should represent Pantry Pride, a jolt to Wall Street that assumed such a bank as Morgan Stanley would never stoop so low. And to act alongside the dreaded Drexel? This was shocking indeed. Michel Bergerac would call Robert Greenhill, Gleacher's boss, to remonstrate with his old ally about consorting with horse thieves, to no avail.

Chemical Bank was another unashamed defector. The bank had rarely joined in a takeover and never in one funded by Drexel's bonds or one aimed at breaking up a target. Ezra knew people in Chemical's boardroom and made his calls urging them to avoid having anything to do with the risky, irresponsible financing that was coming at Revlon with all the force of cash money. Felix Rohatyn of Lazard, on Revlon's team, also called Michael Blumenthal, Ezra remembers, a director of Chemical. Michel himself called his counterpart at Chemical, Walter Shipley, the chairman of the bank. Nothing worked. They had all broken ranks for the first time, and for good.

Ezra's calls to his friends at Chemical Bank took up much of his deposition at the hands of Stu Shapiro, the man who failed to wear what Ezra considered appropriate office attire. "I was deposed in a windowless office at Skadden, Arps," Ezra remembers. "Stuart Shapiro was wearing a green golf shirt and no tie. True, it was Friday, but 'casual Fridays' had not yet become a custom—a custom I don't particularly approve, by the way. The lack of decorum was demeaning. Our lawyers cautioned me not to get angry, but finally I couldn't restrain myself. 'You must think I'm really stupid,' I said to Shapiro, 'because you're asking me the same question over and over again, each time in a slightly different way, and you don't think I can figure it out?' He wanted to get me to admit that in opposing Perelman's tender and calling the Chemical Bank directors, I was interfering, when in fact I was doing my job as a director and defending a company that I did not think should be sold so cheaply."[17]

* * *

THE FIGHT OVER REVLON STARTED WITH A KNOCK ON THE DOOR AT THE HOME OF MICHEL Bergerac by Ron Perelman on the night of June 14, 1985. Later, Bergerac would say to an associate, "Can you imagine this guy, saying he's going to make me a rich man?"[18] It may have been presumptuous, but it turned out to be true—true, at least, that Perelman would make Bergerac a much richer man than he was already.

Revlon quickly adopted a poison pill. It was its second line of defense that backfired, and it backfired brutally in both courts. In August, after Bergerac had barely contained himself from slamming his door in Perelman's face, Perelman announced a hostile bid for Revlon at $45 per share. Michel Bergerac rejected the bid and called Perelman, among other things, a "bust-up artist." The company responded with a poison pill and began buying back its own stock. Perelman came back at them with a cash tender offer at $47.50 per share. On August 26, the Revlon board threw up another defense. It offered to buy back as many as 10 million shares of its stock from its shareholders with notes or debt instruments that would pay 11.75 percent in annual interest, with a principal amount of $47.50. The company's later reaction to the fallout from this plan would prove to be its fatal error.

Unbeknown to Ron Perelman, the Revlon board had opened secret talks with Ted "Teddy" Forstmann of Forstmann Little and a second buy-out firm known as Adler & Shaykin. Forstmann, who died of a form of brain cancer called "glioblastoma" in 2012, was a notorious lothario, Machiavellian, and brilliant businessman, with the phrase "who once dated Princess Diana" forever attached to his name and, later, in the same way, "whose companion, Padma Lakshmi, is the ex-wife of Salman Rushdie."

The writer William D. Cohan, in a profile and obituary in *Vanity Fair,* describes Teddy's autobiographical anecdotes about his early life and his buyout firm.[19] His younger brother, Nick Forstmann, who had joined KKR in May 1976, called Teddy and asked for help in introducing his bosses Jerome Kohlberg and Henry Kravis to Derald Ruttenberg, an acquaintance of Teddy's who was then the CEO of Studebaker-Worthington and one of the country's richest men. After the meeting, Ruttenberg turned to Teddy and asked, "Are you very impressed by them?" Teddy was not. "Well, I was completely unimpressed," Ruttenberg is quoted as saying. The anecdote is one that Kohlberg and Kravis hate to hear, Teddy told Cohan. Ruttenberg then reminded Teddy that the team had already discussed doing buyouts together. "Well, what do they have that we don't have?" Ruttenberg asked. "I'll tell you something that we have that they don't have. We have money. So let's talk about setting something up and doing it." And so began the long march of Forstmann Little, soon KKR's main rival, and the successful victor over the years since in some 30 buyouts, Cohan relates, including Gulfstream, Topps, Yankee Candle, Dr Pepper, General Instrument, and many more.

With Revlon in play and the headlines blasting forth its vulnerability, Teddy rode in to save the day. He, too, faced an implacable Ezra, who was against the proposed deal with Forstmann just as he was against

Perelman's efforts, although this time for different reasons. Ezra considered Revlon's liaison with Teddy to be a potential disaster. "Bergerac made a mistake that proved fatal," Ezra says. "He tried to split Revlon in two and sell its halves separately in a leveraged buyout. Fred Adler, of the buyout firm Adler & Shaykin, would take the beauty business, while the rest would go to Ted Forstmann of Forstmann Little. Not only that, but Michel would run the health-care side of the business for Forstmann. To the Court of Chancery in Delaware, this smacked of self-dealing. Bergerac appeared to be acting out of self-interest rather than in the interest of Revlon's shareholders."

When the Revlon board met on October 3, Ezra was not in New York. His brother Abdullah was celebrating his fiftieth wedding anniversary with a five-day gala in Jerusalem. Ezra and his wife, Cecile, were staying at a suite at the King David Hotel so that he could take the calls from Revlon and, given the six-hour time difference, his wife could sleep. The calls were agonizingly long, four to five hours at a stretch, exacerbated by a rabbi telephoning Ezra in the midst of it all pressing him to donate money to some worthy cause. "The rabbi would have the operator interrupt my New York connection so he could talk to me instead," Ezra says with a smile. "And as you know, rabbis can be very persistent."

Despite Ezra's vehement arguments against the plan, the Revlon board approved the leveraged buyout with Teddy Forstmann. To help finance the transaction, Revlon planned to sell its American Home Products division and Norcliff Thayer to Adler & Shaykin. The price for Revlon's shareholders was set at $56 per share, which topped Pantry Pride's offer at that point. Management was slated to become a 25 percent equity participant in the buyout, using the proceeds of the golden parachutes that the merger with Forstmann was designed to trigger. For the transaction to proceed, there would have to be more borrowing against Revlon's assets. Under the terms of the notes, the company was barred from taking on any further debt. This covenant was designed to protect the value of the notes, as a company with high debt is at greater risk and of less value than it would otherwise enjoy. Revlon was preparing to waive those restrictions so that the buyout with Forstmann could proceed. At this sign of yet more debt looming for the company, the value of the notes began to drop. The notes had already traded widely. Soon, most of the shareholders had sold off their notes, and then the value of the notes took a nosedive. The new noteholders were an angry bunch. The directors had to find a way to keep them happy or massive damages could fall on their heads.

On October 9, Arthur Liman of Paul, Weiss convinced the three sides—Teddy Forstmann, Ron Perelman, and Michel Bergerac—to come together to see if they could make peace. Connie Bruck takes us back to that gathering: "At around midnight on October 9, Perelman and his entourage arrived, for the first time, in Revlon's gilded, rococo foyer on the thirty-ninth floor of the General Motors Building. 'I'll never forget those twenty or thirty guys coming off the elevators,' recalled Bergerac. 'All short, bald, with big cigars! It was incredible! If central casting had had to produce thirty guys like that, they couldn't do it. They looked like they were in a grade-D movie that took place in Mississippi or Louisiana, about guys fixing elections in a back room.' 'What a scene,' Liman concurred. 'All the Drexels were in one room—these guys with their feet up on Michel's tables, spilling their cigar ash onto his rugs.'"[20]

The tripartite summit at headquarters lasted until four in the morning. Nothing was accomplished. Perelman was willing to sell one of the health-care companies to Teddy Forstmann, but Teddy would agree only if Michel Bergerac gave the nod. Bergerac announced the next day that he disapproved, and the long talks went for naught.

Ron Perelman did announce that night to an incredulous Teddy his new and intensely frustrating tactic that his adviser and future colleague, Skadden's Don Drapkin, has just dreamed up. "We were sitting around in Perelman's office," one member of the team recalls, "which was in his townhouse in the Sixties, filled with incredible art—Modiglianis and Giacomettis, just unbelievable stuff—and the deal was just kind of plunking along. Donny Engle and Leon Black and Don Drapkin and me. We were all talking strategy, and Drapkin suddenly had an idea. 'We'll raise them a quarter every time they bid,' Drapkin says. 'They won't be able not to sell to us because we'll raise them by the same amount every time. We won't care what it costs.'"[21]

Of course, a quarter was not just a quarter. It was an increase of 25 cents for every share Revlon had outstanding, around $30 million for each increase of two dozen and one pennies per share. It would prove expensive, but it would be cruelly effective. The Revlon side would fume impotently at what they called the nickel-diming racket. "The whole Revlon case revolved around Drapkin's strategic advice," Stu Shapiro says.

At oral argument at the Court of Chancery, Herb Wachtell of Wachtell, Lipton—counsel to Perelman—revealed the degree of irritation Drapkin's tactic had caused in the Revlon camp. There had been several conversations between Marty Lipton, Revlon's lawyer, and Drapkin himself, and in one of them, Don said, "We have a very, very great respect for Forstmann Little's expertise. In fact, so great is this respect that we have decided to make Forstmann Little our [de facto] investment banker. Anything they bid, if they are prepared to do it, well, we will be prepared to go up another nickel, dime or quarter." In what was amounting to a $3 billion transaction, Pantry Pride was willing to say to whatever Forstmann bid: "Up you a quarter." It was infuriating or, as Herb Wachtell put it, "[t]hat situation was totally intolerable to Forstmann Little."[22]

When the case later came before Justices Andrew G. T. Moore II, John J. McNeilly, and Bernard Balick in the state supreme court, Stu Shapiro defended his client's tactics to the court at oral argument: "Now, a lot was made of this question as to whether there is some sort of invidious feature in what has been characterized by my friends as nickel-and-diming, or twenty-five-cent raises. I would like to address that briefly. Twenty-five cents paid now is worth somewhere close to a dollar a share, 30 million to 35 million dollars on Lazard's calculation, because it is paid now against a deal which at the most optimistic will close in thirty-five days and which the Lazard people advised the Revlon board might not close for several months. You clearly have a significant, not a trivial, economic advantage to shareholders."[23]

At a board meeting on October 12, Revlon still sided with Teddy Forstmann but with a new twist. Management gave up hope of part ownership of a future Revlon this time around. Forstmann and his allies, Adler & Shaykin, were the buyers. They agreed to put a floor under the notes, which would stop them from plunging any further in value. In return, however, Teddy demanded a no-shop clause and a lockup of some of Revlon's most precious assets. This effectively ended the bidding for Revlon, Justice Walsh would later find. There was no point in trying to buy the company if the jewels in the crown would be carved out and sold to one's rival as soon as you paid the purchase price. Perelman went to court, filing his complaint and his request for a preliminary injunction on October 14. From then on, the litigation in the Delaware courts was typically rapid. Between that date and the final opinion from the supreme court on November 1, the entire court war was fought in 17 days—all the discovery, all the briefing, and all the arguments in chancery, the opinion of Justice Walsh sitting as a temporary vice chancellor, followed by the supreme court briefs and the oral argument.

Then it all became rather eerie. Ezra reported to Marty Lipton that he had received phone calls purportedly from Peter Ackerman of Drexel, warning that to oppose Perelman's high price for the stockholders would be "un-American" and alluding meaningfully to Ezra's well-known aversion to publicity. "They were threatening something near and dear to my heart," Ezra says. "My own privacy. I was deeply offended and wanted to tell Drexel Burnham to go to hell. Marty Lipton said, 'Go ahead and tell them that.'"[24] Ezra, ever the gentleman, is too polite to say what he did next.

And then there was the mole, or moles, never identified but always suspected of passing information to Pantry Pride about the secret talks with Forstmann Little. Lazard's Bill Loomis said at the time, "I have never been in a deal where there were leaks like this. The transmission of information was *immediate*."[25] Ezra is even more pointed. He openly suspects, and has published his suspicions, that two pillars of the law world, Arthur Liman and Simon Rifkind of Paul, Weiss, were double agents, the Burgess and

Maclean of the Revlon War.[26] Many in the MEA bar are appalled at the suggestion.

Judge Rifkind, then 84, had been a director at Revlon since the late fifties and had served as the executor of Charles Revson's will. He was renowned and respected. But he had also been the lawyer for a Perelman family member and had recently joined the board of Perelman's company, MacAndrews & Forbes. As for Arthur Liman—Judge Rifkind's protégé and heir apparent at Paul, Weiss, renowned as one of President Nixon's most formidable antagonists, former counsel to the Senate Iran-Contra committee—Arthur Liman had long been Revlon's counsel but had recently taken on Perelman as a client as well. "Neither is still alive," Ezra says, "and the dead cannot defend themselves, but some people suspect there was a mole on Revlon's board who leaked our deliberations to Perelman."[27]

The more it looked likely that Revlon would lose to Perelman, the more the Revlon side grew appalled by this new vicious game and the new breed of opponent, where boardrooms now had to be swept for bugs, phones checked for listening devices; where no one kept his word; where the debt financing was at best unreliable and at worst a nest of carpenter ants that would soon hollow out the company's very life. They themselves were gentlemen. They were important, trusted people. They viewed Peril-man and his allies at Drexel as their opposites. "The directors and their lawyers simply couldn't believe that people in this dirty takeover business could be viewed as legitimate," says Stu Shapiro. "This made them very vulnerable because it made them very impractical."

And then Revlon sullied its own hands. Suddenly, there was the little matter of the missing $25 million. As the Friday approached before the Columbus Day holiday, Revlon revealed that it had agreed to sell itself to Teddy Forstmann's leveraged buyout fund. As an added incentive, Revlon guaranteed to Forstmann Little that even if the buyout firm did not end up with the entire company, it would still have the right to buy several of Revlon's most prized divisions, spoiling any potential victory for any other eventual buyer. With the Monday holiday imminent, Revlon told the Delaware Court of Chancery through its lawyer, Lawrence Hamermesh of Morris, Nichols, Arsht & Tunnell, that no monies would change hands over the long weekend and that the status quo would remain intact so that the judge could safely delay his ruling on the case until the week after the break. The judge accepted this promise and, on Revlon's word of honor, agreed to postpone his decision until the Tuesday after Columbus Day.

There is a little-used courtroom, more like an anteroom, off the Delaware Supreme Court chambers in Wilmington. The bench is large enough to seat all five judges, but the room is very small and very dark, and often very cold. It was to this place that Justice Joseph Walsh summoned the two sides to the bar on Tuesday, October 16, 1985.

For Skadden, it was a bit awkward, as Teddy Forstmann was a highly valued client. Rather than argue specifically against their own client's surprise deal with Revlon, they decided to turn to Bruce Stargatt, a Delaware litigator, to do it for them. But Bruce could not be found. "We put out an all-points bulletin for Bruce, and we found him down in Dover, at his regular poker game with all the important state legislators. We got him up to Wilmington the night before the hearing," recalls one M&A specialist, who was intimately involved in the fight. "When we went into court the next morning, Bruce stood up, and rather than launching into some big argument and yelling and waving his hands around, he said a few words of introduction and then he just turned to Larry Hamermesh and said to the court, 'I think I'll just allow Mr. Hamermesh to explain to the court what happened.' Poor Larry came up with some sort of explanation, but it just couldn't fly."[28]

The opinions that the Delaware courts handed down in the course of the Revlon fight are now part of the architecture of merger law. Yet invocations of the so-called Revlon duties of boards of directors, among other doctrinal incantations inspired by the takeover, reveal little of why the judges decided as they did. Their rulings did not spring fully formed from their Olympian foreheads but instead congealed around a series of rivalries, tactics, written and oral arguments, witness interrogations, and random litigation ricochets, or, as in this instance, blatant insults to the bench.

It was stunning. Over the weekend, Revlon had removed from the corporate treasury, and placed in escrow, not only a tranche of stock in the companies promised to Forstmann Little but also cash in the amount of $25 million that was earmarked for Teddy to compensate him if his deal with Revlon were to fall through. There was simply no reason to do this except to remove these assets from the reach of the court's orders.

Revlon had gone back on its word in what was a rare and egregious defiance of the Court of Chancery and an affront to Justice Walsh himself. Not prone to public revelations of his private thoughts, Justice Walsh nevertheless made clear that he was furious. "They had made a pledge and then days later they just turned around and broke it," says a litigator involved in the case. "It was the turning point for the whole case."

On October 23, one week after Revlon's local difficulties with Justice Walsh, he issued his opinion. He granted Pantry Pride's request for a preliminary injunction, freezing in place everything to do with the deal. The Delaware Supreme Court agreed to hear the case on an expedited appeal. Justice Walsh was well aware of the noteholders and their sway over the Revlon board.

"The board's primary responsibility after the exchange offer was to bargain for the rights of the remaining equity holders," Justice Walsh wrote. "By agreeing to a lock-up and no-shop clause in exchange for protecting the rights of the noteholders, the Revlon Board failed in its fiduciary duty to the shareholders. The board may have been informed, but its performance did not conform to the other component of the business judgment rule—the duty of loyalty. The board's self-interest in resolving the noteholders' problems led to concessions which effectively excluded Pantry Pride to the detriment of Revlon's shareholders. Thus, the element of loyalty may turn, as it does here, on the selection of a takeover defense or a bargaining device that is not proportionate to the objective needs of the shareholders but merely serves the convenience of the directors." Justice Walsh granted Pantry Pride's motion and banned any transfer of assets to Forstmann Little or any placement of those assets in escrow for Forstmann's benefit. All eyes turned to the high court for the appeal.[29]

Stuart Shapiro was thousands of miles away, admiring the gardens and temples of Kyoto. A phone call came in from Mike Mitchell, a fellow Skadden partner: "We've gotten a preliminary injunction, and it's going up on appeal to the Delaware Supreme Court. It's your case. You need to take care of it." He would be going up against an imposing group: A. Gilchrist "Gil" Sparks III, one of the premier litigators in Delaware and in all of M&A, was representing Revlon. Leon Silverman of Fried, Frank was arguing for Teddy Forstmann.

At the Hotel du Pont, Stu puzzled over the case. What should he emphasize at oral argument before the redoubtable Drew Moore? There were innumerable paths to take: Revlon's choices of defenses, its favoritism toward Forstmann Little, the relative strengths and advantages of each bid.

> I remember going in to argue the case, and Joe Flom gets me on the phone, and I tell him what I'm going to argue concerning the board's decisions, and he says in that gravelly voice, "Nah, that's all wrong. The directors have complete discretion to consider what they ought to do on a business basis, and as long as what they're doing makes sense, it's okay. You can't argue that they have an absolute right or absolute obligation to take a certain action. You have to argue that what they did was conflicted and wrong. Not because they chose one course over the other, but because they did it on the wrong basis." Flom was a genius. He looked at a picture, and he saw things that no one else saw. He knew the court wasn't going to say that directors have an absolute obligation to take the highest price regardless of all other factors, because, for example, one deal might be less risky or it might close sooner. A lot of factors would go into the mix. You needed to find something that would make it clear that what they'd done was not motivated by loyalty to the corporation or shareholders but that they were driven by some other motive.[30]

Stu found that motive in the testimony of Judge Rifkind, a member of the board of directors of Revlon:

JUSTICE MOORE: [T]here was testimony from Judge Rifkind, one of the directors, and others, to the effect that they firmly believed that Mr. Forstmann
would walk away from the transaction. Now, why doesn't that leave us in
the realm of business judgment?

MR. SHAPIRO: First of all, with all due respect to Judge Rifkind, he was not a
part of the negotiations at the time. He was relying on, presumably, his
own mental processes but no evidence. Secondly, the question was put to
Judge Rifkind, "Why didn't you call up Pantry Pride and ask them if they
would beat the Forstmann bid?" And his answer was, "There was no reason to do that. We knew that they would beat the bid." This was at page 89
of his transcript. "But Pantry Pride had said they wouldn't take care of the
noteholders so we had no interest in talking to Pantry Pride."

What he was saying quite candidly was that the noteholder problem assumed such proportions that an absolute condition of doing a deal
with Revlon was that you took care of the noteholders. And that is also
reflected in the October 12 minutes at about page 8, I believe, where Mr.
Lewis describes the course of discussion with Mr. Forstmann. And he said
on I believe it's October 10th, "We talked with Mr. Forstmann and we
said, 'If you want to make a new proposal to beat Pantry Pride, there are
two conditions.'" And the first condition was, you have to take care of the
noteholders. And only the second condition was that you ought to make
your best price and put it on the table.[31]

On November 1, the omnipresent Justice Andrew G. T. Moore II wrote
the opinion for the state high court. First, he ruled on an important M&A
issue that neither side had asked him to address, a decision that has been
largely overlooked ever since. Marty Lipton had installed a flip-in pill at
Revlon, a variation on his device that had not yet been sanctioned by a
court. This pill gives shareholders the right to benefits from their own company at the expense of a bidder, as opposed to the flip-over pill that grants
similar rights in the attacking corporation. Justice Moore noted that the
board had later voted to lift the pill for any cash offer of at least $57.25.
With both contending offers equal to or higher than that, the rights had no
further effect on the contest. "This mooted any question of their propriety
under Moran [the Household case] or Unocal." But that didn't stop Drew
Moore. He ruled that the "adoption of the Plan was valid." The Revlon
board had put it in place "in the face of an impending hostile takeover bid
by Pantry Pride." The pill, he said, protected the shareholders from low-
ball offers and gave the board the flexibility it needed to get the best deal
for shareholders. "This part of the opinion often slides under the radar,"
says Lawrence Hamermesh of Morris, Nichols, who represented Revlon in
the fight. "One can miss this about Revlon, but it may be one of the most

important points in the case. He doesn't focus on the flip-in issue, but it was a flip-in pill and it was validated."[32]

One of Justice Moore's declarations most often cited in the world of M&A is the critical tipping point he finds in the Revlon fight: "The Revlon directors concluded that Pantry Pride's $47.50 offer was grossly inadequate.... However, when Pantry Pride increased its offer to $50 per share, and then to $53, it became apparent to all that the break-up of the company was inevitable. The Revlon board's authorization permitting management to negotiate a merger or buyout with a third party was a recognition that the company was for sale. The duty of the board had thus changed from the preservation of Revlon as a corporate entity to the maximization of the company's value at a sale for the stockholders' benefit. This significantly altered the board's responsibilities under the Unocal standards. It no longer faced threats to corporate policy and effectiveness, or to the stockholders' interests, from a grossly inadequate bid. The whole question of defensive measures became moot. The directors' role changed from defenders of the corporate bastion to auctioneers charged with getting the best price for the stockholders at a sale of the company."[33]

Finally, he turned to the noteholders, in a statement that does not ring down through the annals of the law but decided the case for Ron Perelman: "When a board of directors ends an intense bidding contest for the corporation on an insubstantial basis and a significant by-product of that action is to protect the directors against a perceived threat of personal liability for consequences stemming from the prior adoption of an anti-takeover measure, the directors have breached their fiduciary duties to the shareholders."[34] Justice Moore affirmed Justice Walsh's ruling, and Revlon belonged to Perelman for $1.8 billion.

Stu won one of the most important court victories in the history of mergers and acquisitions. "I got the word back ultimately from one of the justices, who made a comment to my father after the case was over that the oral argument had been very helpful," Stu says. The noteholders had become more important than the shareholders, a violation of the board's duty of loyalty to those who own stock in the company. "We did not emphasize this in the briefs. I came across Rifkind's testimony. It just was something I'd read, and after talking to Flom, it became the thing I knew I had to say."

Later in the day, Stu and his father, Irving Shapiro, were having a drink at the Rodney Square Club in Wilmington, cofounded by the senior Shapiro at a time in the not-so-distant past when Jews were not welcome in the city's other exclusive clubs. Gil Sparks came over to their table to congratulate Stu on his oral argument. It was fitting that a luminary in M&A with an initial for a first name and a Roman numeral for a surname would tip his hat to a Jewish lawyer at a club founded in response to discrimination after an M&A victory against an established elite that had scorned a bidder as unworthy of anything but ostracism. At that point, the court had not ruled yet, but Sparks knew from the oral argument that it was Stu's day.

A devastated Michel Bergerac came to see Ezra at 30 Rock just two hours after the Revlon board met for the last time, with Ron Perelman and his team waiting outside for the boardroom doors to be opened to them.

"What has happened?" Bergerac said as he let himself down into a chair.

You have just made yourself $35 million with your golden parachute and the sale of your stock. That is what has happened, Ezra told his friend. It's November, he went on quickly. It's almost tax time. Don't waste your time with me. With me you can talk any time. We have been friends all these years, great friends. I will call my Peat Marwick people for you, Ezra said. Go now and see how you can defer your taxes. "And that," Ezra recalls, "is exactly what Michel did."

*   *   *

LORRAINE BRACCO, WHO PLAYED TONY SOPRANO'S THERAPIST, HAD AN EVEN TOUGHER job than her fictional efforts to resolve a two-bit mobster's phobias in a television series. She tried to bring Ron Perelman and Don Drapkin together for a reconciliation. At her suggestion, they met after work at Manhattan's Le Bilboquet on the Upper East Side for dinner in December 2008, Ronnie and Donnie together for the first time since their split a year earlier. Ron brought along Barry Schwartz, vice chairman of Perelman's MacAndrews & Forbes since the death of his longtime adviser Howard Gittis.

Drapkin, after leaving Perelman's employ, had quickly found a perch at Lazard, headed by his old friend from their days as Cravath associates, Bruce Wasserstein. "I thought you were gonna help us at Lazard," Ron said to Don as the dinner began, according to his deposition. "That's what you keep telling me. You're gonna help us [get deals through the Lazard investment banking network]. Why are you telling me now—'cause you guys are meaningless over there, and nobody cares about you. So that seems like a funny way to do business, but OK," Ron testified. "And I got up and left." And threw a $100 bill on the table as he did. The next morning, Don sent an e-mail to Ron that read, "I loved having drinks with you for the holidays. It made me feel great. I remain your friend and love you . . . and want things to go back to normal."[35] Next up as couples therapist came Vernon Jordan, the Washington lawyer, clout merchant, presidential friend, and Wasserstein's Lazard colleague. Perelman told Jordan that Drapkin had been a "naughty boy," according to sworn testimony by the latter. "At that point," Don said, "I decided this wasn't going anywhere."[36] He filed his lawsuit soon after.

Don Drapkin began his career as an associate at Cravath and left to join Skadden, where he became a partner and Flom acolyte, with the distinction of being the one hundredth lawyer hired by the firm in 1977. In *New York* magazine's issue of April 14, 1986, David Blum wrote a profile of Drapkin that begins by calling him "the hottest young takeover lawyer in America." Bruce Wasserstein is later quoted as saying, "He thinks the business, he dreams the business, he eats and sleeps the business. Let's face it. He *is* the business." Here is Blum's account of Drapkin relaxing at home in front of the television:

> He and Bernice are watching *Dynasty* on television. On the prime-time soap, Barbara Stanwyck (of *The Colbys*) has just given her nephew a gift of $500 million in stock. "What a terrible gift!" Drapkin is thinking. Doesn't she realize he'll have to pay gift tax on the stock—and that the rate of gift tax on stock is higher than on almost any other category? He does the arithmetic in his head. His ballpark estimate is that the nephew will owe the Feds $380 million, leaving him with a net profit of only $120 million. "God," he thinks, "these shows are so stupid."[37]

Drapkin was known to idolize Joe Flom, whom he once called "a spiritual figure," and soon had the office right next to that of his mentor on the thirty-fifth floor of 919 Third Avenue, or "919" as it is still known by Skadden alumni. Former colleagues remember that Drapkin refused to take a corner office and abandon his seat near the throne and that he kept his office phone extension as 3150 rather than take the partner perquisite of a number ending in two zeros. To do so would have meant losing the number closest to Flom's own 3100. Then 38 years old, Drapkin tells Blum that he will probably never leave Skadden. "Why should I? My friends are here. I'd never find a place as much fun as this. I like to think of myself as an entrepreneur, off starting businesses, but deep down, I know I'm a lawyer. That's it."[38]

But it wasn't "it." The Revlon deal was his breakthrough starring role, and he soon left to join Perelman at MacAndrews & Forbes. The two men became inseparable. They had pet names for each other. Don called Ron either "the Putz" or "the Dwarf," in honor of his small stature and bald head. Ron called Don "the Asshole."[39] The Dwarf and the Asshole would breakfast together daily at Ron's splendid townhouse on the East Side, followed by the dealmaking day, lunch at Le Cirque, and then a black-tie dinner for a charity or with fellow businesspeople. They were together at landmark events in their lives: the bat mitzvah for Drapkin's daughter at the Pierre, with Perelman on drums with the band Kool & the Gang; Ron's bachelor party at La Côte Basque before he married gossip columnist Claudia Cohen after divorcing his starter wife, Faith Golding, in both of whose footsteps from wedding to divorce would follow actress Ellen Barkin and serial power wife Patricia Duff. After the two men had their own breakup, they spoke only once, as Don told Andrew Ross Sorkin of CNBC on the air in 2012: Ron called Don to offer condolences on the death of Don's son, Dustin Joseph, who died on March 5, 2010, at Snowmass Village at 23 years of age.

By the time their relationship dragged itself into court, Ron was to testify in his deposition that by 2007 he was no longer enamored of his friend Don. "I became dissatisfied with his performance. He started spending more time on his own investments than he did on MacAndrews' investments." In Don's own deposition, he testified that he gradually found himself at an ever-growing distance from the throne. "He one by one took away any responsibility. . . . He became monstrously abusive to me." By the turn of the millennium, Don said that Ron had behavioral issues with others as well. "[He] screamed," for example, "unmercifully at some handyman or something putting in a light bulb the wrong way." Perelman had recently come close to paralysis after being treated with "massive doses" of progesterone after an epidural damaged his spine, according to Drapkin's testimony, an account that Perelman rejected in his deposition as "false." Drapkin maintained that he spoke to Gittis about leaving the firm, saying, "I just can't take it any more." He testified that Ron called him, "screaming at the top of his lungs, 'OK, I'll let you out but it won't be pretty.'"[40]

The two men signed a separation agreement. Don was to receive $27.5 million for five years. The contract also called for Drapkin, then 63 years old, to relinquish all files relating to MacAndrews & Forbes that were "not otherwise available to the company, after which you delete (and do not attempt to recover) all copies of such files in your possession." The agreement also included a "nondisparagement" clause that banned Don from saying bad things about his former place of employment. Eric Rose, a MacAndrews & Forbes executive, in his deposition claimed that Drapkin had made "denigrating remarks" about Ron at a dinner at Quality Meats in Midtown Manhattan. Two months after their failed reconciliation at Le Bilboquet in December 2008, Perelman, then 68 years old, stopped payments under the contract with some $16 million to go. Thousands of pages of documents poured into court. Subpoenas were served on friends, lawyers, investment advisers, the brother of one of Ron's four ex-wives, and even Don's son. The trial lasted three weeks. Drapkin's lawyer, Elkan Abramowitz, told the jury of eight in his closing in mid-February that MacAndrews was "scrounging around for any excuse not to pay Mr. Drapkin." He asked, "Do these nitpicking breaches really give the company the right to terminate contracts worth $16 million?"

With Ron Perelman's wealth estimated at around $12 billion and Don's own in the hundreds of millions, a question was put to the jury pool:

"Especially with the recent attention to the top 1 percent and the other 99 percent brought about by Occupy Wall Street, I ask you to consider whether you have any prejudices or biases against very wealthy people that would affect your ability to be a fair and impartial juror in this case, where unusually wealthy men are involved in both sides of the case." Perelman's lawyers objected and, in all caps and bold type, declared, "This question is overbroad, and it is neither fair nor accurate to simply characterize this case as a case about money."

Drapkin had a base salary at MacAndrews of $15 million a year, plus 3 percent of any deal done by the firm and 8 percent of any he brought in. Money, indeed, seemed to be a receptacle for far deeper feelings of loss and betrayal, of jealousy and longing, an example yet again of the old adage that there are no new stories in all of human experience. With a backdrop of an enlarged *New York Post* headline that read "Spoiled Rich Guys," CNBC's Gary Kaminsky on January 31, 2012, asked Don Drapkin how it all happened. "Well, I was best friends with Ronald and Howard Gittis for twenty-five years," Don said. "You know, people have disagreements over contracts—can't resolve 'em—they have to go to trial. I was hoping it would be resolved before, but I knew there was a possibility it could go to a jury, [and] there's always a danger when two rich folks are fightin' in court that the jury's not gonna like that, but I have new respect for the judges and for the—you know, we've all watched *Law and Order* a hundred times—the jury really does pay attention and tries to understand what's going on. And I had two brilliant lawyers, Elkan Abramowitz and David Dunne, and they had said to me—the case went to the jury at four o'clock—if the jury comes back before five-thirty, you're a winner. At maybe five twenty-six, they announced the jury was coming back, and I consider myself a fairly sophisticated guy—I'll be back next week to talk about real business stuff—that ten seconds, when the judge says, 'Madam Foreman, have you reached a verdict?' and looks at me—my heart was in my throat. I don't want to do that again." By mid-February 2012, Ron and Don had come to an agreement about that money. The judgment of $16 million was vacated, with the court's approval, and a settlement was reached by the two parties, the terms of which remain private.

Changes come to every life, of course. Drapkin, a respected commentator on CNBC, is now an equally respected shareholder activist, one of the newly dominant breed of M&A practitioners who buys large stakes in companies, not to take them over but to press for better performance. Drapkin is now estranged from his longtime second wife, Bernice. During the trial, his girlfriend, as he allowed Kaminsky to call her without protest, was Elyse Slaine, in court every day, complete with cushions for Don's bad back. Spotted by a "spy," the *New York Post* described her as "Donald Drapkin's femme fatale . . . the ex-wife of David Slaine, the Galleon employee who wore a wire to help authorities investigate and convict hedge fund cofounder Raj Rajaratnam. . . . Now she's clattering her Louboutin heels into court for her new man. . . . Yesterday, Elyse was in skintight jeans and fur-lined snow bunny boots . . . huddling with Drapkin during breaks. Everybody was asking who she was. She told the paper, 'I am just being supportive of my dearest friend.'"[41] The loss of his other dearest friend seems to weigh heavily on Don. "I mourn the loss of that friendship," he says. In his deposition, he testified, "A person goes through life with only a few friends that you can be that close to. I never understood how you could throw them away."[42]

How different it had all been at the now-defunct Quilted Giraffe's table 11, in the mid-1980s, their specially reserved place in M&A history. In June 2013, Perelman filed suit against Michael Milken, to the latter's surprise, charging his old friend with an alleged deception in a 2011 deal. It was nothing personal, Perelman said. Just business.

CHAPTER THIRTEEN
FOUL DUST

Gary Wood's three hunting dogs had been missing for too long for any-thing good to have happened. In the early morning of an unseason-ably warm late-winter day, with the mist curling down from the Blue Ridge Mountains, he set off to search for them again across the sloping meadows and low hills of southern Albemarle County in central Virginia. As a country boy "and proud of it," as he would often say, Wood knew the land intimately, as did his dogs. He lived in a tenant house on an estate that had until recently been known as Oakwood. In keeping with ancient tradition, he and his dogs had long enjoyed the permission of adjoining landowners to roam and hunt freely over their farms.[1]

Three years earlier, however, an aging M&A merchant prince and his trophy wife had parachuted into Wood's world from New York. Rapidly and relentlessly, the couple began buying up what the missus called "his-toric farms," including Oakwood. One Bavarian aristocrat was besieged with takeover offers for her estate, culminating in a blank check that she was told she could fill in for any amount. Countess Marie Therese von Degenfeld-Schonburg returned the check, still blank, with her final refusal. Others happily sold their land, and soon the billionaire and his exotic con-sort had merged their conquests into one 6,000-acre dominion.

Things hadn't been the same since their arrival. The new people didn't seem to know or care about local traditions, and Wood feared for his dogs. It was not like them to stay away overnight, let alone for two full days and nights. He called and whistled at intervals, scanning the valley that un-folded toward the distant purple hills. When he came over a rise, it was the stench that got him first, an invisible plume of rot that made his eyes water. He stared down at the pit, surrounded like an open wound by the red, vis-cous Virginia clay. Then he saw one of his dogs, the young walker hound, hanging by the neck from a trap, its vocal chords cut. It was still alive and had managed to stay on its hind legs for two days.[2]

*   *   *

IT LOOKED LIKE A GIANT BASKET BEING PULLED DOWN THE MEADOWS FROM THE MANOR house by two horses, a rogue escapee from some cyclopean picnic in the clouds. It was lunch for the shooting party, arriving in one of the antique coaches the host liked to collect. "It was a huge, huge, *huge* basket thing made by Asprey's," Ezra Zilkha, who, with his wife, Cecile, was included in that weekend house party. "Somebody opened it, and all the chairs came out, the tables, the utensils, the food, everything."[3]

It had been a good morning in this new-found-land of flowery meads and shadowing hills, and the gamekeeper was pleased. He was an Irish baronet, Sir Richard Musgrave, who managed the 850-acre preserve for the 10,000 pheasants and 3,000 ducks that he and his two assistant gamekeepers raised by hand. Once known as Seven Pine Farm and then simply The Shoot, it is in southern Albemarle County, several miles from the main estate.

Kitted up in specially provided tweeds, the guests had been transported in more of the open carriages in the early hours to their "pegs," or positions in the field. Beaters marched through the tall grass and flushed the hand-fed, nearly tame birds into the air. The shooting master blew his whistle, and the guests opened fire. Ezra did not take a gun. Once, he says, he went shooting at Alexandria with his brother in the Egypt of King Farouk. "I shot a bird. I couldn't stand it. But I don't begrudge others the pleasure."[4]

The Kluges provided their guests with special scorecards with hand-drawn sketches of each species and adjoining boxes in which to write the number killed. One item was titled "Various" so that the occasional regrettable decision by a deer or a fox or a rabbit or a bobcat might also be recorded. To toast their triumphs, the guests used silver goblets engraved with the number of their peg. A day's total could be as high as 800 kills, not counting the category of "Various."[5]

At the midday meal, John Kluge turned to the guest on his right as they sat down. "So tell me, Ezra, how much do you think this lunch cost?"

"John, how could I possibly, I mean I have no idea."

"Take a guess!"

"Twenty thousand dollars."

John laughed. "Two hundred thousand dollars, my friend. Two hundred thousand dollars!"

It was disarming, Ezra recalls. The man was laughing at the absurdity of his own creation. "He was very down to earth," Ezra says. "*Very* down to earth."

Kluge then gestured toward two of the newest additions to his collection of carriages, kept in a 34,000-square-foot museum on the place. "And what do you think they cost, Ezra?"

"How can I know, John?"

"Well, take a guess."

"A million dollars?"

"A million dollars? A million dollars? You don't know. They cost *five* million dollars. But do you know what they charged me for freight and insurance? Five hundred thousand dollars." Kluge frowned and shook his head, disgusted. "Five hundred thousand dollars!"

"But John, if they had told you the price was five and a half instead of five million, wouldn't you have bought them anyway? Just cancel two or three of these lunches and you'll make up the lost money, am I not correct?"

He laughed loudly and thumped his friend on the back.[6]

John Kluge was a short man with a large head set on a wide neck. He was no Jimmy Goldsmith, says one lawyer who worked at the right hand of both John Kluge and Sir James. "When Jimmy walked in the room, you started checking the boxes. Tall? *Tall.* Good-looking? *Good-looking.* Well dressed? *Well dressed.* Articulate? *Articulate.* Smart? *Smart.* Well traveled? *Well traveled.* Rich but understated? *Rich but understated.* Okay, I understand why's he's him and I'm me. But when John walked into the room, you were kind of like, 'Hmmm. Well, *okaaaay.*' He just wasn't an imposing presence. But he done good."[7]

His surname is pronounced "KLOO-gee," but in German it sounds like "kloo-guh"—and it means "clever," in the sense of quick intelligence. There are many stories about the man, many supplied by Kluge himself. Born in 1914 in Chemnitz, Germany, he moved with his mother at the age of eight to Detroit. His first job, he would always say, was on Ford's assembly line. He got a scholarship to Columbia University, persuaded the university grandees to double it, and then lived high on his poker winnings until threatened with expulsion for gambling. Although he was not handsome, he had a way of making people like him. He was a salesman with a compelling smile; he was a persuader.

Kluge began building his M&A empire in the late 1940s, beginning with a Maryland radio station, WGAY, which he founded at a cost of $15,000. Thirteen years later, he got his first television stations when he took over from Paramount Pictures its 24 percent stake in Metropolitan Broadcasting Corp. Renamed Metromedia in 1961, the company ballooned in size. Kluge proceeded to absorb more than 200 businesses, including billboard companies, telephone systems, Fritos corn chips, the Ice Capades, the Harlem Globetrotters, Radisson hotels, and, among others, the Ponderosa and Bonanza steakhouse chains.

In 1984, Kluge decided to take over Metromedia from its stockholders. He needed their approval to do so, and the shareholders of Metromedia assembled to vote on the proposal at an office building on Manhattan's Park Avenue, just before it is bisected by the 808-foot wall that was still known in the early 1980s as the Pan Am building. Kluge wanted to take the company private to remove it from its listing on the stock exchanges and escape the cold eye of the regulatory agencies that supervise publicly traded companies.

He turned to Marty Lipton to orchestrate the acquisition. Marty suggested a leveraged buyout, a takeover financed by debt. Just as one uses a lever to lift a weight far in excess of what one could handle without the rigid little object, in a leveraged buyout a small amount of one's own cash used to lift a vastly greater amount of borrowed money to dump on the stockholders in return for their shares. Kluge proposed to borrow $1.3 billion from a total of ten banks, led by Manufacturers Hanover and the Prudential Insurance Company, which helped by buying up $125 million of the preferred stock. With that money, he offered to pay the stockholders about $40 per share in total—$30 in cash plus a debenture, or promissory note, worth roughly $10. Kluge had already raised the value of that debenture by $1 per share to quell a shareholders' lawsuit challenging the deal.

Metromedia's shareholders, not unexpectedly, voted in huge numbers in favor of Kluge's 1984 deal, as was common in the day when shareholders typically did what management said was best. This time, however, there were at least a few murmurings of dissent among the stockholders in the auditorium of Manufacturers Hanover. Kluge would often retell the story of a woman who, he said, came up to him at the end of the meeting and told him that her son's education money was in Metromedia stock, and she was worried about what would happen to that nest egg. Kluge said he promised the woman that he would put her son through college. It is not known whether he did pay for the young man's bachelor's degree, but Kluge took home $115 million in cash and securities and leapfrogged from an ownership stake of 26 percent of the company to 75.5 percent. It became rapidly notorious, however, that Kluge was facing such financial trouble with this deal that his promise was in jeopardy. Under the banks' terms, he had to pay back a first installment of $200 million by June 1985, which meant he would most probably have to sell some assets.

He was not thrilled. Then, his famous luck kicked in. He happened to meet at one of his senior employee's homes in New Jersey a leading banker from Drexel. We hear you could use some help, the Drexel man said. Soon, Drexel started to refinance Kluge's existing debt, using four kinds of junk bonds with a total value of $1.35 billion against all the assets of Metromedia. "Kluge had to pay a higher rate on the new paper than he was paying the banks, but Metromedia's cash interest payments were lower because $300 million of the new money came from zero-coupon bonds," explains William Shawcross in his book *Murdoch*. These bonds require no periodic interest payments, or coupons, with the face value of the loan repaid at maturity, similar to US Treasury bonds. "He was betting that the value of the [television] stations would compound faster than securities Drexel sold for him were accruing interest," Shawcross writes.[8]

Then Kluge went to Mike Milken's Predators' Ball in 1985, the annual bond conference, legendary for the connections made, both among those who attended and those paid to provide a wide variety of entertainment. Barry Diller, who had left Paramount and joined Marvin Davis at Twentieth Century-Fox, then brought Kluge, Rupert Murdoch, and Milken together at Diller's office on the studio lot. It was the start of the deal between Murdoch and Fox on one side, and Kluge on the other. Kluge demanded $1.05 billion for his television stations in five cities: Washington, DC, Houston, Dallas/Fort Worth, Los Angeles, and Chicago. Hearst Corporation had already snapped up the right to buy the Boston station. Kluge would not agree to sell New York. Diller was appalled at the high price, but Murdoch was rubbing his hands, knowing that such a clutch of stations in such a cluster of major American cities was one of his chances of a lifetime. It would be like buying an entire collection of Audubon prints at once, before they could be dispersed to the four winds. Still, Murdoch wanted more. He demanded New York. Kluge conceded. The group announced their megadeal on May 6, 1985, and the birth of Fox Television Inc. At the time, it was the second-largest media deal in history, second only to ABC's acquisition of Capital Cities in April of the same year.[9]

But there were problems. D. M. Osborne explained a few of the hurdles blocking the way toward Kluge's $2 billion triumph in her profile of Murdoch's general counsel, Arthur Siskind, in the *American Lawyer*.

> [A] thicket of debt-equity ratio requirements in News Corp.'s numerous credit agreements stood between Murdoch and his Metromedia deal, requiring what Siskind terms "an extraordinarily complicated and very unusual financing." The junk bond house Drexel Burnham Lambert Incorporated planned to raise $1.15 billion of the purchase price, but the heavy bond component of the financing at first appeared to run afoul of News Corp.'s debt agreements. Working with Metromedia counsel James Dubin of Paul, Weiss, Rifkind, Wharton & Garrison—who describes Siskind as "a major force in [the] deal closing"— and Drexel counsel Vincent Pisano of Skadden, Arps, Slate, Meagher & Flom, Siskind found a way out: The company could satisfy the restrictions by defining the bonds as preferred stock. "Under Australian [generally accepted accounting principles], a preferred stock, even though it is designed to have all the attributes of debt, would be treated for accounting purposes as equity," Siskind explains. "I always referred to it as 'junk preferred,'" he quips.[10]

Bruce Wasserstein called it "the blockbuster television station deal of the 1980s."[11]

For Kluge there were no problems to slow him down. The sale to Murdoch was only the beginning. His auction rattles on into 1986. He sells the Ice Capades, the Globetrotters, his billboard business, and nine radio stations for yet another billion. Having invested $300 million of Metromedia's funds in cellular telephony in 1983, Kluge sells these properties to Southwestern Bell for $1.65 billion. And what of the shareholders? The $7 billion fortune that Kluge amasses so quickly means that he in effect bought Metromedia for one-sixth of what it was actually worth. As chairman and CEO of the board at the time, he was legally obligated to put the interests of those shareholders above his own in all circumstances. There was a rather stinging appraisal of all this in *Barron's:* "Suppose a trustee for an orphan sold to himself property for which he paid the orphan $5,000, then resold the property two years later for $30,000. In what sense would that transaction differ from the Kluge-Metromedia transaction?"[12]

Of course, there could have been no way to tell what Metromedia's assets would bring once they were put on the auction block. To know that, you would have to have been both as lucky and as *kloo-guh* as Mr. Kluge himself. In two years, his massive garage sale of Metromedia's businesses transformed the $250 million he paid for the company into a multibillion-dollar fortune that made him the second-richest man in America, behind only Sam Walton of Wal-Mart (which had not yet lost its hyphen). Within another three years, Kluge doubled his net worth to $7 billion. This time *Forbes* put him in first place, and John Werner Kluge, child immigrant, former factory worker, and scholarship student, was officially the richest man in the United States. By that time, he also owned the largest house in the country.

John Kluge had married his second wife, Patricia Gay, in splendor six years earlier at St. Patrick's Cathedral on Fifth Avenue on May 24, 1981. "We went to their wedding," recalls Ezra Zilkha. "It was white tie,"[13] he says, with a smile that notes benignly the breach of the tradition that calls for full evening dress to be reserved for state occasions.

The *Palm Beach Daily News* called it "one of the most carefully planned and dramatic weddings New York [had] seen in many years." As evening mass came to an end and the worshipers were walking out onto Fifth Avenue, the limousines were pulling up to the curb with the 500 guests invited for 6:30. The men were in tails and medals and decorations, and the women in ball gowns "covered up in deference to the cathedral." Purcell's "Trumpet Voluntary," along with the organ, announced the start of the wedding procession. On the arm of Baron Damato, who gave her away, the bride wore Arnold Scaasi, a wedding dress the designer described as a cathedral gown, appropriately enough, with a high neck, long sleeves, and a full top, embroidered in white silk organdy and seed pearls—"all very Edwardian."[14]

The matron of honor was Mrs. Anna Murdoch, then still the wife of Rupert, and the bridesmaids were Christina de Lorean, Mrs. Nicholas

Toms, and Mrs. Michael Finkelstein, all in Jonal, who designed a deep-peach moiré gown with spreading skirts and "more ruffles than cuffs," as well as bodices tailored to each attendant. The ushers included Robert Marx, son of Barbara Sinatra by a previous marriage. The reception was held at the Metropolitan Club, and the guests included Gina Lollobrigida, Roy Cohn, Walter and Jane Hoving, Robert and Phyllis Wagner, Norman Lear, Paul Anka, Tony Bennett, and Ivana and Donald Trump. Mrs. Kluge walked down the "club's dramatic art deco stairway, stopping for just a minute to toss her bouquet," as Peter Duchin struck up his orchestra and the dancing began.[15]

Patricia Kluge is the daughter of a British translator and his Scottish-Iraqi wife and was brought up in colonial Baghdad. She fearlessly acknowledges that she has a "past," as these things are so often euphemistically known, and she agrees that newspapers around the world have felt free to have their say. One British tabloid, for example, labeled her "Di's Porn Queen Hostess" in a banner headline when the Prince and Princess of Wales were slated to be the guests of honor at a $50,000-a-ticket charity ball in Palm Beach that Patricia chaired. But the truth, said Patricia, is much more mundane. As a young woman, she married a man 32 years her senior and lived the high life for a short while. In her case, the spouse in this starter marriage was Russell Gay, the publisher of *Knave,* a sex magazine. Yes, she did pose for nude photo shoots ("The raunchier her full frontal pictures, the better, as far as she was concerned," her photographer George Harrison Marks once said). And yes, she did write a how-to column on sexual techniques for the publication. And, yes indeed, she did also appear as a belly dancer in the film *The Nine Ages of Nakedness,* but she kept her clothes on, one of the few cast members to do so. She was also quite an accomplished belly dancer.

She did take off more at other times. "Modeling nude was okay for five minutes. I did it for a lark," she told a British newspaper. "He [Russell Gay] was the antithesis of my Catholic upbringing—so wild and crazy. We fought a great deal. But it was a good experience. I was brought up so strictly and hypocritically that marrying him liberated me from all that. I had a lot of admirers. I was hot-looking in my twenties. I certainly looked a lot more nubile than I do now. I mean at five feet-ten inches, with long dark hair and wearing a mini-skirt, I was gorgeous. It was a no-brainer."[16]

So was their takeover of New York society. In the late eighties, as only one example, the Kluges hosted one of the premier events of the calendar at their Manhattan apartment—the nuptials for Abe Rosenthal of the *New York Times* and Shirley Lord. Guests included Beverly Sills, Nancy Kissinger, the Trumps, Gloria Steinem and Mort Zuckerman, Gay Talese, Estée Lauder, and Senator Moynihan and his wife, Elizabeth Brennan. For John Kluge's seventieth birthday party in 1984, the couple took over L'Orangerie, a private dining room at Le Cirque, and transformed it into an

English garden. The birthday cake was designed to simulate a billion-dollar bill; the wine was a Chateau Lafite from 1914, the year Kluge was born. The dining room seats 100 people, a quarter of what Mrs. Astor's ballroom could contain, and invitations were deeply coveted.

A year after the birthday party, the takeover of Virginia began in earnest. Mrs. Kluge had been on the hunt for a place to build a country seat and had decided on Albemarle County, Virginia. It is reminiscent of an English county, for one thing, with its fox hunting and horse races and house parties. It also has a collection of famous presidential houses: Thomas Jefferson's Monticello, James Monroe's Ash Lawn, James Madison's Montpelier, and Zachary Taylor's birthplace at Montebello. She set about assembling a plantation and a decorative arts collection with the same insatiety as her husband with his companies. She would call it Albemarle House.

She turned to David Easton. "I wanted to build a Georgian house. When I met David I found in him somebody who really understood that period extremely well. And so, literally in one and a half hours, we designed the whole house on the back of a napkin. And Albemarle House was the beginning of that movement in the '80s and '90s of neo-Georgian style, and the sort of grand kind of English-style living." Although its elephantine size implies a mutation in the DNA along the way, Albemarle House turns out to share a common ancestor with the local manors built by the Virginians of the Enlightenment. "Growing up as a child, having discovered Palladio at the age of eleven, I have always dreamt that when I grow up I will build a house like Albemarle House," Mrs. Kluge told Sotheby's in its promotional video for the house sale.[17] The Italian Renaissance architect had also inspired Mr. Jefferson, as he is known in the county, as well as countless others down the ages.

Massive gates open to a long, winding drive that curves up through the valley to the distant shining house on a hill. There is a gingerbread chapel. There are five artificial lakes, liquid circles in square miles of landscaping marked by mature trees planted by helicopters. There is an 18-hole golf course designed by Arnold Palmer. Crowning it all, above mowed meadows and vistas of vineyards, stands the manor house itself.

The interior of the 45-room palace, when intact, was indeed a 1980s fever dream of silk and satin and damask, of marble and plaster, of trompe l'oeil and frescoes. The books-by-the-yard were organized by color and size so that *Elizabeth de Valois* was shelved next to *The Hobbit*. Reproductions of discus throwers and naked quasi-Greek deities lined the sculpture gallery. The windows, hundreds of them, were of specially manufactured German glass with identical flaws to simulate great age. The silence was the only feature that was not quite perfect. Behind everything was the soft vibrato of the vast air-conditioning system sealing off Virginia's summer heat.

The housewarming was a hoedown, which featured an entire buffalo on a spit, as well as Jerry Zipkin and Saul Steinberg in country costume. "A livable palace is a palatial home that is actually relevant in the twenty-first century, because it functions," Mrs. Kluge says. "You know, there's a theater in your house, or you can go shoot and fish any time you want to. You have your own kitchen and you can entertain in your own kitchen, or you can have a magnificently formal dinner in the dining room. And there's space there to be on your own or to be with your family. It's grand. But it's also a place where, even though all the furniture is quite magnificent and the rooms are very rarified, it's still a place where children run and dogs jump, where every room is used all the time."[18]

The English garden behind the house was designed by Lady Xa Tollemache and George Carter to mimic the layout of the interior in a series of intimate garden rooms. The swimming pool lies between the big house and its dependencies. Two empty sarcophagi sit waiting in the crypt below the pretty little church. There are all the accoutrements of country life, the golden Labradors, the prize cattle in their chandeliered barns, the legions of servants in eighteenth-century livery, the feudal villages of farm workers. "It's a world," Mrs. Kluge says quietly. "It's a world to itself, and one that, once you're in it, it's very hard to leave it."

"It is a beautiful house," says Ezra Zilkha. "Patricia is smart. She's fun. She was just a girl living a dream."[19] But foul dust floated in the wake of that dream.

*　*　*

THE DOBERMAN PINSCHER CAME UP TO THE BACK DOOR AS IT ALWAYS DID. THE THREE-year-old dog was whimpering. Courtney Peck, the owner, heard the sound and recognized it immediately. Opening the door, he could barely assess what he saw. His dog had a snare trap dangling from a hind leg and a clean dark bullet hole straight between its eyes. Later, at the trial, Peck would hear an estate employee say that he had tried to put the animal out of its misery, but that the bullet had failed to kill it and the dog had taken off for home, dragging the trap behind him for miles.[20]

Wood and Peck did not yet know that this kind of thing had been happening for months, nor were they aware that a secret investigation had been launched by the US Fish and Wildlife Service and state and local authorities after 61 hawks' feet tied on a string and several hawk carcasses were found in the autumn of 1987 dropped at the roadside at a gate to a subdivision at Lake Monticello. At first, it was suspected that they were the relics from some satanic ritual. Soon, however, it was another sporting tradition that became the object of official interest.

On March 28, 1988, the authorities pounced. They found two large pits at The Shoot, each the size of a tractor-trailer bed and each between 10 and 15 feet deep. They began to dig. By the end of their excavations, they found more than 400 remains of protected hawks as well as several owls. It later emerged that this practice was designed to protect the thousands of duck and pheasant from an early demise and to save them instead for such regular house party guests of the Kluges as King Juan Carlos of Spain, Katherine Graham, Betsy Bloomingdale, Bob Hope, the Sinatras, Abe Rosenthal and Shirley Lord, Senator Chuck Robb, Governor Douglas Wilder—the Old Dominion's first African-American governor, with whom Mrs. Kluge would be romantically linked—and sometimes Sam Shepard, Jessica Lange and Sissy Spacek, fellow Virginia landowners.

The bodies of twelve dogs were also unearthed. "Some were so badly decomposed that you could tell it was a dog but not who it belonged to," Jacky Gillispie, a Fluvanna County sheriff's department investigator, told the press. "One did have a collar and I would say it was freshly killed, within the last week." That dog, a small beagle, wore tags that revealed her name and her owner. She had belonged to Charlottesville police officer Charlie Via. Her name was Molly.[21]

Sir Richard Musgrave and three of his employees were indicted on federal wildlife charges and eventually released on bail that had started out at $75,000 but was dropped to bonds worth up to $7,500. One employee was out of the country but a warrant was also issued for his arrest.[22] At the trial that began May 26 before a jury of eight women and four men, it was revealed that tape recordings of a dying rabbit, a mouse in extremis, and the cries of baby raccoons were used to attract the birds. Thirty seconds of one tape, labeled "cottontail rabbit," were played in open court.[23] There was testimony that the birds and owls were killed sometimes at the rate of 20 per day, either shot or beaten to death.

From the witness stand, Sir Richard maintained that he had "not killed a single thing in Virginia." He said he suspected that his gamekeepers had done it all on their own, "as it's the custom to do so" to keep the shoot from depletion by natural predators. Described by a character witness as "a jovial English gentleman," Sir Richard stressed that the birds were kept as wild as possible to give them a sporting chance to escape. He said that if The Shoot were to be shut down it would be a loss to the community, as many of the pheasant had flown off and were available for hunting by the local populace.[24]

All three of the defendants maintained that the Kluges had not ordered the killings and knew nothing of the practice. As the scandal unfolded over the months from the arrests to the trial, a local child rehabilitation center was renamed for John Kluge in April after he gave it $500,000 for the construction of a new wing and $2.5 million for cerebral palsy research.[25] In May, John and Patricia were presented in London with the Silver Partridge Award by the Duke of Edinburgh. The Kluges won the six-inch silver statue on its walnut base for their $25,000 gift to the American chapter of the Game Conservancy, a conservation and research organization devoted to game birds and other wildlife.[26]

After four and a half hours of deliberation on Thursday, June 2, 1988, Sir Richard Musgrave, 66, and British gamekeepers Paul Shardlow, 25, and David Amos, 20, were convicted of "conspiring to kill hawks, owls, and other protected birds." Sir Richard faced a maximum sentence of two years in prison and a $15,500 fine. Shardlow faced a two-and-a-half-year term and a fine of $20,500. Amos could have been given a six-month prison term and a $5,000 fine.[27] A week later, all three were given suspended sentences and paid a total of $12,575. Moments after the court's decision, the three were detained by agents of the US Immigration and Naturalization Service. A day later, on June 10, 1988, they were released. They promptly went to Dulles Airport to take the 1:10 p.m. flight to London on the Concorde.[28] A parting remark from Sir Richard got a laugh from the courtroom spectators: "It looks like I'm going to be the first criminal in my family since Charles II."

The local difficulties in Charlottesville came at a busy time for John Kluge. He was in the midst of what looked like the opening skirmishes of a takeover battle with the curmudgeonly Sumner Redstone, whose National Amusement Corporation had just bought Viacom, owner of some 20 percent of Orion Pictures. Kluge held a similar stake in Orion, and in March 1988, the two men had just started a game of leapfrog. When one bought a chunk of stock in Orion, the other bought just a bit more soon after.

With the discovery of the grisly predator pits, they had to attend to some serious damage control. Kluge suspended his nascent campaign against Redstone for control of Orion and flew down with his wife to Charlottesville. The barn was packed for the press conference, called for the morning after their return to Albemarle House. Dressed in blue jeans and a white shirt with the sleeves rolled just past her wrists, she wore no makeup and no jewelry. She stood under one of the barn's brass chandeliers, looking solemn. This could work, Patricia's publicist thought to himself.

"The reason I have summoned you here today," Patricia began, and the publicist blanched. "To use the word 'horror' is not even a big enough word, but I'm so exhausted thinking about it that my vocabulary is just stopped with that. It just shows what can happen. You just throw your hands up in the air and just say, 'How could this possibly be?'"[29]

The Kluges were not there for the trial. At greater than the speed of sound, they left for London on the Concorde the day after Patricia's barnstorming press conference. It is not yet known what they knew and when they knew it.

Et in Arcadia ego.

CHAPTER FOURTEEN
FAT MAN AND LITTLE BOY

Robert Campeau was besotted with Bruce Wasserstein, and Bruce Wasserstein was just as intoxicated with his own role as the Canadian's sorcerer. Often referred to as "Bid-'em-up Bruce," a nickname he hated, Bruce regularly urged the combustible Canadian ever onward with Shakespearean soliloquies preaching higher and higher offers that gave Campeau the auction fever that ended in his winner's curse. Mike Rothfeld, then at First Boston, remembers the standard oratory working all too well with the Canadian novice: "Bruce made one of his best 'Dare-to-Be-Great' speeches that I'd ever heard, and, of course, to somebody like Campeau, it played right into [his] ego."[1]

Kim Fennebresque, also at First Boston at the time, witnessed the actual moment of seduction. It was more than a rapport between Bruce and Bob, the American Jew and the French Canadian. It was a bargain between a vulnerable troubled man with many unmet needs and a skilled adviser advancing his career by offering that man a means to satisfy those intense desires. "There is a Wall Street skepticism about real estate developers," Kim said, "so there was some uneasiness in the house about this, but we met with the Campeau people, we talked about their financing, and we embarked as if we had no doubts. We moved ahead. . . . It was clear that when Bruce said, 'You hire me—this is what it costs,' Bruce was saying, 'It's going to cost this much money,' but in effect, Robert was beginning to make his Faustian deal. He basically *said*, 'Okay, I'll pay this amount of money,' [but] it was clear from the dynamic between the two of them that Robert Campeau had capitulated also psychologically to Bruce, that Bruce in fact would be in charge here on out."[2] Indeed he was.

In what must be one of the great howlers of all time, Bruce Wasserstein once said of Campeau: "He knows his limits, he knows he can be exhausting, but he never makes a bad move out of emotion."[3] Stu Shapiro, on the other hand, notes a sad parallel to today's financial world. "Odd, isn't it," says Stu, former Skadden partner and adviser to Federated, "that Wall Street hasn't changed? Instead of convincing ego-driven CEOs to 'bid-em-up' and go bankrupt, they convince clueless investors to buy CDOs [collateralized debt obligations] filled with toxic waste, rated AAA by rating agencies, and go bankrupt themselves with their portfolios filled with worthless, unsalable junk when the music stops."[4]

In 1992, four years after Campeau's blitzkrieg across the department store sector of the North American economy, the National Film Board of Canada, with CTV Television Network, released a docudrama called *Double or Nothing: The Rise and Fall of Robert Campeau*, written and directed by Paul Cowan. It is a somewhat awkward hybrid. Part of the film is a screenplay based on fact, with actors playing Campeau, his two secret wives and two sets of children, his lawyers, his opponents, and his investment bankers, including one very short clean-cut, prep-school-accented man out of a Brooks Brothers catalogue impersonating Bruce Wasserstein. The balance of the movie is a series of interviews with the real people who ran the deals. They are our M&A stars in their prime, most notably Mike Rothfeld and Kim Fennebresque of First Boston, and Peter Solomon of Shearson. They are still young men arrested in time. They speak openly about the two most unusual deals of their careers. There is no bragging. There is dark humor. There is wistfulness and regret, even sadness. There is caustic humor. There is honesty about what they did and what happened. It is a series of episodes of *In Treatment*. It is a priceless artifact of a time now two generations past.

Kim is the primary patient. When the film was released, at least a dozen reviews mentioned Fennebresque by name. "The best performance," one critic wrote, "is turned in by the real-life Wall Street banker Kim Fennebresque, who gives us a crisp play-by-play of the machinations of high finance. You can almost see the testosterone ooze."[5] Kim is often described in newspapers and books as "impish" or "wise-cracking," but that seems to trivialize both his intellect and his willingness to speak directly about his own foibles and the absurdities of his work.

A lawyer by training, Kim began his career as a litigator with Simpson Thacher. He was, however, "bored numb" by the law. An investment-banking client urged him to apply for jobs in finance, and he took the only offer he got, which was from First Boston. He stayed 13 years and became head of corporate finance and mergers and acquisitions. In 1989, he designed and breathed into life First Boston's bid for RJR Nabisco. In *Barbarians at the Gate,* he is described by Bryan Burrough and John Helyar as delivering particularly effective faint praise to *Investment Dealers' Digest* about a competitor. "Wasserstein Perella & Co., although a fine firm, is basically a one-product firm," he is quoted as saying. He goes on to suggest that its 30 bankers try to peddle "the impression that Bruce is really working on [all clients'] deals." Fennebresque, the authors add, "knew the term *fine firm* would rankle the Wasserstein contingent: 'In investment banking,' Kim tells the authors, 'that's like saying she doesn't sweat much for a fat girl.'"[6]

In November 1994, Benjamin Wallace, then senior reporter at *Corporate Control Alert,* found Kim at his new UBS offices. "Fennebresque leans forward in his upholstered chair, one eye scrunched shut, and sights down the shaft of a Head squash racquet, as if lining up a putt," Wallace wrote. "*I really really really love golf,* a sticker on his desk-chair announces. Two weeks ago he was chain-inhaling cigars—inhaling cigars!—and now, for the gazillionth time in his 44 years, he has quit cold turkey. The withdrawal has left Fennebresque with a surfeit of energy, and on this Thanksgiving week afternoon, he grips the racquet and paces anxiously, cleaving the air with forehands and backhands. His slicked-back dark hair hangs to his shoulders, and as he swings, so does it. 'This is not a statement,' he says. 'I just haven't had a haircut.'"

> Back in his office, Fennebresque is now poised in a batting stance, the squash racquet cocked over his shoulder like a Louisville Slugger. He swings. Along the windows, which together frame a panoramic view of the East River, tchotchkes pack the radiator top and form a collective monument to Fennebresque's career and tastes. Beside multiple photos of his wife and children are signed glossies—"To Kim"—obtained through friends and colleagues with connections—of Cybill Shepherd, Linda Evans, and Vanna White. "They're babes," Fennebresque says. Some of the twenty-odd books in his radiator-top library include *The Cynic's Lexicon, The Portable Curmudgeon,* and *Political Babble.* A mounted *Wall Street Journal* article from September 29, 1992, headlined, "Lazard Taps Rattner and Fennebresque to Co-Head Banking," recalls another turn in the investment banker's working life.[7]

At the time, Kim expected that he would stay at Lazard for the rest of his career, where he was not only a partner and co-head of investment banking but surrounded by people he considered his friends, rather like Don Drapkin at Skadden. Steven Rattner, for example, once said of Kim that he was the funniest person Rattner had ever met. After only three years, however, Kim would move to Union Banque Suisse and then on to his own investment firm, where he is today. In 1994, Kim told Benjamin Wallace that in his letter of resignation to Felix Rohatyn, he thought Lazard would be "the zenith of his c.v." "I believe that," Wallace quotes Fennebresque as saying, "I think when I am laid to rest, if my kids have anything about which they are inclined to brag, with respect to me, it will be in order: He was an unbelievable father, and he was a partner at Lazard Frères. That's what they could brag about."[8]

Looking back on the Allied and Federated saga, Kim had a final thought on his former client. In a mock whisper, he said, "Campeau was a fucking nut."[9] Bob was not alone. The department store wars took a long two years. From the beginning, nothing and no one were normal. At Campeau's first meeting at Cravath, he wore a floppy hat adorned with a tall feather and filled his mouth from a bag of cherries. At his fortieth-floor suite at the Waldorf Towers, which became his central command, Campeau would receive the cream of New York investment banking while he was dressed in a jogging suit or an open shirt with a gold chain plunging down his chest and a huge Rolex on his wrist. "The Hairy Navel Meeting" became infamous among the potential advisers, when one banker came calling to find him sitting on a sofa, his legs tucked under him, and an open button on his shirt exposing his belly button.[10]

Campeau was lurching from idea to idea at the time, first eyeing Macy's as a possible target—"Get me Finkelstein!"—but Macy's was in the midst of an LBO in December 1985, and, although a senior vice president was assigned to meet the Canadian visitor, Macy's chief, Edward Finkelstein, did not drop by his subordinate's office to meet Campeau. Macy's, after all, had a market cap of $2 billion, and Campeau's outfit barely crested $200 million. Finkelstein and Campeau would later find themselves rivals for Federated, but in the meantime, Campeau turned back to Allied. He code-named his takeover plan "Project Express."[11]

After several investment banks, including Merrill Lynch, Goldman, and Salomon, turned down Campeau's overtures to become their client, Peter Slusser of Paine Webber took on the task. "I got this feeling that at first, Campeau had no idea what I did for a living," Slusser recalled soon after the battles were over. "He kept referring to me as his broker."[12] Paine Webber was looking for a big deal, having recently failed to sell Carl Icahn's junk bonds for his takeover of TWA, quickly ceding that role to Drexel. He did need another investment bank onboard to add to his somewhat meager resources. This was the first of many hurdles.

Eric Gleacher, then head of M&A at Morgan Stanley, said that after leaving the Waldorf Towers with his colleagues, he waited until reaching the safety of the street before asking them what they thought. "I said to the guys with me, 'I don't know about you, but I didn't understand a word he was saying.' Turns out they didn't either."[13] Gleacher remembered sitting in front of Campeau, bemused. "As I sat there listening to him, it occurred to me that nothing the man was saying made any sense."[14] He called Cravath's Allen Finkelson to say, "Count us out." Paine Webber's Slusser eventually found success in his search for a willing and an unconflicted law firm for Campeau, when he turned to an old rugby pal from Harvard, Cravath's Sam

Butler, who agreed to take on the bizarre client as a favor. Butler handed the matter over to Allen Finkelson and Rob Kindler, now a partner. As for an investment bank, First Boston got a call from Campeau to say they were his first choice, and they jumped at the job.

On September 4, 1986, in a scene that reveals a bit of what the world was like before cell phones, Campeau met Allied's chairman, Thomas Macioce, and left the meeting convinced he had a deal. He frantically searched for a phone to call Cravath's Allen Finkelson and finally found one in a nearby rooming house that wanted $20 for ten minutes, which Campeau knocked down to $10.[15] A week later, on September 11, 1986, a day that would later live in infamy, Campeau's offer to buy Allied at $58 per share was summarily rejected. Allied raced to find a rescuer and enlisted Ed DeBartolo, a well-heeled Ohio businessman, and his large empire. With Shearson, advised by Simpson Thacher, as the investment banker for the white knight, and Sullivan & Cromwell representing Allied, the target girded itself for a hostile battle.

A hostile takeover was always infinitely more fun and lucrative for the bankers and lawyers of the day. "The prospect of this being a hostile transaction had a high recreational value for us," First Boston's Fennebresque recalled at the time. "Wall Street, obviously, is not for the people who are secure, [who] have good sentimental hygiene. It's for a lot of broken-down jocks. It's a place for emotional babies. People who like highs and lows. And so the greater the hostility, the higher the pleasure factor."[16]

As the bidding between Campeau and DeBartolo oscillated wildly back and forth over the autumn of 1986, money was, as they say, no object. "Robert Campeau, I'm sure, had a price in his mind over which he would not go," Kim Fennebresque recalled. "We had no price in mind. Obviously, we didn't care. It was his money, and that was the nature of the time. So we really hadn't thought about it. We knew how much he could finance, and every time we decided to help him raise his threshold of pain, we had to find some financial Novocain around the Street. And we did. We found it. . . . Bob was good because he could ultimately be persuaded. He would rant and rave and look like a five-year-old when you take away his LEGOs. He would do the commercial equivalent of lying on the floor and holding his breath." But each time, in the end, Wasserstein could get him to take the next step down the labyrinth. "As the price escalated," Kim Fennebresque recalled later, "we legitimized each other. Edward DeBartolo would say to himself, 'Geez, well, if those guys want to spend X dollars, what's X-plus-one?' And we'd say, you know, 'That proves X was the right price because Edward DeBartolo is willing to bid X-plus-one.' And of course, you can see how we both kind of made each other feel good. Not intentionally. Week Six: price at X-plus-ten. Campeau no longer feels good. Price up by half a billion dollars."[17]

Two flashes of genius from Wasserstein sealed the Allied victory for Campeau. The first was the bridge loan, and the second was the street sweep. First Boston did not, at first, offer its own money to Campeau to finance his bid for Allied. The investment bank had issued to Campeau a "highly confident" letter, a qualified assurance that it would successfully raise $600 million worth of debt through junk bonds. This letter had already cost Campeau $1 million. In September 1986, Wasserstein was getting worried about Campeau's uncertain financing. As so often happened, he had an epiphany: Why shouldn't First Boston use its own capital to give Campeau an immediate loan that he would repay later? A bridge to the future with money needed now, coming back to the bank later? This had rarely, if ever, been done in a hostile takeover by an adviser to the bidder. Peter Buchanan signed off on it, and First Boston was on the hook for an immediate $455 million and a total of $865 million, reduced from an initial offer of $1.8 billion by the arrival of Citibank as a fellow financier for the takeover. First Boston also got a fee for doing this, which would otherwise have gone to a conventional lender, for $7 million. Wasserstein, no fool he, insisted that Campeau send the money by wire transfer rather than a check.

In his book *Going for Broke,* John Rothchild describes the moment of triumph: "Wasserstein was sitting in his office, which was decorated in what could be called British Empire High-Tech—dark wood and faux bamboo, a round desk with brass fittings, two computer screens (one of which was reportedly dysfunctional), plus a Quotron, installed, say colleagues, to give the impression that Wasserstein was adept with numbers, although in fact he was terrible with numbers—when he received a message that Campeau's wire transfer had cleared. 'Heh-heh,' Wasserstein chortled. 'We just made seven million dollars.'"[18] The loan fired up Campeau, and he bumped his offer yet again, on his way to the nearly $4 billion sticker price for Allied Stores. Later, First Boston, after Bruce left to form Wasserstein Perella, would end up losing $100 million on Robert Campeau. Wasserstein never loaned the client a cent.

The street sweep clinched the deal for Campeau. His team knew that the trader Boyd Jeffries could decide the winner. Jeffries was what Sullivan & Cromwell's George Kern called a third-market trader, a kind of off-hours stock exchange, who, like others in his field, bought and sold and brokered stock when the markets were closed. Jeffries had in his hands enough stock in one block to give Campeau the majority he needed. Campeau could conceivably end his tender offer, avoid all the rules and restrictions that came with it, and sweep up ownership of his target. Kern, who started his firm's M&A practice in the 1970s, was advising Allied and served on the board of the company. He had never trusted Campeau, and he had been warning that Allied's defenses could crumble in an instant if Campeau swept the market. Here is Kern, a quiet, methodically sardonic man just entering his 60s at the time, speaking into the camera for the National Film Board of Canada's docudrama about Campeau made in 1992 about the events of 1986:

> I was kind of from the beginning somewhat suspicious that Bob Campeau had in mind something more extravagant than what he was first talking about. . . . Originally it was the idea that we ought to make beautiful music together by a consensual agreement. . . .
>
>   The main thing I was worried about was there might be a drop-and-sweep. Now, a drop-and-sweep is where somebody who is making a tender offer announces one minute that the tender offer is over and then the next minute goes out and buys all the stock that's around. . . . [Paul] Bilzerian [an ally of Allied's white knight, rival to Campeau] kept telling me, "No, no, no—there's no problem," and so forth, and then he asked me to hold for a moment—there was something coming over the wire, and it said, "Campeau Has Dropped His Tender Offer." So he came back and said, "Well! We've won! Campeau's finished." . . . I said, "What do you mean, he's finished? That's just a prelude to doing a sweep." He said, "No, no, no. There's no possibility of that." . . . And then he said, "Excuse me a minute." He went back and looked at the tape again. He said, "Well, you know, there's something new on the tape." . . . They'd swept the Street. They owned 51 percent of the stock. So this was kind of an extraordinary telephone conversation where the man who was supposed to be the expert was saying it couldn't happen, and it was happening in front of him while he was saying that. I haven't had anything go quite that dramatically wrong in my experience.[19]

It was a risky decision, and, as Rothchild tells it, the dangers were not lost on Bruce. What if a court allowed Campeau to buy the stock and then invalidated his voting rights, for example, leaving him stuck with a large block of impotent shares? Bruce was well aware of the risks, as Rothchild tells it:

> Wasserstein himself was uncertain enough of the ramifications that he wavered Hamlet-like through dinner at Il Nido Restaurant on the night of October 23. "Am I nuts?" he wondered out loud to himself and two dinner companions. "Does it make sense?"
>
>   Later that same evening, Wasserstein met with an old friend, lawyer Don Drapkin, and some other associates in Drapkin's office at Skadden, Arps to mull this over some more. (Drapkin would soon leave Skadden to become Ron Perelman's right-hand man at Revlon.) Wasserstein polled the room, and everybody said, "Do it," and the papers were drawn up.[20]

On October 24, roughly seven weeks after Campeau tried to find a phone on the streets of New York to tell Cravath's Finkelson the mistaken news that Macioce had agreed to a friendly deal, a large crowd gathered at the forty-second-floor office of First Boston's William Lambert, a close ally of Bruce Wasserstein, with a small conference room connecting their two offices. They had swept the street, and now they were waiting to hear if Boyd Jeffries would call. He did. The phone rang into the silence. Jeffries was on the line. By Halloween, Campeau had won.

The struggle was on to secure the financing for the deal. By Christmas, things were tense. First Boston's Kim Fennebresque was no stranger to Bob's needs: "He would often call my home at 6:30 in the morning, I having been up very very late the night before, working on his deal," he says. "He would call at 6:30 with another seemingly trivial thing. It got to the point where my wife just would pick up the phone and hand it [across] to me and say, 'It's him.' So he was a very important part of the bedroom activity in our marriage for a long time." On Christmas Day 1986, Kim reached a tipping point. He couldn't take it anymore. The phone rang. Kim was in the midst of carving a goose. It was Bob, for the third time that day. Kim's wife and children were sitting at the dining room table. Bob was angry and desperate and demanding. It was a typical manic episode. "Bob," Kim said, as his children's eyes widened. Kim, now standing in the doorway to the kitchen, told his client where he could put the goose. "Bob! It's Christmas Day! Go fuck yourself!"[21]

Things did not go well with Allied from the start. Campeau hired and fired, and hired again; he scheduled interviews for a top executive position that left the applicants mystified as to whether he recognized them or knew why they were there. Following the plan to sell divisions to raise money for debt service, Campeau thoroughly frightened off Felix Rohatyn and the Limited's Leslie Wexner who came shopping. They scurried away after a late night of talks during which Campeau suddenly stood up and began pacing the room. "Do you think I did right in buying Allied? I hope I didn't overpay. I think I didn't overpay."

He had overpaid. In November, Campeau released the numbers for the first nine months of 1987: Operating earnings were $44 million, the tiny capital spending budget pushed free cash flow—the amount legitimately available to pay interest—to just over $100 million, but interest paid was $244 million. "So what do you do when you have a limping retailer in tow?" *Fortune*'s Carol J. Loomis asked rhetorically in one of her masterpieces, the landmark analysis of the Campeau debacle in 1990. "If you're Campeau, you buy a spry one and cripple it as well. In the late summer of 1987, he began making plans to go after Federated, owner of an avenue of names: Abraham & Strauss, Bloomingdale's, Bullocks, Burdines, Filene's, Foley's, I. Magnin, Lazarus, Rich's, and—an apple among pears—Ralph's Grocery, a California supermarket chain."[22]

In Campeau's search for another giant to kill, the choice was between May Department Stores and Federated. In October, the market crash cut the price of Federated stock from the mid-40s to the low 30s, and he began to buy. His code name for this effort became "Project Rose," since Federated shared a hometown, Cincinnati, with baseball star Pete Rose. His vice chairman, Bob Morosky, was against the plan: "I tried to talk him out of it. I said it's like acquiring the US Navy. I asked him if he had any idea of the complexity of the financing, and the good old-boy system, and the management politics that had caused Federated's deterioration. Federated had great consumer recognition with its famous department stores, but Federated was poorly managed."[23] And that was before Campeau. By this time, Bruce Wasserstein and Joe Perella had left First Boston and set up their own investment bank. Campeau refused to lose Bruce. He hired them both. First Boston, under Peter Buchanan, was out to prove that they had lost nothing despite the departure of Bruce and Joe; Bruce and Joe, for their part, were determined to show that they could make it on their own. Both sides would use Campeau for their own ends.

There were at first six potential bidders for Federated: KKR, the Pritzker brothers, the Simon Property group, the Dillards of Arkansas, Campeau, and Donald Trump. Skadden's Jim Freund, working for Federated with Joe Flom, recalls Trump's quick exit: "I have a memory of getting on the phone to Trump, who had bought 5 percent or so of the shares, and I said, 'Get rid of those shares, or we're coming after you.' And he did. I was not nice in that phone call."[24] Freund, now 78, is an imposing man, still playing singles in tennis and still proud of his record as athlete of the year at Horace Mann, when as a senior classman he played football, basketball, and baseball before going on to become a first-team halfback on the NYC All City private school team. Trump backed off.

On January 25, 1988, Campeau bid $47 per share for Federated, not long after the stock market price was as low as $33. By early February, KKR had folded, and Campeau looked set for another victory, come hell or high loans. At last, on February 25, it looked as if Federated had capitulated. Campeau had raised his offer yet again to $66, much higher than Federated could reach with its restructuring proposal.

Federated had fervent hopes of rescue by May Department Stores in the final hours as it writhed on the deck of Campeau's trawler. At 8:00 a.m. on February 16, 1988, in New York, the board of directors of May Department Stores was waiting to start their meeting. Stewards of what was the third-largest US department store chain, May's directors were set to lead the charge as a white knight galloping in to buy Federated at the last minute. "Across town Federated's representatives, themselves poised to enter a board meeting, were eagerly anticipating May's call—and an offer they expected to be $67 a share," *Fortune*'s Carol Loomis writes. "But May's 54-year-old chief executive, David Farrell, normally punctual to the second, was late this morning. 'When he finally came in,' says one of the waiting May directors, 'his face was long. I knew then we weren't going to be approving any deal.' Soberly, Farrell explained that he and his executive team had concluded that the challenge of taking over Federated—huge, sprawling, and run by managers who would not necessarily cotton to May's exacting ways—seemed too great to risk."[25] The May team called Federated. There was to be no rescue.

On February 25, the battalions gathered like sorrows at a conference room at Skadden. It was a bloody confrontation and destroyed at least one working relationship. Lehman's Tom Hill, representing Federated, who had joined forces with Campeau this time, left the room to make a telephone call, according to John Rothchild in *Going for Broke*. When he returned, a member of the Campeau team went to the same phone and found a yellow pad left there with a list of Federated bidders and the prices each had offered for Federated. He and his colleagues saw that, if they were right, Campeau could be the highest bidder if he agreed to jump to $68.[26] But where was he? Many involved in the Allied and Federated takeovers, including the board of Federated itself, would never lay eyes on him. "We never knew where he was or whether he'd show up," says Jim Freund. "In fact, I never actually met him."

A clutch of Campeau advisers rushed to Wasserstein's new headquarters, still decorated for the holidays by E. F. Hutton, the firm that had decamped quickly after agreeing to a bailout merger with Shearson Lehman. Back to Skadden they raced, with the assembled multitude growing increasingly tense at the enforced hiatus. A German-speaking paralegal was found, and a call was placed to Campeau's Austrian chalet. He was finally tracked down at a local restaurant. He agreed to pay $68.

Wasserstein was elated. He urged Federated to sign up the deal that night. He had not reckoned with Skadden's Jim Freund, adviser to the Federated board. "That was my finest hour," Jim says. "I really just refused. Bruce went crazy. He was ranting and raving, pressuring us and yelling at us. 'Campeau will go away,' Bruce said. 'The offer will go away. You can't risk this. We've got a deal. We've got a deal.' I just took a very strong position—Nope. We'll talk to you after the weekend.' Oh, Bruce was upset. He wasn't happy with me. We were never really friends after that. But it was the right thing to do."

Wasserstein's fears proved right. On Monday morning, it turned out that Federated had been talking to Macy's after all, with Weil, Gotshal's Dennis Block advising the latter. "Nobody wanted Campeau," Jim Freund says. "Federated much preferred Macy's." The two sides signed their $6.1 billion deal on March 1, an agreement far too complex to have been negotiated in all its detail since the previous Friday.

During those leonine days of March, Federated was in court fighting to keep its poison pill in place. One of Bob's many problems was his absence of verbal inhibitions. In a conference room at Skadden, in the teeth of the pill fight, Bob Campeau uttered 11 memorable words: "What would you expect from a Jewish judge like Leonard Sand?" Judge Sand, a senior US federal judge for the Southern District of New York, was known as an eminent jurist, responsible, for example, for such rulings as his declaration in 1985 that the city of Yonkers had illegally and intentionally segregated the city's public housing and its public schools since 1949. Stu Shapiro, who was conducting the deposition, turned to Fritz Schwarz (the grandson of toy empire founder F. A. O. Schwarz), a senior Cravath partner representing Campeau. "Let's go off the record," Stu said.

He took his adversary to one side. "If you want, Fritz, we can take that out of the deposition. I'll give you a gift." To this day, Stu is not sure why he did this. "Campeau was raised in a small, very Catholic town. He had real blinkers on. He didn't have any idea what the real world was about. I didn't want Fritz to be put in a bad position because his client was a creep, because *he* wasn't. I like Fritz. I think he's a wonderful guy." Could it have been because, as a tactician, Stu did not want the judge to be laboring to avoid any appearance of having been affected by such a comment from one side? "I'm not sure I had that calculation in the front of my mind. I just felt there was something wrong about it, that this was dangerous for me as well as Campeau."

This was not the only time Bob would make odd statements that were either clueless or evidence of bias, or both. In May 1989, the New York United Jewish Appeal gave a fund-raising party at Bloomingdale's to honor Campeau. As he promised to contribute $50,000, Campeau rambled on about the tendency of Jews toward oversensitivity and even paranoia. "I like Jews," he said helpfully and mentioned his frequent interactions with such people in Canada, whom he often found "honorable." He then strolled into history, comparing Hitler and Napoleon, both "murderers," one with Jews as his targets.[27] It was what the English call a "fanny-squinching" moment. No one knew where to look.

Campeau made yet another public relations blunder that gave Stu a victory before Judge Sand. Federated had put in a poison pill in its efforts to fend off the takeover. Fritz Schwarz was arguing that the board should lift the pill because it was preventing the shareholders from getting the highest possible offer. "We're in this big ceremonial courtroom down in the Southern District, and the whole room is filled with reporters and arbs," Stu remembers. "Those are the only people in the room, 300 or 400 of them. Mike Rogan, a corporate partner, comes in with something off the broad tape. Remember the broad tape? It's Campeau saying, 'I don't care what Judge Sand rules; we're going to keep bidding.' Fritz is getting up to argue that Judge Sand ought to enjoin the pill, and I actually handed him the broad tape. I said, 'Fritz, you'd better look at this.' He didn't want to look at it. So he finished, and I took it back and I said, 'Your Honor, here's what Mr. Campeau just said on the broad tape: 'I don't care what Judge Sand rules; we're going to keep bidding.' That was the end of that argument. 'I'm going to keep bidding.' Why would you enjoin the pill if the guy's going to keep bidding?" In late March, they did keep on bidding. On March 22, Campeau jumped to $73. Macy's raised the price to $74.50. Campeau topped that toward the end of March with an offer of $75.

What propels deals and those who run into these sustained spikes of auction fever? "The thing that drives the team in a transaction like this," Kim Fennebresque mused in the Campeau documentary, "is hard to differentiate after a period of time. At the beginning, it's 'Let's analyze this. Let's see the best way to get this transaction done.' But as time passes, you get caught up in it. And one of the things that separates the good and the bad in our business, I think, is people who can step back and say, 'Okay. We've invested a lot of time and a lot of money, but the smart thing to do is to stop.'"[28]

One of the few who did know when it was time to stop was Joe Flom. "There are certain things, sort of old chestnuts, that Joe Flom used to say: 'If you wouldn't be prepared to see it on the front page of the *New York Times,* then don't do it. Right? You'd better decide whether you're going to take that risk,'" Stu remembers. "So if you would not be willing to see it disclosed, if you're not willing to embrace it publicly, then you sure as hell shouldn't be doing it. And if you *are* willing to embrace it publicly when everybody else turns their nose up, then it doesn't pass what's called the smell test, and you'd better reconsider what you're willing to hug in public. That was Flom's mantra from the first time anyone ever worked with him to the last day."

Flom had grown up on the margins of society, where life is more dangerous, where sudden turns can lead to imprisonment, serious injury, poverty, or death itself. "He was willing to take risks, but only risks that he understood. He never wanted to be on the wrong side of the line that could lead you to go to jail, whether metaphorically or literally. You have other people who just don't seem to have that sensitivity," says Stu. "Friends of mine went to jail for insider trading, for securities fraud—lawyers and investment bankers—for amounts of money that couldn't possibly have been worth it, or for trying to win in situations where the risk-reward ratio made no sense. There really is a huge divide between people who understand that if you step over the line, you can get your foot chopped off, and people who simply don't appreciate that, and when their foot does get chopped off, they think it's someone else's fault. 'The judge just doesn't know what he's doing. This judge has never had a name partner from a major New York firm in his courtroom—that's obviously why he's treating me this way.' Joe was not like that."

Joe educated the Federated board just as he did young associates and partners. They were a sophisticated group of directors that included Kathryn Wriston, the wife of former Citibank chief Walter Wriston; a former chairman of the Ford Motor Company; and Mike Blumenthal, former secretary of the treasury under President Carter. There was Joe, a small man, with a propensity to construct elaborate geometric designs on yellow pads and to create his own slightly off-kilter aphorisms, who could snarl at white-shoe lawyers in proxy fights like a bridge troll, a man who had been blackballed at a co-op board that would have fawned over the likes of the Federated directors—here he was asking them questions they should have been asking of him: What are we doing here? We are charged with getting the best deal for shareholders, but we can all see that if we encourage this guy to keep on bidding higher and higher, he won't be able to deal with the debt he's taking on. What then? How many department stores will go belly up? How many thousands of jobs will disappear? "Selling the company for a price that will bankrupt the buyer and result in the company being destroyed is not consistent with the board's fiduciary duties. There are other considerations than just price."

At Flom's behest, the Federated board announced a halt to the auction. Joe wanted a truce before the village was destroyed in order to save it. Campeau would get Federated for $73.50 in cash, lower than his last offer. Macy's would buy three West Coast divisions of the company from Campeau for $1.1 billion. The Federated deal was done. The Faustian bargain, however, was not yet complete.

CHAPTER FIFTEEN
A BIG BLOODY OUTCRY

Rob Kindler was on a customer call in his father's plumbing van. It was the hot summer of 1977. Reggie Jackson was mesmerizing fans at Yankee Stadium. David Berkowitz, first christened Richard David Falco, was terrorizing potential murder victims from his lair on Warburton Avenue in Yonkers. New York was being told to drop dead by the White House as it faced its own real fiscal cliff. In mid-July, the blackout hit everywhere but Queens and the Rockaways, and the city that never sleeps went into a sweltering, cowering nightmare.

Then 23 years old, Rob found himself passing by Vanderbilt Hall at New York University Law School, adjacent to Washington Square Park. There was an empty parking place for emergency vehicles, and he presumed the cops would see the van's license marked as a plumbing and heating vehicle and leave it unmolested, so a ticket was unlikely. He had been working for S. Kindler Plumbing, his father's company and his father's before him, ever since dropping out of law school after his first semester in the fall of 1976. He thought he might as well hop out and check to see whether he had passed his law exams.

Rob started NYU right after college and was living in the Village. It was a difficult time. "I just kind of melted down." His father's business was in trouble and about to go under. He had massive loans and no possible help from his struggling parents. "I didn't know why I was in law school. It was just awful. I thought I'd done very poorly. I took the first two exams and I told the law school I didn't want to finish. They said, 'No. You started. You have to finish.' So I took the last two exams by myself in early January and then dropped out. Went to live with my mother-in-law. Worked for my father's plumbing company again. Those were particularly good times."[1]

There is at least one good memory from his days as a young plumber, however. Rob was working on the boiler in Walter Cronkite's brownstone one hot summer day. He heard footsteps approaching. It was the man himself, the globe-trotting conscience of America. "I thought you might like a cold drink," The Voice said. Rob gratefully accepted the Coke and the handshake. Years later, in the boardroom of CBS as a chief adviser to the network, Rob told Cronkite about the kindness of a client to a kid sweating over a boiler in a sweltering basement. "It was kind of a thrill to connect those dots."

Growing up in Beechhurst, where you can walk to both the Whitestone Bridge and the Throgs Neck, he and his family, including younger brother Andy Kindler, the comedian and television actor, "lived a very nice middle-class life." His father was from Jackson Heights, and his mother, from Mamaroneck. They met at Indiana University. His father was a teacher, then a social worker, and then took over his own father's plumbing business, founded in the1920s. Rob, having started classical flute lessons at the age of seven, was accepted at the High School of Music and Art. Before graduating, he had a serious talk with his flute teacher, the well-known Harry Moscovitz. "Look," Moscovitz said to the young Rob, "you're almost at the level of a virtuoso. But the odds of you being one of the top in the world are very small. Only a handful of people make a living. So, if you're doing it for that, I wouldn't." So, recalls Rob, "I didn't." He transferred to Bayside High School.

The flute did carry him through the admissions process at Colgate. He was a reasonably good student in high school, but he didn't break 1200 on the SATs. Thankfully, the Colgate orchestra needed a flutist. He took many music courses, as many English courses, and graduated with a degree in the latter, specializing in romantic poetry. "You play the flute. You majored in romantic poetry. You actually write poetry. These are not good things for people to know if you're an M&A guy." He also graduated Phi Beta Kappa and magna cum laude. "Of course, my kids tell me that's just because I took all easy courses. And they're not wrong. They're actually right."

After graduation, what? Plastics? How about a PhD in English? "You had to get scholarships to do that. And it was hard. I didn't think, frankly, that I was even equipped to write a doctoral thesis." Law school? Well, why not? Here's why not. Rob has a peculiar auditory memory. He cannot take notes at a lecture or meeting without canceling out both his hearing and his ability to write. So, he listened his way through the notoriously difficult first semester of his first year at NYU Law. He didn't own a notebook. Ever. He joined no study group. But he went to every class, and he read every case. "Took me a long time. I'm a slow reader. And when you're in law school, and you see all these students, everyone else, furiously taking notes and they're all in study groups, I was sure I was missing everything. Maybe it's ADD—I hate that phrase. I used to call it bibliophobia. I couldn't even be in libraries. I never figured out the Dewey Decimal System. But I have a memory—it's not a photographic memory, but I remember everything. I can tell you what page of a novel a sentence appears. I remember everything."

He locked the plumbing van and walked into Vanderbilt Hall to see what he might find. First-year results were posted on the bulletin board. "I was astonished to see that my grades put me among the top few kids in the class." He decided to reenter law school and graduate a year late in 1980.

Meanwhile, Rob had an epiphany: "I had lived in the Village, where there were all these frozen yogurt parlors popping up and all these cappuccino places popping up—you're probably wondering where this is going—I was just going downtown in Katonah where I was living and I saw an empty storefront. There it was. Right there. I said, 'Wouldn't this be a great place to have an ice-cream parlor and a frozen yogurt place?'" He soon had his sign up: RAZZLEBERRY'S FROZEN YOGURT AND ICE CREAM PARLOR. FOUNDED 1977. The name was taken from *Mr. Magoo's Christmas Carol.* The place served cappuccino, espresso, frozen yogurt, ice cream, penny candy. Rob went back to law school, but Razzleberry's was his love. "Didn't go often to the school. I mostly ran the ice-cream bar." He also made law review.

The last hurdle of his academic career was the law school's writing requirement. Instead of producing a scholarly analysis of some arcane issue for the law review ("I already had my job at Cravath—what did I need them for?"), he got permission from his professional ethics professor, the famous Harry Subin, to fulfill the requirement by writing an epic poem. It is a journey through the canons of professional ethics, titled "The Canonization of Henry Quidnunc." As our lawyer-hero, Henry, works his way through each of the canons, he is so scrupulously honest in adhering to each one that he is invariably unable for ethical reasons to take on any of the clients who seek his counsel. Thus, Henry, by following every rule, never gets work as a lawyer and ends up bankrupt. "It took me forever to write. For-*ever.* I can still remember the intro. I'll give you the intro." And without pause he recites from memory the preamble:

> *In halls and haunts of lawly academe,*
> *We learn of things that were, or should have been.*
> *With untaught eyes and untrained ears,*
> *We see and sense the wisdom of the years.*
> *And for what is all this golden ideology?*
> *So we may learn the art of quick and cute apology?*
> *That we, with well-oiled tongues, can fox our foes*
> *With reasoned wherefores, therefores, and hithertos?*
> *Rather, we all hope, and I surmise,*
> *That scholarly pursuits will make us wise,*

That the weak and weary of our lot
Will seek the long-taught virtue that we've got.
It's for this, three blessed years we've spent
To learn that all help springs from us,
And isn't heaven-sent.

Rob takes a job as a young associate at Cravath, Swaine & Moore, one of the oldest and most prestigious firms in the country. He cloaks his acumen and ambition in slapstick and irony. He makes his way quickly through the ranks, in part because he shows little of that typical associate awe for superiors that the established can often find cloying.

Soon after Rob started at the firm, he was assigned to help Hank Riordan, a senior partner who had cornered the market on railroad-lease financing that longtime client Salomon Brothers had taken on in the early 1980s. A looming change in the tax law let loose a torrent of these deals, which had to be done while the tax shelter remained in place. Harry, as he was known, and Rob were churning them out as fast as they could, dozens and dozens at a time. There were many long hours, as Cravath did an estimated 75 to 80 percent of all the railroad-lease financing in the United States.[2] "Harry was very, very well known, a kind of dean of the corporate bar," Rob says, "and a very big golfer. He loved golf. Not particularly good, but he loved golf. So I was pulling an all-nighter, and I just fell asleep on his couch in his office. He woke me up like at 7:30 or 8 in the morning and he says, 'Well! What are you doing here?' I propped myself up on one elbow and said, 'Oh, Harry. What happened—did you get lost on the way to the golf course?' He just laughed. The fact that he just laughed—right? As you know, my brother's a comedian, and Cravath was totally willing to accept my sense of humor. Cravath is nothing like what people visualize it to be."

Negotiating opponents would come to know Rob's quirks just as did his colleagues as he advanced through the Cravath system. In her story about rising young stars in the *American Lawyer* in late 1988, Karen Dillon described Rob as "cocky, calculating and irreverent," a man who had not lost his Queens accent and was "oblivious to his occasionally mismatched clothing and tousled hair."[3] As a 31-year-old associate representing Bob Campeau in the post-acquisitions clean-up that involved the rather panicked sales of certain assets of Allied Stores, Rob made a series of flash cards that he and his team would hold up silently in front of their counterparts at tricky moments in the talks: "Big Point," "Little Point," "Give Up On This Point." Campeau's US president Ronald Tysoe said the unexpected gimmick worked well. "It makes people back off a little and take a fresh look at the points we're haggling over." Others have not found such efforts to their liking. One lawyer quoted in Dillon's story said rather acidly: "Whether he becomes a superstar or not may well depend on his ability to outgrow that kind of behavior."

One afternoon, when the firm's offices were still down on Wall Street at One Chase, Sam Butler wandered down to the set of conference rooms where the tax shelter leasing factory had set up shop. "Clients were coming in and out, the lawyers were coming in and out, and I was just watching what was going on," Sam remembers. "All of a sudden this young handsome kid comes in, sort of disheveled, tie loose and one thing and another. He comes in, he's got a handful of papers in his hand, and he's looking really tired. The kid says, 'I can't keep up with this, Mr. Riordan. This 24/7 thing is just killing me. These deals have got to end.' Harry is dismissive at this whining. Impatiently and gruffly, he demands, 'Did you get the check?' Rob answers, 'I am really exhausted.' Again, Harry asks, 'Yes, yes, yes—did you get the check?' This goes back and forth. Rob repeats his complaint. Harry asks yet again, each time more worried and loudly more insistent. 'Did you get the *check?*' Rob seems to shake himself into focus and stares ahead in panic. There is a long silence. Then this kid whips out the check and says with a big smile, '*I got it!*' Harry laughed and laughed and laughed. When Kindler left again, I said, 'Who was that, Harry?' After that, Rob came to work for me."[4]

Rob's work for Sam would take him to the center of the country, and for two years, from 1988 to 1990, it was an experience that "the handsome kid" from Queens would never forget.

* * *

IN DENNIS BLOCK'S CONFERENCE ROOM ON MANHATTAN'S MAIDEN LANE, NOT LONG after he left Weil, Gotshal to join Cadwalader, Wickersham & Taft, and thence to Greenberg Traurig, two courtroom artist's sketches had a place of honor. Both depict Lord Hanson undergoing cross-examination during his hostile bid for SCM Corporation in 1985. During that trial, he was asked why he was fighting to take over the American chemicals and typewriter group, his first hostile bid in the United States.

"I liked the pictures in the annual report," Lord Hanson said insouciantly.[5]

The courtroom buzzed with consternation. So did the world of M&A for many a year. Lord Hanson, or Lord Moneybags as one London newspaper dubbed him, died of cancer on November 2, 2004. His partner, Sir Gordon White, died in August of the next year. Together, they were among the defining figures of contemporary mergers and acquisitions from the mid-1970s through the mid-1990s. "I worked on just about all of Lord Hanson's transactions. He was a very nice man who really cared a lot about his reputation for creating shareholder value," Block said.[6]

Born in Huddersfield in Yorkshire in 1922, James Hanson, the son of Bob Hanson, a prosperous and ruthless businessman, grew up somewhat overshadowed by his younger brother, Bill, a war hero and bemedaled show-jumping champion. For some time, James was known mostly for his photographs in the newspapers in the company of such celebrities as Jean Simmons and Joan Collins. He was engaged to Audrey Hepburn in 1951, a relationship that foundered partly on the distance between Hollywood and Huddersfield.[7]

His social whirl was helped by the nationalization of most of the family business in 1948, which pumped another £4 million into the already-bulging Hanson coffers. With that money behind them, the brothers spent much time in Canada, taking advantage of the opportunities in the New World and escaping their domineering father. Bill Hanson died of cancer in 1952, leaving his devoted brother devastated.[8]

Hanson joined forces with Gordon (later Lord) White, a close friend of his late brother and a fellow playboy businessman and Hollywood deal-maker. "We're twins, really," Hanson once said. White agreed, but added a note of difference: "If he were climbing a mountain, James would follow the footpath. I would look for a short cut." In 1959, Hanson married an American, Geraldine Kaelin. Drawing on their American connections, Hanson and White began importing greeting cards, as the first of their many ventures together. Soon, they drafted Jim Slater, an accountant and stock market genius, who would lead them into the fertile pastures of public company stock.[9]

In the early 1960s, Hanson and White returned to Britain, but not to the family road-haulage business, which the former was happy to leave in the hands of his father. Their first efforts to build an empire were frustrated by the fact that banks were reluctant to lend to a private company. So they did a reverse takeover, selling their own businesses and acquiring a controlling stake in Wiles Group, a publicly listed company. The twosome then began their long and tumultuous series of conquests on both sides of the Atlantic, drawing on Slater's accounting techniques for acquisitions and divestitures, to build their own Hanson Trust, a conglomerate that eventually owned businesses as disparate as batteries, tobacco, homes, typewriters, and bricks.[10]

The juggernaut really started to roll when White moved to the United States in 1973. Here was a brave new world, with none of the restraints of tradition and class that clothed corporate Britain. Here was a culture that rewarded a ruthless, focused, dynamic business style. Here was a savanna of sleepily grazing giants under the care of smug boards of directors.

* * *

CHAMPAGNE BEFORE DINNER IN THE HOLLYWOOD HILLS IN THE EARLY 1990S. TWO sleek, though now slightly elderly, corporate hawks stand by the window, regretting that they have never swooped on General Motors together. The bosses at GM are "timeservers" and "pygmies," the two startlingly tall men observe with English disdain; it would be doing a public service to toss them out. Of course, jobs would have to go, but a fortune is waiting to be unlocked. Eventually, Gordon White (the mastermind of the American side of the Hanson takeover machine) admits the truth: "You just couldn't do it. Washington, the American establishment: there would be the biggest bloody outcry ever." "But that would be the best bit," smiles back Jimmy Goldsmith.[11]

That was the opening paragraph to the *Economist*'s obituary for Sir James Goldsmith on July 24, 1997. The two men never did attack General Motors, but Lord White, as the chief of the American side of Hanson PLC, did move in on another industrial company beloved in the heartland, where he caused a big, bloody outcry indeed. Their target was Cummins Engine. This time, they met their match.

As Rob and his colleagues began their descent into the small airport, they could look down on an American idyll, a model of what the country, and capitalism, should be. Cummins Engine was and still is the beating heart of the city of Columbus, Indiana. The company, a maker of diesel engines, and the town, a pleasant and progressive place of some 44,000 souls, have thrived together for decades. The company was founded in 1919 by Clessie Cummins, the chauffeur and mechanic for William Miller, who financed his employee's ambitious new venture. The late J. Irwin Miller, William Miller's great-nephew, joined the company in 1934. He became the clan patriarch and champion of Columbus philanthropy. At what was once the family seat, the Italianate late-nineteenth-century mansion that is now the Inn at Irwin Gardens, there sits on a table in the hall near the library a copy of *Esquire*'s October 1967 issue with J. Irwin Miller on its cover. The caption reads: "This man ought to be the next president of the United States." This man did not run for the office but he convinced Nelson R. Rockefeller to enter the race.[12] "Whatever you do in this world," Miller said once, "you've got a responsibility and the privilege of doing it the very best way you can, and whether it's architecture, cooking or drama or music, the best is none too good for any of us."

He brought the best to Columbus, not only engineers from MIT but architects, plenty of them. More than 60 public buildings in Columbus are subsidized by the Miller family and Cummins Engine: works by I. M. Pei, James Polchek, Deborah Berke, Harry Weese, Richard Meyer, Cesar Pelli, Eliel Saarinen, and his son, Eero Saarinen, designer of the TWA terminal at JFK. In the 1950s, the city fathers saw the baby boom rumbling toward them and realized that they would have to build an elementary school every two years to keep up. The first new school was an aesthetic and functional disaster, so Irwin Miller made a suggestion to the school board: Pick an architect from our list of five choices, and our foundation will pay the fee. It was not long before the program spread across the town: firehouses, a jail, schools, a bank, the newspaper building, a courthouse, city hall, a golf course—all built under the same program. Irwin Miller once spoke as a modern Plato in defining what is good, with a businessman's twist at the end: "The better a building serves its purpose, the longer it will last before you have to tear it down. Mediocrity is expensive."

Irwin and his wife, Xenia, commissioned Eero Saarinen to build their own house, where they raised five children. It sits behind a wall of sculpted evergreens at 2760 Highland Way, a quiet street. Huge steel-and-glass doors open to a unique place. It is obviously midcentury modern, completed in 1957, but it has private spaces, including a sunken sofa-surrounded square in the center of the open sitting room. The interior has uninhibited color and is surrounded by one of the most important and successful modernist gardens in the country. It is a national historic landmark. The town itself was in sixth place on the American Institute of Architects' recent list of the top ten American cities, along with Chicago, San Francisco, and New York.

At a Cummins plant outside town, just as gleaming and modern as Miller House itself, 500 workers make around 500 midsized diesel engines every day, mostly for Dodge Ram pickups. There are another 5,000 employees in the United States and some 44,000 around the world. Cummins is now a company with a market cap of $22 billion. We are reliably told that a sign in the ladies room at the plant outside town reads: "Treating people with dignity and respect is a core value at Cummins." All of this in a place of parks, ethnic festivals, excellent public schools, a branch of Indiana University, low unemployment, and rich contacts with the world beyond the United States, in the midst of the clear air and endless green lines of the soybean fields of south-central Indiana, an hour from Indianapolis and Louisville.

Rob and Sam Butler, himself a Hoosier from Logansport, Indiana, were flying in with Jim Wolfensohn, then the head of his own investment bank, on the latter's plane to defend Cummins against Hanson PLC. Perhaps Lord Hanson and Lord White, and fellow corporate raider Sir Ronald Brierley of New Zealand immediately after them, were not aware of just what they would find themselves up against, although James Hanson and the Cummins company had met before.

In the early seventies, Cummins got pipped at the post when it sought to buy Holset Engineering Company, Ltd., a turbocharger business in Britain. Cummins's financial vice president, Dr. John Hackett, discovered that Hanson had just bought the target four months before, with plans to take over Rolls Royce and install Holset's founder, Paul Croset, to run it for him. When he couldn't get Rolls, he offered to sell Holset to Cummins after all. He drove his usual ruthless bargain and got from Hackett only a bit less than the full $27 million he demanded. It was the largest acquisition Cummins ever made.[13]

This time around, Sir Gordon White, in charge of the American side of Hanson PLC, put Cummins itself in play. On December 23, 1988, a filing with the SEC revealed that Hanson PLC had acquired an 8.3 percent stake in Cummins, which amounted to around 886,000 shares. Cummins stock jumped from $50 per share to $64, and almost 11 percent of the stock changed hands, mostly into the eager palms of arbitrageurs. Hanson said in its filings that its stake was for investment purposes only, but that could be changed in an instant.

Henry "Hank" Schacht, then Cummins's president and later head of Lucent Technologies, is a tall man with white hair. He speaks directly and clearly and, as the saying goes, says what he means and means what he says. Hank moved quickly. He set up a team of his own, including vice president for corporate strategy Chip Gulden, general counsel Steve Zeller, and treasurer Peter Hamilton. He installed them in a secret situation room, a windowless chamber in the basement of the company's Fifth Street headquarters, and charged them with their first task: Find out what Hanson wanted. Then he brought in Sam Butler and Rob from Cravath, Jim Wolfensohn, and Michael Schmertzler from Morgan Stanley.

The New York advisers were not a sanguine lot. They told Hank that Cummins was in mortal danger. Even if Hanson could be diverted, the company could soon be chum to a roiling sea of sharks. They weren't talking to a hayseed. "We made it very clear," Hank says, "that we didn't want to be taken over. Period. And we made it very clear that we wanted to be represented by somebody who believed that we could mount a successful defense. We were well aware of the conventional wisdom at the time that if you're attacked, then in fact it's only a question of price. There is one banker on the aggressive side, representing the potential acquirer or greenmailer, whatever the case may be, and another banker on your side saying, 'I can get you top dollar. Of course, we can sell you. You should engage us. We'll sell you for a higher price than the other guy.' Very few people would take on just plain defense. That's why Sam and Rob and Mike and their colleagues, well, they were pillars."[14]

With his teams at work around the clock, Hank and his chief of operations, James "Jim" Henderson, made an unorthodox move. They went directly to Sir Gordon, "Gordie" to his friends. They met at Sir Gordon's office on Park Avenue in February 1989. Hank was, as always, direct. "If you think you can buy the company," Hank said to Gordie, "impose your operating standards on it, and get your money out, you're wrong. You will be like the person who is in the middle of a big circus tent, pulls the center pole out, and tries to get to the exit before the roof falls on him. You won't make it. You can't get there fast enough."

Sir Gordon responded, over and over again in virtually the same words, by saying simply that Cummins was a great American company, enormously undervalued, and that Hanson took positions in many similar companies. There was less consistency from other Hanson people. One Hanson executive mentioned the possibility of combining Cummins with General Motors, independent for the moment but a possible target, and handing over the resulting behemoth to Hank and Jim as their fiefdom within the Hanson empire. It might have been a medieval king trying to co-opt his enemies by offering them a province or two to rule. "Absolutely not," came the answer from Hank. "We can't operate your way, and you can't operate our way."

Hank and his colleague came back again to see Sir Gordon soon after. Again, Hank was frank, this time about the harm Hanson's presence was wreaking on Cummins. The search for new executive talent was now impossible. Customers and potential business partners were wary of the company. Manufacturers were distancing themselves and looking for other suppliers. Daimler-Benz, for example, had just backed away from a joint venture with the warning that as long as Hanson loomed over the future of Cummins, there could be no partnership. Sir Gordon expressed surprise that Hanson's stake could appear so threatening. He also intimated for the first time that Hanson might be willing to sell its Cummins stock.

Immediately, Hank went in search of a buyer for the Hanson stake. He traveled all over the United States and scoured the globe for potential saviors. He had with him this time William I. Miller, the 33-year-old son of J. Irwin Miller. Over the July 4th weekend, Hank was in London to see Sir Gordon. He told him that he had found a buyer willing to pay the market price for the Hanson shares. Sir Gordon turned that down with great hilarity. There seemed likely to be no independence celebration for Cummins on the Fourth, just as a pall had been cast over the previous Christmas. On the Monday of the holiday weekend, Hank returned to Columbus with nothing.

Reluctantly, the Cummins executives called an impromptu meeting at headquarters with the Millers to inform them that the company's future was still in limbo. At this point, events took a dramatic turn. As the Millers made their way out to the parking lot after the meeting, Will Miller began thinking out loud. Hanson wanted to make a profit on its stake. Word had it that Hanson would sell for a 15 percent premium to market. This would mean it would take about $10 million to buy them out. Cummins was then a $3 billion company. Should the kingdom be abandoned for want of a $10 million nail? Let's assume, he said to his father on the way to the car, that Hanson takes us over. The Miller family—J. I., William, and J. I.'s sister, Clementine Tangeman—will be fine. Columbus, their beloved city, will not. Cummins will be sold for parts. "I suspect that as a family, we won't feel very good about that," Will said to his father.

In New York's meatpacking district, this set of stairs can still be found at the Triangle Building, leading to what was once the Hellfire Club, an infamous retreat in the 1980s. Through the wind-machine-driven street garbage and down these steps, Bridget Fonda follows Jennifer Jason Leigh into the world of Single White Female. *Many on Wall Street did the same.*
Photo credit: Michael A. Smith/ smithshot.com

As a star M&A partner at Cravath, Swaine & Moore, Rob Kindler posed for the cover of American Lawyer's *April 1998 edition, a time when he was at the peak of his career in the law. Since then, Kindler has taken his long-running hit show on the road and is now vice chairman and global head of mergers and acquisitions at Morgan Stanley.*
Photo credit: Rafael Fuchs

Ronald Perelman, with the omnipresent cigar, in his townhouse in September 1987, two years after shocking the business elite with his coup at Revlon. Junk-bond-funded and adrenaline-fueled, Perelman was initially dismissed as an arrogant annoyance, both audacious and odd, until he and Skadden's Lucky Sperm Club engineered one of the most startling takeovers in history.
Photo credit: Rob Kinmonth/Getty Images

An elixir of youth, the love of beautiful women, a bargain with the devil for worldly riches, the legend of Faust goes back to the Middle Ages. Here, at the February 1, 1990 opening of Gounod's treatment of the saga at the Metropolitan Opera, we find (from left to right): LBO king Henry Kravis; John Kluge, who turned Metromedia into one of the world's great private fortunes; his wife Patricia Kluge, who built a Virginia palace with those riches; and Kravis's wife Carolyne Roehm. Three months later, the Kluges would announce their divorce. Three years later, Roehm and Kravis would announce their separation.
Photo credit: Ron Galella, Ltd./Getty Images

Robert Campeau, the French-Canadian real estate developer, on his way in September 1988 to an evening in his honor at the Temple of Dendur after taking over corporations that owned hundreds of department stores in North America. This was his second star turn at the temple within two years. This time, because he had made more headlines and captured Bloomingdale's itself, more actual guests showed up, as opposed to investment bankers in disguise.

Photo credit: Ron Galella, Ltd./Getty Images

At the St. Regis in 2005, Carl Icahn (right) *talks about his typically quixotic but inspired proposal to overthrow the Time Warner board, break up the conglomerate into four companies, and appoint CEO chief Frank Biondi* (center) *as the CEO of Time Warner. At left is Icahn's chief strategist for the battle, the late Bruce Wasserstein, head of Lazard.*

Photo credit: Michael Nagle/Getty Images

Sir Gordon White, here escorting Elizabeth Taylor, was in charge of the American operations of Hanson PLC, an investment company that he founded with his friend Lord Hanson, who was himself once engaged to Audrey Hepburn. Sir Gordon ("Gordie") led the first of two assaults on Cummins Engine in 1989 and 1990, an icon of the heartland. Rather than sacrifice the company and the company town along with it, and unimpressed with the glitz, the founding family successfully turned away both Hanson and, soon after, New Zealand raider Sir Ronald Brierley.

Photo credit: Time & Life Pictures/Getty Images

Sir James Goldsmith (left) and Robert Maxwell during Malcolm Forbes's seventieth birthday party in the summer of 1989 at the Tangier Country Club in Morocco. Both men were out-sized public figures and powerful raiders from across the Atlantic. Goldsmith crushed one of Marty Lipton's early poison pills. Maxwell (also known as the "Bouncing Czech") captured Macmillan in a scandalous takeover.
Photo credit: Ron Galella, Ltd./Getty Images

Here at a recent Toronto conference is Chancellor Leo Strine, the head of Delaware's Court of Chancery, the preeminent business bench in the country. He is not your usual éminence grise. *The chancellor sprinkles his rulings and his speeches with references to hip hop, sports,* Parks and Recreation, *Hollywood stars, and* Moby Dick. *He uses words such as "freakin'" and neologisms like "hinky." He also has one of the keenest contemporary legal minds at work today, and holds sway over deals worth billions of dollars that shape global law and commerce. Photo credit: Michelle Siu/National Post*

Viacom's CEO Philippe Dauman (left) pays tribute to one of the great lions of entertainment and media, Sumner Redstone, during the latter's star ceremony on the Hollywood Walk of Fame on March 30, 2012. Redstone fought Barry Diller for Paramount in a takeover like no other, one that has never before been given the treatment it deserves. Photo credit: Paul Buck/Corbis

William "Bill" Ackman, one of the most powerful shareholder activists of the day, has muscled his way into companies that he sees as trapped in needless atrophy, including Borders, Target, the giant Canadian Pacific railroad, and 111-year-old department store J. C. Penney. He is always busy tackling those he sees as naked emperors, including bond insurance giant MBIA and health supplement company Herbalife. He is also known for his long and very public feud with Carl Icahn, and he recently quit the J. C. Penney board in frustration.
Photo credit: Bloomberg/Getty Images

Former M&A prodigy Ilan Reich stands next to the plane he bought to replace the one he flew for a medical charity that crashed in 2005 during a tumor-induced blackout. It was not the first disaster that failed to stop Reich. He has come back from a felony conviction for his involvement in the infamous insider trading ring of the late 1980s, a prison term, ostracism, divorce, unemployment, bankruptcy, and a second brain tumor.
Photo credit: Ilan Reich private collection

"In that event, I'm sure we'll feel we have to step up to the plate philan-
thropically on a lot—maybe even more than ten million bucks' worth. So
what would you think about what I would call 'preventive philanthropy'?
What if the family stepped forward and just ate the Hanson premium,
and viewed it as a less expensive way of doing the philanthropy? Is that
something that would make sense to you at all?"[15]

Irwin thought it made perfect sense. On to Clementine, his sister, the
largest single shareholder in Cummins Engine. Irwin thought this might
prove difficult. "Will took a long time with Clementine, because he wasn't
sure she got it the first time. But she did. She got it right away." On to Hank,
who was shocked. "We were flat out of ideas," he remembers. "We didn't
have any prior warning. It didn't occur to us that the Miller family would
releverage themselves at their ages and take that kind of risk. But they did."
The board approved the deal at a special meeting in New York. On July 12,
eight days after Hank and Gordie met in London, Will Miller flew to Los
Angeles with Hank to meet Lord White for the final time.[16]

Outside Gordie's house in Beverly Hills was a swimming pool, which
had his crest painted on its floor. His cars also had the same insignia painted
neatly by the door handles. "It's what I've been granted," he would say, "and
I'm proud of it." He was often seen with glamorous women, including Joan
Collins, Cheryl Tiegs, and Elizabeth Taylor. He also loved horses. He was
a devotee of Margaret Thatcher. She recommended him for a knighthood
in 1979 and then a life peerage in 1990. Like Jimmy Goldsmith, he became
known for an aphorism quoted in the press: "Never marry a young girl.
They only want babies." All this stood in dramatic contrast to the midwest-
erners who came to him with their proposal.

It took two days of negotiations. Will reduced the premium to 7.5 percent rather than the expected 10 percent. The Miller family thus paid an
estimated $72 million, about $5 million above the market price, for the one
million Hanson shares. Hanson made a profit of $17 million. The Miller
family tripled its investment in Cummins. White also agreed to a ten-year
standstill, barring Hanson PLC from buying any more Cummins stock
without the family's permission. "Gordon White is an absolutely charming person and conducted the whole negotiation in a businesslike manner,"
Will told the press afterward. "I'm sorry, but there wasn't a whole lot of
drama."[17]

This was technically greenmail: the payment of a premium over the
market price of a stock to buy out an unwanted interloper. The Miller family's move, however, is the only known time that a stockholder has done
so instead of the corporation itself. "We ate the premium," Will also said
later. "It was not a very eighties thing to do." He described the 1980s as "the
decade of the grasshopper" and his hometown of Columbus as "a town of
somewhat nerdy, hard-working ants, taking pride in our labors."[18]

Cummins and Columbus had only nine days to celebrate before finding themselves under attack once more.

* * *

IN 1990, THE CITY OF COLUMBUS BASICALLY HAD ONE HOTEL, THE HOLIDAY INN, WHICH also had the only decent restaurant in town. The Cummins team assumed this would be the place they would find their adversaries, who were flying in for the company's annual meeting. They were right. The process server found the room he was seeking on the ground floor. He knocked, and the door swung open.

There before him was the scene from the movie *Fargo*, set in 1987 in North Dakota, in which William Macy's Jerry Lundergaard is trying to climb out the bathroom window of his motel room to escape the police. An aggressive lawyer who represented Industrial (Pacific) Limited (IEP) is looking over his shoulder at the sound of the process server's knock, with his hands on his client's backside, pushing him out the window to make his escape. It didn't work. The IEP executive was duly served with process.[19]

IEP was the North American branch of the notorious New Zealand corporate raider Sir Ronald Brierley's Brierley Investments Limited. Sir Ron, then a bachelor in his 50s, had created a global financial empire, having started out as the publisher of an obscure investment newsletter, and had crept into the picture in July 1989 with a 9.9 percent stake in Cummins, for which his company had paid some $60 million, just over a week after Cummins and the Miller family had rid themselves of the Hanson people.[20] IEP had been a Cummins shareholder for some years, but this move was different. It was not good news for the guys in the white hats in Indiana. Ron and his companies had a long history of reaping huge profits by raiding public corporations. Until the early 1980s, their targets were companies in New Zealand and Australia, including Herald and Weekly Times, Carlton and United Breweries, and MLC Insurance.[21]

The first defense was to change the Cummins pill. The Cravath team had the company lower the flip-in threshold—not to the 10 percent level of Indiana's five-year freeze-out statute but to 15 percent of company stock. The trigger for the flip-in, which allows company shareholders to buy more of their company's stock at a steep discount, diluting the attacker's stake to a lower percentage of the total, was deliberately reset at a higher point than Indiana's official trigger to lure the Brierley people across the statutory line. The Indiana law would bar IEP from merging with Cummins for five years if the acquirer stepped over the 10 percent line without the approval of the Cummins board.[22]

IEP jumped. In September 1989, the New Zealand buyer boosted its stake to 14.9 percent of Cummins stock, crashing right through the statutory barrier. Kramer, Levin's Josh Berman at the time scoffed at the notion that Cummins managed to draw IEP across the state threshold by setting the pill trigger at a higher level. "The ten percent mark was irrelevant to us," he argued, "because we never intended to make a bid for the company." Perhaps. But now they couldn't. State law would outlaw that for five years.[23]

Nevertheless, Brierley and IEP could still start a proxy fight to try to get enough shareholder votes to kick out the board of directors. They could still put to a vote a troublesome shareholder proposal for some change in the company's internal rules. They could make a move that would put Cummins in play and start a full-scale bidding war among other potential buyers. They could start lobbying for a seat of their own on the Cummins board. Virtually all of this is exactly what they did and what they had said they would not do in their filings with the SEC in July when they first crossed the 5 percent mark.[24]

Sam Butler called in his litigators from New York in full battle gear. Francis "Frank" Barron, then in his late 30s and described by Stephen Adler in the *American Lawyer* a year earlier as "boyish" and "disarmingly earnest," immediately began a carpet-bombing campaign. In the amended complaint, which he and his colleagues filed in federal district court for the Southern District of Indiana, the Cravath team exhaustively described the IEP's pattern of perfidy over the years since they first began trolling in US waters in 1981:

> Defendants are pursuing against Cummins a strategy which they have used repeatedly against other publicly held companies in the United States. First, defendants acquire a substantial stake in the common stock of the target, violating Federal law in the process by falsely describing themselves as passive investors. By falsely describing their intent, defendants are able to acquire shares from unsuspecting sellers at prices lower than they would be required to pay if they had made truthful disclosures. Their purpose is to creep up to a significant enough ownership position to allow them to influence, and perhaps ultimately control the affairs of the target company—without paying a price that reflects their intentions. Second, once the defendants have acquired their stake, they threaten to disrupt the target's affairs unless the target accedes to their demands—for board membership, for greenmail (i.e., the repurchase by the target of the company's shares at a price not available to the target's other shareholders), or for some other action by the target that defendants could not otherwise obtain. In at least one instance, defendants have used the seat they gain on a target's board of directors to engage in insider trading in the target's stock.
>
> Defendant's raid against Cummins has followed that strategy. First, claiming to be passive investors, defendants acquired approximately 14.9% of Cummins common stock—falsely stating in Schedule 13D filings that they acquired those shares "for investment." Second, defendants revealed their true intention

(privately to Cummins but not to the Securities and Exchange Commission ["SEC"] or the investing public) to gain representation on the Cummins Board, and have made various threats if the Cummins board does not acquiesce.

Among other things, defendants have threatened that if the Cummins Board does not acquiesce in defendants' undisclosed request for board representation, they intend to disrupt Cummins by commencing a proxy contest, announcing a takeover bid for the sole purpose of putting Cummins in play, or taking some other disruptive action. Defendants' intent to engage in such tactics likewise has not been disclosed to the public or the SEC.[25]

In the nine years since IEP showed up in the United States, it had used the same strategy against Ameron, Oglebay Norton Co., CalMat Corp., Handschy Industries, and Steego Corp., among others. Its record was pockmarked with violations of Australian and American law. The Supreme Court of Victoria, Australia, in 1986 ordered IEP to disgorge its shares and turn over the sales proceeds to the government for violating disclosure laws in its raid on North Broken Hill Holdings. The Supreme Court of New South Wales found the same chicanery in IEP's acquisition of Woolworth stock, a matter settled out of court with a $780,000 penalty. The New Jersey Casino Control Commission ordered IEP to divest its holdings in the Del Webb Corporation. Amid all this strife, the company pocketed $100 million from its skirmishes Down Under and another $100 million from its American raids. According to Cravath, IEP had also paid "virtually no U.S. tax on these profits," turning to "an elaborate web of foreign and domestic entities—including various shell companies and nominal foreign offices— in an attempt to evade payment of U.S. taxes."[26]

"On or about September 25, 1989," Cummins alleges in its complaint, "[IEP's North American chief executive, Robert Sutherland] telephoned Henry B. Schacht, Chairman and chief Executive Officer of Cummins. During that conversation, Sutherland repeated that the IEP Board wanted IEP to have representation on the Cummins Board—a fact that had not been disclosed in IEP's Schedule 13D filings. Sutherland explained that IEP did not want Cummins to say 'no' to IEP's request because if Cummins did say 'no,' then it might become involved in 'a proxy contest and all that nonsense.' The clear purpose and intent of Sutherland's statements was to threaten Cummins with the disruption of a proxy contest and thereby carry out its intention (still undisclosed in its Schedule 13D filings) to obtain board representation and influence and participate in the management of Cummins."[27]

IEP advisers acknowledged that the New Zealand group wanted board representation, but they denied that they pressured Cummins to relinquish a board seat. Kramer, Levin's Josh Berman pointed out that IEP purposely allowed the annual meeting notice deadline for board nominees to pass without taking any action. In a February 5, 1990, letter to Representative John Dingell, then chairman of the House Committee on Energy and Commerce, Brierley Investments chairman, Bruce Hancox, insisted that "IEP's conduct belies any notion that IEP threatened or had any plans to launch a proxy contest. IEP never attempted to exert any influence over Cummins or the way it carries on its business."

On October 10, 1989, at a meeting in La Jolla, California, IEP's outpost, Bruce Hancox and Rob Sutherland unsheathed their real plans, despite having filed with the SEC the precise opposite of what they now disclosed, according to the Cummins team. To Hank Schacht and Peter Hamilton of Cummins, Hancox said that IEP did not view itself as "just an investor." It was now the largest shareholder in Cummins. It should have a seat in the boardroom. If this did not happen, Hancox said, "Then there would be trouble. You will be responsible for the consequences. Whatever happens will rest on your shoulders. If you bring a lawsuit, you will not find any documents that say we have a master plan for Cummins."[28]

It didn't stop. Hancox and Sutherland met Hank Schacht and Jim Henderson in mid-January, this time on the company's home turf. Hancox repeated IEP's demand for a board seat. Hank told him that he would be recommending to the board that this request be denied. Hancox said that if they didn't get what they wanted, there would be consequences. They might launch a bid, even though they didn't have enough money to buy Cummins, hoping that would trigger a bidding war. IEP would "do something," Hank was assured. "We're not going to just sit there," Hancox stressed. "We have never engaged in disruption that we have not benefited from."[29]

Soon after these discussions, IEP amended its filings with the SEC. It changed its story. "They effectively admitted that they had violated 13D," says Cravath's Frank Barron, looking back on the fight. "I'm not saying they admitted it outright. They would never say, 'Yes, yes, we violated 13D.' But in their amended filing, they cited exactly what we claimed had happened. Then you ask yourself, 'Well, these things are true now, so they were also true back then. And didn't the shareholders who sold their stock to you back then deserve to know the same information?'"

IEP, as it promised, was not just sitting there. It filed a counterclaim against Cummins management, alleging that the board had amended its pill, established an employee stock ownership plan, and bad-mouthed IEP in the press in order to entrench itself at the expense of the company's stockholders. Seeking damages of $1.8 billion, IEP asked the court to void the pill and enjoin the directors from any further conduct designed to protect their own jobs. They took particular aim at Hank Schacht:

His public statements are part of a carefully crafted, duplicitous public relations campaign—carried on at Cummins' expense—to portray Schacht as

"Mr. Rust Belt," a hands-on manager committed to revitalizing America's industrial manufacturing base.... That image is at odds with reality.... Schacht
and other inside directors have imposed upon Cummins a management structure designed to free Schacht from spending the time on Cummins affairs that
would ordinarily be required of a chief executive officer and enable him to do
what Schacht likes to do best—hobnob with individuals of national power and
influence in industry and government on matters having little, if anything, to
do with Cummins.[30]

Frank Barron and his colleagues began deposing witnesses, one of whom
was Roger Penske, the famed car racer in the 1960s, when he was named
Sports Car Club of America's Driver of the Year. He was the owner of a NAS-
CAR racing team, an avid car collector, a General Electric board member,
a former chairman of the Detroit Super Bowl XL, owner of the corporation
Detroit Diesel, and professional larger-than-lifer. Frank Barron began to suspect that IEP had been sounding out Penkse as a possible ally in its planned
efforts to put Cummins in play. He was a tricky person to try to depose. "I
have no reason to believe that Roger Penske wasn't telling the truth in his deposition," Barron says. "But he was cagey, as deposition witnesses frequently
are, particularly a highly intelligent, highly accomplished deposition witness.
So, he didn't deny that he had met Hancox on at least two occasions. It may
have been more than that. He put more emphasis on what he called just a get-
acquainted set of meetings, visits to a nearby company for a tour, that sort of
thing. When I pressed him, when I finally got him cornered he said, 'Yeah,
yeah, we did discuss the possibility of a combination.' There wasn't any question in my mind that the IEP people were approaching Detroit Diesel and
Hanson, and maybe some other companies, with the at least general goal of
trying to create interest in putting Cummins into play.'"[31]

The stakes were high. The town of Columbus watched it all, like At-
lanta awaiting General Sherman. Hank Schacht and his team were not the
sort of law-abiding midwestern-based people who take kindly to deception and threats. Their army continued to attack on all fronts. Rob Kindler
drafted a new anti-takeover law for the state of Indiana. "That was Rob's
show," says Frank Barron. "That was quite a tour de force." The new version specifically eschewed the traditional Revlon requirement that boards
champion shareholders above all and added other constituents that directors should be encouraged to take into account when faced with a buyer for
the shares. This makes it easier for companies to stiff-arm bidders and keep
the company independent and, in the likely case of Cummins, intact. The
legislation also includes a clause that allows a board to stagger its elections
by fiat rather than a shareholder vote to allow directors to be elected at different times. It was diplomatically delicate. Cummins did not want to be in
the front lines fighting for this new bill in the midst of the threat of losing
control to a high-bidding buyer. It took several years for the self-staggering

provision to win approval, but the legislation passed the rest of "Rob's Law" with alacrity.

The company also turned for help to the Indiana congressional delegation. Hank Schacht visited every Indiana representative and senator, each of whom signed a letter to Representative Dingell asking him to instigate an SEC investigation of IEP. Dated January 29, 1990, the letter asked Dingell to support Cummins in its efforts "to stand up to other tactics employed by the corporate raiders of the 1980s—now adopted by an entity with a history of greenmail." Dingell jumped right in. He sent a letter to the Federal Trade Commission voicing his suspicions of IEP and its compliance with antitrust laws. He wrote to SEC Commissioner Richard Breedon telling him that Indiana congressman Philip Sharp thought that IEP had not registered as an investment company and that the SEC should investigate.[32]

Spring drew nigh and with it the Cummins annual meeting in the first week of April. Hancox held court before a group of about 20 journalists at his hotel and then took the microphone at the meeting to decry the takeover of Cummins by what he called "lieners," or "lienholders," his euphemism for the Miller family. The shareholders were not impressed. They gave Henry Schacht, in contrast, a standing ovation.[33] IEP was feeling slightly besieged. Bruce Hancox, for example, hadn't had the chance to try to escape a process server through a motel window. The Indiana Securities Commission, also galvanized by Cummins and also on the hunt, met him at the door of the local high school, where the shareholders were gathering, and served him with papers.[34]

This may have been the final blow. IEP faced endless discovery and depositions. The poison pill blocked any further purchases. Washington regulators and their Indiana counterparts were poised to pounce. Any incentives IEP might have had to attempt either a takeover or greenmail at this point had been squelched. Cravath had multiple rounds of ammunition firing at once. One bullet at least was bound to hit.

IEP asked Kramer, Levin's Josh Berman to contact Cravath's Rob Kindler and sue for peace. Within a month, after one meeting between Kindler and Berman and a routine exchange of drafts, IEP accepted a standstill agreement containing a series of stunning limitations on its role as a Cummins shareholder. IEP could not increase its stake beyond 14.9 percent of the stock for a decade. If it sold its block of shares, subject to other restrictions in the agreement, it could buy back no more than 4.9 percent of outstanding shares during the ten-year period. IEP could bring no claims against the company based on any actions approved by a majority of the company's independent directors. IEP was barred from seeking a board seat. For five years it would have to vote its stock in proportion to the other stockholders, nullifying its voting power, since it could only duplicate any existing ratio of votes. IEP could submit no shareholder proposals and was barred from asking for any votes by proxy. IEP could sell its shares to anyone as long as the new buyer ended up owning a maximum of 2 percent of Cummins stock. Any higher and IEP would have to give notice to Cummins, and the company would have the right of first refusal. IEP was allowed to tender into any offer for all Cummins shares, and it could request meetings with Cummins executives to discuss company business. "We got tired of it," Rob Sutherland later said.[35]

Josh Berman at the time compared all Cravath's defenses to a man standing on a street corner frantically waving his arms. A passerby asks him what on earth he is doing. "I'm keeping away the elephants," the man says. "But there aren't any elephants," the passerby answers. "You see! It's working." "Yes," says Frank Barron, "that was the tune they were singing all along. When you're hired as a lawyer, you have an ethical obligation to give your client the best defense that you can possibly do. Now, I'm very fortunate. I haven't had very many of those situations where I kind of have to hold my nose and say, 'Well, I'm their lawyer, so I gotta defend them.' But in the Cummins situation, it was just a real pleasure and honor to be an advocate for a company of that caliber and that sort of ethical timbre. It was really a highlight of my career."[36]

Rob Kindler remembers arriving at the annual meeting. In the parking lot of the high school is a large crowd of shareholders, Cummins retirees, factory workers, and people from the town and the surrounding farms who have come to join in. Large Cummins engines built in local factories are placed around the lot, counterparts to the city's collection of contemporary sculpture. There are old people, young people, children, and pets. There are tents and chairs, handicrafts on offer, and bake sales aplenty. It's like an old-time county fair. He watches quietly for a while. The cynical New York takeover lawyer is quite moved: "You just realize sometimes that we get caught up in what we do for a living, this M&A thing, and you forget that it's real people, real jobs, real communities—that's what's at stake. It's real life. It's more than just a tactical game. We should never forget that."[37]

In late 2011, Sir Ronald Brierley announced that he was giving up on retirement. At 74 years of age, he took control of a listed investment vehicle called India Equities Fund with about $28 million in ready assets. He said his latest foray was "nothing too big, nothing too ambitious," just part of plans to rejoin the corporate world.

"I never encountered Brierley except as a name," Frank Barron says. "He was sort of like the Wizard of Oz, you know? Hidden away on his emerald isle."

* * *

"THIS HAPPENED ALMOST OVERNIGHT," STEPHEN SCHWARZMAN, PRESIDENT OF THE Blackstone Group, said in January 1990. "Only occasionally do things change fundamentally in our business. This is one of those times."[38] The

M&A boom of the 1980s stopped abruptly at the end of the decade, almost to the day. The classic hostile acquirer of the 1980s—financially driven, funded by junk bonds, with a bid structured and marketed at enormous profit to bankers and lawyers—was uprooted and tossed to the side. There would come another time of great change, and Mr. Schwarzman's event to mark his sixtieth birthday would become something of a symbol, or poster child, for that change. But all that was still 17 years in the future.

In 1987, two years before doomsday, Rob Kindler, in London on business with his Cravath partner Allen Finkelson, looked out his hotel room window at the devastation of Hyde Park. The hurricane damage of what became known as the Great Storm of October 1987 reminded commentators of Hitler's bombing of London. Some 15 million trees came down, including six of the famous seven oaks in the town of that name in Kent. Rob looked at the sky and wondered if the heavens were sending a message. It was still dark gray, the air was cold, the capital shut down, and the park a bleak place of ruin. Three days later, on Friday, October 16, he was back in New York to sign the contract on the house he was buying in Rye, New York. He was looking forward to living in the town. The next-door neighbor was Ron Nesson, who was busy advising Paramount on its fight to capture Time, Rob's client. The third day after Rob paid a not-inconsiderable sum, the New York Stock Exchange sank by just over 500 points, the worst crash at that time since the Great Depression. "I've always had perfect timing," Rob says. On Black Monday, some inexplicable market psychology surfaced that autumn day. It returned with a vengeance almost exactly two years later on October 13, 1989. By the end of that year, it was obvious that the world of M&A was as blasted a heath as Hyde Park.[39]

In all the serial crises of market history, there has come a moment when the human collective acts as one. The bubble takes time. Slowly and then steadily more rapidly, investors take a while to inflate it. The burst is instant. No one has yet to come up with an adequate explanation for group delusion. James Buchan, for one, in his book *Frozen Desire,* dismisses one popular analysis of such events by Charles MacKay, who, in his 1841 work *Extraordinary Popular Delusions and the Madness of Crowds,* devotes a chapter to the Dutch *tulpenhandel,* "the speculation in the bulbs of variegated and plain tulips that reached its peak in Haarlem and the Dutch cities at the beginning of 1637":

> With its warning of the unreasonable conduct of people in mass, the book tends to be reissued in the United States at the peak of bull markets or just after they have broken. Indeed, the lecture has become so wearisome that the economists now claim that the tulip trade of the 1630s, but for its final phase, was eminently calm and sensible: naturally, if you believe the market is all-wise, then, well, so is any particular market.

Financial booms and crashes are exemplary forms of history, for they appear to present that fata Morgana, an empirical or measurable psychology. You
need merely record the money price of the security, or of an index, at the
height of the boom and the depths of the crash to have what seems to be a quantity of human joy and misery; rather as the experience of battle is measured in
the number of dead men and captured guns.[40]

There were dead deals and captured takeover offers aplenty in 1989.
Since 1980, the M&A cycle has run from boom to bust exactly three times.
Magically, every 10 years for the last 30, the good times have given way
to lean at or very near the turn of a new decade. Lawyers and investment
bankers, when asked the reasons behind each bust, repeat the cryptic
phrase, "Trees don't grow to the sky." It seems that there is some unspoken
and unseen force in the species that decides when money can no longer
be made because things have grown too high and too wide, that to make
money once again, there must be growth, and that growth by definition can
come only from small things that get larger. Everything must be cut down
once again so that it can grow back because, yes, trees don't grow to the sky.

Blame has often been assigned to the cratering of the United Airlines
(UAL) transaction on October 13, 1989, and it was indeed quite the debacle,
just days before the Great Storm in London and the grim plunge at global
markets. The airline's management and its employees were buying their
company for $6.75 billion in the late summer of 1989. Citibank was eager
to make its mark in takeover finance, and, in support of the bid, it made
its largest-ever commitment to an M&A deal—$2 billion. But the chance
for glory abruptly turned into one of the most embarrassing episodes of
financing history, when not a single other US bank would join lead lenders
Citibank and Chase Manhattan Bank in the proposed loan syndication.[41]

Lenders who turned down the UAL transaction—executives from
British Airways, which was providing $750 million in equity, advisers to
the unions, and lawyers and investment bankers involved in the deal—all
agree that specific decisions by UAL management, the pilots, and Citibank
scared off the banks and shattered the proposed buyout by mid-October.
Shunning the services of an investment adviser, UAL management participants in the buyout—Stephen Pope, chairman and president, and John
Pope, chief financial officer—pushed the proposed sale as even better than
the recent Northwest Airlines takeover but made fundamental miscalculations about the company's future earnings and its ability to service its debt.
By treating the deal like an airplane financing or bank line of credit, and
chiseling on the fees and interest rates, Wolf and Pope undermined the loan
syndication from the beginning.[42]

Citibank and Chase only exacerbated the wrongheadedness. The two
commercial banks' syndication effort quickly descended into chaos when,

in direct competition with the very bankers on whom they were trying to push primary commitments, Citibank and Chase scoured the secondary market for lenders to take a piece of their own $3 billion stake. And at a time when Japanese financial sources accounted for a significant amount of lending to US-leveraged buyouts, Citibank did not have any official in Tokyo fully informed on the deal who could address the concerns of potential Japanese bankers. It would take nearly ten more years of trying before UAL finally transformed itself in 1994 into the country's largest majority-employee-owned company.[43]

Meanwhile, other storm systems moved in, merged with the mushroom cloud around the UAL failed deal, and uprooted M&A until almost the middle of the next decade. The junk bond market shut down. There was a crisis in the Russian bond market. Large securities houses halted the flow of bridge loans. All levels of debt financing came under pressure. Alan Stephenson, a former Cravath partner who would return to his law firm after a stint as vice chairman of Wasserstein Perella & Co.'s mergers and acquisitions advisory group, described the wreckage at the time: "Banks became more and more skittish, reflecting their increasing concern over the future economic outlook, and they came under increasing regulatory pressure to avoid too much exposure."[44] As with so many market collapses, it was the sudden disappearance of money that did it. It had not leaked away slowly. One minute credit was sloshing happily through the system. The next minute, all was dry and silent. "When there's no credit, it's hard to do deals. Credit is the lifeblood of M&A. You're dead if you can't borrow money," says Stu Shapiro.[45]

It had all looked so good midway through 1989. Having meandered along somewhat lazily for the first three months of the year, M&A activity hit a stretch of rapids once again in the summer months. M&A lawyers and bankers insisted they had seldom been in greater demand. They attributed the earlier calmer pace to peculiar bends in the river now left far behind: the completed marketing of the junk bonds spawned by the previous October's $30.6 billion buyout of RJR Nabisco; concern over rising interest rates and a possible recession; the unpopularity of the leveraged buyouts, with Congress very hot under its collective collar after RJR; and seasonal hibernation after the frenzied final quarter of 1988.

By the end of 1989, however, the number of M&A transactions dropped 32.6 percent from the previous year, and the dollar value of leveraged buyouts sank by 54 percent from 1988 levels. "And last year," Stephen Schwarzman said, "there was a good junk bond market. There will be a continuation of the decline in the overall number of transactions this year [1990], and large buyouts could easily drop by as much as 50 percent to 60 percent and possibly much higher. We just don't know yet."[46] Mr. Schwarzman would turn out to be right.

For the next two years, M&A found itself in toxic shock. Deal volume for the first quarter of 1991 fell to its lowest point since 1982, a full 57 percent below the figures for the first three months of 1990, which was hardly a banner year. Stuart Shapiro said then, "It's very very slow. It's as if the M&A machine runs on oil, with the banks having all the oil and not letting any loose."[47] It was impossible for most CEOs to go to their boards and get approval for a large acquisition at a time when employees were being fired and subsidiaries spun off, said Steven Wolitzer, then co-head of M&A at Lehman Brothers. But at the end of the first six months of 1993, M&A would fill up with fuel once more. From January 1 to June 25, 1993, there were 2,782 domestic M&A deals worth a total of $74.5 billion. That compared favorably to 2,703 deals worth $62.9 billion in the first six months of 1992 and 2,278 deals worth $69.3 billion in the same period in 1991. It is telling that at this point, M&A had not yet metastasized around the globe, and it was American statistics that counted and were counted.[48]

Media, banking, insurance, high-tech, and natural resources were all roiled by consolidations. "The business trend is up," said Jack Levy, then co-head of M&A at Merrill Lynch. "This renewed activity does not feel like a transient surge. There could be some sustainability here. Our backlog of business—which we monitor very carefully—is steadily increasing both as to dollar value and quality of the deals. Having said that, it's still hard to get deals done." Simpson Thacher's Robert Spatt was even more optimistic: "Activity levels are up—there is a new energy in M&A. My sense is that there are greater financing sources in both banking and the high-yield market. I am substantially busier. There is a resurgence, a new vitality in the market."[49]

Many saw the 1980s as a historical anomaly, a time so frenzied and complex that its like would not be seen again. Were it not for the 1980s, Lehman's Steven Wolitzer said, the quality and quantity of deals in 1993 would be cause for rejoicing. "Everyone's reference point is the 1980s. But that is the wrong reference point. Never before and probably never again will M&A reach such heights."[50] Mr. Wolitzer would turn out to be wrong.

CHAPTER SIXTEEN
ORION AND THE WOLVES

Fittingly enough, the nineties begin with a bankruptcy. There are many instances of M&A acting as a guarantor of corporate health that eliminates the weak and rehabilitates the sick, ensuring the inheritance of the genes most perfectly geared for survival. But data also reveal M&A, not as some Darwinian force, but as merely a vast shell game played at the expense of the little people. The demise of Orion, the storied film studio, falls in the latter category.

The fight between two old men riveted the M&A world. John Kluge was a laconic man, less prone to the explosions of temper for which the faded-red-haired Sumner Redstone had long been known, but they had their similarities. Neither was young: Kluge was then 74, and Redstone 65. Each ruled over a media empire, and both were well known for their deal acumen. Yet in this case, Orion was a debt-ridden, troubled film studio. What were they doing?

Kluge was seen as a loyal friend to Arthur Krim, Orion's chief executive. Kluge was on Orion's board of directors, both he and Krim were on the board of Occidental Petroleum, and both were huge benefactors of Columbia University. Was Kluge buying up Orion stock to block Redstone from taking over his friend's company? Kluge might be positioning himself as a white knight, ready to ride in to save Orion and its executives from an unfriendly buyer who would install his own management team. Was Redstone accumulating stock in Orion to try to own the whole company or merely to lure Kluge into buying him out to protect Krim's position as CEO? Redstone had already made millions from similar strategic moves at 20th Century Fox and Columbia Pictures.

Full-scale war was expected to ignite at any moment, but it all came down to telephone negotiations in May 1988, led by Philippe Dauman, then general counsel and now CEO of Viacom. "Kluge is notoriously reclusive, and he and I didn't need to meet," Redstone recalls in his 2001 autobiography, *A Passion to Win.* "Philippe handled the deal, fielding the offers and relaying them to me. It was done on the phone. Kluge offered a subprice, I came back with a higher one, and the deal was settled like a stock trade. Kluge came away with the company, we came away with a nice profit to put toward the removal of our debt, and everyone was happy. Every deal should be so easy."[1]

Kluge would later call his purchase "an investment that was made as a personal favor in a white knight situation." Was it also a classic Redstone head-fake, as two of his advisers maintain? "Did I want to run a studio?" Sumner asks rhetorically in his book. "Not that one. As an exhibitor I understood the complexities of the movie business. I had no intention of getting involved at that time with that company. To keep the fever high, however, I did not want to appear anxious to unload my stock and therefore intimate that a lower buyout price might be acceptable. When Ace Greenberg of Bear Stearns called and basically said, 'I talked to Kluge. I can arrange a trade here,' we responded, 'Let's resolve this.'" Redstone made an $18 million profit on his sale to Kluge and left his rival to preside over a decade-long deathwatch at Orion.[2]

Orion made great movies. Two of Orion's founders, Arthur Krim and Robert Benjamin, were industry legends. Krim and Benjamin were renowned for having taken over a flailing United Artists in 1951 and turning it into a prestigious powerhouse with low expenses and a high regard for artistic talent. Over the next 27 years at United Artists, Krim and Bernstein oversaw such classics as *High Noon, The African Queen, In the Heat of the Night, Last Tango in Paris, Midnight Cowboy,* and *One Flew Over the Cuckoo's Nest.* After founding Orion in 1978 with their colleagues Eric Pleskow and William Bernstein, Krim and Benjamin had similar triumphs at Orion, including *Amadeus, Platoon, Dances With Wolves,* and *The Silence of the Lambs,* as well as many of Woody Allen's films. With such a record of success, John Kluge felt in the spring of 1988 that he could safely turn his attention to a host of other matters, including the local difficulties in Virginia as the trial of his gamekeepers riveted Albemarle County.[3]

Two years after John Kluge's deal with Sumner Redstone, Orion stumbled back onto Kluge's radar. The company was bankrupt in all but name. How could he cut his losses? How could he rid himself of the turbulent and aging priests at Orion, in particular his old friend Arthur Krim? He had to do something fast. To stave off bankruptcy proceedings, Kluge loaned Orion $29 million to release *Mermaids,* with Cher as the lead.[4] Often seen by those not in the know as a "regular Joe," Kluge showed little charity. In return for his cash, he insisted on a substantial cut off the top of any profits *Mermaids* might make. If the movie did not do well—and it bombed—he got the right to tap into the receipts of *The Silence of the Lambs*.[5]

Kluge called in Salomon Brothers and told the bankers in early 1991 to find Orion a buyer. Salomon urged Kluge to pump money into the studio and to strike a deal with the bondholders, the company's lenders, as fast as possible. The time to save the company, the investment bankers stressed, was while it was still a going concern, with its staff still onboard, new movies in the pipeline, and a distribution network intact. Otherwise, the studio, like a dying patient, would enter terminal agitation as each of its organs failed in turn.[6]

Salomon dutifully peddled the company to its dozens of contacts around the world, but Columbia had already snatched up the foreign theatrical and home video distribution rights to 50 future Orion films for $175 million.[7] For Salomon to try to interest foreign firms in a company that had sold the foreign rights to much of its product proved an impossible sell. Such conundrums would dog the deal until the end. Kluge could not bring himself to give up control of the company. He wanted his own people at the top. He did not want to give up any stock. He couldn't bear to dilute his stake. He was reluctant to pour yet more of his own money after bad. Yet he could hardly have failed to see that other people's money would mean other people's ownership, at least to some degree. As a result, deal after deal would be painstakingly assembled, and then a crucial piece would be dislodged and the whole edifice would crumble. To save Orion, he seemed bent on destroying it.

By the early spring of 1991, Orion was desperate for cash. High executive salaries and perks, and duplicate offices in New York and Los Angeles, were driving its overhead past $60 million, at least 50 percent higher than its running costs should have been by industry standards. Orion cofounder and company president Eric Pleskow urged the sale of *The Addams Family*, then in production, to raise money. When you sell your movies, and when you sell your Christmas movie, you are saying to the world, "We are going out of business." There is nothing a hit movie won't cure. But you have to own the movie. The company's chief financial officer, William Bernstein, negotiated the deal with Paramount, and *The Addams Family* turned out to be a hit for Orion's archrival.[8]

Billy Crystal, in his element as host of the sixty-third Oscar ceremony, began the night with a joke at Orion's expense: "*Awakenings* is a film about people coming out of a coma. *Reversal of Fortune* is about someone going into a coma, and *Dances With Wolves* was made by a studio in a coma." It got the laugh he wanted.

Many of the era's celebrities walked down the red carpet that March night in 1991 at the Shrine Auditorium in Los Angeles. Madonna, then recently estranged from Warren Beatty, came as Marilyn Monroe in a tight, white sheath with outsized ermine boa, on the arm of Michael Jackson. So-phia Loren, Carlo Ponti, and their two sons stopped traffic on the red car-pet. But the actual nominees—the actors and directors and the films they created—made it a vintage year. The contenders for best film were *Dances With Wolves, Awakenings, Ghost, The Godfather Part III,* and *Goodfellas.* For best director, the nominees were Kevin Costner for *Dances,* Francis Ford Cop-pola for *The Godfather Part III,* Stephen Frears for *The Grifters,* Barbet Schro-eder for *Reversal of Fortune,* and Martin Scorsese for *Goodfellas.* Jeremy Irons, fresh from playing Claus von Bulow in *Reversal of Fortune,* and Robert De Niro, for his role in *Awakenings,* were up for best actor. Meryl Streep, Al Pacino, Joe Pesci, Whoopi Goldberg, Lorraine Bracco, and Annette Ben-ning were all Oscar hopefuls that year. And there was Kathy Bates, the star of Rob Reiner's *Misery,* a nominee for best actress, along with Julia Roberts for *Pretty Woman,* in which she played a prostitute saved by Richard Gere in his role as an M&A raider.

Despite such competition, it looked likely that it would be the year of *Dances With Wolves,* directed by and starring Kevin Costner and nominated for best picture, director, actor, supporting actor, and supporting actress, as well as costume design, original score, sound, film editing, cinematography, and writing. It was an Orion film, and it was an important night for the stu-dio's people. The way they figured it, they deserved a break. Everyone in the theater knew how much they needed one.

Reba McEntire's band and her manager had just been killed in a plane crash in San Diego. She had decided to go on in their honor. In black, but with the requisite if more subtle glitter, she stood in the middle of a blue neon circle and sang "I'm Checking Out of This Heartbreak Hotel." It was the nominee for best song from Meryl Streep's headliner, *Postcards from the Edge.* It was a poignant moment. If only Orion could "pull back them dark and dusty drapes and let in some light." It looked like that light was indeed beginning to pour in when Tom Cruise announced Costner's win for best director, and Barbra Streisand presented *Dances* with the award for best picture.

Orion had done well to get itself involved in *Dances.* In early 1988, Mike Ovitz, then a massive gravitational force in Hollywood at Creative Art-ists Agency (CAA), got a whisper in the ear that Kevin Costner was not happy at the William Morris Agency. Costner's pet project had landed with a thud on the desks of studios all over town: a western, written by a friend, that would have a host of unknown actors all speaking a Lakota dialect for some three hours. Ovitz asked if Costner would join CAA if Ovitz would get someone to green-light the project. Ovitz suggested to Orion that CAA would be helpful in shepherding more of its A list toward the studio if Orion would take on Costner's "Indian movie." Orion, already in full panic that Costner would leave the studio, after such hits as *Bull Durham* and *No*

Way Out, fell over itself saying yes to both Costner and Ovitz. Everybody was happy.

More welcome good news hidden from the public this time came just weeks after the Oscars, when it looked as if Orion were about to have its own awakening. As it turned out, when Rob Reiner kissed Kathy Bates twice on her right cheek on her way to the stage to collect her Academy Award from Daniel Day-Lewis, Reiner, who directed her in *Misery,* was already immersed in a campaign to acquire Orion. In late March and early April 1991, Reiner's Castle Rock Entertainment—partially owned by Sony Corporation, the parent of Columbia—floated a proposal that Salomon bankers told Kluge was the best way to save the studio. Columbia had already acquired its $175 million stake in Orion's foreign film rights. It looked like all the players were virtually all in the family already.[9]

One of the most successful independent production companies of its day, Castle Rock was founded in 1987 by Rob Reiner and four other partners. Reiner—"Meathead" in *All in the Family* and director of *When Harry Met Sally* and *Misery*—now saw his chance to work with his idol, Woody Allen, an Orion director. "Rob would have had an orgasm if Woody had to pitch his story ideas to him," one former Castle Rock employee said.[10] Fortuitously, or so it seemed, Kluge got rid of both Krim and Pleskow in early April, which meant Castle Rock could move in immediately. But Stuart Subotnick, Kluge's right-hand man at Metromedia, refused to allow anyone from Castle Rock to take over as the new Orion chief. Orion's Bernstein was placed in charge instead. Kluge then decreed that he would not be selling his stock in Orion to anyone, in part because to do so would mean losing millions in tax-loss carry-forwards that would be in jeopardy with any stock sale. Castle Rock stormed off.[11]

What to do now? Kluge began considering an exchange offer to the bondholders, a device that gets rid of onerous debt payments by paying off the debt to bondholders with new stock in the company. His investment bankers at Salomon Brothers discouraged the idea. Salomon's then head of restructuring, Gordon Burns, warned that unless Metromedia injected more money into the company, an exchange offer would extinguish its Orion shareholdings. While Kluge continued to balk at the idea of increasing his exposure, he became ever more tempted to try a restructuring of the company's subordinated debt. It seemed a way to give the beleaguered film studio a financial jump-start at minimal cost to Metromedia. Meanwhile, Kenneth Moelis, a managing director at the Los Angeles office of Donaldson, Lufkin & Jenrette, another Metromedia adviser, had long been promoting the idea of such an exchange offer. Kluge gave Moelis the green light, and Salomon quickly faded from the scene.[12]

Orion's bondholders turned to Wilbur Ross as their investment adviser. Then a senior star with Rothschild Inc., Ross has since become one of the preeminent investors of modern times as head of his own WL Ross & Co., single-handedly restructuring America's steel industry and now assembling an empire from the smoking ruins of international banking. He is a quiet man, with a voice that is often difficult to hear. He has a wry sense of irony but delivers jokes in a monotone that obscures his humor. He looks fragile and irresolute, but he is the ultimate ratiocinator. When his then wife, New York lieutenant governor Betsy McCaughey Ross, ran a somewhat unlikely campaign for the Republican Party's nomination for governor of New York in 1998, for example, he refused to donate to her cause because he saw it as a waste of money. The marriage ended soon after.

In late May 1991, still looking at around $287 million in subordinated debt, $229 million in bank debt, and $40 million owed to trade and other creditors, Orion filed an S-4, which gives the SEC a look at the details of exchange offers. The company offered to exchange the $287 million in interest-bearing bonds for roughly 70 percent of the equity, plus zero-coupon notes that would accrue but not pay interest until maturity in the year 1998. This was designed to save Orion approximately $400 million in principal and interest payments for the next seven years. But after nearly seven months of negotiations, Orion and the unofficial bondholders committee could not reach an agreement, and the exchange offer went nowhere.

Both sides accused the other of cratering the deal. "In effect, the bondholders turned down the offer," said James Dubin, Metromedia's longtime counsel at Paul, Weiss, Rifkind, Wharton & Garrison. Another adviser to Metromedia also said at the time that the bondholders were too greedy. "Overreaching would be an understatement," this adviser maintained. Kluge's side also said the bondholders were poised to force Orion into bankruptcy in a Los Angeles court, a jurisdiction supposedly less favorable to management than New York. Wilbur Ross disagrees with all of this: "The bondholders did not turn down the deal. The sad thing is that the bondholders had never voted to file an involuntary petition [for bankruptcy]. Orion misinterpreted our position and filed the petition." Orion filed for bankruptcy at the end of 1991.[13]

The case came before Judge Burton Lifland, then the chief judge of the US Bankruptcy Court of the Southern District of New York. Judge Lifland joined the court in 1980, was named chief justice in 1984, and has yet to retire, well into the second decade of the twenty-first century and his own eighth decade. He would preside over some of the most monstrous bankruptcies to result from the debt binge of the 1980s: Manville Corporation, Eastern Airlines, LTV Corporation, *New York Post,* and Macy's. He has also been the judge overseeing the fallout from Bernie Madoff's massive Ponzi scheme.[14]

It takes a special kind of jurist to specialize in bankruptcy law. Judge Lifland has been criticized for being testy, impatient, and conservative with fees, one who plays favorites with lawyers. He is also said to be patient, generous, evenhanded, courteous, and inclined to trust the lawyers he knows and respects. What no one can dispute is that he was born in 1929, went to Syracuse University (class of 1951), and three years later took his juris doctor degree from Fordham University School of Law. He had a bankruptcy practice in the sixties and seventies, which was absorbed by the infamous Finley, Kumble, Wagner, Heine, Underberg, Myerson & Casey, where Lifland was a 50-year-old associate, and which itself went bankrupt. One statement epitomizes the man and his approach to his work. In the courtroom in the old US Custom House in Lower Manhattan, a sheepish-looking lawyer suggested that Judge Lifland was overly skeptical about the lawyer's fee request. "I don't *want* to be skeptical," His Honor almost pleaded. "I want to be *forgiving.*"[15]

There is a reason that a bankruptcy proceeding can last for years, even decades. When a corporation explodes, those scalded include lenders of all classes, some with rights and some with almost none, shareholders and their potentially worthless stock, tradespeople and their unpaid invoices, workers with threatened IRAs and their unpaid salaries, pensioners, health insurers, and executives, all fighting each other for what can be salvaged from the wreckage. All will get less than they should in a perfect world, and as a result, they are typically an unruly bunch.

To manage this mob, a bankruptcy judge has great power. In a Chapter 11 proceeding, a reorganization of the company, a judge might do everything from appointing a trustee, deciding a tort issue, approving the fees of lawyers and bankers, arbitrating the priority of liens, mediating a dispute with the IRS, to converting a case to Chapter 7 (liquidating a business for good). Two of the most important of a bankruptcy judge's responsibilities are granting extensions of the 120-day exclusivity period the Bankruptcy Code gives the bankrupt company to come up with a reorganization plan of its own, and ultimately signing off on any agreement the company and its creditors reach. Judge Lifland would make full use of his powers when confronted with Orion.

Fewer than two weeks after coming before Judge Lifland, the studio had another of its tantalizing encounters with a potential savior. New Line Cinema, a New York–based film production and distribution company, struck a deal with Metromedia. The two companies submitted to the judge a joint restructuring proposal that would have placed 49.5 percent of Orion's stock in New Line's hands. The plan contemplated paying off the trade creditors in full and awarding the bondholders 41.5 percent of the stock plus $30 million in principal amount of new Orion notes. Metromedia's stake would be reduced to 7.5 percent, with an option to purchase a further 2.5 percent of Orion's shares from New Line. Negotiations with the cumbersome group of Orion constituents were both glacial and volcanic.

Days of talks would creep forward, finally erupt into a meeting with creditors, and reach no conclusion. After a month of bargaining, New Line and
Metromedia sweetened their bid. In January 1992, they offered the bondholders 45 percent of the stock in a reorganized Orion, plus $60 million in
principal amount of new Orion notes, with New Line guaranteeing up to
$4 million in annual interest payments. Unsecured creditors were also to
receive a 5 percent stake in New Line itself.[16]

New Line would own 46 percent of Orion. The bidder planned to fold
Orion's distribution network into its own system and promised in writing
to cut Orion's $60 million in annual overhead to $7.5 million per year. Metromedia and New Line would each donate $12.5 million in cash to Orion,
and the trade creditors would be paid in full. Metromedia also agreed to
assign the roughly $29 million it was owed in connection with the *Mer-
maids* film to New Line. In early February 1992, the Orion board approved
the terms of the joint acquisition plan. Columbia gave Orion a verbal commitment to support the deal. The battered film studio was awaiting only
the approval of its unsecured creditors before launching into discussions
with the banks.[17]

But it was all in vain. And yet again, each side blamed the other. It was
a large and restless group of unsecured creditors who gathered for a breakfast meeting at New York's Intercontinental Hotel in April 1992 for what
looked like Orion's last chance to be saved by a fellow studio. Wilbur Ross
insists that New Line backed off after realizing they could not afford their
own offer: "After they did their due diligence, they began to understand the
thing and they realized they just couldn't perform. From the point of view
of the unsecured creditors, it was a very attractive deal. The problem was
New Line just couldn't deliver it." New Line's lawyer, Richard Blumenthal
of Blumenthal & Lynne, remembered it all differently. He said that Ross's
clients claimed to reject the deal in a misguided attempt to get a better
one: "At the huge breakfast meeting at the Intercontinental, Ross told us
the creditors were turning us down. It was sorely disappointing. New Line
could have given that company a future."[18]

Meanwhile, in the first week of April 1992, Orion reported that in its
latest fiscal quarter, it had incurred a net loss of $29.2 million on revenues
of $94.8 million. The loss included a theatrical write-down of roughly $12.5
million as various films pulled in less than expected at the box office. Also
included was the $4.9 million in expenses generated by earlier negotiations
with subordinated debtholders over the proposed exchange offer. That
spring, after New Line's efforts cratered, three other suitors emerged, each
of whom made tentative proposals to save Orion: Savoy Pictures Entertainment, Inc., Republic Pictures Corporation, and MGM-Pathé Co. None
generated much enthusiasm. Despite the encroaching disaster, Orion had
yet another triumph at the box office and the Academy Awards when *The*

Silence of the Lambs swept all five major Oscars in March 1992. Again, it was not enough.

Metromedia and the unsecured creditors committee, still represented by Rothschild's Wilbur Ross, began to hammer out a stand-alone plan of reorganization with John Kluge's wealth as the anvil. These talks culminated in an all-night session on June 3. The talks began at the offices of Stroock & Stroock & Lavan, the law firm for the unsecured creditors; the parties moved over to the offices of Paul, Weiss at 5:00 p.m. and finally signed off on a term sheet the next morning at 7:00 a.m. And still it went on and on. Three times the negotiators had to go before Judge Lifland and ask for an extension of the exclusivity period to allow them to reach a consensus. The night before the third hearing on June 18, advisers could not predict whether it would be a "lovefest," with all the parties joining in a request for more time, as one adviser to Metromedia described it, or a "slugfest." Barely a half hour before Judge Lifland took to the bench at 2:00 p.m., the lead banks at last agreed to come onboard, and Columbia agreed not to press its objections to an extension.

On the afternoon of June 18, 1992, at the US Custom House, Judge Lifland glared at Zachary Kass, an attorney for a bondholder owning $22 million worth of Orion debt. Kass objected to Orion's request for more time to win support for its plan. He asked the court instead to open up the process immediately to other potential bidders. "May I ask where you have been all this time?" Judge Lifland asked coldly, as the courtroom fell silent.

For over a year, the judge says, he had "flayed" the lawyers before him, urging them to come to an agreement as quickly as possible to save the film company from bleeding to death while in bankruptcy, only to have a steady procession of merger proposals and acquisition offers that amounted to nothing march through his courtroom while Orion slipped ever deeper into the red. Judge Lifland dismissed Kass's objection as a craven attempt to gain bargaining leverage on the brink of a long-awaited and painfully negotiated consensus. He swiftly granted Orion's motion for an extension.

On July 13, 1992, Orion made the deadline and submitted its plan for its future. Kluge's Metromedia would contribute to a reorganized Orion $15 million in cash and its rights to the proceeds of *Mermaids*, which had a face value of $29 million. Some 85 percent of Orion's cash flow would go to its bank lenders and certain other creditors until they were paid in full, with the remaining 15 percent going to trade creditors and the holders of certain rights to film revenues until they, too, were paid in full. Subordinated debtholders were to receive 49 percent of the stock of the new company and nine-year zero-coupon subordinated debentures with an aggregate face amount of $100 million and an annual interest rate of 10 percent. Cash flow would go toward payment of this interest at maturity after the banks and other creditors were made whole.[19]

It proved too late. Negotiations had dragged on so long that Orion's talent had fled, its library of films had largely been sold, and its distribution system had unraveled. Nothing was left but the rights to some future cash flow and a few unreleased films. Greed, obstinacy, and male primate behavior kept Orion in limbo until 1996, when it finally emerged from bankruptcy, a wizened version of its former self. In 1997, Metromedia sold Orion to Metro-Goldwyn-Mayer, a deal that closed in 1998. The last of the final handful of films released by Orion bore the title *One Man's Hero*.

In 1994, Orion's chief operating officer, William Bernstein, added several ironic twists to the story's spiral. First, Bernstein was the man who organized the sale of *The Addams Family* to Paramount, signaling Orion's distress. Bernstein was also the one Kluge had insisted should run Orion, a decision that smothered the Castle Rock deal. Finally, in 1994, Bernstein would leave Orion in disgust and move to Paramount, the very studio to which he had sold the prize Orion movie. That same year, Sumner Redstone fastened his steely gaze on a studio that he very much wanted to run, unlike Orion, and the fight for the glamorous house of movies known as Paramount Pictures, the last of the Hollywood greats, would become one of the most storied takeover fights in history.

CHAPTER SEVENTEEN
THE HEART OF HOLLYWOOD

From the 15 volumes of documents totaling some 7,251 pages presented to the Delaware Supreme Court in the fight for Paramount, the justices themselves excavated the transcript of a deposition taken on November 10, 1993, in Houston and found the gleaming nugget of Joe Jamail likening opposing counsel to the larva of a brachyceran fly: "Don't 'Joe' me, asshole. . . . You could gag a maggot off a meat wagon." Mr. Jamail, thought to be the richest practicing attorney in America, had won fame in 1985 for his roughly $345 million fee from Pennzoil for wrestling Texaco to the ground and humiliating Marty Lipton in the process. This time, representing the head of Pennzoil, J. Hugh Liedtke, he would become a law school case study for all time.

The fight between Barry Diller's QVC Inc. and Sumner Redstone's Viacom Inc. for Martin Davis's Paramount Communications Inc. was a hostile takeover second to none, pulling into its vortex legions of lawyers and bankers, including some of the greatest names of the day. Paramount turned to Simpson Thacher's Joel Hoffman and Richard Beattie—the latter a veteran of KKR's eighties takeovers, including RJR Nabisco—as well as highly successful litigator Barry Ostrager. Simpson had a long and intimate relationship with Paramount, having represented the company in its failed hostile bid for Time in 1989, and with former partner Donald Oresman, now Paramount's general counsel.

Felix Rohatyn and his partners Steven Rattner and Peter Ezersky at Lazard Frères were Paramount's investment bankers, themselves advised by veteran M&A specialist Arthur Fleischer. Viacom was advised by Robert Greenhill, the renowned Morgan Stanley banker who jumped ship to Smith Barney Shearson in 1993. Viacom's lead lawyer was senior partner Stephen Volk and his team from Shearman & Sterling. Just as former

Simpson partner Donald Oresman was now head in-house lawyer at Paramount, former Shearman partner Philippe Dauman had just been promoted to general counsel at Viacom. Barry Diller, chairman of QVC, had his trusted counselor Marty Lipton and Lipton's litigation partner Herb Wachtell on his side, as well as famed media investment banking house Allen & Co. Wayne Huizenga of Blockbuster Entertainment Corporation had Roger Aaron of Skadden.

The board of directors of Paramount was an equally distinguished group: Pennzoil's Liedtke; Lawrence Small, president of the Federal National Mortgage Association, or Fannie Mae; Franz Lutolf, former general manager and executive board member of Swiss Bank Corporation; and Lester Pollack, a partner at Lazard Frères, formerly a general partner of Odyssey Partners, a director of Loews Corporation, and a former chairman of the Conference of Presidents of Major American Jewish Organizations. Pollack was the honoree at the dinner in November 1975 at which Marty Lipton and Joe Flom first put on public display their growing rivalry with a game of grab-the-microphone one-upmanship. Lester and his fellow directors of Paramount were in for quite an experience in the Paramount battle, particularly when Delaware's chancery and supreme courts forced Paramount to abandon its first merger agreement with Viacom as unfair to QVC and instead to auction itself to the highest bidder, each court lacing its opinion with acidic comments about the board's ignorance and bias in favor of Viacom, publicly embarrassing the directors.

On this deal, entire law firms hummed 24 hours a day. There were lawyers from Delaware and partners and associates in New York, Washington, and Los Angeles specializing in securities and corporate law, tax and employment, and litigation. Other media giants that considered making a run at the last available Hollywood studio included Comcast, based in Philadelphia, and Liberty in Denver, Colorado, each with its own teams of advisers, and advisers advising advisers. Potential rival bidder TCI, whose president, John Malone, was also chairman of the board of Liberty, found itself embroiled in Viacom's antitrust suit, for which he, too, sent out a call for legions of mercenaries. There were public relations specialists from both coasts, as well as financial printers, secretaries, and herds of bike messengers. The deal became the subject of a *New Yorker* cartoon, the ultimate cultural accolade, drawn by the famed Al Ross, who died at the age of 100 in 2012. Observed by a scowling, large, behatted, and beheeled Upper East Side matron pulling a tiny dog, a bearded and berobed prophet carries a sign that reads: "THE END OF THE SALE OF PARAMOUNT IS NEAR!"

The beginning of the sale of Paramount can be traced to April 1993. The end never seemed to be near but did finally come in mid-February 1994. The result was a combination not just of Viacom and Paramount but also of Viacom and Blockbuster, as well as Viacom and Macmillan Inc.

Viacom turned itself into the world's second-largest media company after Time Warner Inc., with $12 billion in annual revenue and 60,000 employees. The skirmish between Viacom and QVC turned into "open warfare," as Redstone put it, with large groups of allies ranging themselves alongside each bidder, a clash of rival consortia of telecommunications companies, cable programmers, cable operators, and video rental companies. Few if any deals in modern M&A have been so full of new case law and arcane financing techniques; of odd similarities between the bidders; of historical ironies and double disappointments, of new auction rules, simultaneous acquisitions, lost tempers, stinging court reprimands, and, as in the case of Joe Jamail, raucous depositions. "Although I'm an M&A lawyer, I've never seen anything like it," said Philippe Dauman, the former Shearman partner, then Viacom general counsel, and now Redstone's dauphin at Viacom. Steve Baranoff, chairman of global mergers & acquisitions at Bank of America Merrill Lynch, who watched the Paramount battle from afar, agreed: "This deal was the most fascinating hostile battle of the past thirty years. More interesting than RJR. As important as Revlon itself."[1]

It is odd, then, that the story of the sale of Paramount has largely failed to be given the full treatment in books or movies, particularly as journalists at the time were fascinated by it and turned it into the story of the year. They were right to do so. This takeover was a battle for the last available Hollywood studio at a time when M&A was in full flower toward the middle of the 1990s. The latest in takeover assault weapons and defensive shields are on display. The players are not corporate raiders, greenmailers, or private investor groups. They are some of the world's most powerful media chiefs fighting to expand their empires. Why then has its story fallen into relative obscurity?

The victor is now old, in the last year of his 80s, his star recently unveiled on the Hollywood Walk of Fame. His heir faces troubles in the provinces, but the empire is intact, and it is the continued survival of that empire that may be the very reason why the saga of its birth has rarely been told. Viacom controls many of the film and television studios, cable channels, and publishing houses that might have put its own history on full display well before now. Its time has come.

*   *   *

ON THAT NOVEMBER DAY IN HOUSTON IN 1993, THE LAWYERS AND THE WITNESS THEY were deposing were stuck in the same room together for roughly five hours. Joe Jamail was representing the deponent, Hugh Liedtke, a member of the board of directors of Paramount and himself the head of Pennzoil. Simpson Thacher & Bartlett's Peter Thomas, counsel to the Paramount board, was also at the proceedings, as was Lawrence Sucharow, of Goodkind Labaton

Rudoff & Sucharow, one of several firms representing disgruntled Paramount shareholders.

QVC counsel William Johnston of Wilmington's Young, Conaway, Stargatt & Taylor, was questioning Liedtke, pressing on doggedly, asking him to recall dates of meetings, telephone calls, and negotiations in the takeover effort in an attempt to unearth what the board knew of QVC's competing offer and when it knew it. Liedtke was repeatedly asked if he had ever seen a large collection of documents, ranging from faxes of attorneys' letters to amendments to amended SEC filings and investment bank analyses, all labeled and numbered, few of them bringing any memories to Liedtke's mind. "Mr. Liedtke—how can I phrase this—doesn't appear to me to be a personality that deals in details," said Sucharow soon after the ordeal. "He is a barrel-chested guy. He takes things in gulps, a big-picture kind of guy. He looks at things not in tiny sequences, but in outcomes, in my estimation. For this kind of person, this kind of questioning is necessarily tedious."

Tempers were beginning to slip. QVC lawyer William Johnston's line of questioning continued, clearly designed to support the thesis that Paramount directors had wrongfully stiff-armed Barry Diller and his QVC, and that Paramount's executives had been feeding their board what the directors wanted to hear. Johnston asked Liedtke why he thought Paramount general counsel Donald Oresman wrote in a note to the Paramount directors on October 28, 1993, "Worth reading is Item 4 on Page 14 which sets out the reasons why the Paramount board of directors recommended the Viacom offer and merger."

PETER THOMAS (SIMPSON THACHER; COUNSEL TO THE PARAMOUNT BOARD): Do you remember reading that statement in Mr. Oresman's letter?

HUGH LIEDTKE (CEO OF PENNZOIL; PARAMOUNT BOARD MEMBER): I vaguely recall that letter, but—and I do think I probably have that material on my desk. I think I did read it, probably.

WILLIAM JOHNSTON (YOUNG, CONAWAY; COUNSEL TO QVC): Did you read the letter?

JOE JAMAIL (COUNSEL TO HUGH LIEDTKE): Material.

LIEDTKE: I did read the material, that section four.

JOHNSTON: Okay. Do you have any idea why Mr. Oresman was calling that material to your attention?

JAMAIL: Don't answer that. How would he know what was going on in Mr. Oresman's mind? Don't answer it. Go on to your next question.

JOHNSTON: No, Joe—

JAMAIL: He's not going to answer that. Certify it. I'm going to shut it down if you don't go to your next question.

JOHNSTON: No, Joe, Joe—

JAMAIL: Don't "Joe" me, asshole. You can ask some questions, but get off of that. I'm tired of you. You could gag a maggot off a meat wagon. Now, we've helped you every way we can.

JOHNSTON: Let's just take it easy.

JAMAIL: No. We're not going to take it easy. Get done with this.

JOHNSTON: We will go on to the next question.

JAMAIL: Do it now.

JOHNSTON: We will go on to the next question. We're not trying to excite anyone.

JAMAIL: Come on. Quit talking. Ask the question. Nobody wants to socialize with you.

JOHNSTON: I'm not trying to socialize. We'll go on to another question. We're continuing the deposition.

JAMAIL: Well, go on and shut up.

JOHNSTON: Are you finished?

JAMAIL: Yeah, you—

JOHNSTON: Are you finished?

JAMAIL: I may be and you may be. Now, you want to sit there and talk to me, fine. This deposition is going to be over with. You don't know what you're doing. Obviously someone wrote out a long outline of stuff for you to ask. You have no concept of what you're doing. Now, I've tolerated you for three hours. If you've got another question, get on with it. This is going to stop one hour from now, period. Go.

JOHNSTON: Are you finished?

Later it was Liedtke himself who lost patience with Johnston, who then suffered a second attack from Jamail:

JOHNSTON: I'll show you what's been marked as Liedtke 14 and it is a covering letter dated October 29 from Steven Cohen of Wachtell, Lipton, Rosen & Katz including QVC's Amendment Number 1 to its Schedule 14D–1, and my question—

LIEDTKE: No.

JOHNSTON:—to you, sir, is whether you've seen that?

LIEDTKE: No. Look, I don't know what your intent in asking all these questions is, but, my God, I am not going to play boy lawyer.

JOHNSTON: Mr. Liedtke—

LIEDTKE: Okay. Go ahead and ask your question.

JOHNSTON: I'm trying to move forward in this deposition that we are entitled to take. I'm trying to streamline it.

JAMAIL: Come on with your next question. Don't even talk with this witness.

JOHNSTON: I'm trying to move forward with it.

JAMAIL: You understand me? Don't talk to this witness except by question. Do you hear me?

JOHNSTON: I heard you fine.

JAMAIL: You fee makers think you can come here and sit in somebody's office, get your meter running, get your full day's fee by asking stupid questions. Let's go with it.[2]

The Delaware Supreme Court was not amused. Chief Justice Norman Veasey, Justice Andrew Moore, and Justice Randy Holland attached a 16-page addendum to their Paramount opinion condemning Jamail and all but openly demanding that he explain himself to the court or be banned from appearing in Delaware, the font of M&A law and practice.

The court found that Jamail "abused the privilege of representing a witness in a Delaware proceeding, in that he: (a) improperly directed the witness not to answer certain questions; (b) was extraordinarily rude, un-civil, and vulgar; and (c) obstructed the ability of the questioner to elicit testimony to assist the court in this matter." The justices acknowledged that Jamail's conduct did not appear to have prejudiced the witness or the parties to the litigation. "Nevertheless," the justices wrote, "the Court finds this unprofessional behavior to be outrageous and unacceptable. If a Dela-ware lawyer had engaged in the kind of misconduct committed by Mr. Ja-mail on this record, that lawyer would have been subject to censure or more serious sanctions."[3]

Finally, the Delaware justices issued a warning barely costumed as an invitation: "[T]his court will welcome a voluntary appearance by Mr. Ja-mail if a request is received from him by the Clerk of this Court within thirty days of the date of this Opinion and Addendum. The purpose of such voluntary appearance will be to explain the questioned conduct and to show cause why such conduct should not be considered as a bar to any future appearance by Mr. Jamail in a Delaware proceeding."[4] This was as close to an *order* to show cause as one can get.

On February 14, four days after the opinion came down from the court, Brenda Sapino of *Texas Lawyer* quoted Jamail as saying, "I'd rather have a nose on my ass than go back to Delaware for any reason."[5]

* * *

SUMNER REDSTONE AND WAYNE HUIZENGA STOOD NEXT TO EACH OTHER AT THE URINALS. Huizenga (pronounced HIGH-zing-uh), the head of Blockbuster Enter-tainment Corporation, stared straight at the wall. Then he spoke. "Sumner, this deal is not rich enough. Give me more stock. I want you to add a dollar."

Huizenga thought he had sold Blockbuster too cheaply, and he wanted more. An increase of $1 sounded innocuous, but Redstone of course knew that one extra dollar would add millions to the cost of his $8.4 billion acqui-sition of the video-rental company and potentially deconstruct the entire $9.7 billion takeover of Paramount itself.

"Your stockholders have a fair deal," Sumner said. "I can't guarantee the movement of our stock. That wasn't a condition of our deal." He moved to the sink and washed his hands.[6]

Sumner Redstone was born Sumner Murray Rothstein. His parents were native-born Americans, a fact that gave them great status in what Sumner calls "the tenement world of Jewish immigrants." His father's surname was Rohtstein, or "redstone" in the original German. When his grandparents came to America, immigration officials, "in their infinite wisdom," transcribed it as Rothstein with the "h" and the "t" in reverse order. Sumner's father, born Max Rohtstein, then changed his first name to Michael and the family name to Redstone. "It's a much better name," he told the young Sumner. "It's easier," his father insisted. "It's what our name should have been translated to by my father when he came here. Other people did it." It was now 1940, with European Jewry in the midst of a modern pogrom. To Sumner, the name Redstone "sounded so solidly American, so ecumenical, so Christian." He was troubled by what he saw as a jettisoning of their Jewishness.[7]

The Redstones were poor, at first. "Our apartment in Charlesbank Homes in Boston's West End had no toilet; we had to walk down the corridor to use the pull-chain commode in the water closet we shared with the neighbors," he recalls in his autobiography. From the West End to Brighton, the family moved on up, to paraphrase the theme song from *The Jeffersons,* Paramount's hit television show in the 1970s. His father, Michael, was putting together his fortune and bought the family a large two-bedroom house in what was a prosperous suburb. But life wasn't much easier for young Sumner. "In 1935, Brighton was an Irish neighborhood which didn't have much tolerance for Jews, and almost every morning on my way to James A. Garfield Intermediate School it was like taking my life in my hands. The level of violence was not nearly as high then as it is now and I saw no knives, but I would get smacked around, and along with my bruises I'd hear a lot of threats and name-calling. I fought back as best I could, but I often had to face five or six tough Irish kids and I was always pretty much outnumbered."[8]

As a young businessman in 1979, the owner of a small chain of movie theaters, most of which were drive-ins, he checked into Boston's Copley Plaza to join a party for a Warner Bros. branch manager. That night, there was a fire in the hotel. The branch manager opened his door and stepped into the corridor. He was killed. Redstone opened his door as well. "I was enveloped in flames." He managed to get a window open in his room and crawled out onto the ledge, with fire shooting above his head. With one arm he held on to the inside of the windowsill to keep himself from falling. That arm had to be held still while fire surrounded it. His legs had already been burned to the arteries. Finally summoned after the hotel realized it had to admit to a problem, a fireman reached him by ladder and carried Sumner in his arms to the ground.

There was no such thing then as artificial skin. Redstone would later fund the research that led to its development. "[T]hey had no choice but to flay me." For five months, at the Burn Center at Mass General, Redstone was in agony. He survived five operations totaling 60 hours. When his bandages were unwrapped for the final time, with the toes of one foot still nailed in place, his doctor said the word "Congratulations." Years later, Redstone would write: "Determination, physical, or any other kind, is the key to survival. If I hadn't learned that lesson before, I knew it well now."[9]

On Valentine's Day 1994, it looked like a very determined Redstone, with fully 75 percent of Paramount shares in his hands, had pulled off the conquest of Paramount Communications, one of the great coups d'état of modern M&A. The great studio's future had preoccupied, seduced, or betrayed almost everybody in the business: Barry Diller and John Malone as well as Redstone, Ted Turner, David Geffen, Michael Ovitz, Brandon Tartikoff, Laurence Tisch, Arthur Liman, and Felix Rohatyn; corporate chieftains such as Steve Ross, Jack Welch of General Electric; all three major networks; European players such as Thorn EMI and PolyGram; and Hollywood's Japanese pillars, Sony and Matsushita. Redstone was closer to the prize than so many who had fallen short before.

Essential to the deal had been Redstone's alliance with Huizenga's Blockbuster. By absorbing the video-rental company, after labyrinthine and often testy negotiations, Redstone got his hands on its $600 million in cash flow. He added $1.5 billion to his war chest. He avoided taking on yet more debt that would require payments so high that it might have killed his hopes of victory. He had eliminated the need to sell luscious Paramount assets to pay for any acquisition, and he was able to raise his offer for Paramount by enough to win the battle. Sumner Redstone was to become not only the CEO but also the majority owner of the new behemoth, having bought both Paramount and Blockbuster with nonvoting Viacom shares. But things were not good between Wayne and Sumner. Neither the Paramount acquisition nor the purchase of Blockbuster had closed. The Viacom/Blockbuster merger still needed the approval of the Blockbuster shareholders at a meeting not to be held until September, more than six months in the unpredictable future.

Redstone and Huizenga were now on a road show in February to persuade large Blockbuster shareholders to vote for the merger with Viacom. They had taken a break from their spiels, which Sumner felt were going nowhere, to head for the men's room at the headquarters of a Boston investment fund. For weeks, Wayne had made it clear that he was suffering a severe case of "winner's curse," hinting that he wanted out of the deal. Now he was trying to rip apart their agreement by reopening the essential issue of price. Sumner was livid. They had been through all this before.

Huizenga's negotiating techniques had grated on Redstone throughout their months of talks. It might be called the elevator tactic, honed during Huizenga's serial acquisitions of video stores across the country. Just as the video-store owner was planning on how to spend the sale proceeds, Wayne would suddenly announce that because of some roadblock he couldn't do the deal. Coats put on, handshakes all around, and a brisk walk to the elevator. Typically, the crestfallen seller would chase after the Blockbuster delegation and concede everything.

Sumner soon took to reversing their roles in this drama. "Huizenga tried to get you where you could taste the deal and then whisk it away," Sumner remembers. "At two in the morning in a conference room we would make a proposal, Huizenga and his cohorts would go talk about it privately, come back and tell us, 'We're at an impasse. Sorry we couldn't work this out. Best of luck.' We let them go. Huizenga would get to the elevator and no one would run after him. One time he waited there for fifteen minutes before it dawned on him that we weren't going to chase him. He got to his car. Nothing."[10]

This time there was no elevator. And this time, Wayne had an extremely valid point. The stock of both Viacom and Blockbuster was plunging and had been ever since the deal was announced on January 7. The morning after Viacom announced that it had won the support of a majority of Paramount stockholders, Viacom's share slipped from its perch in the high 30s and fell to $27 per share. Viacom's shares had slumped in value by 34 percent in the few weeks since then, and Blockbuster was watching its stock sink from a high in November of $33.50 to roughly $21. The value of the Blockbuster/Viacom merger had therefore decreased from $8.4 billion to roughly $5 billion.

The two men faced each other in the middle of the men's room. "You don't get it," Sumner shouted, the slight echo in the men's room amplifying his rant. "You're complaining because the price of our stock is down. *You are driving it down!* Every time you criticize, every time you talk about the price of our stock, every time you say it is not adequate for Blockbuster shareholders, it goes down some more. *It is a self-fulfilling prophecy!* How can you do this? You're double-crossing us. We did everything you wanted. We cooperated with you, we made a deal that you liked, and it was premised—*and you know it!*—it was premised on your commitment to the Paramount deal." As Redstone remembers the scene, "Huizenga simply growled in response." The deal within a deal was beginning to dissipate before Sumner's eyes.[11]

There was another deal within the Paramount deal, an auction that got little attention amid the trench warfare and artillery shelling of the main battle. This deal did not involve the bidders for Paramount. In this deal, Paramount itself was the buyer.

* * *

THE TAKEOVER OF MACMILLAN IN 1988, THE PUBLISHING HOUSE WITH THE IMPECCABLE
pedigree, is a congeries of ancient stories, familiar, like so many others, to
both Shakespeare and the Greeks. A father abandons his son, who remains
tortured by years of paternal tyranny. An adviser overreaches and suffers
the public opprobrium of judges. A scorned intruder triumphs and takes
control of the company but is fatally burdened with the winner's curse. The
fight for Macmillan also stands in M&A lore as the example of hubris and
overreaching that all defenders against takeovers should avoid.

It involves some of the greatest combatants of early modern M&A:
Henry Kravis, a year or so away from winning the mythic war for RJR
Nabisco, one of the bidders; Robert Bass, the Texas oil baron who first put
Macmillan in play; and Robert Maxwell, the eventual victor over Macmillan, a legendary Czech-born Jew who fled the Nazis, whose parents died in
the death camps, who fought with distinction in World War II, and who was
periodically a pariah in England, the land he adopted but that never quite
gave him welcome.

One telephone conversation became emblematic of the deal. Edward
Parker Evans, known as Ned, the head of the publishing house, does not
want Robert Maxwell to get his company. Ned prefers the New York investment house of KKR. For one thing, KKR's Henry Kravis was a prep school
classmate of Ned's brother. For another, Ned and his team were at first set
to keep their jobs through their alliance with KKR. At this point, Maxwell
and Kravis are fighting it out in an auction run by Macmillan management.
Ned has turned to special outside counsel, Stephen Jacobs and Dennis
Block of Weil, Gotshal. He has also retained Bernard Nussbaum, Lawrence
Lederman, and then-associate Pamela Seymon of Wachtell. Ned's investment bankers include Bruce Wasserstein and Mack Rosoff of Wasserstein,
Perella & Co.; and Lazard's Steven Golub and Jonathan O'Herron, who are
advising the company's special committee of outside directors. It was not an
easy relationship between client and advisers, as Miriam Rozen explores in
her *American Lawyer* article in 1989 entitled pointedly, "Headstrong Client,
Cowardly Counsel." Ned was no Mr. Milquetoast. His lawyers and bankers
were summoned only when needed, and otherwise sequestered alone in
conference rooms. "Number 26, your cake is ready," was how one investment banker described it all. Word would spread quickly of Ned's open
criticism of team members: "Bruce just wants to sell my company," was only
one example."[12]

Just before the deadline for final bids, Ned makes a phone call and
tips off his favorite. It is September 26, 1988. Earlier in the day, Ned spoke
to Michael Tokarz of KKR and told him to expect a call at around 7:00
p.m. that evening. At the appointed time, Tokarz, another KKR colleague,

and both Casey Cogut and Richard Beattie from Simpson Thacher, long KKR's counsel, all gather around the Panasonic Easa-Phone. It is Ned and his president, recruited from W. R. Grace, William Reilly:

NED EVANS (MACMILLAN): The other offer is eighty-nine dollars all cash.

MICHAEL TOKARZ (KKR): Great! We've won!

[*Silence*]

TOKARZ: This is super! We've won!

[*Silence*]

TOKARZ: Uh, you guys don't sound enthusiastic.

EVANS AND BILL REILLY (*talking over each other*): Well, it's a little close. . . .

[*Silence*]

Tokarz gestures to his lawyers, moving his hand in a slicing motion back and forth under his chin to signal that he is about to hang up. He whispers to Casey Cogut and Richard Beattie, "Let's cut the phone call."

Michael Tokarz thought the call was to be Macmillan's formal notification of the results of the auction and that he was being told that KKR had the highest bid and had won control of Macmillan. "With the pauses, it made me suspect that the phone call wasn't what I thought it was," he said later. "I said I'd call him back but I never called him back. The bottom line was we had done everything perfectly and by virtue of the phone call it would look bad on the record. Irrespective of what happened, it would look bad." Indeed, it did look bad. It looked like what it was. The two senior executives of Macmillan, in violation of their duty to shareholders, had secretly tipped off their favorite bidder so that KKR could offer to pay just a fraction above Maxwell's $89 offer and win the company. It looked just as bad as the gob-smacking recapitalization plan that Bruce Wasserstein had erected to keep Robert Bass away, just a short time before. The two episodes remain infamous in M&A.[13]

Like the takeover wars at Cummins Engine raging away in the Midwest at the same time, the fight for Macmillan on the East Coast turned into two different campaigns in a long war for independence. First, Robert Bass made his move, just two days after Black Monday had sent its tremors through Wall Street, with hostile takeover bidders presumed to have taken cover. Next, Ned Evans turned to KKR as a safe repository for his company. This turned into the second half of the saga after Bass folded and Robert Maxwell rose up to challenge Henry Kravis for the prize.

Ned Evans had grown up with takeovers. His father, Thomas Mellon Evans, was one of the leaders of the first great modern M&A movement in the 1950s and 1960s. A descendant of Andrew and Rebecca Mellon, who founded the Pittsburgh dynasty, his father was a first cousin of Paul Mellon. Young Thomas had no money of his own to give him a start in life, but he lived in intimate proximity to the branch of the family that was one of the richest clans on the planet. This fired his ambition. He rose from the blackened air and earth of industrial Pittsburgh, imbued with a Protestant work ethic like no other, and ranged across America, practicing a craft that had not yet been named M&A.

In her book published in 2000, *The White Sharks of Wall Street: Thomas Mellon Evans and the Original Corporate Raiders,* Diana Henriques describes Tom Evans as part of something new in the world of business. "When Evans looked around at the American business landscape in the last days of the war," Henriques writes, "he saw dozens of cash-rich companies, fattened by their lush wartime profits, whose stocks were trading for a small fraction of what the companies were actually worth. Most of his contemporaries, and virtually all of his elders, saw a very different scene. To them, the corporate landscape was littered with former casualties of the Depression that had been rescued by a temporary wartime windfall, one that might well have to sustain them through seven more lean years."[14] Tom Evans would more than once reach into a "community and [grab] a piece of the local economy to serve his own ends." It would mean that suddenly "[p]ower—over the company's payrolls, its property, its purchasing, its people—was no longer wielded by some wealthy citizen with a stake in the local culture. It was in the hands of some ambitious young man in a big muscular city in the midst of the Allegheny Mountains. . . . The anxiety that this shifting pattern of ownership created was no more than a wisp on the air as the war ended. But it would grow."[15]

In 1947, like so many other M&A warriors or their heirs, including Henry Bradley-Martin, Edgar Bronfman, and John Kluge, Thomas Mellon Evans found a respite from his turbulent life in the Virginia countryside. He bought what was then known as Buckland Farms, now called Buckland Hall, six miles east of Warrenton, Virginia, and turned it into a respected stud farm. The two-storied, stone, Federal-style house with a double portico was built in 1774 for Samuel Love on land that had been owned, like much of the entire state, by Robert "King" Carter. Richard Bland Lee II bought the place in 1853, and his descendants lived there until 1935. It was the site of one of General J. E. B. Stuart's major Confederate victories known as the "Buckland Races," in honor of General Custer's speedy retreat to the north.

Although Washington sprawl licks at the edges of the estate, just nine-tenths of a mile from the entrance off a busy Route 29, it is a place of quiet elegance. On a side table in the downstairs drawing room, still, is a water-color of Buckland painted in 1887 by John Singer Sargent, a cousin of Mrs. Richard Bland Lee. Just outside the front entrance, under a copse of trees, is a memento mori to the thoroughbred racing establishment it once was: the grave of Pleasant Colony, winner of the 1981 Kentucky Derby and Preakness, foaled and trained at Buckland under Thomas Mellon Evans.

From a place drenched in early American history, Evans spent the next 40 years after buying Buckland changing American business. In an earlier twentieth-century era of M&A, now largely overlooked, he was criticized as a liquidator, which Henriques calls unfair. He built an empire, and he championed the rights of shareholders. As he continued what Henriques calls his "lifelong shopping trip through corporate America," he became known as "Jaws."[16] He was not an easy man to be with, either as a husband or father, obsessed as he was with his corporate campaigns and growing industrial power. The first of his three marriages began coming apart in the early fifties, during which he was described as "a tyrant of the breakfast table, pounding the table and shouting at the boys."

Both boys would endure the shouting for decades. Ned's brother, Shel Evans, barely managed to escape being thrown to the curb when their father decided to sell Crane in 1984 to one of its directors, Wall Street legend William Donaldson. Shel had worked at Crane since 1974 and was now an executive vice president and member of the board. He was to be left out of the future of the company and was told by his father to return to work on the floor of the New York Stock Exchange. Shel fought back, however, in an oedipal battle that deposed the father and installed the son as the leader in his place.[17]

Ned Evans got the top job at Macmillan when he and his father engineered a boardroom coup at the publishing company, and Ned was elected chairman of its board in January 1980. Ned had been working at one of his father's companies, H. K. Porter, but at Macmillan, Ned was no longer his father's employee. Just as he took over at Macmillan, his father was cited in *Fortune* magazine in 1980 as one of the "Ten Toughest Bosses in America." Other former executives had felt the same humiliations. One former Macmillan executive told *Fortune* that Evans deserved first place in its ranking. "Peter Grace [of W. R. Grace and Company] is tough. Armand Hammer [of Occidental Petroleum] is really tough. But next to Tom Evans, they are pussycats. He's the toughest man I have ever known." Even at Macmillan, purportedly captain of his own ship, Ned could not escape. "Several times recently, while Ned was interviewing candidates for jobs at Macmillan," Diana Henriques quotes from *Fortune* magazine, "a side door opened and the sturdy square figure of his father steamed into the room. The father listened for a while, barked out a few questions, expressed his opinion about the candidate's qualifications, and then departed as abruptly as he had entered."[18]

At Macmillan, Ned was working with much paternally inherited and emulated temper and drama to improve the business. Macmillan had long been an ungainly company, with legal research services and school band instruments among its disparate divisions. Within six years, Ned had reshaped the company and sent its stock from the mid-teens to the high fifties.

In the midst of these efforts, Thomas Mellon Evans announced abruptly in 1982 that, as chairman of the executive committee at H. K. Porter, he was selling Porter's stock in Macmillan just as the publisher's long-term prospects looked better than ever. It took $42.9 million of Macmillan's money to buy back those shares, a cash stockpile that Ned had planned to use to continue Macmillan's rise. Ned, by now described by employees as "like father, like son" for his tempestuous reign, was by all accounts crushed by this abandonment and "sulked for two years."[19]

Ned feared a takeover at Macmillan as only one can who grows up in the midst of so many in both his professional and personal life. He became even more obsessed with protecting his company when Robert Maxwell made a run at Harcourt Brace Jovanovich in the spring of 1987, successfully stopped in its tracks by a recapitalization of Harcourt by Bruce Wasserstein and his colleagues at First Boston. Ned brought the same team in to Macmillan to construct similar barricades for his own redoubt. A number of takeover defenses were set up, including an employee stock ownership plan. In August 1987, under Wasserstein's guidance, Macmillan began to consider a recapitalization that would split Macmillan into two entities, an information company and a publishing company.

On October 21, 1987, just after the stock market earthquake that sent the market down by more than 500 points, it was announced that Robert Bass had acquired roughly 7.5 percent of Macmillan's stock. From the fall of 1987 through the spring of 1988, the guns fell silent as the restructuring plan took shape and the annual meeting approached. On March 22, Macmillan granted a total of 130,000 restricted shares to Ned, to president and chief operating officer William Reilly, to general counsel Beverly Chell, and to chief financial officer Charles McCurdy. The company also decided to ask the shareholders at the annual meeting to approve the issuance of blank-check preferred stock. Bass fired his opening round on May 17, 1988, the day before the gathering of shareholders, offering in a letter to Ned to buy all of Macmillan for $64 per share. Bass was "scared to death"; his lawyer Michel Klein of Wilmer, Cutler & Pickering explained at the time that the day after getting the blank-check preferred authorized by the shareholders, Ned would issue himself supermajority voting stock. Bass's offer, Klein said, was an act of self-preservation to protect his $150 million purchase of Macmillan stock.[20]

The next day, the shareholders did indeed approve the stock issuance. The board convened right after the shareholder vote to hear Ned's analysis of the proposed restructuring, which would split the company into two and give Macmillan executives control of the far more important and profitable half, to be known as Macmillan Information. The board also appointed a committee of five outside directors to evaluate both the Bass offer and the restructuring proposal. The first meeting of the special committee came a week later. In attendance for most of the session were Ned Evans, Beverly Chell, and William Reilly. The committee listened to a presentation on the restructuring and chose its own advisers, including Wachtell as legal counsel and, at Ned's suggestion, Lazard Frères as the investment bank. Bruce Wasserstein, now chief executive of Wasserstein, Perella & Co., Inc., was already on the case.[21]

On May 30, the Macmillan board rejected the Bass offer of $64 per share and threw its support to the restructuring plan worth $64.15, scheduled to be put in place 11 days later. On June 4, the Bass Group announced two alternative offers, either a $73 cash payment for each Macmillan share or a restructuring similar to the one proposed by Macmillan management, except with Bass as the new owner without management. Three days later, Bruce addressed the board. He maintained, according to minutes of the meeting, that "selling equity to management" was an entirely different proposition than doing the same with the Bass Group. If Macmillan restructured itself into two companies, as management proposed, and management acquired 39 percent of the entity into which Macmillan's valuable information businesses were placed, this structure would "preserve the upside of the enterprise for shareholders." There would therefore be no change of control, Bruce insisted, which was a trigger that would impose a host of duties on the company to get the best deal for shareholders and to refrain from any defensive measures disproportionate to any threat posed by a takeover offer.

A change of control would occur, according to Bruce, if Macmillan were split into the same two companies and the Bass Group were to acquire the same 39 percent of Macmillan Information. "While there [is] a superficial similarity between the two restructuring proposals, from a shareholder's point of view, Bass is an extraneous force, while management through its efforts is the generator of profit. The present structure preserves the upside of the enterprise for the shareholders," Bruce insisted, according to the board meeting minutes. Robert Bass took Macmillan to court.

Vice Chancellor Jack Jacobs issued his revised opinion on July 18. He was having none of Wasserstein's arguments. There was more than a "superficial similarity" between the management and Bass restructuring proposals, the judge wrote. They were identical or, as the judge put it, "materially indistinguishable." One was an offer that the shareholders should be able to accept or reject, as they saw fit. The other was a disproportionate response to the nonexistent threat posed by the Bass bid. Management's efforts were nothing more than a carefully orchestrated maneuver to transfer control of Macmillan to its executives, without paying anything to shareholders for that change of ownership, and driving off the competing offer without giving shareholders any chance to consider it.

Vice Chancellor Jacobs also questioned Lazard Frères and its supposedly unbiased analysis of the Bass offer compared to management's plan.
He found their study to be "highly questionable." He also criticized Evans and his executives for describing Bass as a greenmailer out to extract
money from Macmillan. This criticism was a "mischaracterization" exacerbated by the board's failure to investigate Bass for itself. The group's $64
offer specifically asked for negotiations on the price, and the raised offer of
$73 was well within the range of prices that the board's own financial advis-
ers had set as fair. Jacobs pointed out that Macmillan had ample defenses
in place and that a reasonable response to whatever threat Bass might have
posed would have been "at a minimum" to "offer stockholders higher value
than the Bass Group offer, or, at the very least, offer stockholders a choice
between equivalent values in different forms." As it was, management's restructuring was coercive and inferior.[22]

After Ned's elaborate defense lay in ruins, he turned to KKR. Would
Henry Kravis like to buy Macmillan in partnership with Ned and his fellow executives? Robert Bass promptly launched a tender offer for all of
Macmillan stock at $73.50 per share. Three days later, Robert Maxwell
strode forth with his own bid of $80. Bass folded, and battle was now joined
between the British press tycoon and the American private-equity giant.
They both soon had their jaws locked on the company, and management
had no choice but to launch an auction. Like the lateral head-shaking that
sharks use to debilitate their prey, the bids oscillated between the two, each
bumping the other to ever-higher prices.

Macmillan announced on September 12, 1988, that it had agreed to a
leveraged buyout with KKR. Within a day, Maxwell raised his tender offer bid to $86.80. There were three other bidders, aside from Robert Bass,
Robert Maxwell, and Henry Kravis: Rupert Murdoch, McGraw-Hill, and
Gulf + Western. Bruce Wasserstein called all of them and said that if they
wanted to participate, their final offers had to be submitted by Monday,
September 26. Maxwell's adviser, former Skadden partner and champion
of Hanson's fight for SCM, Robert Pirie, was in his office as the deadline
approached, waiting for word from his client.

If Pirie could engineer a victory, it would mean not only a $12 million
fee for him, the newly named president of Rothschild Inc., but also a personal vindication as the new spear carrier for the Rothschild clan in North
America. He had just had lunch in the dining room opposite his office at 1
Rockefeller Plaza, according to William H. Meyers in his piece for the *New
York Times:* turbot quenelles, partridge, and tarte tatin, washed down with
the house wine (Chateau Lafite-Rothschild '79). He waited, "sipping claret
and puffing on his third Davidoff cigar of the last hour."

Finally, at 3:30 p.m., Maxwell called from London. "'Is it a winning
bid?' the foghorn voice booms through the receiver. Pirie replies in soft,

measured tones: 'It's a very bold number, Bob. You're paying top dollar.' He advises his client that KKR will undoubtedly get a chance to top his bid. 'It's your call, not mine,' says Pirie. Without hesitation, Maxwell gives the order to charge ahead. He will pay $2.6 billion for Macmillan—his biggest single commitment ever."

The afternoon lumbered on and on with no word from the Macmillan board. "The longer the silence, the more suspicious Pirie becomes," Meyers writes. "'I smell a rat,' he mutters to his second-in-command, Gerald Goldsmith. Could Macmillan have leaked Maxwell's bid to KKR? If so, that would constitute an unfair advantage in the auction. The telephone rings. A banker from Lazard Frères, representing the Macmillan board, is calling to inform him that KKR has won Macmillan with a bid of $90.05 a share in cash and notes." Pirie was instantly determined to go to court, but again, he could not get hold of his client. Maxwell was in meetings with French government officials at the Élysée Palace and not taking calls. Finally he spoke to Bob. "Sue them" was the command.[23]

The lawsuit would have come to nothing and no one would ever have known about the tip-off had not Simpson's Casey Cogut and Richard Beattie, advisers to KKR, insisted that they were under an obligation to tell the court what had happened. Once everyone did know about it, the secret advantage that Pirie suspected had been awarded to KKR seemed certain to seal the case. The deposition of Ned Evans was now even more crucial.

Stu Shapiro, the Skadden partner on Maxwell's litigation team who questioned Ned, is still bemused by what happened. All would have been solved for everyone concerned, he feels, if the lawyers for Ned Evans had immediately announced that their client had wrongly called KKR without their knowledge and that as a result all bidders would be told what the bids had been before a final round of offers would be solicited. But that didn't happen. "It was just stunning," Stu says. Before deposing the hapless Ned, Stu had a word with Dennis Block of Weil, Gotshal, Macmillan's lead litigator, telling him this phone-call tip would be a killer. Oh no, it's no problem, Dennis said. It's not material, so it won't matter.[24]

Robert Pirie was eager for Stu to be as tough as possible on Ned Evans in the deposition. Like Justice Moore, Pirie was always abrasive and never much liked. He made one well aware of his lineage as the nephew of Adlai Stephenson and an heir to the Carson Pirie Scott department store fortune, of his cousinhood with the Astors, his 100-acre estate outside Boston, his equestrienne wife who transported her horses on 747s to European competitions, of their stay at Windsor Castle as guests of the royal family, of his wine cellar, his collection of rare books and later Asian art, his Christmas tree decorations that were the same as those used by the Metropolitan Museum for its tree because her family had donated the second set to the museum. His motto, which he often repeated, was, "A gentleman is never unintentionally rude." Pirie was very close to Guy de Rothschild and was brought in to launch the family firm in the New World, although he was later dismissed and went on to Bear Stearns and then Société Générale, where "the kitchen was much better."

Well known for his intelligence, for his typical night's sleep of four hours, as well as his brutal treatment of subordinates and unconventional colleagues, Pirie was often rude and dismissive of Bruce Wasserstein when Bruce was a young, fat, funny-haired, famously unkempt Jewish kid. Then Bruce grew up. However, Stu says, "I was un-bullyable." Colleagues and former partners say that Stu and Robert Pirie sometimes found it difficult to be in the same room. They came to a modus vivendi. Stu remembers the gift of a book on Chateau d'Yquem from Pirie, for example, "when he was making nice."[25]

Pirie wanted Stu to go for the Ned Evans jugular at the deposition. Stu had no plans to do any such thing. "I've often had fellow lawyers, corporate lawyers, and clients who say, 'I'm looking for a junkyard dog,' and I always say, 'Well, you gotta go get one then. I'm not one,'" he says today. "I'm just a lawyer. I ask questions. You want somebody that snarls and drips saliva on the table? Get someone else. You want an asshole? Go find an asshole. I learned from Joe Flom that everything you do is going to be communicated to somebody you're trying to persuade, whether it's a judge or a jury— every e-mail you send, every letter you write, every brief you submit. People have bizarre notions of what the process is about, as if you're supposed to club somebody into submission. This doesn't mean you win if you're nice and you lose if you're nasty. It means you make it harder to persuade if you're behaving like a junkyard dog."

Stu was not feeling well when the deposition began at around ten in the morning. He was wearing glasses with so-called progressive lenses for the first time, and he felt dizzy and nauseated. Ned didn't seem to be feeling any better. "He was an emotionally battered child," Stu remembers. At the deposition, Ned had before him a glass of dark liquid with ice cubes. At regular intervals, about every 20 minutes or so, during a long deposition, Ned stopped the proceedings for trips to the men's room. He would come back to the conference room, bright-eyed and rubbing his nose. Rumors flowed through the ranks of lawyers and investment advisers. By the end of the deposition, he seemed unusually tense and abrupt. Most of his answers were variations on a constant theme: "I can't recall; I can't remember; I don't know."

Since it is well known that judges don't often examine the exhibit books, which they openly admit, a smart lawyer will quote from an important deposition in the briefs submitted to the bench. You string together a dozen or so "I don't knows" and "I can't recalls," and you make your point. The stream of Ned's evasions was presented to both Jack Jacobs in chancery and then Drew Moore at the state supreme court. Justice Moore noted sardonically at oral argument that, for a CEO, the guy didn't seem to know much. To make his point, Stu did not have to snarl and drool after all.

The black-and-gold-bound volume on the Macmillan fight is three and a half inches thick and weighs eight and a half pounds. Exhumed from history, it feels like some holy book found preserved in the Sinai caves. The briefs for each side show how bitter the Maxwell team had become over the course of the fight and how determined the Macmillan side remained not to concede that anything at all had gone awry with the auction process. In his deposition, excerpted in Skadden's October 5, 1988, brief, Tokarz describes the call:

> Mr. Tokarz: Evans called, announced that he and Bill and the attorney and others were in the room, and then proceeded to tell me that the other offer was $89 all cash.
>
> Q. And he identified—
>
> Mr. Tokarz: Maxwell's offer was $89 all cash.
>
> Q. What else did he say?
>
> Mr. Tokarz: Nothing. Then I said, "Great, we have won."
>
> Q. Did he say anything else?
>
> Mr. Tokarz: That's all [he] said. Then I said, "Great we have won." Then I heard nothing. There was a little pause and I said, "This is super. We have won." There was another pause and I said, "You guys don't sound enthusiastic." They said, "Well, it's a little close."
>
> Q. Who said that?
>
> Mr. Tokarz: Ned and Bill. They basically said it together. "It's a little close." Then I looked over at my attorneys and said, let's cut the phone call.
>
> Q. Who said that?
>
> Mr. Tokarz: Me.
>
> Q. Why?
>
> Mr. Tokarz: Because I thought the phone call was to inform us of the results and that we were going to be told that we won or lost and the way— through that point with pauses, it made me suspect that this phone call wasn't what I thought it was.
>
> Q. What did it make you suspect the phone call was?
>
> Mr. Tokarz: That they were trying to let me know what happened [in the bidding], that it wasn't a formal communication . . . it would look bad.[26]

Skadden, in its October 5 brief, goes on to discuss the aftermath of the call:

> Evans and Reilly deliberately never disclosed to their board (or evidently to Macmillan's advisers) that they tipped MCC's bid to KKR. Macmillan's

outside directors testified that they only learned of the 7:00 p.m. September 26 tip for the first time in preparing for discovery on September 30, long after the board had granted KKR the lockups and accepted KKR's bid on September 27.

KKR also consciously determined to keep the tip secret pending approval of its bid and, apparently, did not even tell Macmillan's financial advisers when they called at 8:00 p.m. Only on September 29, 1988, days after these events, was the secret tip-off disclosed by KKR in a filing made by their counsel.

Evans was cross-examined October 3 only after the KKR filing and Tokarz deposition had established what he had done. Evans was forced to admit that

- He and Reilly called Tokarz;
- He told Tokarz the exact price of MCC's bid, $89 cash;
- He did not tell anyone including Macmillan's directors he had tipped Tokarz;
- He did not even tell Macmillan's financial advisers;
- He did not alert the board to the tip during repeated requests for assurance that the bidding process had been fair.[27]

The Macmillan team was led in Delaware by A. Gilchrist Sparks III, the imposing litigator from Morris, Nichols, and included E. Norman Veasey from Richards, Layton & Finger, Bernard Nussbaum from Wachtell, and Dennis Block from Weil, Gotshal. This side pointed to Maxwell's decision not to enter a higher bid at the end of the auction as a choice he must now live with without whining. In its October 7, 1988, memorandum in opposition to Maxwell's motion for injunctive relief, they argued that Maxwell's objections to the auction were disingenuous and misleading:

MCC [Maxwell] misrepresents completely the import of this telephone call. In the first place, even if the phone call could be said to have "tilted the playing field," it did so only momentarily and for a period of time during which no decisions were made and no actions were taken because just one hour after the Evans phone call, whatever imbalance existed was set right when the bankers phoned both bidders and told them that the advisors could recommend neither bid and that each bidder was being given the same message. In the auction context, this had an unmistakable meaning: the bids were virtually even and each party was at risk that the other would bid again. Thus, by 8:00 p.m., KKR and MCC both knew that the other bidder had been invited to bid again and whoever bid the highest in this final round would win. . . . This is not a situation, such as *Revlon, Inc. v. MacAndrews & Forbes Holdings, Inc.*, Del. Supr. 506

A.2d 173 (1986), where the auction was ended in midstream by directors acting
out of self-interest to protect themselves from litigation. To the contrary, this
board knowingly exposed itself to the certainty of litigation from Maxwell by
taking the higher KKR offer.

> . . . MCC's response, predictable from the outset, is that the bidding pro-
> cess was a "sham," and that it lacked sufficient information to make a decision
> to increase its offer. However, MCC decided to stick with $89.00 not because it
> lacked information, but because it wanted to acquire the Company for $89.00.
> MCC never told Macmillan or its advisors it was willing to pay $90.00 in cash;
> rather, it simply tried to pay as little as possible, and accepted the risk that its
> bid would not be the highest. Now, after the auction has been completed, MCC
> is trying to reopen the bidding. Like any disappointed bidder in an auction,
> however, MCC must accept the responsibility for its failure to bid when the
> auction was being conducted and cannot have this Court usurp the role of the
> directors.[28]

In its reply memorandum, Skadden asserted that the court had before
it actual evidence of "a management tipping its cohort-bidder, a board that
was misled and later actively chose to ignore troubling information, an
'auction' subverted, and a poison tax lockup approved to end an ongoing
auction in favor of management." Skadden took particular umbrage at the
argument that Maxwell should simply have bid more. "Most offensive of
all," the lawyers wrote in their October 9 memorandum, "is the continued
suggestion that Maxwell is himself to blame for failing to put his highest
bid on the table. Here, then, is the pitcher, caught red-handed with tar in his
mitt, blaming the batter for missing the pitch."[29]

Vice Chancellor Jack Jacobs was not impressed with Macmillan's claim
that the investment bankers, in the person of Bruce Wasserstein, had made
it clear to both sides after the tip-off call that their bids were too close to
call and that each now had the chance to win with a higher bid. At 8:15 p.m.
on September 26, Bruce Wasserstein called each bidder and read the following statement:

> We are not in a position at this time to recommend any bid. If you would like
> to increase your bid price, let us know by 10:00 p.m.

However, the vice chancellor noted, Bruce read an additional paragraph to KKR:

> Focus on price, but be advised that we do not want to give a lockup. If we
> granted a lockup, we would need (1) a significant gap in your bid, (2) a smaller
> group of assets to be bought, and (3) a higher price for the assets to be bought.

At 10:00 p.m. that same night, Rothschild's Robert Pirie called
Wasserstein:

> PIRIE: If you have a higher bid, then please inform us of that bid, and we will
> tell you promptly whether we will raise our bid to top their bid. If you
> don't have a higher bid, then regard this as our highest bid. Will you get
> back to us?
>
> WASSERSTEIN: We have gotten back to you. If you have anything further to
> say, tell us by midnight. We reserve the right to get back to you, but you
> should assume we won't unless we hear from you.[30]

To say "we are not in a position at this time to recommend any bid" does
not automatically mean the two bids are "substantially equivalent," the vice
chancellor wrote. Robert Pirie had testified in an affidavit that Bruce's statement was "completely uninformative," and Vice Chancellor Jacobs virtually
agreed: "[T]hose carefully chosen words were susceptible of various mean-
ings. They did not unambiguously convey the clear message that the defendants ascribe to them. The 'signal' given to KKR that ultimately led KKR
to raise its bid was not similarly provided to MCC. And Wasserstein's decision during the 10:00 p.m. telephone conversation not to tell Pirie whether
Macmillan had received a higher bid, can only be viewed as another missed
opportunity to induce MCC, directly and straightforwardly, to increase its
offer." The vice chancellor went on to describe the auction as "deficient."
It was "not even-handed." KKR, management's "favored bidder," enjoyed
"pointed and explicit" communications. Maxwell suffered from what "fell
short of being model disclosures designed to maximize the likelihood of
MCC raising its bid."[31] Well, precisely, the Maxwell side might have said.

Sadly for Maxwell, however, the vice chancellor, to distill his words to
their somewhat unconvincing essence, just didn't feel it was all that bad. After all, Jacobs declared, "Messrs. Pirie and Maxwell are highly sophisticated
businessmen, experienced in the corporate takeover field. They knew that
to win the auction, MCC would have to submit the highest bid." Well, yes,
the Skadden lawyers could well have muttered to themselves. "During those
critical final hours," the vice chancellor noted, "MCC's representatives were
repeatedly told that MCC should submit its highest bid. Macmillan's representatives could have been more pointed or emphatic, but they did convey
that message. The advice to Pirie—that MCC should submit its best offer—
was truthful and could not have deceived a reasonable bidder. It may be that
if Pirie had been told that KKR had submitted an equivalent or higher offer,
MCC would have increased its bid. But Macmillan's representatives did not,
in these circumstances, violate any duty by not disclosing such information.
And it has not been shown that their conduct misled or otherwise inequitably induced MCC into standing on its $89 bid."[32]

True enough, as far as it goes, but the top Macmillan executives also conveyed to KKR's people that if they left their bid as it was, they would lose. No one told Maxwell that he needed to raise his bid in order to win. The vice chancellor concedes that the blind auction was blind in only one eye, yet he concludes from all this that Maxwell was not "misled or otherwise inequitably induced" to stand on its $89 bid, which is exactly what happened. Advisers on the losing side to this day are mystified at Jacobs's ruling. Now on the Delaware Supreme Court, Justice Jacobs may simply have decided that by canceling the Wasserstein restructuring plan for Macmillan, he had done enough.

On to the Delaware Supreme Court on appeal, where, with his colleagues Chief Justice Christie, Justice Randy Holland, and Justice Andrew G. T. Moore II awaited. Skadden's team included Rod Ward, Keith Sattesahn, and Andre Bouchard of the Wilmington office; Stu Shapiro of the New York office; and Thomas Dogherty, George J. Skelly, and Dennis Kelleher of Boston. They pointed out to the high court that Robert Pirie had been leery of the looming auction and over the weekend before the bidding opened had specifically challenged Macmillan's advisers for assurances that it would be fair. He told them in a letter that they must realize that for Macmillan to shop a Maxwell bid to KKR and to keep any increased KKR bid a secret "kills the auction process."

At oral argument, the Skadden side began to see some hope. Larry Lederman in his book *Tombstones* recalls a sinking feeling on his team:

> [Gil] Sparks began his presentation. Sparks rose and addressed the court: "If it please the court, I am counsel for the outside directors—"
>
> Justice Moore immediately broke in from the bench: "As counsel for the outside directors, are you and your clients disturbed that senior management of this company tipped the bid?" . . . Justice Moore leaned over the bench and demanded, "Why didn't they fire them?"
>
> Sparks: "Fire them?" Sparks was incredulous.[33]

"And why not? That's exactly the right question to ask when you've got somebody who does something this outrageous," says Stu Shapiro.[34]

> Before Sparks could recover, Justice Moore said, "Yes, it seems to me that if it was such a breach of duty. . . ." And then Sparks tried to argue, but never got a chance. . . . [Justice Moore] found that the board had been misled. Ned Evans hadn't told the board that he'd intervened in the process. As a consequence, the board didn't have adequate information at the appropriate time, tainting everything from the beginning. Moreover, the board had been too pliant, and the advisers, the lawyers and bankers, should never have allowed Evans and his management to participate in or be informed about the status of the bidding.[35]

As for the conversations with Bruce Wasserstein on auction night, Justice Moore went further than Vice Chancellor Jacobs and found that Maxwell and Pirie had "reasonably, but erroneously, concluded" that they actually had the higher bid and didn't need to top themselves when their victory was already at hand. "The voluminous record in this case discloses conduct that fails all basic standards of fairness," Justice Moore wrote with characteristic bluntness. Later in his opinion, Justice Moore was equally direct: "As for any 'negotiations' between Macmillan and Maxwell, they are noteworthy only for the peremptory and curt attitude of Macmillan, through its self-interested chief executive officer Evans, to reject every overture from Maxwell." He decried the "tone and substance of the communications between Macmillan and Maxwell," which, he wrote, "dispel any further doubt that Maxwell was seen as an unwelcome, unfriendly and unwanted bidder."

Finally, Justice Moore turned his ire to the secret phone call to KKR. "[T]here can be no justification," he declared, "for the telephonic 'tip' to KKR of Maxwell's $89 all-cash offer." He then accuses the Macmillan side of lying. "Although the defendants contend that this tip was made 'innocently' and under the impression that the auction process had already ended, this assertion is refuted by the record. The recipient of the 'tip,' KKR, immediately recognized its impropriety. Evans' and Reilly's knowing concealment of the tip at the critical board meeting of September 27th utterly destroys their credibility."

> Defendants maintain that the Evans-Reilly tip was immaterial, because it did not prevent Maxwell from submitting a higher bid in the second and final round of the auction on September 26th. However, this "immaterial" tip revealed both the price and form of Maxwell's first round bid, which constituted the two principal strategic components of their otherwise unconditional offer. With this information, KKR knew every crucial element of Maxwell's initial bid. The unfair tactical advantage this gave KKR, since no aspect of its own bid could be shopped [under the terms of a no-shop agreement], becomes manifest in light of the situation created by Maxwell's belief that it had submitted the higher offer. Absent an unprompted and unexpected improvement in Maxwell's bid, the tip provided vital information to enable KKR to prevail in the auction.
>
> Similarly, the defendants argue that the subsequent Wasserstein "long script"—in reality another form of tip—was an immaterial and "appropriate response" to questions by KKR, providing no tactical information useful to KKR. As to this claim, the eventual auction results demonstrate that Wasserstein's tip relayed crucial information to KKR: the methods by which KKR should tailor its bid in order to satisfy Macmillan's financial advisors. It is highly significant that both aspects of the advice conveyed by the tip—to "focus on price" and to amend the terms of the lock-up agreement—were adopted by

KKR. They were the very improvements upon which the board subsequently accepted the KKR bid on Wasserstein's recommendation. Nothing could have been more material under the circumstances. It violated every principle of fair dealing, and of the exacting role demanded of those entrusted with the conduct of an auction for the sale of corporate control.

Given the materiality of these tips, and the silence of Evans, Reilly and Wasserstein in the face of their rigorous affirmative duty of disclosure at the September 27 board meeting, there can be no dispute but that such silence was misleading and deceptive. In short, it was a fraud upon the board.[36]

The Delaware Supreme Court overruled Vice Chancellor Jacobs, and Robert Maxwell's bid won the day. And to think it was all needless humiliation. Why didn't one of the bankers or lawyers simply call Robert Pirie, tell him that KKR had somehow found out about their last bid, reveal to him what KKR had offered, and declare one more final round of bidding? Instead, the lawyers and bankers argued that the tip-off wasn't "material," that it didn't matter. It did, to Drew Moore at least, and that was all that mattered.

A month or so after the Delaware Supreme Court invalidated the Macmillan auction and guaranteed Maxwell's final victory, Wachtell's Larry Lederman is in Bernie Nussbaum's office, his partner on the Macmillan case. Bernie has a confession to make. He made a deal with God. If he could win only one case, let it be his cousin's case. His cousin, an aide to Queens borough president Donald Manes, had been accused of soliciting a bribe for Manes. The cousin was convicted by a jury, but Bernie convinced the court on appeal to reverse the conviction for insufficient evidence and free his cousin. Larry suggested that Bernie might have made a better deal by offering up only one of the two Macmillan cases, rather than both.[37]

Maxwell paid some $2.6 billion for Macmillan, more than $20 per share above the price at which the conventional wisdom valued the publishing house. It turned out to be Maxwell's poisoned chalice. Just two years after he won the auction, Maxwell was watching his publishing empire devolve into dysfunction. Three years after his victory in New York, Robert Maxwell was dead. He went missing from his yacht, the *Lady Ghislaine*, his floating command post named for his daughter and symbol of his power, off the Canary Islands and was found drowned on Guy Fawkes Day in 1991. Although no one can ever know exactly what happened or where his mind was traveling as his life ended in the wine-dark North Atlantic, it has been widely assumed that Robert Maxwell killed himself. The debt he took on to overpay for Macmillan in 1988 was seen as the nest of carpenter ants that ate away his business.

Robert Maxwell was a Jewish immigrant who changed his name three times and was consistently snubbed by the city establishment, either bluntly or with exquisite subtlety. With typical English felicity, his nickname—the Bouncing Czech—captured in two words the man's girth, his foreignness, his loud personality, and the questionable business practices that forever swirled around him. In his day, he was a worthy rival of the early Rupert Murdoch, growing his media and publishing empire faster than was wise. He left a gap in the world. The former Jan Ludwik Hoch, Leslie du Maurier, and Leslie Jones lost his parents to the death camps, fought against the Nazis, both in the Czech army and later the British army, and was presented with the Military Cross by Field Marshal Montgomery. After the war, he was elected to Parliament as a member for Buckingham, but his real forte turned out to be the world of commerce.

He always lived flamboyantly, renting Headington Hill Hall from the Oxford City Council, which inevitably ever after became known as Maxwell House. He was always ebullient, always in the boardrooms and headlines of papers on both sides of the Atlantic, always suspicious and mistrustful. He ended up owning the British Printing Corporation, Mirror Group Newspapers, and Macmillan. But he was ever the rogue. After his death, for example, it was discovered that Maxwell had looted the pension funds at the Mirror Group to stave off bankruptcy. By the time of his last sail on the *Lady Ghislaine,* the banks were circling viciously, demanding immediate repayment of his massive debts.

Once again, Macmillan was for sale. It took two years to find an owner for the respected publishing house. In November 1993, while the world stared fixedly at Viacom and QVC dueling over a famous movie studio, it was Paramount, that very company, which quietly won Macmillan in another auction, picking up the most significant item left in the everything-must-go sale of bankrupt Maxwell Communication Corporation PLC (MCC). The media took little notice, but Paramount is still the only known target of a hostile bid that won an auction while selling itself.[38]

The Macmillan purchase, which cost Paramount almost half its cash reserves, or more than $500 million, happened because Viacom and QVC let it happen. Both contenders for Paramount, rather than view the expenditure as a misuse of funds earmarked for paying down takeover debt, were in favor of the Macmillan buy. In fact, according to Paramount adviser Wilbur Ross, then senior managing director of Rothschild Inc., the Macmillan bid "turned out to be the only thing QVC and Viacom agreed on throughout their fight."[39]

For the world of M&A, the deal provided an epilogue to the infamous scandal of 1988, which tarnished the reputations of Macmillan's management and board as well as the company's advisers at Lazard and Wasserstein, Perella. For Henry Kravis, who lost that fight to Maxwell and whose K-III was a contender in the latest bout, Paramount's victory must surely have smarted.

Paramount had known all along that it could afford to bid more for Macmillan than any of the three other bidders: Harcourt General Inc., K-III, and Pearson plc. Paramount's Simon & Schuster, a trade publisher, and Prentice Hall, a college publisher, could profitably be merged with Macmillan's trade and college division. "It was a real opportunity, given the synergies involved," recalled Paramount board member Lester Pollack after the victory. "Paramount was the best possible buyer."[40] But price was not the only issue. Macmillan management, albeit a pawn in the bidding rather than a principal, was known to favor K-III, some of whose executives, including William Reilly and Beverly Chell, were ex-Macmillanites. Because K-III had fewer synergies, it was not likely to fire as many people as Paramount, and the chairman and CEO of Paramount Publishing, Richard Snyder, had a reputation as a demanding and difficult boss.

Because K-III's parent, KKR, had taken part in the 1988 auction through which Maxwell had come to own Macmillan, Paramount also feared Henry Kravis might now prove to be a ferocious bidder. "There was a danger that they might be more aggressive," says Rothschild's Wilbur Ross. "Reilly had run it before. We also wondered if they might be planning to do a second acquisition of another book publisher, and then combine that with Macmillan to get the synergies."[41] Did others worry that K-III, with its Macmillan defectors, have an advantage? Said Beverly Chell, only half in jest, "I would hope they did."

K-IIII was only one of Paramount's worries. MCC's international bankruptcy, with all its legal brambles and gyring creditors, was about as inviting as a malarial swamp. "There were many contingent liabilities: a huge wrangle over the lease on the Third Avenue Macmillan building, environmental liabilities, executory contracts, potential claims in the UK or US bankruptcy cases," says Wilbur Ross. Paramount had a bit of an image problem to combat as well. The QVC/Viacom fight had undermined the Macmillan auctioneers' confidence in Paramount's ability to sign on the dotted line. "Macmillan was very worried that one side or the other would dispute the deal, file an injunction, somehow prevent the closing." And because Macmillan had a joint venture with McGraw-Hill in an area in which Paramount was well established—elementary and high school textbooks—Paramount knew that the specter of antitrust actions could not have escaped the notice of the auctioneers.

Given the unpredictable gusts of sentiment swirling around K-III, the auctioneers, and Paramount itself, Paramount decided its task was to focus attention on the bottom line. "Our strategy was to keep whacking away at the subjective factors so that the objective factor of price would win out," Ross said. Paramount did what it could to prove its commitment. "Both QVC and Viacom gave their informal approval to the deal. Macmillan wanted much more in the way of formal assurances. Paramount said it couldn't agree as a matter of principle. Paramount said it would give them a binding contract and that was it."

History still does not know what each bid actually turned out to be. Both Milbank's Goroff and JP Morgan's Donahue have long refused to say, citing the confidentiality order. "I can't tell you the spread of the bids because of the gag order," Donahue said. "Under pain of death. Or contempt in Judge Brozman's court. Which are probably one and the same."

Geraldine Fabrikant reported in the *New York Times* on November 11, 1993, that "according to several executives close to the auction, Paramount paid about $40 million more than the next highest bidder, Harcourt General, and perhaps as much as $100 million more than Pearson plc and K-III Communications Corporation." The latter's Beverly Chell said at the time, "We were led to believe that Harcourt was above us and Pearson below us. That's been the rumor." Wilbur Ross, then at Rothschild and advising Paramount, agrees with Chell's ranking but suggests that the bids were more closely clustered than public reports have long held. "We think the other bids were north of $500 million, but south of $550 million."[42]

Macmillan's protracted tour of the auction circuit reveals that the M&A world is a small one indeed. Paramount hired Rothschild, a former adviser to Maxwell. Pearson retained Lazard, which advised KKR in the first infamous Macmillan auction. Lazard and Rothschild had offices in the same Manhattan building on Sixth Avenue at the time. K-III came a-courtin' with its ex-Macmillanites and retained Simpson Thacher, which, besides representing Paramount in its own auction, was advising Paramount on bankruptcy issues in the Macmillan deal.

Henry Kravis was deprived of the counsel of his old friend, Simpson Thacher's Richard Beattie, who was busy advising Paramount in its own endless saga with QVC and Viacom. Simpson partner Gary Horowitz, who advised K-III on the Macmillan deal, says that a Chinese wall prevented any conflict of interest at his firm. Had Horowitz noticed his then-partner Joel Hoffman, Simpson's Paramount counsel on the deal, rushing about the halls any faster than usual on the day Macmillan bids were due? "Absolutely not. I actually see him rarely," Horowitz said at the time. "If he had been running through the halls, I probably would have assumed it was Viacom."[43]

There was one person whose name never appeared on-screen or in the credits of *Macmillan: The Sequel:* the auctioneer the first time around; the one who advised the very same Macmillan executives who later moved to K-III before he advised the Macmillan board of directors; the renowned investment banker accused by Delaware Supreme Court Justice Andrew G. T. Moore II of a maneuver that the justice said "violated every principle of fair dealing."

The missing banker's colleagues at the time refused to confirm or deny whether their firm had been retained by any party involved in the Macmillan auction. Louis Friedman would only say that his investment bank was "active in the media field." Another managing director at the same firm, Michael Biondi, would say only that none of the final four bidders had been a client. And who was this famous M&A mandarin who remained unseen? Bruce Wasserstein. Ned always refused to comment on Bruce: "I'd like to live in peace."[44] Ned died on New Year's Eve of 2010 at his Virginia Horse Farm.

* * *

SIX TIMES IN SEVEN MINUTES: THEY MAY TURN OUT TO BE THE LONGEST SEVEN MINUTES and the most challenging six interruptions of Barry Ostrager's life. Arguing on behalf of Paramount before Delaware's Justice Moore, Chief Justice Veasey, and Justice Holland, Ostrager was trying to show that the board of Paramount, advised by his Simpson partners, had been evenhanded, that the directors had been open with Barry Diller, that they had not stonewalled him to ensure that Sumner Redstone won the company.

It was painful to watch. And it was not just those in the actual courtroom who did so. By this time, Steve Brill had launched Court TV. The oral argument before the Delaware Supreme Court was thus seen by all of Wall Street as Justice Moore burst in with variants of the same pointed question: "Where is it shown in the record [that the Paramount board was fair to QVC]? . . . Please tell me, where is that found in the record? . . . Where is that in the record?" Ostrager did his best to parry these thrusts, but he could not say what many at Simpson Thacher to this day would still like to stand up and announce to the world. Simpson was "thrown under the bus," in the words of one veteran of the Paramount wars, by its own client. That would be the board of Paramount itself, and not only the Paramount directors but also a man who had started his career at Simpson Thacher, where he had been a colleague and partner of the board's law firm for 26 years: Paramount general counsel Donald Oresman.[45]

Donald Oresman had a long, intertwined history with Paramount, formerly known as Gulf + Western. It transformed his life, and he helped re-create the company. In the early seventies, Oresman, who had already been at Simpson for 16 years and a partner for half that time, was absorbed by management issues at the firm and was long considered a mere administrator. He had been given the distinctly unglamorous job, for example, of reorganizing the trusts-and-estates department. A decade later, in the early 1980s, however, he had become the chief outside lawyer for Gulf + Western, he was instrumental in the rise of Martin Davis to the chairmanship of the company, and he was filling Simpson's coffers with $3 million every year.[46]

Charles Bluhdorn, the legendary leader of Gulf + Western, had relied since the late 1950s on a lawyer named Joel Dolkart, a partner at Fried, Frank. In the mid-1960s, Simpson Thacher's Edwin Weisl, a senior corporate partner with such clients as Lehman Brothers and the Hearst Corporation, set his cap for Bluhdorn's ever-growing conglomerate. Bluhdorn was seen as an egomaniacal boor whom Fried, Frank partners refused to receive; Dolkart was similarly snubbed when he demanded to be made a name partner at the firm in return for all the work Gulf + Western generated. Bluhdorn was already pleased with Weisl's work on Gulf + Western's acquisition in 1966 of Paramount Pictures, and he was quite taken with Simpson's political clout, given Weisl's connections with the Johnson administration and New York political circles. Dolkart was also eager to move on. In 1967, Simpson Thacher offered him a partnership.[47]

Oresman, chiefly known then as Weisl's assistant, was examining the firm's books in the summer of 1974 and found some intriguing anomalies. After a secret investigation on his own that took three months, he unearthed an improvised explosive device in Dolkart's accounts: two fake bank accounts. Dolkart was charged with quietly embezzling from both Simpson and Fried, Frank a total of around $2 million over the previous four years. Leon Silverman, then a Fried, Frank partner, said at the time that Oresman, a former newspaper reporter, "did the sleuthing of a detective." Cyrus Vance, head of Simpson Thacher, when informed by Oresman, did the honorable thing as the head of the firm. He, accompanied by the sleuth, tendered to Bluhdorn the firm's resignation as counsel to Gulf + Western.[48]

Bluhdorn would have none of it. Instead, he anointed Oresman as his lead outside counsel, Weisl having died two years before the scandal. Dolkart was fired, and Oresman filed a complaint against him with the Manhattan district attorney. In 1976, Dolkart, with 50 counts of grand larceny and forgery lowering over him, retaliated. He went to the SEC and claimed that Gulf + Western was guilty of financial chicanery. The SEC launched itself into what would become a five-year investigation. Oresman brought in Arthur Liman as special counsel to Gulf + Western, Edward Bennett Williams as Bluhdorn's attorney, and Skadden's Joe Flom as counsel to the other company directors. Oresman led the team. Martin Davis was by now an executive vice president under Bluhdorn, responsible in part for the company's legal affairs. He famously refused to let the SEC's attack sidetrack the company's business and decreed that no legal work could start until the end of business hours at 5:00 p.m. Martin Davis said of Oresman when it was all over, "He broke his tail. He used to live in the office. I developed a lot of respect for him." So, it turned out, had Bluhdorn.[49]

The result of the SEC ordeal: complete exoneration of Bluhdorn and Gulf + Western, Dolkart's guilty plea of one count of forgery with no jail term, and the ascension of Donald Oresman as Bluhdorn's trusted

confidante with a seat on the board of directors. They might have seemed
an odd pair: Bluhdorn was an immigrant from Vienna who began his working life as a cotton trader. Oresman grew up on the Upper West Side as the
son of a rich lawyer. But they spoke the same gruff, demanding language.
And Oresman knew client management.[50]

He also knew how to manage the board of directors. When Bluhdorn
died of a heart attack at the age of 56 in February 1983, Oresman moved
quickly. He set up a board meeting two days after the funeral. There were
four candidates for CEO: David Judelson, already G+W's president, and
the press favorite; and three executive vice presidents, James Spiegel, Lawrence Levinson, and Martin Davis. Oresman counseled Bluhdorn's widow,
lobbied the other directors, and quickly put together a unanimous vote for
his own favorite, Martin Davis.[51]

Brian Burrough found Oresman in the throes of another battle at Paramount in February 1994. By this time, Oresman was the general counsel of
the company, with established access to the redoubtable Martin Davis, and
it was soon to go on the auction block:

> "We're like pigs in clover," laughs Oresman.... "Martin and I don't shock very
> easily—we've been around too long," he says laconically. "You have to under-
> stand, there are people like us who have no interest in the outcome but who
> revel in the process.... I'm interested in books. I'm interested in literature. I'm
> interested in birds." He whips a pair of binoculars around as a bird soars past.
> "Did I tell you I saw a peregrine falcon up here the other day?"[52]

The sale of Paramount looked like it would never happen, so long had
so many gentlemen callers pressed their suits. "If it were a movie, it would
be *Wall Street* as directed by Hitchcock," Brian Burrough wrote in his February 1994 article in *Vanity Fair,* which focuses on the confluence of events
leading up to the takeover, a piercing look at all those in the media business
who were stalking the last Hollywood studio. The late Martin Davis, the
Paramount chief who died just five years after the takeover, might be seen
as the Hitchcock of the piece, as Burrough may have been implying. For
years Davis held his company just out of reach of his eager industry rivals,
and then he plotted, bullied, and maneuvered to give Paramount to Redstone rather than Barry Diller, whom Davis disliked and distrusted. Just
after the sale, Davis said to Burrough, "This is the most complicated plot
you've ever heard."

Burrough describes that plot as, on one level, "the ultimate clash between New York and Los Angeles," with Davis as "the tough streetwise kid
from the Bronx" and Diller "the playful rich kid from Beverly Hills." With
Danny Thomas as a neighbor, Diller became one of the youngest studio
emperors in history at the age of 32, and launched ABC's *Movie of the Week,*

with friends who included David Geffen, Warren Beatty, and Calvin Klein. He and Davis did not get along, and Diller left to start the first television network at Fox in many years and thence, to the puzzlement of his world, on to QVC, a home shopping network of all things, in West Chester, Pennsylvania. Diller is now head of IAC, married to Diane von Furstenberg, and laird of a stunning headquarters on Manhattan's far West Side, designed by Frank Gehry. In the mid-1990s, Burrough writes, "Diller wanted nothing more than to legitimize his hype, and the test he soon set for himself was a full-throttle attempt to wrest Paramount from his old nemesis Marty Davis."[53]

Davis had a rough early life in poverty and family dysfunction, stealing copies of the *Daily News* and selling them at street corners for two pennies. He "grew up to be the most hated man in Hollywood," as Burrough puts it. He was known as the ultimate "suit," who watched with cold equanimity as Diller, Michael Eisner, and Jeffrey Katzenberg all fled Paramount. He had little to do with the L.A. artsy types at Morton's and Le Dome, Burrough says, and quotes a former aide's description of Davis as "just plain mean, a mean with a tiny, cruel heart."[54]

Sumner Redstone liked Marty Davis of the tiny, cruel heart: "Martin Davis did not exude warmth. He had a reputation as a screamer, and there were few people who had worked for him who did not view the experience as particularly pleasurable. But I had never seen that side of Martin, and we had great affection for each other."[55]

Paramount dazzled with its riches: a library bejeweled with 890 films that in the modern era alone included the *Godfather* series, *Star Trek, Beverly Hills Cop,* and *Indiana Jones;* such television shows as *Frasier, Cheers, Taxi, Laverne & Shirley;* theme parks, Madison Square Garden, the publishing houses of Macmillan, Simon & Schuster, Scribner, among others; the New York Rangers and the New York Knicks; co-ownership of USA Networks; and seven television stations.

As the owner of Viacom International, Sumner Redstone already controlled MTV, Nickelodeon, and Showtime/The Movie Channel, as well as five television stations, eight radio stations, and the syndication rights to *The Cosby Show* and *The Honeymooners.* He was tantalized by the possibilities of taking on the storied studio and its stable of media businesses. "The fit was indeed extraordinary," Redstone writes, with his typical exclamation marks. "Viacom possessed a vast array of outlets for Paramount products. We also possessed the growth engine of the entertainment industry, MTV Networks, while Paramount had a vast potential for crossover of Viacom products. Talk about shared opportunities! The acquisition of Paramount and the marriage of the Paramount studio, television operations and library to MTV Networks would allow me to realize my dream of creating the premier software-driven media company in the world."[56]

Sumner had long lusted after Paramount and, like so many others, had suffered a series of interrupted seductions by Davis for years. "*Years!*" as Redstone puts it in his autobiography. So when Robert Greenhill proposed to host Marty and Sumner at a private dining room at Morgan Stanley, Sumner expected little to come of it, this latest in a series of frustrating assignations with Davis, forever gripped by his own power. Nevertheless, Redstone and his protégé Philippe Dauman, who had just left Shearman & Sterling to join Viacom in February 1993, devised what they hoped might entice Davis out of his CEO man-cave once and for all. It worked. For years, Davis had been looking for a junior partner in a merger, proclaiming that he would remain monarch of all he surveyed. This time, at the dinner on April 20, 1993, at Robert Greenhill's invitation, Davis acknowledged for the first time that in the new empire he envisioned, he would have to abdicate and allow a new leader to ascend the throne. Redstone and Dauman began to see a deal taking shape.[57]

There were, in the end, two deals between Viacom and Paramount. The first they negotiated together between April 20 and September 12, when at a three-hour meeting the Paramount board unanimously approved a merger with Viacom at $69.14 per share. Then, on September 20, Barry Diller lobbed in a letter to Davis offering to buy Paramount at $80 per share, for a total of $9.5 billion. In October, he went to court, and, on November 24, Vice Chancellor Jack Jacobs took the Viacom deal apart and tossed it aside. On December 9, the Delaware Supreme Court agreed with him, adding its own vitriol for good measure. The first deal between Viacom and Paramount was officially dead. Simpson then decided that the best way to respond to the court rulings was for Paramount to auction itself, with victory to the bidder who offered the best deal to its shareholders.[58]

The court losses stung Simpson Thacher attorneys, as did the criticism that welled up around the firm from its peers in the M&A world. First, they, along with lawyers at QVC's law firm of Wachtell even before this fight, believed that the case law was on their side and that the Delaware courts had done unexpected backflips. Second, they felt, and still feel, deeply frustrated that they could not publicly reveal how their client had brushed off their tactical advice.

When Barry Diller made his bid at $9.5 billion, Paramount and Viacom thought that the parallels to a recent takeover would protect their friendly deal. In that fight, Paramount had taken the role that Diller played in this one, roaring in at the last minute with an offer for Time valued at $200 per share, a huge premium over the $126 at which Time's shares were then trading at nearly three times the $70-per-share value ascribed to Time's impending union with Warner. Just as QVC would later argue, Paramount maintained that the Time board had a duty to accept the best deal for its shareholders since it had put the company up for sale.

Both courts found ways to lecture their audience on the real meaning of the Revlon decisions of 1985, which required directors to get the best deal for stockholders when there is a sale of control of the company. A dichotomy emerged between cash and stock deals. If a buyer is paying cash, the argument ran, then there is a change of control. The shareholders walk away with money and own no part of the newly merged company. But if a buyer is paying with stock, then those who get paid with those shares are still able to participate in company profits and in the public markets, and there is essentially no change in control and therefore no duty to get the best price.

The Paramount decisions seemed to reiterate that cash deals are subject to Revlon and stock deals are not. Except, the courts said, when they are. The fact that Sumner Redstone would end up owning a supermajority of the stock of the new company seemed suddenly to be a "double super secret" exception. This would be a change of control, and Paramount was under a duty to get the best deal for its stockholders. Delaware found that Paramount had failed its duties to shareholders by placing huge protective barriers around its deal with Viacom, in the form of stock options and breakup fees, and stiff-arming QVC.[59]

These are all distinctions that only lawyers can love. The courts might well have been mesmerized by the big-screen story behind the legal niceties: the bad blood between Martin Davis and Barry Diller that had long been Greek in its intensity, Paramount's recent history as a sudden spoiler when it tried to thwart the friendly deal between Time and Warner, and Paramount's more ancient history as a steely-eyed vicious company under its previous name of Gulf + Western and its nickname of EnGulf + Devour. All this, when Barry Diller merely wanted to get a good look at the company's books and try to give Paramount shareholders more money. How could one argue with that? One needed to display a paper trail that would lead the courts to conclude that Paramount had not argued with that.

In this fight, unlike the board's election of Davis as CEO, two meetings of the directors would not be counted as Oresman successes. Simpson Thacher had been urging Oresman and Davis to protect their Viacom deal with ample evidence of the board's neutrality so that the law firm, if need be, could argue that Paramount's directors had been fair to both bidders out of concern for the welfare of their shareholders. The board could safely maintain that Viacom was the best alternative only if it could show that it had carefully considered QVC's offer and found it wanting.

Simpson Thacher prepared an appropriate paper trail, but Oresman and Davis went off course. In discovery, Paramount turned over "outlines" that Davis used to conduct at least two board meetings that drew particular fire from Delaware judges. These documents, which in his deposition Oresman said he prepared, are not lists of discussion points.

They read like scripts, written in conversational language, and evoke a carefully controlled forum that did not make the board look impartial in the least.

The October 24 meeting occurred just after QVC had filed suit in chancery court. At this meeting, Paramount agreed to let Viacom drop its original merger agreement and match QVC's tender offer. The target won significant additional concessions from Viacom, including a price increase of $1.3 billion and a fiduciary out, which would allow the Paramount board to terminate the Viacom deal if it believed a competing offer was better. Much of the rest of the September 12 deal remained intact.

At this gathering, the board was given less written information than usual, a fact that QVC would turn to its advantage. When the directors considered the original Viacom merger proposal in September, for example, they were given a "book," or written presentation from Lazard. At this October meeting, the directors were given a one-page sheet outlining the deal. Also, Lazard's fairness opinion on the new Viacom proposal was presented verbally, whereas for the original deal, the investment bank put its opinion in writing for the board.

In his deposition, Oresman was questioned about these omissions. "Given the substantial change in the form and substance of the transaction," asked Wachtell, Lipton's Michael Schwartz, "did you not consider it important that there be a written presentation from your financial adviser to the board?"

"No," Oresman answered. "I did not think it was important." This did not look good.[60]

Oral argument before Vice Chancellor Jack Jacobs was the very next day. Simpson Thacher argued to Oresman that it would be impossible in such a short time to prepare a thorough record to show the court. Before the meeting, Oresman sent all the directors a three-page memorandum titled "Conditions and Uncertainties of QVC's Offer," asserting that QVC didn't have much chance of lining up financing nor was it likely to get the antitrust clearance it needed to buy Paramount. The directors duly voted down the QVC offer.

The next day, in a preview of his performance before the state supreme court, Herbert Wachtell announced dramatically to Vice Chancellor Jacobs that on the very day that the board rejected his client's offer, QVC had won final clearance from Washington's antitrust authorities to buy its target. He also insisted that financing would not be a problem and presented affidavits from investment banks to support his contention. Then he announced that QVC's revised offer was worth $1.3 billion more than Viacom's $9.5 billion bid.

Vice Chancellor Jacobs dismantled the Paramount/Viacom merger, and on appeal to the state supreme court, Paramount and Viacom fared even worse. In its written opinion, Justice Moore, Chief Justice Veasey, and Justice Holland went even further than their earlier order from the bench or the lower court ruling they upheld. The justices criticized Paramount's directors for the November 15 meeting. "When Paramount directors met on November 15 to consider QVC's increased tender offer, they remained prisoners of their own misconceptions and missed opportunities to eliminate the restrictions they had imposed on themselves," the high court declared. "Yet it was not 'too late' to reconsider negotiating with QVC. . . . Nevertheless, the Paramount directors remained paralyzed by their uninformed belief that the QVC offer was 'illusory.' This final opportunity to negotiate on the stockholders' behalf and to fulfill their obligation to seek the best value reasonably available was thereby squandered."[61]

M&A people at the time criticized Simpson Thacher for allowing the board to look both biased and ignorant. "The board looked stupid and its counsel looked stupid," was a typical comment by one senior investment banker soon after the debacle. But a different consensus has emerged over time in discussions with M&A specialists, members of the Paramount board, Viacom's chairman, the company's general counsel, former Paramount executives, advisers to all sides, law professors, proxy solicitors, arbitrageurs, and industry analysts: Simpson was too harshly criticized. Its legal advice was sound. Its tactical advice was rejected or ignored by Paramount's executives. The board's choice of Viacom was an intelligent decision, vindicated in the end when QVC fell away.

There is no prominent lawyer who doesn't understand that sometimes you have a client who doesn't listen. "Simpson talked until they were blue in the face about one thing and another," says one adviser on the deal. "Oresman did whatever the hell he wanted. Oresman had done dozens of transactions for Paramount. He didn't necessarily think he needed lots of advice from an outside law firm."[62] What do you do as a lawyer when you have a client like that? You stand up and take the heat, like Barry Ostrager did before the Delaware Supreme Court.

There was one moment of secret vindication for Simpson Thacher. Soon after the Delaware rulings, Donald Oresman came to the offices of Simpson Thacher, where he had spent the first 26 years of his career. In a speech to the senior members of the litigation and corporate departments, he acknowledged all their hard work and said he understood that they were dealing with an irascible and demanding client, namely him. In his own way, Oresman was thanking his lawyers for falling on their swords.

* * *

WITHIN A WEEK OF THE DELAWARE SUPREME COURT'S DECEMBER 10 ATTACK ON Paramount's first merger agreement with Viacom, an auction in some form was inevitable. Two Simpson lawyers were assigned the task of designing the rules for the sale.

Viacom and QVC were both offering what is known as a two-tiered bid. Such offers can often spark a stampede of sellers. Shareholders who sell into the front end, as it is known, get cash. Those who sell into the back end get stock or securities, which are usually less desirable than actual money. Once the bidder wins the company by getting 50.1 percent of the stock, all others who want to sell are forced to the back end. A typical offer subject to federal tender offer rules must be kept open a minimum of 20 business days and an additional 10 business days if that offer is raised or changed. The offer that closes first will often win a majority of stockholder support even if it is worth slightly less than its rival. As Dennis Block explained during the Paramount battle, "If a bid is one dollar less, but closes a day earlier, there would be a strong temptation to take that bid. You don't want to risk being part of the losing offer and getting only the stock, which is harder to value, less liquid, and often not worth as much as the cash portion."[63]

Under the scorching lights of public and court scrutiny, John Finley, now the general counsel at Blackstone, sat down with his colleague Alan Klein, now a star partner and member of Simpson's executive committee, for several all-nighters. They came up with a procedure designed to reassert target control over what had become a chaotic scramble for the hearts and votes of the shareholders and to make sure those shareholders were completely free to choose between the two rival bids so that no further court criticism would have to be endured. The system they created was designed to move the two offers along in tandem and to eliminate all advantages of timing and all sense of a stampede.

First, they decided that there would be no deadline for final bids. The bidding would go on—and on and on—if necessary until one bidder finally exhausted the other. An auction typically will last for a fixed period, with final bids required at the very end, and a drop-dead date at which point the winner is announced. Not this one. A new round of bids would be due December 20. The board would then decide which offer it would recommend to shareholders. That bidder would sign a merger agreement with Paramount, and the target would agree to lift its pill should that tender offer win the required majority of shares over the ten business days it would remain open. If the bidder with the lower offer then decided to sweeten its bid, both offers would be extended for ten more business days. As soon as one bidder won the support of 50.1 percent of the shareholders, the other side would concede defeat and withdraw its offer.

Both QVC and Viacom also agreed that neither would increase its bid just to trigger an automatic extension. If one party appeared on the verge of winning 50.1 percent, its rival could conceivably announce a small increase in its offer, force an extension of both bids for another ten days, and deprive the first bidder of victory just before the finish line. To trigger an extension, therefore, the rules decreed that a bidder would have to increase the cash portion of its bid by a minimum of $460 million.[64]

The lawyers also came up with a quick way to embody these agreements on paper and activate the appropriate contracts depending on who had the highest bid at any stage in the auction. The bidding rules were incorporated into a merger agreement, which both sides approved in advance of the auction. There was also a separate auction rules contract. Each time one bidder topped the other, the merger agreement would be canceled with the lower bidder, and the auction rules would reignite. This would go on for as long as needed. "They wanted an auction," says Alan Klein, "so we gave them an *auction*."

John Finley and Alan Klein could have no idea which of the two bidders would be willing to commit the most money or which would be the most persistent. "We just stood back and let them go at each other," Alan says, looking back today. "The system made it possible for the best offer to win." John Wilcox, then a specialist in shareholder votes as head of proxy solicitation firm Georgeson & Company Inc., retained by Viacom, still admires the plan: "It was a very complicated time, with two complicated offers, and this procedure made order out of chaos."

Not all was as orderly as it might have been. At one point, for example, Barry Diller swept into the offices of Simpson Thacher with great flourish, those involved say, to sign the merger agreement with Paramount, assuming his was the highest bid. But Viacom bid again, and the process rolled forward once more. Back in October, QVC had shown similar overconfidence. The home-shopping channel announced plans for a two-tiered bid on October 21, but it did not formally launch the tender offer until October 27. By that time, Viacom had formally started its offer two days earlier on October 25. This meant that the Viacom offer would expire first and most likely win. This was a misstep. "The delay in launching the offer was premised on the belief that Viacom was just going to give up," one investment banker recalls. "It was not the cleverest thing to do. It was a potential disaster."[65]

The deadline for the first round of bids under the new auction rules was December 20. On that day, QVC submitted a bid of $92 per share, surpassing Viacom's existing offer. Two days later, Paramount duly signed the merger agreement with Diller's company. Viacom now had until January 7 to top QVC. To do so, to pay any more money, Redstone needed Blockbuster.

Now it was Sumner Redstone's turn to have a heart-stopping moment. The talks with Blockbuster, essential to Viacom's ability to make ever-higher bids for Paramount, collapsed just before Christmas. Since Viacom planned to use its own nonvoting stock to buy Wayne Huizenga's Fort Lauderdale–based video-rental giant, Blockbuster wanted protection from any drop in the value of that stock. Without such a deferred collar, Huizenga said there would be no deal. Redstone hated the idea. He refused to give Wayne a stock-price guarantee for Blockbuster shareholders. Exhausted by the interminable struggle for Paramount, angry at the high price he was contemplating having to pay for his prize, humiliated by this time by the Delaware courts, bitter about his treatment in the press, and now frustrated in his talks with Huizenga and the Blockbuster team of advisers, Redstone all but walked away. "He had had it," recalled one adviser close to the chairman. He had no interest in the sort of deferred collar that Huizenga wanted so intensely. "I hate collars," Redstone told his demanding erstwhile ally. "Forget about it."[66]

After the negotiations fell apart, the Viacom team took a break between Christmas and New Year's. Redstone went to the West Coast. Viacom CEO and president Frank Biondi went to his place in Scottsdale, Arizona. Smith Barney Shearson chief Robert Greenhill, Viacom's investment banker, went skiing in Utah. Shearman & Sterling's Steve Volk, Viacom's main outside lawyer, went to Lake Tahoe.[67]

The deadline approached inexorably. Friday, January 7, 1994, was days away. Of the rival bids, Barry Diller's offer to buy shares for $90 each was getting more support than Viacom's $85. If QVC's offer were to close by the end of the day on Friday with the support of 50.1 percent of Paramount's shareholders, then Viacom's offer would automatically dissolve, under the terms of the auction rules. Only if Viacom could raise its own bid by that deadline would the clock stop and be reset for another ten days, giving Viacom another chance. Meanwhile, QVC's supporters now included Comcast, Condé Nast, BellSouth, Nynex, and John Malone and his Telecommunications Inc., a frightening show of strength.

After the Christmas break, the Viacom people returned to the frozen East and tried furiously to reach an agreement with Blockbuster in time to make another lunge for Paramount. "We worked over seventy-two hours straight," recalled Blockbuster assistant general counsel Adam Philips, now a partner at the Palo Alto office of Kirkland & Ellis. "We were all at Shearman & Sterling's office, and no one had any sleep."[68]

Finally, Redstone decided he could live with the deferred collar, usually known as a contingent value right (CVR), and agreed to issue one for each outstanding Blockbuster share purchased. The mechanism was rechristened a variable common right (VCR) as a pun on the Blockbuster video-rental business. By whatever name, the principle is the same: If Viacom's stock, which it was using to buy Blockbuster shares, dropped in value a year after the closing, then Viacom would make up the difference by giving the former Blockbuster shareholders more Viacom stock.

With his VCR in hand, Wayne signed up the deal with Sumner, the $8.4 billion sale of Blockbuster to Viacom. The Huizenga team also committed itself to buy $1.25 billion worth of Viacom stock, contingent on Viacom's success in the Paramount battle, not on the closing of Blockbuster's merger with Viacom. Viacom had made a two-tiered offer to Paramount shareholders. It would pay cash for the first 50.1 percent of the shareholders who agreed to sell their stock to Viacom, and everybody else would be paid with Viacom shares. In effect, Blockbuster undertook to purchase shares from the back end of Viacom's tender offer for Paramount, enabling Redstone to apply that money to the cash portion of his bid, Shearman & Sterling's Stephen Volk explained.[69]

Viacom agreed that one year after its deal with Blockbuster it would determine the highest average closing price of its stock over any 30 consecutive business days during the final three months before the first anniversary of the closing. If that value were to be between zero and $35.99, then the VCR holders would get .13829 of a Viacom share for every VCR owned. If the average price were to be between $36 and $52, they would get .05929 of one Viacom share; and if the average trading price were to exceed $52, they would get nothing.

First, however, documents had to be drawn up and signed, and SEC filings had to be prepared and electronically filed in Washington. Everything had to be done by 3:00 p.m. Friday, January 7, two hours before the QVC deadline, so that the papers could be placed on the SEC's computer system. QVC's $92-per-share offer of December 20 was the highest bid on the table. With hours to spare before the QVC tender was set to close—and it looked extremely likely that Barry Diller would have a majority of Paramount stock in hand when its offer expired—Viacom announced the Blockbuster merger and a new bid for Paramount. It raised the cash portion of its tender offer from $85 to $105, moving to the front end a total of $1.6 billion from the package of securities at the so-called back end.[70]

Herbert Wachtell, Barry Diller's lawyer, was angry. He argued that Viacom's latest bid was made in bad faith because it was designed merely to win an extension of both offers and threatened to take Viacom to court. He accused Redstone's team of raising its offer just to force an extension of the bids and get more time to corral the shareholders he needed. The Paramount side did not take the protests seriously. Viacom had just committed itself to a multibillon-dollar merger with Blockbuster just so it could raise its bid for Paramount. "Both Blockbuster and Viacom would have to be demented to do that just to announce some illusory increase in an offer," one Paramount adviser scoffed.

In the end, QVC was hoist on its own petard. Having demanded an auction so that ostensibly Paramount shareholders could get the highest price, they did not realize that Viacom would just keep coming at them and coming at them with higher bids. Barry Diller had two smashing victories in his court battles, but he lost the war. "It was a classic example of that old saw," says one Paramount adviser. Says another, "We outfoxed them."

Redstone writes of the final moments before the January 7 deadline. Interestingly, as he turns to the little emperor for inspiration, he makes no mention whatsoever of his capitulation and the magically transformative VCR:

> Napoleon Bonaparte said, "An army travels on its stomach." He understood that to win a war you need a steady supply of resources. We were in an all-out war for Paramount and we were running a wartime operation. The price had gotten so steep that both sides were now scrambling for cash. The other side had begun with Comcast and TCI and when Malone was forced out, they'd brought in Cox and Advance and the very deep pockets of BellSouth. We had begun with our own resources and brought in NYNEX and Blockbuster. Diller had his troops in order, he had ample supplies and a solid pipeline. We were about tapped out. If we could raise no more money to make another bid by January 7, 1994, we were dead. . . . I convened a meeting at my apartment which included Blockbuster's Wayne Huizenga and Steve Berrard, NYNEX's Fred Salerno and CEO and Chairman Bill Ferguson, Frank Biondi and Philippe. I told our investors, "The future course of this battle is up to you. . . ." We needed another $600 million.
>
> Bill Ferguson said he would support whatever we decided to do but that NYNEX's board could not invest more cash in our bid. This was a surprise; they were the ones with deep pockets. Huizenga, who had been sitting and listening quietly, was considerably more impassioned. He stood up to speak.
>
> "We're on the brink of greatness here," he said heatedly. . . . We have gone this far and we should do everything we can do to prevail. These opportunities come rarely in this life and we cannot let it slip away. We must dare to be great!"
>
> I just about cheered.[71]

The market was unimpressed. Stephen Volk, at the time a partner at Shearman & Sterling and an adviser to Viacom, who has gone on to be chairman of Credit Suisse First Boston and now a senior executive at Citigroup, was chagrined at the response. "It was a stunning move," he said, "but in the eyes of the market, it just wasn't enough."[72] It was time for Sumner to do for Paramount what he had done for Blockbuster. On January 18, 1994, he finally gave in. On February 1, after submitting Viacom's final bid one minute before the 5:00 p.m. deadline, Shearman & Sterling lawyers went to the Manhattan steakhouse Smith & Wollensky to celebrate their victory over QVC in the long fight for Paramount. Their *victory?*[73]

Neither side's tender offer was set to close for two more weeks. With each bid a complicated mixture of cash and stock, what assurance could the lawyers have had that the market would find either of the two rival offers obviously superior to the other? "We believed we were ahead. Absent a blow-out bid from QVC, we felt we would stay ahead," said Stephen Volk, then at Shearman & Sterling, counsel to Viacom.[74]

A large measure of Shearman & Sterling's somewhat premature confidence at their celebration that wintry Tuesday night stemmed from the CVR, the rare stock-price guarantee that had suddenly been added to their bid for Paramount. Redstone had long refused to include any device that would force him as the buyer to pay more if his stock dropped. Once he gave in to Wayne Huizenga's demands for this sort of protection, however, Redstone finally agreed on January 18, 1994, to give Paramount's stockholders similar protection. "This was one of the tactical turning points of the whole Paramount battle," Stephen Volk maintained.[75] Viacom owes its $10 billion victory in large part to the stock-price guarantees that Redstone, with much bad temper and grave reluctance, at last gave to both his ally's shareholders and those of his target.

Diller, like Redstone, was not a big fan of the CVR and regularly and vehemently rejected the idea. One arbitrageur with a substantial stake in Paramount stock remembers the argument well. "We all told Diller over and over again to put a CVR into his bid. He just kept saying it was a stupid idea."[76] Diller, according to his advisers, said using such a device was tantamount to inserting a time bomb in his own company. Although QVC could have retained the right to pay off the CVRs in stock rather than cash, as Viacom did, such a move could conceivably dilute existing stockholders and flatten the stock price.

Both QVC and Viacom offered a mixture of cash and their own stock to Paramount shareholders. Whichever bidder finally acquired Paramount was widely expected to see its stock price drop because of the debt that the victor would be taking on and the scary prospect of digesting its huge prey. Through the five-month struggle for Paramount, the market value of bidders' shares rose and fell in inverse proportion to the waxing and waning of their perceived success on the battlefield.

On January 21, Paramount terminated its merger agreement with QVC and linked arms with Viacom. Still, the fight was not yet over. The two tender offers were set to expire on February 1, so Viacom and QVC had one last chance to increase their bids. Across the hushed battlefield, QVC made a secret offer to withdraw its bid if Viacom would pay QVC $50 million to cover the expenses the home-shopping network had incurred in the fight. Viacom refused and held its breath. Then, after QVC filed an increase to its offer on February 1 of $104 per share for 50.1 percent, Viacom responded with an improved back end and a new offer of $107 a share for 50.1 percent. A week later, on February 8, Diller hinted at a meeting at Allen & Co. Inc., his investment bankers, that his ally BellSouth might agree to buy QVC stock to shore up its price after the bid. This would have achieved the same effect as the CVR he had so often disparaged. Nothing came of it.[77]

Other last-minute game changers loomed. What if neither bidder had a clear majority by the time the bids expired? Alan Klein and John Finley had included a ten-day pour-over period, designed to protect shareholders who chose the loser from being barred from selling their stock to the winner. But might shareholders simply wait to tender to either side until those ten days had elapsed? Nervous Simpson lawyers scrambled to get the rivals to agree to award victory to whichever one of them first hit 40 percent, but their efforts were spurned by each. On February 13, QVC announced that it would not be altering its bid, sealing the outcome of the contest.

On the evening of February 14, Sumner and his closest advisers went to 21, the Manhattan club with the famous array of miniature iron jockeys along its front balcony. At 8:30 p.m., a telephone was brought to the table. Viacom's proxy solicitor was on the line. They had crossed the 50 percent finish line. They would own Viacom as long as they could come up with the $9.7 billion by the closing date.

The next day, Barry Diller would issue his valedictory "They won. We lost. Next." Sumner Redstone's toast at the moment of victory the night before was equally simple. He raised his glass and said, "Here's to us who won."[78]

*   *   *

AMY CHOZICK OF THE *NEW YORK TIMES* OPENS HER FEATURE ON THE VIACOM OF 2012 with a celebration on the Hollywood lot of Paramount Pictures. It is the studio's one hundredth birthday[79]:

> Roughly 100 have gathered on this June day on the Hollywood lot of Paramount Pictures to celebrate the studio's centennial. . . . Mr. Redstone, lord of the Viacom empire, enters slowly. He is 89, and on this day so heavy with Hollywood history, it is remarkable to think that when he was born Sumner Rothstein to a modest family in Boston, the first feature talkie, "The Jazz Singer," hadn't been made. He wears a dark suit and flashy tie and looks frail but bursting with accomplishment. At his side is Philippe P. Dauman, 58, his figurative heir and the dauphin of Viacom—"the son Sumner wishes he had," as one executive close to the company puts it. This is the man who would be Redstone. It is an emotional moment for two men not known for displays of emotion, at least not the warm, teary kind. Two decades ago, in an epic struggle for control of Paramount, Mr. Redstone and Mr. Dauman beat back A-listers like Barry Diller and John C. Malone and walked away with their prize. Mr. Dauman tells the crowd that Mr. Redstone "transformed my life." He goes on: "We shed a lot of blood, sweat and tears in a very long process."
>
> Then, he echoes a toast Mr. Redstone gave when the $9.75 billion takeover of Paramount was sealed: "Here's to us who won."

CHAPTER EIGHTEEN
ICARUS FALLING

Elizabeth picked up her telephone. She frowned. She felt cold. The goose bumps crawled up her arms as she hung up. It was the compliance department at Merrill Lynch. Could she come down immediately? She was on the forty-ninth floor at One Liberty Plaza with a view of the harbor and Liberty and Ellis Islands. The lightless lower floor, where the enforcers lived, stared straight into another building. She faced two men. One she remembers as Steve, also known as the door rattler, since his job was to check to make sure the doors were locked around the office at the end of each day. The other was a staff lawyer. He began asking her questions about Brian Campbell. They seemed to accept what she said, and she was allowed to get back to work. "It was terrifying," she remembers. "Absolutely terrifying."[1]

It got worse. The next day, she was called down again. There was a speaker box on the table out of which emanated a disembodied voice that reminded her of *Charlie's Angels,* only it wasn't. It was the voice of Gary Lynch, the new head of enforcement at the SEC. How well did she know Brian? Were they boyfriend and girlfriend? They were the same age, weren't they? Wouldn't it be natural to be friends? Was there any romantic connection? Why had she been writing tickets for Brian Campbell, who had just left for Smith Barney? She said she had done it as a favor. He had told her he was closing out his positions and could use some help, as he was swamped at his new job. She didn't know Brian very well. She didn't find him very interesting. She said he was known as a dork. Besides, she was engaged.

They brought in Ken, her fiancé, and began asking him similar questions. No, we are not friends with Brian. I think he's an asshole. He flirts with my fiancée. He punches stuff onto her Quotron, and she buys the stocks. She gives me the info. I do the same thing. The next day there's a merger. It's piggybacking, for crissake, and I happen to know it's not illegal.

No, we don't know where he gets all this. Everybody's got a tip. Everybody knows somebody who knows somebody. It's all rumors all the time. What do you think goes on around here? There are strippers in the office, for fuck's sake. Do we need a lawyer?[2]

Ken and Elizabeth did get a lawyer, the head of the securities practice at LeBoeuf Lamb, which later merged with Dewey and went belly-up in the spring of 2012. He told both of them that they had done nothing wrong. You don't have inside information. You know nothing. Remember. You're both idiots. So you don't have to worry. The lawyer was intrigued. What was the SEC up to?

Brian Campbell sounded edgy on the telephone. His calls grew rapidly more desperate. He started calling Elizabeth at home. He wanted her to send him research reports on a range of stocks. He wanted to show that his buys had been based on official recommendations from Merrill Lynch. Why do you need that stuff?, she asked. There's been this letter from Caracas. I can't go into it. Can you do this for me? I'm begging you. Brian, you can't call here again. Ever. Good-bye.[3]

*   *   *

THE AWKWARD MOMENT WAS APPROACHING. THE EX-LAWYER AND HIS NEW COLLEAGUES were putting together a deal in 1995 for their publishing company, and the hour was getting late, although nowhere near as late as he had once been used to working as an M&A partner not so very long ago, when he was routinely at his desk well past midnight. This time, in his first week at his new job, there was an unavoidable reason he could not stay past a certain hour, but if the group decided to quit for the night, he might not have to bring it up. Finally, however, at 10:30 p.m., he told the team that he would have to leave. There were puzzled looks.

Ilan Reich then told them that he had to be back in his bed at the Project Return Halfway House off Times Square before 11:00 p.m. or he might face a return to prison. No one knew what to say.[4]

Eight years before, Ilan was living as a convicted felon at the Federal Correctional Institution in Danbury, Connecticut, a minimum-security prison. As a partner at one of the most respected and frenzied M&A practices in the world, a firm renowned as a font of innovation and sought after by the country's most powerful corporations, Ilan was accustomed to days filled to the second with conference calls, SEC filings, heated negotiations, and serial deadlines. "I never thought of myself as overworked," he would say later. "I loved what I did." At Danbury, for the first time since he could remember, he had time on his hands.[5]

In December 1995, Ilan agreed to talk about his prison time. He was just into his 40s. He no longer looked like a nineteenth-century tragedian or a wide-eyed Coptic saint, having lost the haunted, hollow-cheeked look that dogged him at the height of his turmoil. His phone rang regularly, and he treated his secretary with deference as he told her to take all his messages. He spoke confidently, as he does to this day, glibly, unstoppably, looking directly, unapologetically at his listener. His tie was loose, his cuffs rolled up, and he draped himself in his chair limply, elegantly, as he looked back on his then-more-recent incarceration.

On March 27, 1987, Ilan's first day at Danbury, he found himself in the midst of what he calls a small town—some 200 inmates, many in for drug-related offenses, held in a 300-acre camp that is part of a larger prison but that is left alone for the inmates basically to run under the supervision of one guard. It was a place ruled by elaborate politeness, to avoid the kind of trouble that would mean swift dispatch to a stricter prison. It would seem to be a rigorous academy for those who do not find social cues and nonverbal communication easy to perceive or interpret.

The population as a whole divided itself along ethnic lines, with Italians, Irish, Jews, and African Americans forming their own cohesive support groups. Smuggling was rampant, organized by those lucky enough to secure assignments as drivers, who deposited freed prisoners at the town bus station, rented videos, and made deliveries. "No one was allowed cash," Ilan recalls, "but somehow these guys were bringing in bagels and lox, Chinese meals, and every sort of contraband imaginable." At the top of the social hierarchy were "the Mafia types," and on the lowest rung was the untouchable caste of alleged informers.[6] There were no locks, very few rules, and only one outbreak of violence. A "wiseguy," in the more innocent meaning of the word, insulted Michael Jordan during a televised Bulls game and "basically got the shit beat out of him," Ilan recalled.[7]

Ilan was assigned the task of teaching English to fellow inmates. His students were uninterested, so he would let them fill the time as they liked, as long as they remained in the classroom. When prison officials found out, he was reassigned to the grounds crew. This was quite fun. One could drive a tractor, enjoy the outdoors, and "play with power tools," Ilan says. He also did time in the kitchen, although he never rose to the rank of cook. Ilan read an average of two works of fiction per week and played hours of chess at night.

Time is measured differently in prison, he found. Inmates who face sentences of one year tend to block out time in months; those who are in for five years think in terms of seasons of the year. "You can't count every day or you'd be too miserable," Ilan says. "You can't wake up and think, 'I've got two thousand more days.' That's too big a number." Also, each inmate finds another who has a more onerous sentence and comforts himself in comparison. "They would say, 'I couldn't stay in here one day past my five years. Not one day. And look at that guy—he's in for nine.'"[8]

Prison can actually improve one's health, Ilan says. A fellow inmate, convicted of running an illegal pornography business, arrived with extremely high blood pressure. Freed from the stress of his work, he would take long walks on the grounds every day. Within weeks, his doctor was able to take him off his blood pressure medicine and pronounce him more fit than he had been in 30 years.

One of the greatest hardships for Ilan was the fact that his wife was in effect serving time as well, raising three young children alone, driving to the prison every Saturday or Sunday, returning home to Manhattan at nightfall, bundling the three tired toddlers out of the car and into a dark and empty house. "There's so little you can do," he says. "You can't solve anything for the other person. You can't be there with them as a fellow adult. You can't *help*."[9]

For Ilan's wife, Diane, it all began at Mount Sinai. The hospital, founded in 1855 as The Jews' Hospital in the City of New York, then only the second Jewish hospital in the country, is a favorite charity among the upper strata of the M&A crowd and a beloved institution across American Jewry. On the night of May 12, 1986, Ilan and Diane went to the latest fund-raiser for the hospital at the Waldorf Astoria on Park Avenue. It was black-tie. Many in the world of M&A were there. One person who would have fit right in and had planned on attending was notably missing. That afternoon, Dennis Levine had been arrested for insider trading, and the SEC filed a $12.6 million lawsuit against him. Brian Campbell had led the authorities to Bernie Meier at Bank Leu in the Bahamas, and thence to Dennis, and on to the likes of Marty Siegel, Ivan Boesky, and Mike Milken himself. When Diane saw Ilan's face that night, while the gossip about Dennis Levine swirled through the crowd, Diane for the first time suspected that her husband had a secret.[10]

On July 8, 1986, the SEC issued a subpoena, demanding that the firm of Wachtell, Lipton disgorge volumes of its own records and those of a partner, Ilan Reich, including all of his personal records, bank accounts, travel and expense vouchers, and telephone logs for the past six years. On the afternoon of that July day, Ilan went to Larry Lederman's office. Larry remembers his first question to Ilan and the answer: "What will the records show?" "Nothing." "Do you have anything to worry about?" Then, Lederman paused to look at his young colleague:

> In the strong afternoon light his prematurely gray hair looked almost white and his skin glowed the way it would with a lamp behind it, pink and luminous, nearly baring his finely wrought bone structure. Everything about him was at rest: even his long, lean fingers, usually curled around a pencil, were relaxed. Sitting comfortably in a slouched position, one leg slung over the arm of his chair, he seemed at total peace with himself. As I observed him, he leaned forward and drank slowly from the can of soda he held, his eyes finding mine.[11]

On a business trip to Los Angeles, driving along the coast, a week or so later, Ilan was tempted by a cliff. "A sharp right" was all it would take. He felt trapped. His death would solve everything. He drove aimlessly all day and gradually abandoned thoughts of suicide.

Ilan was a young god of M&A, a surrogate son to Marty Lipton himself: Daedalus and Icarus, the father providing the son with his wings, and the son flying too high and too fast to save himself. At a time when Wachtell's partners were generating an average revenue of $715,000 a year, Ilan had been made a member of the elect a year before his time on the first day of 1985, just as he was turning 30 years old. He flourished in tandem with the multifoliate explosive blossoming of M&A in that year of years. Ilan had found what so few in life ever do: a vocation that was also his avocation, a way to earn a living that would also fulfill his life. He had, as the saying goes, everything to live for.

He stood a good chance of escaping notice. He had done so little, and he could deny all. On the flight back, he made a list on a yellow pad. He could not think of a single "external fact," as he put it, that would implicate him in what would become the largest insider-trading scandal in contemporary history, stretching from low-level employees such as Brian Campbell to the bankruptcy of Drexel itself.

Sporadically, between 1980 and 1984, Ilan succumbed to the blandishments of Dennis Levine and gave him inside information on takeovers in time for Levine to profit from the surge in stock prices that can accompany the announcement of a fight for corporate control. The virtually friendless Ilan had found the obsequious Levine irresistibly seductive. When Levine suggested lunch after a meeting over a conference table, for example, it was the first time anyone had ever done so, as many of his colleagues found Ilan distant and supercilious. Levine, in contrast, saw the loneliness, and he trained all his con-man's skills on satisfying or titillating his target's unmet needs: the need for a friend, the competitive urge to provide better information to his new buddy than other sources did, the need to be appreciated and understood, admired and listened to, the need to be loved.

The conspiratorial confidences and sudden friendship turned Ilan's head. He began revealing the details of pending merger deals to Levine before they became public. Levine and his cohorts would then buy stock in those companies just before the share prices rose, when plans for a takeover became public. They would meet for lunch, or in Central Park, or talk on pay telephones on street corners. Appalled at himself, however, Ilan began giving Levin false information to devalue himself in Levine's eyes. He began canceling meetings at the last minute. He would pull out of the conspiracy, only to fall back into it once gain. Finally, he withdrew entirely, hoping that the episode would never come to light.[12]

Ilan had given Levine tips on 12 deals, spread over several years. He had taken no money, although Levine had earmarked $300,000 as Ilan's share of the profits. There was no paper trail. There was no bank account. There were no records of expenses or deposits. No one knew anything about his involvement except Levine. He was isolated from the rest of the saturnine rings of the conspiracy. He loved his life, his children, his wife. He would get through this.[13]

On July 14, 1986, two months after Levine's arrest, Ilan's life changed forever on that Bastille Day. At about ten in the morning, one of his partners, Lawrence Pedowitz, called Ilan and asked him to come by. Martin had clerked for Justice William Brennan Jr. and had left Wachtell to run the Southern District of New York's criminal division before returning to Wachtell in 1984. When Ilan got to Pedowitz's office, they walked over to a conference room. There, Ilan faced the three other partners chosen by the firm to deal with the crisis: Herbert Wachtell, Allan Martin, and Bernard Nussbaum.

For six hours, Ilan did not leave the room. He ate noting. He denied everything. He took refuge in his legal pad. As the team leader for a takeover, the fight for NL Industries, Ilan was still indispensable. The Truth Squad funneled information to him, and he worked it as the maestro he was, bringing the deal to the required crescendo from his interrogation room. "Sitting in the conference room, Ilan tore off the pages of doodles that were the product of his nervous energy, and on a clean sheet of paper tried to calculate whether he was caught," Larry Lederman recalls. There was still no sure sign of his unmasking. He worked through his checklist on the legal pad for 45 minutes. For all that time, the partners watched in unbroken silence."[14]

At last, exhausted, Ilan confessed in a series of sobbing contractions. He told his partners that he had considered killing himself, that he hated his life, that he had always envied his older brother, that he was all but estranged from his parents, that his marriage was crumbling. Robert Morvillo, Ilan's chosen counsel who had arrived during the conference room ordeal, said later that he had never seen anyone so distraught. One of those present remembered the ordeal as tantamount to the unraveling of a personality. Ilan calls it "a total shattering of one's existence." His lawyer said he should be on a suicide watch. That night, at around 9:00 p.m., Ilan walked out of the offices of Wachtell, Lipton for the last time, carrying nothing.[15]

Meanwhile, Marty Lipton had called Larry Lederman at home earlier in the evening to relay the news of Ilan's confession. "Lipton was shaken," Lederman writes, "and told me that Ilan had apologized to him and to me, recognizing that he'd hurt us and hadn't meant to do so. Lipton told me that Larry Pedowitz was also concerned about Ilan committing suicide and that Ilan would stay at Pedowitz's home for the evening. Ilan, he said, wanted to speak to me and would call me. When I hung up the phone, I cried."[16]

On January 23, 1987, Ilan was sentenced on two counts of an indictment charging him with securities fraud, insider trading, and mail fraud. Ilan admitted misappropriating nonpublic, material, and confidential information in connection with the purchase and sale of the stock of G. D. Searle & Co. and passing this information to Levine, who used it to trade in stock. Ilan also admitted telling Levine that one of Wachtell's clients was planning a bid for SFN Companies, which allowed Levine to make a profit of $129,316.[17]

No one felt vindicated or pleased with any of this, including Judge Robert Sweet as he delivered the sentence. Thirty-two of Ilan's friends, former partners, and clients wrote letters to the court, pleading for leniency. Ilan's rabbi wrote to the judge, as did his mother, his wife, his mother-in-law, and, interestingly, Alan Elton, vice president and general counsel of Uniroyal, Inc., who had lived through Carl Icahn's greenmail of his company with Ilan's help. Marty Lipton also joined in the appeal to the judge: "The flaw in Ilan that has brought him disgrace and destroyed his career is not something I understand. I do know, however, that there is much goodness and talent in Ilan. If he is given a chance promptly to pick up the pieces of his life, I believe he can build something much, much better."[18]

The judge sentenced him to a year and a day in prison, and, because of his felony conviction, Ilan was automatically disbarred. He had to pay a fine of $485,000. One of the prosecutors in the scandal said at the time that Ilan got "the severest sentence yet imposed on a lawyer for insider trading." But Judge Sweet read a statement to the court, complete with paraphrases of Tennyson and references to Proust, that gave Ilan hope. "But for that statement," Ilan said in 1995, "I don't think I would have considered it." Here are the words of Judge Sweet, spoken to a silent and composed Ilan, with Diane beside him:

> Mr. Reich. I've read the many letters which have been written on your behalf by distinguished lawyers whom I respect—it is the kind of respect that results from confronting them in court professionally. . . . From these letters and the memorandum from your very skilled counsel, from my own experience, I believe I know you. As in Ulysses, I am a part of all that I have met and I have met you throughout my life. . . . This is not a case of greed or self-aggrandizement. This is a case of a brilliant lawyer, one of the brightest and the best, who has done a lot of good things. To quote Mr. Rogers from Proust: "One should never feel resentment against men, never judge them because of the recollection of an act of malice for we do not know the good that at other times they have singly willed and achieved." That's appropriate here.
>
> You have acted in an open and a free society and taken advantage of that mobility and risen to the top. You are by all accounts an excellent father and

perhaps a difficult but improving husband. You have received careful religious training, your family has a strong belief in the ethical basis of our society, the Judaic-Christian tradition. You were a highly regarded partner in an outstanding firm—and at an early age. Both your secretary and your senior partner respect you and have written letters of support.

By giving Dennis Levine inside information, you betrayed your trust, your family, your firm, and all of us. The SEC has taken assets of almost half a million dollars from you. Your career has been destroyed, at least for the time being. An almost intolerable burden has been placed upon your family. . . . How did all of this come to pass? Why do we find ourselves here at this sad and tragic moment? It was not greed or ambition. As a valued associate in that firm with a potential of partnership, which was later realized, you were at the peak of your profession. You were powerful, secure, on the edge of very substantial wealth. But your perception was different. You wanted to belong, to have a special relationship with a friend, to be part of a social and business world where appearances count. Dennis Levine took you. He gave you that special feeling of belonging, as well as a sense of guilt, because you knew what you did was not right, but wrong—a knowing violation of law. . . . Simply stated, a breach of trust at this level requires a jail term as a deterrent. . . . You have, it is very sad to say, become a symbol of the sickness of our society and of that lost integrity which cannot be condoned, whatever the cost. However in imposing this sentence I want to make it clear that if ever reinstatement to the bar is appropriate—and it is after a felony conviction—this is such a case.[19]

The judge knew that Ilan and Diane were expecting a baby within days of the sentence. He gave Ilan two months after the birth to report to federal prison. The Reichs held a bris for the newborn boy. It was well attended not only by friends and family but also Wachtell associates and Ilan's clients. Larry Lederman, however, was the only one of the firm's partners to be there. "I told Diane that I thought there was a good turnout," Lederman writes, "and she told me, in an acerbic way, not as good as eighteen months before, for the second son."[20]

From the moment of his sentencing, Ilan began planning his resurrection, in what he once called his "maniacal pursuit of the unattainable," a phrase he now finds slightly florid and embarrassing. There were setbacks, year-long delays, insulting rejections. His chances of becoming a lawyer again were infinitesimal. There are so few readmissions to the bar for those convicted of a felony that it amounts to a permanent ban. Ilan was relentless. Judge Sweet, who agreed, probably in peril of his sanity, to write a supporting letter, said, "That kind of uni-directional strength and fixation is bound to irritate people," the judge told Jennifer Reingold, a *Fortune* senior writer who chronicled in 2007 the rise and fall of Ilan Reich for the magazine.[21] "I don't mean to be flippant," Ilan said when it was all over, "but it was a little like that scene in *Alice's Restaurant*, where they keep asking, 'Are you rehabilitated? Are you rehabilitated?'"[22]

With credit for good behavior, Ilan was released from prison to the halfway house in Times Square on December 17, 1987, having served a total of seven months. Later, Danbury became a women's prison. Ilan has some colorful fellow alumni, both real and fictional: Leona Helmsley for tax evasion; Sun Myung Moon, also for tax evasion; Ring Lardner Jr. for contempt of Congress for refusing to answer questions about alleged ties to the Communist Party; and Robert Lowell for conscientiously objecting to World War II. John Sacrimoni, the boss of his eponymous Mafia family, is jailed during the sixth season of *The Sopranos*. Phil Leotardo, a captain in the Lupertazzi crime family, refers to Sacrimoni as "folding laundry in Danbury."

At the halfway house, Ilan faced few restrictions, other than an 11:00 p.m. curfew and random drug tests. Toward the end of the year, he joined Western Publishing. Two years later, he convinced Judge Sweet to end his five-year period of probation. His insurance broker had neglected to pay a premium, and his life insurance policy had lapsed. No company would issue him a new policy as long as he was still under the shadow of the judicial system. The US attorney's office and the probation office argued against granting his request, arguing that such clemency would encourage other convicted felons to let their policies lapse intentionally to win court approval for a similar lifting of probation. "People my age do die," Ilan said at the age of 41. "The judge recognized that my family was at risk and he granted my request."[23]

Ilan still had to wait a total of seven years to apply for readmission to the bar. "You live your life. We had another child. The kids were growing up. You know the seven years is out there, but you don't think about it." Except you do. Or you do if you're Ilan Reich. As the deadline drew closer, Ilan pursued his own resurrection as indefatigably as he had his work in M&A. He could have done what was once known as "the decent thing" and moved away or, at least, stayed away. Carlo Fiorentino, for example, Wachtell's other insider-trading felon, was last heard of selling used furniture in Queens. Not Ilan.

It was a challenge, in so many ways, on so many levels. He prepared assiduously. He did charity work. And he wrote letters. And he wrote more letters. He wrote to friends, former adversaries, famous lawyers he barely knew, and he amassed a long list of supporters. He asked Rob Kindler, then at Cravath and once a fellow associate of Ilan's wife, for an introduction to Cravath's Frederick A. O. Schwarz. He sought help from Leon Silverman of Fried, Frank and Larry Lederman, who had left Wachtell after the publication of his book to join Milbank, Tweed, Hadley & McCloy; he turned to the prosecutor in the case, Charles Carberry, and in a brilliant political move, even Judge Sweet himself.

Ilan submitted his petition in October 1993. He wrote a long statement of his own to the disciplinary panel, describing what he had done and why his plea to become a lawyer again should be granted. First he led the panel through his crimes, then his tortured confession to the Truth Squad, and then, finally, his twisted response to Levine's blandishments:

> Since 1987, as I struggled to build a new career, confronting the daily remind-ers that I had failed to realize the promise of my youth, I have come to appreci-ate several factors which led me to provide inside information to Mr. Levine.
>
> First, I feared failure in my career as a young associate, and I was initially swayed by the allure of easy profits through insider trading as an attractive alternative in the event I could not succeed as a lawyer....
>
> Second, I enjoyed Levine's easygoing manner and apparent sophistica-tion; my friendship with him served as a strong counterweight to my shyness and lack of friends. Frankly, for many years I had unfilled emotional needs which were typified by a difficulty in developing and maintaining personal relationships. I understand today that the bond formed with Levine at various times during 1980–1984 addressed those needs and made me susceptible to be-ing manipulated in furtherance of his illegal objectives.... Third, while I knew the law and understood the prohibition against insider trading, at the outset I was arrogant enough to think that because my involvement was cloaked in secrecy, it was unlikely to be detected....
>
> Finally, I now perceive Levine as the consummate con artist, whose forte was recognizing and manipulating those who might be vulnerable, who could be seduced to exchange their morality for friendship and "a sense of belong-ing," as U.S. District Judge Sweet said.[24]

Ilan practically begs for reinstatement. "It is clear to me," he writes, "that there was a dark undercurrent in my legal career which ultimately led to my disbarment." Twice in a subsequent paragraph, he uses the term "self-esteem" with the law as its source. "My wife is a lawyer, as is my older brother. The law is part of the life of my family, part of my children's heri-tage. Readmission to the bar would place me in the position to discourse within my family on an equal footing about the process and progress of legal developments. It would help to replace a part of my life that I sorely miss, and that is not replaceable through any other means."[25]

After a hearing in April 1994, the staff of the appellate division told the full panel that it had no objection to Ilan's petition for reinstatement to the bar, but it took a year for the Departmental Disciplinary Committee for the Appellate Division, First Department to issue its own recommendation to the court. The news was not good. Two of the three committee members were scathingly unimpressed with Ilan's words, his demeanor, and his sin-cerity. Solo practitioner Beverly Sowande and Citibank executive Howard

Stein said that his character was dominated by "lethargy." They dismissed his emphasis on his refusal to take money from Levine. "Reich was paid richly in the currency that was most important to him, which is no better or worse than money. . . . It is not surprising that a well-fed person doesn't steal food."[26]

They noted that Ilan had confessed only after he was caught, that he abandoned Levine but then rejoined the conspiracy, that he seemed "reluctant to deal with hard matters," that he was not direct in his dealings with people. "[H]is was a weak character seduced into criminal behavior." The two committee members were particularly withering about Ilan's supporting letters. "We were somewhat off-put by what appeared to be a 'campaign' for reinstatement, supported by letters from prominent persons who had no particular knowledge of Reich." They also questioned his charitable work "as possibly of recent origin."[27]

Ilan's petition would now go before the five judges of the appellate division, dragging behind it a vote against him of two to one. "I was demoralized," he confessed in 1995. Ilan was particularly stung by what the twosome wrote about his letters of support from people who did not know him that well. "The people who had been my friends were no longer my friends. Which is understandable. I betrayed them." One example was enough: "I called Marty on the day of my sentencing in 1987. He was very sympathetic. He wished me well. I haven't spoken to Marty since that day." Ilan's lawyer, Milton Gould, had a more colorful reaction to Sowande's statement: "This was psychobabble. She should have been saying this to her psychiatrist. This was a woman speaking from her umbilicus rather than her brain."[28]

In a kind of fitting irony, a lawyer at Skadden represented Ilan, a former partner at arch-rival Wachtell. Jonathan Lerner, the chairperson of the committee, wrote a powerful 30-page dissent, urging the court to ignore the two votes against Ilan and to approve his reinstatement to the bar. In an interview at the time, Lerner explained his passionate support of Ilan: "Reich did something that was terrible. He was punished severely, which he richly deserved. But this issue was whether or not he had the character required to be reinstated. I felt he met the very, very high hurdle that I imposed. The contrary view was based on the nature of his offense. But what is at stake here, going forward, is the protection of clients and society. The chances that Mr. Reich will stray again are zero."[29]

In a unanimous decision, the five judges followed Lerner's lead and voted to reinstate Ilan to the bar. He is still the only lawyer to achieve this against similar odds and apparently the only one to have had the sentencing judge, the prosecuting attorney, and so many prominent members of the bar support his petition and applaud the ruling. Milton Gould said at the time, "The decision shows that we as lawyers have a capacity for compassion."[30] Ilan wept that night. "I just closed my door and cried." He wrote to those who had written for him. He said to Gould, "You achieved the sweetest victory: the restoration of my dignity."[31]

Ilan at last got his absolution. What he didn't get was a job at a law firm. No one would hire him. One of the lawyers who had written in support of his cause, Rob Kindler, in contrast, had more clients and deals than most mortals would ever have been able to control.

*   *   *

ROB KINDLER, NOW IN HIS LATE FIFTIES, STOPS AT THE COFFEE CORNER ON THE WAY TO his desk at Morgan Stanley's offices on Times Square. He meets a colleague and introduces him to a visitor. Rob shares the fact that he is looking for the decaf but can't seem to see any. "Don't you have people to do this for you?" his colleague asks, smiling at the visitor. Rob starts shaking the boxes of coffee, grimacing, wildly opening and shutting the cupboards, lurching around the small alcove with eyes shimmering, scavenging through the shelves, trembling: "I just want the decaf! I just want the decaf!"

His colleague ambles off down the hall, shaking his head. It's just another day at Morgan Stanley, with Rob as vice chairman and global head of mergers and acquisitions. "This place wouldn't function without him," an assistant confides.[32]

A dozen years before the day of the decaf, Rob posed for what would become a famous photograph. He sits cross-legged and barefoot, in quite an accomplished lotus position, his left foot just managing to appear at the crook of his right leg and his right foot more securely positioned on his left. He is dressed in a dark suit, a blue dress shirt, and a wide red and white tie. He sits on a field of green artificial grass with a clouded blue sky behind him. Chin lifted and eyes closed, he holds in each hand the receiver of two phones. Three others, translucent blue and yellow, then high-tech land lines with their inner workings exposed, are arranged before him, their cords curled across the grass. He has not a single gray hair. It is April 1988, and Rob Kindler is on the cover of the *American Lawyer*—"Deal Nirvana: As mergers boom, Cravath's Rob Kindler rings up a big year," by Emily Barker and Krysten Crawford. Inside, there is another picture of our meditating yogi grinning straight at the camera. He has one phone to his ear, and he holds another in his left hand. His dark blue baseball hat is inscribed with the words: Merger Inc. The caption reads: "An M&A partner relentlessly in search of new business."[33]

In 1997, while still a lawyer at Cravath and approaching his mid-40s, Rob began a run of deals that would take him through the $10 billion merger of Dean Witter and Morgan Stanley, where he would eventually parachute in as vice chairman; the $10 billion fight between Norfolk Southern and CSX for the hand of Conrail, a rush of smaller deals ranging in value from $2.2 billion down to $73 million, and finally the largest merger of the year, WorldCom's $37 billion battle with GTE for MCI. It was thirteen years after his memorable time with Robert Campeau, back when Rob was 31 years old. Now, in the latter half of the nineties, Rob found himself responsible for the infamous Berenie Ebbers at WorldCom, who would later, no longer with Rob as his counselor, bring about the largest financial fraud in US history to date. Rob could well have become known at Cravath as the partner in charge of loony Canadians. He was at the apex of his career as a lawyer.

Kindler has long been known as a great marketer masquerading as a lawyer. "I take potential clients to Yankees games sometimes and after the fifth time I just come out and say, 'Hey, do you think I do this for my health? Are you going to give me some work or what?' It always gets a laugh. And some work."[34] Press coverage is no small part of the plan. The publicity for just one of the many successful dealmakers in 1997 grated on some. "He must be loving this," one investment banker said with an eye-roll and a groan, as the plans for the cover story quickly spread through the ranks of M&A.[35] And Rob was indeed enjoying it—shamelessly, craftily, joyfully—all without turning himself into a galley slave pulling on the oars in the dank bowels of the ship.

"Kindler doesn't exactly fit the stereotype of the overworked M&A attorney," wrote Barker and Crawford. "His forty-sixth-floor office overlooking the Hudson River has a decidedly casual feel. Pictures of his . . . three children, ages seven to 15 years, adorn the walls, as well as a framed newspaper article about his brother Andy, a Los Angeles comedian who hosts an irreverent late-night cable TV talk show called 'The Pet Shop.' He billed a solid 2,120 hours last year—a respectable if hardly frenetic pace. Normally, he doesn't work Saturdays and Sundays, Kindler says, and last year he put in only four to six weekends at the office. Nevertheless, he's become what he set out to be: a player. In Cravath's merciless meritocracy, a kid from [Beechhurst], New York, who dropped out of New York University Law School for a time . . . has made his mark."[36] The deals that he and his team did in 1997 brought in just over $30 million to Cravath's coffers before WorldCom's bills were sent out. Conrail alone accounted for $12.5 million in fees.[37]

In that war of the three railroads that began in the autumn of 1996, Rob was as relentless in his efforts to save the deal Conrail wanted with CSX as he was when he tried to find the decaf some 16 years later. For Conrail, he was the emergency medical technician who is finally pulled away from the victim lest he start to require cardio-pulmonary resuscitation himself. Even after the original deal had flat-lined, Rob was just as relentless in his salvage efforts as he was when the deal was alive. "I don't give up," he says matter-of-factly. Then he adds, "Ever."[38]

Conrail was a direct descendant of the Erie Railway, famous for the late-nineteenth-century fight between Cornelius Vanderbilt and the Erie Gang, also known as Jay Gould, Daniel Drew, and James Fisk. Lacking only armed goons, 12-inch cannon, and, presumably, bribed legislators, the Conrail wars began innocently enough in September 1996, when Rob and his mentor at Cravath, Sam Butler, were retained by the railroad to run its merger talks with CSX. By October, the two railroads had an $8.4 billion merger plan. "The deal was too good to be true for the guys at Conrail because they were to merge with CSX and Conrail's management would take over," Rob says.[39] "David LeVan, the CEO of Conrail, would succeed CSX chief executive John Snow as head of the combined company, and John Snow, who later went on to be treasury secretary, was going to walk into the sunset." The headquarters would be in Philadelphia. Kindler and Butler were always wary of John Snow, who was advised by Marty Lipton at Wachtell. "We were just very nervous about whether they would actually follow through, because the deal, the original deal, was just so good for Conrail."

There were miles to go before that exploded. CSX was to buy Conrail in two stages, first a payment of $92.50 per share for 19.9 percent. At that point, Conrail would call a special meeting of its shareholders. At the meeting, they would be asked to change Conrail's charter to exempt it from the Pennsylvania takeover law that required a shareholder who crosses a 20 percent threshold to pay on demand a "fair price" to all the other shareholders. The statute defined a "fair price" as a price not less than the highest paid to all other shareholders. CSX needed this opt-out because its offer came in two stages: first, the cash tender for 19.9 percent of the shares and then, after the vote presumably waiving the "fair price" requirement, an identical cash offer for another 20.1 percent of the railroad's stock. Once CSX acquired 40 percent of Conrail with cash, a merger vote could be held. If the merger were approved, CSX would purchase the remaining 60 percent of Conrail by exchanging 1.86519 CSX shares for each Conrail share. By November, CSX traded at about $44.50 per share. The agreement also provided for a $300 million break-up fee payable to CSX if the deal did not go through and to Conrail if the CSX board changed its vote recommending it.[40]

Rob thought all this was far too risky. He wanted to avoid the shareholder vote at all costs. "Rather than CSX buying us, which would require this vote under Pennsylvania law, I wanted to reverse the deal," he says. "We'd say: 'Shareholders—either you approve the deal on the table, which is, we get a premium price for our shares but we run the company, or we will buy CSX and give them a premium and no shareholder vote will be necessary.' But I couldn't convince anyone—other than me—to do this." This is exactly how a shareholder vote was averted, and Paramount was thwarted in the Time Warner merger, which Rob also worked on. Rob says flipping the deal into a Time Warner would have similarly kept Conrail united with its chosen partner and in charge of its own destiny, but he says he could not sway Joe Perella at Morgan Stanley, Felix Rohatyn at Lazard, or Marty Lipton, advisers to CSX. He calls himself a lone voice in the wilderness, a wilderness that responded with monumental indifference. "To this day, I believe we could've prevailed if I could've gotten Lazard and Morgan Stanley to be more aggressive. Felix Rohatyn and Marty Lipton could not get comfortable with the whole concept of flipping the deal. They just didn't want to. They just seemed to want to get the deal done. And it was the shareholder vote that sunk us."[41] Indeed it was.

In mid-November 1996, all Philadelphia watched. The newspapers and the television crews scribbled and flashed and filmed it all for the nightly news and the next day's banner headlines. Inside, after the first day, the trial had to be moved from Judge VanArtsdalen's usual chambers to the district's ceremonial courtroom as the press of humanity was so great. "It was a madhouse," said John Beerbower, at the time the lead trail counsel for Conrail and a partner of Rob's at Cravath.[42]

Just three weeks earlier, Norfolk Southern had suddenly reared up and made its own hostile offer of $100 in cash for each Conrail share, topping the CSX bid by about $1 billion. An odd ceasefire took hold as the rivals for Conrail held talks aimed at sales to Norfolk Southern of some of the assets a combined CSX and Conrail would own. The talks dissolved into nothing, and Norfolk reaffirmed its bid. CSX then raised its price. It offered to purchase the first 40 percent of Conrail for $110 in cash per share, with the back end transaction, the 60 percent to be bought with stock, to remain unchanged. CSX's revised merger agreement with Conrail also extended the deal's exclusivity period by three months, pushing back further the time in which Conrail's board could not consider any bids to rival that of CSX. Norfolk Southern, one day later, came back with a $110 cash offer for every single share, not just a block of 40 percent of the stock.

Norfolk Southern was faced with a line of cannons against its advance. The target's poison pill would not apply to CSX, the favored bidder, but any other bidder could trigger it. CSX had veto power over any further changes to the Conrail pill. Conrail decreed that only those directors currently on the board could vote to change the pill in any way. The merger agreement, as it stood in early November, had a 270-day exclusivity period during which Conrail could not negotiate with or open its books to any other suitor. Rob calls it his "this-deal-or-no-deal provision," which no one had ever done before.[43]

Norfolk Southern turned to litigation. It took CSX to court, arguing before Judge VanArtsdalen that the CSX offer was illegal, a two-tiered, front-end-loaded tender offer that would cause a stampede as shareholders rushed to be part of the 40 percent that would be eligible for a cash pay-ment, rather than face being lumped in with the remaining 60 percent of stockholders, entitled only to stock as payment for their shares. Norfolk Southern was asking the court to block the CSX tender offer, but the main issue before the judge was whether the Conrail board had failed in its duty to shareholders by doing everything it could to ensure that the sharehold-ers voted to exempt the company from the Pennsylvania requirement that all stockholders get the same price. This became known as the vote to "opt out" of the takeover statute.[44]

The Pennsylvania statute did indeed frown on two-tiered offers that give a portion of the shareholders a better deal. Norfolk Southern could point to the CSX bid as a classic of the kind of bid the statute was aimed to derail. But there was a second edge to the sword. The statute also allowed a board of directors when considering rival offers to take into account not merely the interests of shareholders but also those of employees, suppli-ers, customers, creditors, local communities, as well as both the short- and long-term prospects for their company. The directors could also weigh the resources, intent, and conduct of anyone trying to take control. Judge Van-Artsdalen had no choice. Conrail's board of directors had innumerable rea-sons it could cite to justify its decision to choose CSX. They had violated no duty to the shareholders because they had a duty to so many others. He refused to grant an injunction banning the CSX offer. Just days later, however, he would turn around and grant that same request on different grounds in yet another twist of the spiral. Then Conrail would make a suc-cessful end run around the judge's decision.

The week before Christmas 1996, the numberless mercenaries of the three railroads once again found themselves gathered in the Philadelphia courtroom. It was less crowded this time. "We don't have quite as full an audience as we did for the last hearings," the judge said with a smile of what looked like relief. A smaller audience, but a more momentous ruling, for this time the friendly merger of Conrail and CSX would suffer its first legal setback.[45]

Norfolk Southern was asking the judge to bar Conrail from postponing its shareholder meeting, scheduled for December 23, at which the stock-holders would be asked to decide whether to opt out of the Pennsylvania takeover statute. The late Steven Rothschild, of Skadden's Wilmington office, rose first and stepped to the lectern. He would succumb to a rare form of brain cancer in 2004, but on this day in 1996, Rothschild was in his element. Dressed in a dark double-breasted suit, he argued that the judge should step in and stop the shareholder meeting from drifting ever further into the future. Conrail, he said, was manipulating the vote on the opt-out issue. The target was telling its stockholders that there was "not really the right to vote," but "the right to have a straw poll, or repeated straw polls."

The judge did not seem impressed and subjected Rothschild to a series of blunt interruptions. He noted pointedly that Conrail had explicitly stated in its proxy materials that it might well change the date of the special meeting if it lacked the votes it needed. "It was to me rather obvious that this possibility could arise."

Rothschild was undaunted. He insisted that it was "wholly contrary to any concept of corporate democracy" to tell Conrail shareholders that "if you vote against the opt-out, we will not count your vote." He compared it to the electoral practices of the old Cook County Democratic machine and to Russia under imperial rule. Judge VanArtsdalen, then 77 years old, looked up at Rothschild and said, "Did they have elections in Tsarist Russia? I don't remember. I was young at the time." Rothschild argued that, although Conrail appeared not to know exactly how many shares it had outstanding, "obviously they must be of the view that they don't have the votes to get the opt-out approved." The judge seemed mystified. "The merger will never go through, which is what you want," he said. But Rothschild pointed out that Conrail and CSX could also get their deal with a straight vote on the merger itself, without having their shareholders opt out of the fair price provision.[46]

Stuart Savett, of Philadelphia's Savett Frutkin Podell & Ryan, took the podium next. A raspy-voiced lawyer with a white moustache and shiny cufflinks, he represented three Conrail shareholders who were suing the Conrail board of directors for failing its duties to the stockholders and for untrue statements in their filings with the SEC. He argued to the judge that he must allow the shareholders to vote and to vote quickly. "At every step along the way," he said, "Conrail has been telling its shareholders, 'Drop dead.'" He agreed that Pennsylvania law allowed Conrail to call and therefore to cancel a special meeting of shareholders, but he urged the judge to be fair. "They have taken the Pennsylvania Business Corporation Law over the line. It's just plain inequitable." With all the defenses against a deal that the directors didn't want arrayed against them, the shareholders were powerless. "There is not one thing the shareholders can do to stop this march unless the court intervenes."

The judge began to reveal a poker tell. Thomas VanKirk of Pittsburgh's Buchanan Ingersoll and later the firm's chairman, a serious and dour lawyer with straight gray hair and sloping features, tried to convince the court that there was nothing in the record that showed any unfairness or fraud. Shareholders in Pennsylvania have no right to call a meeting for a vote, and that's that. The judge, however, didn't seem to buy it. "Isn't there something fundamentally unfair about saying we're going to hold an election but we're only going to hold it if we're going to win the election?" Not to be outdone, VanKirk pointed out that the shareholders would get to vote on the merger at some point, but the timing of that vote was up to the board. "I do not believe we should be required to go forward and have a vote if we are going to lose."

Wachtell's Paul Rowe, representing CSX with the firm's Ted Mirvis as first violin, rejected Rothschild's analogy to politics, Russian or Chicagoan. "Shareholder votes and shareholder meetings are a very different species from political models," he said. "It would be an injury against the board of directors using its normal power. This matter is being closely watched by the media. Everything the court does is being read as if it's tea leaves." Rothschild rose to rebut. "I have respect for my adversaries. But I don't think there can be another word to describe the conduct of Conrail and CSX than arrogance. I can't imagine anything more unfair than telling shareholders if you don't vote a certain way our vote will not be counted." Conrail's lead trial counsel, John Beerbower of Cravath, seemed frustrated when he stressed that shareholders do not have the right to vote against something whenever they want to. "There are probably some in this room who would like the opportunity to vote 'no' if I were to run for president."[47]

Eric Herman, then the senior reporter at *Corporate Control Alert*, described the next scene: "The judge announced a ten-minute recess. Lawyers from opposing counsel tables met in mid-room and against walls, talking pleasantly. Rothschild sat down on a bench in the front spectator row with his arms spread on the bench behind him. He looked at Beerbower and said, 'John, should we call you "Mr. President"?' Judge VanArtsdalen reappeared after twenty minutes. He had made his decision. He would not allow Conrail to cancel the shareholder vote just because it was doomed to defeat. This was just unfair. 'It effectively disenfranchises those shareholders who may be opposed to the proposal. That makes, as far as I can see, practically a sham election.' His order enjoined Conrail from canceling, postponing, or adjourning the December 23 special meeting 'by reason of Conrail or its nominees not having received sufficient proxies to assure approval' of the opt-out proposal."[48]

After Judge VanArtsdalen adjourned the hearing, Rothschild praised his ruling as a victory for Conrail shareholders. Lawyers for the other side dismissed it as inconsequential and then proceeded to make sure it was. CSX raised its offer for the final time, adding $16 in convertible preferred stock to the back end of the deal to lure shareholders to its cause. The new proposal also meant that it could legally postpone the shareholders meeting once again: January 17, a month away, would now be the day the deal would be decided.[49]

Rob Kindler took a break. Back five days before the vote, Rob knew that the dream deal for Conrail with CSX was stumbling toward the electric chair. He and his team would be asking Conrail shareholders to get less money for their shares from CSX than they would from Norfolk Southern. CSX chairman John Snow had basically thrown the switch when he announced that there would be no higher bid. Nevertheless, Rob took charge of the public relations campaign, including a barrage of daily full-page print ads in the *Wall Street Journal* and a script for Conrail CEO David Le-Van to read at the shareholders' meeting. Then Norfolk Southern offered yet more. It said it would pay $115 per share for the first 9.9 percent of Conrail shareholders who agreed to vote with Norfolk Southern at the meeting. "We knew we were not going to win even before the shareholder vote, but we had to have the vote anyway," Kindler said at the time.[50] Norfolk Southern had in hand enough proxies to win. The CSX offer of $60 was just not enough.

One would not have known things were so dire at the actual meeting. The shareholders and the lawyers and the bankers, the proxy solicitors, media people, the company executives from the three railroads, the board members and their advisers assembled in their hundreds at Philadelphia's Academy of Music, one of the greatest nineteenth-century concert houses in North America and the oldest still fulfilling its original purpose. To the surprise of all, Conrail employees, at least 20 in total, took to the microphone to support the deal with CSX. Still, Rob says, "the shareholder vote wasn't a lot of fun." From his front-row seat, he lost his temper with Skadden's Michael Rogan, who proposed a ballot designed by Skadden. Rob used a term that family newspapers traditionally do not print. "I can't remember what I called him now," Rob says. "I don't usually do that. I was just a little determined."[51]

After the loss at the meeting, when the shareholders refused to opt out of the statute's requirement that all shareholders get the same price, Kindler was still working it. A contingent value right (CVR), a right to get paid more later if the stock did not do as well as expected? Reverse the structure and have Conrail buy CSX, as he had urged on the advisers earlier in the saga? Lobby the Pennsylvania legislature to nullify the fair price provision? Nothing came of any of it. Indefatigable, Rob then focused on how to make the deal as advantageous as possible for his client. He put together a deal that got Conrail shareholders an excellent price from CSX of $115 per share, or about $10.5 billion. And, although CSX then turned around and divided the spoils with Norfolk Southern, as Rob feared would happen all along, it was more money than the shareholders could otherwise have expected. Rob also won a benefit package for Conrail employees that included six months to two years of severance pay in case of layoffs. Conrail executives still praise Rob's devotion. Rob, however, is grim to this day. "We got an incredible price. It was a blow-out price at the time. But I didn't keep the company independent. I have always considered it a failure."[52]

On to the next deal.

*   *   *

THE CODE NAME WAS B.M.W. "B" STOOD FOR "BLUE" (BRITISH TELECOM), "M" FOR "magenta" (MCI), and "W" for "white" (WorldCom). "I could never get them straight," Lewis Steinberg, the Cravath tax partner, told Emily Barker and Krysten Crawford for their April 1988 story in the *American Lawyer*. "I always had a problem figuring out who was white and who was green."[53]

In the middle of the largest takeover of 1997 and one of the most complex deals on record, the two reporters find Rob Kindler out on the golf course on an October day. His client, the notorious Bernie Ebbers of World-Com, had just offered $30 billion in stock to buy MCI Communications, just before MCI could seal its deal with British Telecom. The battlefield had been quiet that morning, and Rob had decided to get a group together for some golf. The Rolling Stones were in the midst of their "Bridges to Babylon" tour, playing the Meadowlands. An accomplished amateur musician himself, Rob invited Michael Cohl, the Canadian promoter and touring impresario for the Stones, and two of their backup horn players to the illustrious Winged Foot Golf Club in Mamaroneck. They played for $2 a hole. Rob always likes competition with at least some kind of edge. He won $10 and was very happy.

Back in the clubhouse, Rob glanced at CNBC and heard that his client WorldCom suddenly had a three-way fight on its hands—GTE had just offered $28 billion, all in cash, to snatch MCI away from both British Telecom and WorldCom. The surprise offer was $2 billion lower than World-Com's $30 billion, but it was all cash, whereas Bernie Ebbers was offering stock, a currency generally less desirable than actual money. Before going back to Manhattan for what would be weeks of jousting, arm twisting, court fights, and grandstanding, Rob turned to his golf group and said, "I'll win."

MCI had signed a deal in November 1996 to sell itself to British Telecom for about $24 billion. Then MCI saw a slump in long-distance and local phone businesses. After heading for the door, saying it was abandoning the deal, British Telecom came back to the table with an offer cut by $5 billion. Bernie Ebbers saw an exposed jugular. He asked his investment bankers at Salomon Brothers to recommend a law firm for his first hostile deal. At a late August meeting at Salomon's New York headquarters, Rob remembers, Bernie asked him to describe his track record. "I told him, 'Look Bernie, we haven't lost a hostile bid in over ten years.'" Rob's partner, Allen Finkelson, told Ebbers that the Cravath team was 18 to 1 on hostiles.

"Over the course of the next five weeks," Crawford and Barker write, "Kindler and a group of about nine Cravath lawyers worked feverishly on WorldCom's sneak assault. The game plan was to launch a two-pronged attack on October 1: first, filing a formal bid; and second, filing a Delaware suit to block the MCI/British Telecom transaction. . . . Cravath, in Mario Puzo's great phrase, went to the mattresses. By Tuesday, September 30, everything was in place. Kindler, Finkelson, and the rest of the team spent the day finishing the documents detailing WorldCom's bid. 'Everyone was living at the printer,' recalls [Robert I. Townsend III, a Cravath colleague of Rob's at the time]. Kindler spent the night at Merrill Corporate Printers reviewing the final pages himself, a task typically delegated to associates. At one point, he took a break to accept a Cravath summer associate's challenge to a push-up contest. (Kindler claims he won.)"[54]

Rob doesn't remember now whether he did or not, but he does remember that the secrecy with which he and his team had clouded their plans worked exactly as hoped. "By late Wednesday morning [October 1, 1997], WorldCom's bold play became public. Together Kindler and Finkelson fielded press calls. They contacted MCI's lawyers at Simpson Thacher & Bartlett and British Telecom's attorneys at Shearman & Sterling. Jeffrey Lawrence, a Shearman & Sterling partner in London, heard about World-Com's bid after the *Wall Street Journal* posted an article on the Internet while his colleagues in New York were still sleeping. Lawrence says he was stunned," Barker and Crawford recount in their article. "Like other British Telecom and MCI officials, he had known that the revised merger agreement risked a third-party bid. But he thought that threat had diminished significantly during the five weeks that had passed. 'That somebody would come in and be prepared to pay so much was surprising,' says Lawrence. 'Also, WorldCom was not exactly a household word in England.'"[55]

Rob knew that British Telecom (BT) would no longer be a factor in the takeover fight. "We came in fast with our $30 billion stock bid," says Rob. "This wasn't a question about whether or not MCI was going to stay independent because MCI had already acknowledged that it was for sale, right. BT had cut their price and we came in and bid because we knew that they couldn't bid again. Having cut their price, how could they possible justify coming back again and offering a higher price? They would just look stupid. And they didn't." GTE, says Rob, made a fundamental error of judgment. They assumed that British Telecom was in control of the process and showered attention on the first bidder. "They were so wrong," Rob says now. "We were not worried about BT coming back. They were in an impossible political position. Their shareholders were all over them for doing the original MCI deal and they cut the price. We figured there was no way they could come back."

It was MCI that could turn the deal, Rob was convinced. So he set about turning MCI lawyer Pete Ruegger, a lawyer at Simpson Thacher and a neighbor of Rob's in the Westchester suburb of Rye, New York. They both took the same train to Grand Central every morning, and Rob would search for him on the platform or at Grand Central itself, urging him to consider that GTE would be a disastrous merger partner, with its heavy debt, its callous treatment of management and employees at other companies it had absorbed, and the looming danger of antitrust barriers to any deal between the two. Kindler remembers that Ruegger was "very circumspect" but not averse to listening. Ruegger told the *American Lawyer* that the negotiations and renegotiations with fickle British Telecom over the summer had "left a slightly unpleasant taste."[56]

It was not only that GTE was wrongly focused on British Telecom, says Rob. It was also that British Telecom itself had a skewed belief in its own power. MCI, as part of its merger agreement with BT, had agreed to put in a poison pill for a set period of time to deter other bidders from muscling in on their deal. Toby Myerson, a Paul Weiss partner advising British Telecom, locked horns with Rob over whether the pill would be triggered the instant MCI signed a merger agreement with anyone else. The pill gives the shareholders of a target the right to buy more shares in its company at a deeply reduced price, once a hostile buyer has taken more than a set percentage of the total, which dilutes the hostile buyer's stake by turning its shares into a lower percentage of the total. "He was pounding the table," Rob remembers, "because he had told his client that we couldn't even sign an agreement with MCI without triggering the pill. He said that if you sign a deal, you are deemed to beneficially acquire the stock, blah blah blah. I said, 'Toby, what do we care whether the pill is triggered? We don't own any stock, so you can't dilute us from nothing to nothing.' It literally had never dawned on him. He had just missed the entire point. He thought, 'Poison pill—you never trigger the pill.' His client was there too. I kept saying, 'Look, we can sign a merger agreement and then we can close after whenever your blocking rights expire.' He said, 'Yeah yeah yeah, but you can't redeem the pill then because by signing the merger agreement you will already have pulled its trigger.' I said, 'I don't agree that that's true, but even if it is, so frikkin' what?'"

The Cravath team of nine lawyers ran the numbers on GTE and was convinced that its debt load would prevent it from going any higher. After the markets closed on Friday, November 7, 1997, Bernie called MCI's chairman, Bert Roberts, and raised the offer from $41.50 to $50 in WorldCom stock, with one condition. He would hold the bid open only until the market bell rang on Monday.

Bernie Ebbers set himself up at a command post—Rob's desk. The final 48 hours began. GTE executives, hoping against hope that their revised bid would win the day, moved back and forth between the Midtown Manhattan offices of Shearman & Sterling and those of Rothschild Inc. GTE waited and called and lobbied from the offices of Fried, Frank at One New York Plaza at the southern end of the island. On Sunday night, late, Bernie raised his offer to $51 per share for a total of around $37 billion. He wrote down the terms of the deal on a yellow legal pad. Kindler had this framed and placed in his office at Cravath. It is nowhere to be seen in his Morgan Stanley office. When at last the two sides had an agreement, Rob remembers Bernie letting out a yell of triumph. Rob said, "I guess we're now 19 and one." That's the way he likes it.

What Rob does not like is to have his association with Bernie Ebbers discussed without the fact writ large that he had nothing to do with Bernie's local difficulties with the law. "I was the M&A lawyer for Ebbers and never did any work on their disclosures or accounting. And the legal issues they faced happened well over five years after I was their M&A lawyer," Rob stresses. In 2005, Ebbers, nicknamed the "Telecom Cowboy," was convicted of fraud and conspiracy based on WorldCom's false financial reporting and the loss to investors of some $100 billion. It was the largest such fraud in American history, until the advent of another Bernie. On July 13, 2005, Ebbers was sentenced by Judge Barbara Jones of New York's Southern District to 25 years in a federal prison in Louisiana. The earliest date he can be released is July 2028, when he will be 87 years old.

Rob points out that history might have been different had US regulators done the sensible thing with Bernie's proposed acquisition in 1999 of Sprint Communications. "Remember," he says, "after they did the MCI deal, they continued to be a high-flying stock for a long time. That deal was only good for them. Not only were they a high-flying stock, they performed well for years. Verizon tried to buy them for over a hundred billion dollars. Bernie turned it down, because he didn't think it was high enough. Then Bernie tried to merge with Sprint for over $115 billion in a stock-for-stock deal and the regulators blocked it. Think about how ridiculous that is, with MCI gone and Sprint so weakened. They did it because they thought there was such a thing as a consumer long-distance market. We said, 'You've got to be kidding us.' All the regional phone companies were getting into long distance, and now, guess what? There isn't such a thing as long distance anymore. You've got cell phones. The thought that they couldn't merge with Sprint makes no sense. As if you can really monopolize long distance! What a joke! We weren't doing it for the long-distance market. We were doing it because of the business aspects of the deal, the commercial parts, but the government blocked it. They didn't listen. And think how wrong they were. Had that deal happened, it would have been a two-hundred-and-fifty billion dollar company. Scott [Sullivan, former CFO of WorldCom] and Bernie wouldn't be in jail now. The whole world would have changed. In any event, by the time they had issues and things blew up, I hadn't been their M&A lawyer for a very long time and was a banker at JP Morgan."

The year 1997 was a trillion-dollar year for M&A. It transformed global commerce, with M&A people racing from transaction to transaction. Still, they couldn't help puzzling over how long it could all last. Would the stock market crash? Would interest rates rise? Would liquidity evaporate? Would Asia topple the market? Would some other political crisis spoil the party? Or would it all end for the simple ineluctable reason that nothing lasts forever, that "trees can't grow to the sky?"

It was without question a year of the unexpected: the eclipse of cash as the ruler of deals; the widespread use of multiples between target and acquirer; the escalation of hostile bids in Europe; the emergence of a real estate company as the new owner of venerable ITT; WorldCom's sudden power in telecommunications; and, above all, the pandemic of transactions across virtually every sector of the economy. Michael Carr said at the time, when he was still with Salomon and had not yet joined Goldman, "You see consolidation in industry after industry. One or two pebbles roll down the hill. People snap to attention. Before long, you have a landslide."[57]

Few were anything but in awe of the business. Steven Wolitzer, then managing director of Lehman Brothers, said at the time, "Everything is active. Nothing has been left behind. Pick any region, pick any industry. Generally, you see at least one area that is slow. But that has not been the case. And we don't see that ending. We're not upset. Just busy." John Tehan, now retired from Simpson Thacher, agreed: "I thought last year was a terrific year, but this has been non-stop. In 1996, there were a couple of points where things slowed down. This year, there has been no slowdown at all. At all." At Bear Stearns, then-senior managing director and co-head of domestic corporate finance David Glaser was similarly struck by the levels M&A had scaled after the slump a mere seven years before: "At times like this, you begin to wonder if the trees will grow to the heavens. You feel like you're violating some fundamental law of physics. And deals are getting larger. Everything's hot. I can't think of what isn't hot. It's hard to find sage words to say about all this. It's like fine wine. You should just enjoy it."[58]

There were worries. Over breakfast in one of the score of private dining rooms at Salomon, Michael Carr was worried. Then the firm's co-head of M&A, Michael pointed out that 1997 was the year of the stock deal. Such transactions, he said, give dealmakers a much wider panoply of possible structures than is true of cash deals, which trigger special seller's duties more readily. In addition, cash deals do not lend themselves as easily to innovative tax treatment, to stock collars and contingent value rights, to the double barrels of cash and equity. WorldCom's acquisition of MCI and Starwood's capture of ITT, as two examples, both succeeded primarily because each enjoyed greater flexibility and buying power as stock deals. "Cash did not win. This violates page one of the M&A handbook," Michael said. "Eighty percent of my business is in equity-based currency and that is getting skewed even further with larger and larger deals. With stock, you have thousands of ways to keep the conversation alive. If the market does weaken, all this could come to a screeching halt. There is more to a deal than the fact that it must make sense on the day before a market correction and still make sense the day after. CEOs have to feel positive about the deal. Many people don't agree with me, but M&A is an emotional process."[59]

Gerald Rosenfeld, who was head of investment banking at Lazard, predicted that the surge would roll on. "Huge waves of consolidation are washing over industry after industry at the same time. It's pretty staggering. And that won't stop. The continuation of this massive consolidation will be the story of 1988." And so it was. But not for too much longer. Take a look at three of the investment banks whose senior practitioners analyzed the market in 1997: Salomon Brothers, Lehman Brothers, and Bear Stearns. Not one exists today; neither, for that matter, does Salomon's former headquarters at the original World Trade Center.

*   *   *

THE LAST BIG DEAL BEFORE THE DOT-COM CRASH OF 2000 WAS ALSO ROB KINDLER'S last big deal as a lawyer. He joined JP Morgan Chase just after representing Time Warner when it agreed to be acquired by AOL. It all began in 1999 in Tiananmen Square, when Time Warner's Jerry Levin happened to sit in front of AOL's Steve Case at the fiftieth anniversary of the People's Republic of China. The idea soon ballooned: a combination of the world's leading Internet company with the world's largest media company that would make a great leap forward into the new century. It turned out to be a long march in retreat. Within a mere two years, the merged mess saw advertising revenue dwindle, job losses spiral, retirement accounts decimated, lawsuits and investigations by the SEC and the Justice Department, and its stock price dropped by a total of $200 billion. The concept was flawed, the two companies hated each other, and the Internet itself began quickly to devour the newly formed company that was meant to thrive in the new online web world.

As vice chairman of Time Warner and head of the cable division, Ted Turner famously opposed the merger with all he could muster. One of Ted's closest friends and confidantes maintains that those in favor of the deal were hoping that Ted would be sufficiently distracted by his recent marriage to Jane Fonda and his new penchant for "playing Boy Scout with his philanthropy" to prove much of a threat to their deal. A critical board meeting, this friend says, suddenly burst onto the calendar just as Ted had landed from a cross-country trip. He had the flu and was exhausted, but he flew back across the country to join in the meeting. "Hey, you're selling magazines here right?" Ted asked his fellow directors, according to his confidante. "Why are you putting them online? You're selling them for three dollars on the newsstand and you want to give them away for free? I don't like this." Outnumbered and outplayed by colleagues in awe of the riches the deal was expected to unlock, Ted stood aside. "When Levin was up there in the press photographs doing his bro-mance clench with Steve

Case," Ted's friend says, "Ted was off to one side looking like a deer in the headlights."

Two years later, as the technology and dot-com bubble burst nastily, the oddly shaped hybrid faced a loss of $99 billion. It became known as the worst merger in history. Ted had been right all along. Meanwhile, his restricted stock in the new company languished in his portfolio, costing him $10 million a day for two years. He lost 80 percent of his net worth, his friend claims. "I'd like to forget it," Ted said in 2010 at a reunion of those involved. "That's what goes through my mind. I almost didn't do this interview because I didn't want to dig it up again. Let it pass into history. The Time Warner–AOL merger should pass into history like the Vietnam War and the Iraq and Afghanistan wars. It's one of the biggest disasters that have occurred to our country." If Ted had appeared to his friend as a stunned deer at the famous press conference in 2000, for Ted, another large mammalian ruminant came to mind. He is said to have called the deal "a giant cow-tipping by savages."

It took five years for M&A to recover from the busted deal and the burst dot-com bubble, but by 2005, dealmaking had the best year since the turn of the millennium. The volume of announced deals in 2005 soared around the world to more than $2.7 trillion, a 38.4 percent increase from the $2 trillion in 2004. European M&A surpassed the trillion-dollar mark for the first time, increasing by 37 percent to $1.2 trillion from the year before. The endangered species known as the conglomerate continued to dwindle. "The market is rewarding those who get to their core business," Rob said. "No new conglomerates have been formed in the past five years— no Tycos, no General Electrics—and many will be broken up."[60]

Rob had a special way of knowing that trouble was on its way, that it was clearly time for another bust. "Back in 1987, I bought my house in Rye just before Black Monday. I just bought a house on Cape Cod—a pretty expensive house," he said at the time, "and I think they're all going to hell. It won't all crash soon. The cost of debt is low, but more important, the amortization of loans is out there, sometimes five to six years. There will, however, be trouble in the future." He became known as a Cassandra, warning all who would listen about the tulipomania in M&A. "There is a tulip craze in credit availability. It will come home to roost. I absolutely assure you that a lot of very bad deals are being made." The LBO army has more than $125 billion in dry power, Rob would repeat to anyone who would listen, which, when combined with historically low interest rates and high leverage levels, leads to ever-larger buyouts and higher multiples. "People are paying very rich prices to get deals done." Rob, like Cassandra, turned out to be right.[61]

The year 2006 got off to a stunning beginning. Some 622 deals worth $49.9 billion were announced in the first 11 days of January, more than in any year except 2000, and the numbers for that year were distorted by the

AOL–Time Warner behemoth. Not since 1998 had dealmakers seen such an 11-day beginning to a new year, when 861 deals hit the headlines, for a total of $45 billion.

On it roared. On a single day in early January 2007, Simpson Thacher's Alan Klein handled e-mails and conference calls on four non-US hostile deals, each of which had a value of well over $10 billion. "It was certainly a personal high for me," Alan says, "but more importantly it shows that these deals—huge hostile battles that would normally be front-page news—have been treated as reasonably run of the mill. You ask yourself: 'How is this conceivable? Why haven't they been getting their share of attention?' And the answer is simple: Deals like these just get relatively overlooked because there is just so much going on in M&A around the world." By 2007, M&A burgeoned into an estimated $4.4 to $4.6 trillion global business.

It would last another year.

CHAPTER NINETEEN
BIRDS OF AMERICA

I n late April 1988, just a few weeks after Bob Campeau conquered Federated Department Stores, a man named Henry Bradley-Martin died at the age of 82. The symmetry may never have occurred to him, but he was an heir to one of the greatest of the nineteenth-century merger fortunes and reached his eighth decade just as the 1980s merger frenzy reached its zenith. His mother was born Helen Phipps, the daughter of Henry Phipps Jr., a childhood friend and business partner of Andrew Carnegie. Together, Henry and Andrew, two sons of penurious Scottish immigrants, cobbled together a steel monopoly from a host of mergers and acquisitions in the late nineteenth century, between the Civil War and the First World War. What they bequeathed to their heirs has lasted four generations with no sign of exhaustion.

Bradley-Martin preferred his Virginia farm to the big city's bright lights. In this, he was unlike some members of his family, who had long been and continue to be prominent socialites among what used to be known as the jet set. Cornelia Guest, for example, his cousin, was named "Deb of the Year" in 1982, with repeated appearances in newspapers, on the covers of magazines, and on celebrity television shows.

Armed with his portion of his grandfather's riches, which gave him a net worth in the hundreds of millions, Bradley-Martin owned a fine American house called Rose Hill on a swath of some 400 acres of Thomas Jefferson's Albemarle County at the foot of the Blue Ridge Mountains, some of the loveliest land the East Coast has to offer. The original house on the property was built in 1903 as a summer place for Susan Williams Massie, who created the gardens for which the place became famous. In 1930, the house was destroyed by a fire, and the architect, William Lawrence Bottomley, was immediately commissioned to replace it. He created a brick-and-stone-trimmed two-story manor house with two single-story wings that look like arms stretching out in a circle from the main structure. The architectural historian William B. O'Neal placed it on his list of the 12 best structures built in Virginia between 1776 and 1958.

As soon as he bought the estate, Bradley-Martin added a new library to the house. He needed one. Just as his grandfather collected businesses, so did Bradley-Martin collect books. Armed with a bachelor's degree in architecture from the University of Michigan as well as tutelage at the Cranbrook Academy of Art, he was nevertheless unable or unwilling to carve out a career in either art or design, turning instead to the collecting, collating, and cataloguing of the artifacts and works of others—an estimated 10,000 of them. Henry Bradley-Martin bought his first book in 1924 while at Oxford, a first edition of *Tom Sawyer.* Over the next six decades, he added Sir Thomas More's *Utopia,* printed in 1516; George Washington's copy of the Federalist Papers; Edgar Allan Poe's *Tamerlane,* published in 1827; the first translation of St. Augustine's *Confessions;* the second of Chaucer's complete works; and one of the last privately held copies of the first printing of the Declaration of Independence. Of all the works in his collection, he loved his bird books the most. Ornithology made up more than half the library, or some 7,000 books. He was not just a collector of books. He also knew his birds on the wing, although having suffered damage to his hearing in the Second World War, he no longer able to identify them accurately by their songs. Of particular interest to his rare-book cataloguer was the complete copy of Audubon's *Birds of America,* as well as Audubon's 438-page journal from 1826, the year of his trip to England to seek a publisher. She hated to see all this, of all things, broken apart and dispersed to the winds. She implored her former employer Paul Mellon to save the works from this fate, to no avail. In the late 1980s, the Bradley-Martin collection was described by the head of Sotheby's books and manuscripts department as "one of the most magnificent private libraries to come to sale in this century." It was valued at $30 million. The auction house sold it all off at six sales over 12 months.

When the house and collection were still intact, the rare-book cataloguer came upon an interesting volume when Bradley-Martin was not in residence. She pulled it off the shelf cautiously, looking over her shoulder to make sure no one was about to surprise her, particularly the odious brother of Bradley-Martin's younger second wife, the dreaded Herman Almond, he of the reddish-hued comb-over who had a happy sinecure as manager of Rose Hill. As she held it in her hands, wondering what it might contain, she was aware of the borborygmus of the house, the omnipresent creaks and sighs and groans that are accessible to human ears only in a near silence. At first distracted by the possibility of being discovered, she was soon absorbed by what she saw opening up before her in all its monarchical splendor, an infamous event six generations before, given by the paternal grandparents of the master of Rose Hill: the Bradley-Martin ball of 1897.

One morning over breakfast, four years after the Panic of 1893 and 24 years since the Long Depression began in 1873, Bradley-Martin said to his wife, "I think it would be a good thing if we got up something. There seems to be a great deal of depression in trade. Suppose we send out invitations for a concert?" The idea was to help the unemployed by employing them. Mrs. Bradley-Martin, nee Cornelia Sherman, vetoed the idea of a concert. "And, pray, what good would that do?" she asked. "The money will only benefit foreigners. No, I've a far better idea. Let us give a costume ball at so short notice that our guests won't have time to get their dresses from Paris. That will give an impetus to trade that nothing else will."[1]

Mrs. Bradley-Martin, who had added a hyphen to her name and married off her daughter to the Earl of Craven, was already established in society. As the *New York Times* put it in 1897, "It is only necessary for the rumor to be started that Mr. and Mrs. Bradley-Martin are planning an entertainment, when, presto! the world of New York society is stirred from centre to circumference." Famous for her balls, the Bradley-Martins would become infamous for this one. It was to be held at the Waldorf on February 10, 1897, one of the first of such events to take place at an actual hotel rather than a private house.[2]

The *New York Times* published a long list of the costumes and called the story "History Ransacked to Provide Fancy Dress for Those Who Are to Be Present"[3]: "ARTHUR, CHESTER ALLEN—Mousquetaire, in red and white velvet and satin, with bucket boots; ASTOR, MRS.—A superb dark-blue velvet gown, designed by Carolus Duran and in which he painted her portrait. The gown is trimmed around the neck with folds of lace. The costume will represent Marie Stuart. Mrs. Astor will wear an elaborately jeweled headdress and stomacher of precious gems, also a necklace and pendants of diamonds and other gems." There is John Jacob Astor as Henry of Navarre, chosen to lead his hostess in the *quadrille d'honneur* to open the ball and destined later to die on the *Titanic;* J. P. Morgan in a "Molière costume"; his daughter Anne as Pocahontas; at least two George Washingtons; assorted Mary Stuarts; and three Marie Antoinettes, two of them not as authentic as Cornelia Bradley-Martin, who planned to wear a ruby necklace that had actually belonged to Marie Antoinette and a dress once owned by Mary Stuart.[4]

The threat to the establishment came from a combination of outrage and ridicule, a lethal cocktail, as the great and the good stood outside in the cold in full costume waiting for their carriages. One of the more unorthodox of the costumes, for example, was worn by Otho Cushing, 26 years old in the year of the great ball, an artist and graphic designer for *Life* magazine. Otho, the *Times* wrote, "was, in fact, thought to have gone rather too far in his impersonation of an Italian falconer of the fifteenth century. His costume consisted of full tights and a short jacket, with a little cap and long locks, while a large stuffed falcon was perched on his left wrist. The costume left little to the imagination, as far as the figure was concerned, and, although historically correct in every detail, was so decidedly pronounced that he caused a sensation wherever he moved."[5]

One large man dressed as the Shah of Persia, the *Times* reported, was told that his carriage had been ordered for 4:00 a.m. and that he would have a half hour to wait. "Mr. Florence waited and smoked cigarettes. The hurry and bustle of guests getting away continued. Mr. Florence stood around and attracted great attention from the policemen, footmen, and cabmen because of the lavish display of jewels on his headgear. His purple cap, around which was a fringe of pearls, was well covered with diamonds. Several large emeralds surrounded with diamonds decorated one side of the cap, and a pearl pendant hung down the centre of his forehead. 'Did you notice that pearl?' said a Sergeant to a Central Office man. 'Wait till he turns round again. That's all real stuff he's got on his head.'"[6]

Plans for the ball had not been greeted with unanimous approval. The Reverend Dr. William S. Rainsford, rector of St. George's Episcopal Church, thundered to the *Times* that such a display at such a time would be "ill-advised," and he urged his congregation to send their regrets. He noted pointedly the "widespread discontent expressed in the National election by the casting of 6 million votes against existing social conditions."[7] The reverend may have achieved at least some success. Of the estimated 1,200 to 1,800 invitations, only an estimated 600 to 700 guests actually showed up.

The grumbling grew steadily louder after the event. The police, under the direction of Deputy Chief Cortright, kept 33rd Street from Fifth Avenue to Broadway clear of pedestrians, while the guests were making their way to the ball, a decision that was criticized as "unwarranted protection of the rich." Theodore Roosevelt himself, ironically later admired for his trust-busting, anti-robber-baron crusades, was moved to speak. As a New York City police commissioner, he had supervised security for the ball, with his wife inside as one of the guests. "The complaint," Roosevelt said, "is such nonsense that it hardly deserves an answer. The street was not closed to any person having business there, but as the first carriages began to arrive it was found that the crowd was so dense that accidents might easily have happened, and the crowd of people who had no business there were moved away just as similar crowds are moved away any day when for any reasons they obstruct traffic. In other words, precisely the same course was followed that is followed when there is a clambake or picnic on the east side, a fire, or any gathering of any kind. It is the course that has been followed during the last thirty years."[8]

Oscar Hammerstein I wrote and produced a ruthless spoof of the event, titled *Mrs. Radley Barton's Ball; or In Greater New York,* which was mounted at his Olympia Music Hall in March 1897. A critic at the *New York Times* described the piece, condensed by the author into two concise acts, as a "spectacular extravaganza in which are introduced a number of mechanical features and specialties, including a floral fountain which throws flowers into the air, and other attractive novelties." It would appear the libretto and score are no longer extant. Oscar "Andy" Hammerstein III, author of *The Hammersteins: A Musical Theatre Family,* and a grandson of the beloved librettist and lyricist Oscar Hammerstein II, has found no trace of either. "Lyrics to these sorts of spoofs are often lost to the ages," Andy Hammerstein says.

The Bradley-Martin ball turned out to be a tipping point that changed the public's view of the Gilded Age, not only bringing down upon the Bradley-Martins a much-increased tax bill, prompting the family to move to England for good, but also, and much more dangerously, making it all seem risible. People began to laugh, always an insurgency's most powerful weapon, at the oddly dressed merger emperors of the day.

On Valentine's Day 2007, almost 110 years to the day after the Bradley-Martin ball, a party was held at the Park Avenue Armory. It was a clone of its ancestor, complete with awestruck publicity before the event, the opulence of the actual party, the public backlash with calls for tax reform when it was all over, and the slightly petulant counterreaction by the hosts. Steve Schwarzman, head of the private-equity giant the Blackstone Group, gave the party to mark his sixtieth birthday. There were catcalls at one conference attended by Schwarzman—"No more birthday parties!" It came to be seen as the end of an era.

No expense, as they say, was spared at the Schwarzman party. Martin Short was the comedian. Marvin Hamlisch played a piece from *Chorus Line.* Patti Labelle sang. Rod Stewart covered a number of his own hits. A large portrait of Schwarzman by Andrew Festing, the president of the Royal Society of Portrait Painters, greeted the guests. A large replica of the Schwarzman apartment was installed at the Armory by Philip Baloun, a favorite society party planner. This was yet another link to the past. Steve and his wife live at Number 15/16B, 740 Park Avenue. They bought it from Saul Steinberg, a 1980s M&A star. Before the Steinbergs, it was owned by John D. Rockefeller Jr., at one time the richest man in the world, the son of the greatest corporate acquirer of the industrial age.

Saul Steinberg's fiftieth birthday given by his wife Gayfryd at their Quogue beach house in August 1989, also a year when M&A went into hibernation, had a party tent turned into a seventeenth-century Flemish drinking house. Liz Smith described it for *New York* magazine: "In ten vitrines were actors posing in re-creations of some of the world's finest paintings. These included two by Vermeer—*The Kitchen Maid* and *The Artist in His Studio*. An actors' agency provided people who could stand stock-still in costume for twenty minutes at a time. The Steinberg beach house overlooking the Atlantic rocked and rolled with hundreds of flickering terra-cotta pots, identical twins posing as mermaids in the pool, dancers in seventeenth-century garb, heralds, and banner wavers. The guest list was A-list nouveau riche and rising. I will never forget the late Steve Ross of Warner Bros. dancing with the Vermeer girl with the pitcher during her 'rest' period. Saul toasted his wife like this: 'This may be a bit of history. Honey, if this moment were a stock, I'd short it.' He joked that his wife had done a lot for the economy and 'anyone who is talking about recession—well, forget it!'"⁹ Shades of Cornelia Bradley-Martin and her efforts to give work to tradespeople during tough times.

It seems to be something of a tradition among M&A men to give themselves landmark birthday parties that typically star aging rock musicians to help ease the passage of time. David Bonderman, known to his friends as "Bondo," a cofounder of TPG Capital, formerly known as Texas Pacific Group, held a seventieth birthday party attended by some 700 friends at the Wynn resort in Las Vegas. Robin Williams did stand-up, John Fogerty played, and Paul McCartney did some Beatles classics, including, fittingly enough, both "Revolution" and "The Long and Winding Road." Again, the cry for changes in the tax code arose in the press.

Leon Black, once of Drexel and now of Apollo Global Management, had a sixtieth birthday party at his house in the Hamptons in 2011. Yet again, the subject of tax reform rolled through press accounts of the event. Michael Milken came, as did Senator Chuck Schumer, Martha Stewart, Howard Stern, and some 200 other guests, including Vera Wang. One notable guest was Lloyd Blankfein, head of Goldman Sachs. Before Elton John took the stage, wrote Peter Lattman of the *New York Times,* just as the full moon rose over the Atlantic, Blankfein turned to Steve Schwarzman at the foot of the stairs to the beach and said, "Your sixtieth got us into the financial crisis. Let's hope this party gets us out of it."

* * *

A MARGIN CALL AFTER THE ONSET OF THE GREAT RECESSION BROUGHT DOWN THE KLUGE principality at Albemarle House. In 2010, the messuage was disemboweled at a massive Sotheby's auction, one of the rare times in recent memory when a single collection, an entire estate, was on the block at once. Hundreds came to the estate as if to a nineteenth-century public hanging. They wandered through the rooms, which seemed in suspended animation, still intact but lifeless—the jewels, gowns and bison heads; silver-framed photographs of Reagans and continental kings; model ships; the 13-foot,

575-pound blue marlin Patricia caught off Bora Bora suspended from the ceiling in one of the guesthouses.

One ticket holder to the Kluge auction was quoted in the local paper as saying she wanted to attend just to see how vulgar it all was. One of Patricia's close friends notes that margin calls can descend on anyone at any time, and that too much schadenfreude and snobbery are not a good thing, particularly when shown by those who "ate much salt" with her, as the Urdu expression goes, or sought perhaps in vain to do so. The Kluges were generous in Albemarle County, giving to medical institutions, the University of Virginia, and, famously, to a local gentleman of ancient African-American lineage who befriended their young son and taught the lonely lad how to fish in one of the many lakes. The boy's mother started several local businesses, reinvesting her husband's M&A riches in the county economy. She is also invariably polite, extending a hand to all and insisting that one call her by her first name. All this is over now. Sic transit gloria mundi.

John Kluge did not live at Albemarle House for the last 20 years of his life. When he and Patricia had their famously amicable divorce in 1990, he left her with the oft-reported and oft-denied stipend of $1.6 million a week, the annual interest on $1 billion, and the place she had built and loved so much. She started her vineyard business, and he bought a neighboring house called Morven, an authentic eighteenth-century jewel that he recut and polished just enough to return it to its quiet glory. He and his new wife lived among its ancient gardens and honey-colored fieldstone in reticent splendor. No bankruptcy for Mr. Kluge: He died in 2010 a very rich man indeed and bequeathed both Morven and thousands more acres to Thomas Jefferson's University of Virginia.

After the auction, Albemarle House was put on the market for $100 million, cut the day after its listing to $48 million and sold for $12.7 million. Albemarle House, once the epicenter of ten square miles of M&A-begotten riches, now sits alone atop its valley, echoing and sepulchral and Trump-owned.

* * *

IT WAS AS QUIET AS IT EVER GETS AT THE OFFICES OF WACHTELL AT 7:30 A.M. ON A Monday. Rob Kindler looked like he felt, unshaven and tired and still in what one might loosely call vacation attire, as captured for all time by Andrew Ross Sorkin in *Too Big to Fail*.[10] The deal had been struck. But Rob knew only too well that a deal is never done until the money is in hand. He expected it to be delivered without fanfare. The Japanese rarely do anything important without formality. Ceremony is paramount. Once again, Rob would be responsible for an important check, this one slightly larger than the one he had pretended to lose at Cravath as a young man.

The Wachtell receptionist got word to Rob that Takaaki Nakajima, general manager for the Bank of Tokyo-Mitsubishi (UFJ) and a group of his immaculately dressed colleagues were waiting to be received. "Kindler was embarrassed; he looked like a beach bum," Sorkin writes. "He ran down the hall and quickly borrowed a suit jacket from a lawyer—but as he was buttoning the front, he heard a low tear. The seam on the back of the jacket had ripped in half. The Wachtell lawyers could only laugh."

Rob stood before the Japanese delegation, unshaven, gray-faced, in khakis, flip-flops, and a dark unmatched two-winged suit jacket. The Japanese showed only the slightest sign of what Sorkin calls bemusement. Rob apologized with as much fervor as he could muster, explaining that had he known that Mr. Nakajima planned to come to the firm himself that John Mack would also certainly have made sure to be there as well. Hank Riordan's voice from nearly 30 years before might well have echoed through the halls as Rob gripped the life preserver: "Did you get the *check?*"

Checks are always on the minds of investment bankers, but at this point, morale is lower than ever among investment advisers in M&A since the financial crisis and the drop in deals. The large banks have become volatile places to work. Morgan Stanley fired around 1,600 people in early 2013, many of whom were expensive senior bankers. Those with strong clients and personal relationships often peel off to join smaller places or found their own M&A advisory boutiques. At the same time, it's difficult to change jobs because compensation is now typically deferred for as long as three years. To hire a person who is expecting to be paid large sums in the future means that he or she won't move unless that is replaced by the new job. This is by design. It helps prevent poaching, but it can make people feel trapped.

What's more, they feel unloved. "You go into a boardroom today, and a larger percentage of the directors are contemptuous of those who come in from an investment bank," says one senior banker at Lazard. "You are presumptively at best amoral, if not actually immoral. It's assumed that you're going to sell them down the river and do whatever's good for yourself rather than give them good advice. That's the prejudice of a much larger group of people today than was true in the past. The eighties and nineties were more fun. You were much less vilified."[11]

Peter Weinberg, of Perella Weinberg Partners, agrees with his fellow investment banker from Lazard.[12] "You level on top of [the troubled state of finance], the vitriol. I think we all agree, in part it's deserved. Wall Street has been under attack because they—we—were at the center of many of the problems that caused the crisis. But if you cut through it all, I really feel that the vitriol has affected the relationship between Wall Street and its clients, between Wall Street and boards of directors, and between Wall Street and chief executives. Wall Street is taking it on the chin."

Three of the five independent investment banks vaporized. The last two giants, Goldman and Morgan Stanley, were forced to become bank holding companies and are now subject to far more regulation by the authorities than ever before. All the other investment banks, familiar for so long, have become portions of commercial banks. They are now basically M&A departments serving as bait to draw clients to the bank's other more important services. An instant debate has arisen between those who see the smaller, boutique investment banks outpacing their far larger cousins, since the former can establish close personal relationships with clients and are not barnacled with as many conflicts as are the more dominant behemoths.

Weinberg did a recent study and taxonomy of the financial institutions business. He divides that world into four categories of banks. The largest are what he calls integrated firms, which include Morgan Stanley, Goldman, and JPMorgan Chase. These behemoths are in every line of financial work: equity money management, fixed income money management, private equity, hedge funds, market making, securities distribution, and institutional client solutions. They have a combined market value of $527 billion.

The second group he calls client fiduciaries. These include BlackRock and State Street. "This group is in equity money management and fixed income money management. They're client-only organizations," he says. "BlackRock happens to have about $3 trillion under management, so they're an enormous organization. But they're not really in the private-equity business. They are not in the hedge fund business. They definitely don't make markets. They're in the advisory business but not really in the M&A business. Yet."[13] This group has a combined market value of $90.4 billion.

The third group comprises the alternative asset managers, with KKR and Blackstone as prime examples. They are in the private-equity and hedge fund business, with a total market value of $35.4 billion. Finally, there is the group in which Peter counts his own firm, Perella Weinberg: the independent advisers, with a combined market value of $10 billion. "We're tiny relative to the rest of the market. If you look at the M&A market, the restructuring, and the private capital market, we—the independent firms—are about 10 percent of the market," Peter says. "We're not going to 50 percent of the market, I can promise you that. We shouldn't. Our concept would become outmoded if we did. But we could certainly get to 20 percent."

There are now three types of institutions encroaching on the big firms, Peter says, in the field of M&A advisory work. "I think that's probably a healthy thing. The client fiduciary and alternative asset managers are going to gain scale in asset management. They're going to continue to grow asset management significantly—scale has been king in that business. The integrated firms are going to get a bit smaller in the near term but will always play a critical role in the M&A business. I don't think there's a chance that these big firms are going to be more than 25 percent of that market. The concerns about conflicts are just growing every single day. That will also characterize what firms get into the business and which ones succeed."

* * *

BRUCE WASSERSTEIN, THE LATE HEAD OF LAZARD FRÈRES, DIED ON OCTOBER 14, 2009. At the memorial service at Lincoln Center's Vivian Beaumont Theater, Bruce's daughter, Pamela, told the crowd that her father loved James Bond movies. A particular favorite of his was *Live and Let Die.* It is the eighth Bond film and the first to star blond, solid, blue-eyed, Anglo-Saxon Roger Moore. For someone who must have suffered greatly for his unconventional appearance, what did Bruce see in this character, the epitome of someone who belongs, who is never laughed at, who is never ostracized, who always has the perfect phrase for any given moment? Told of the death of one of his colleagues, for example, Bond says without missing a beat, "Ah, Baines. I rather liked Baines. We shared the same bootmaker." Impossible aplomb.

The film opens with a series of three assassinations of MI–6 officers, known only by their surnames. The first is Dawes, at the UN, "keeping an eye on San Monique's prime minister, Dr. Kananga." An aerial shot of the East River moves into a high-ceilinged conference room of blue walls and blond wood, where the Hungarian representative, sounding like John Cleese speaking Russian in *A Fish Called Wanda,* is droning on. The scene cuts to the translation booth, where we hear what he is saying in English: " . . . was so ably pointed out by the secretary general in his opening remarks, but, and I must emphasize this, no formula can or will cover each case. For instance . . . when three or more applicants have been recognized, which is direct contradiction to subparagraph. . . ." Did all this remind Bruce of some of his less interesting times in the law? A hand reaches into the frame and unhooks the earphone of the doomed Dawes and replaces it with a cord that sends a high-frequency blast into the Englishman's ears, sending his head to the desk with a thud. No one is quite sure at first whether he has collapsed from boredom.

Thence to New Orleans, pronounced by the English actors as "Nyew Awe-Leee-Unz." At a corner of Dumaine Street, Hamilton, a second MI–6 man "on loan to the Americans," leans against a lamppost as a funeral appears. The Olympia Brass Band plays a lugubrious version of "Just a Closer Walk with Thee," a nineteenth-century spiritual whose author remains unknown. The character "Baby-Faced Killer" appears at Hamilton's side, played by the band's actual trumpeter, Alvin Alcorn. "Whose funeral?" Hamilton asks. "Yours," comes the inevitable response from BFK, who slips a stiletto between the hapless ribs of Hamilton. As the funeral procession nears the slumped body, the pallbearers place the coffin on top of Hamilton's remains. When they lift the coffin again, the Englishman is somehow inside it, and the procession continues. It is but a few more steps before the band breaks into a rousing, blood-tingling version of "Joe Avery's Piece," and the lugubrious procession turns into a dancing parade with parasols open and trumpets blaring.

Pamela Wasserstein stood silently after describing her father's love of the scene, and at that moment, the brass band she had commissioned to come to the Vivien Beaumont burst through the doors playing the same number to the astonished crowd of Wasserstein friends and former colleagues. The death of Wasserstein, in the doldrums of the greatest of M&A depressions, brought an era to an end. It is as if "M" revoked without warning 007's license to kill.

The real New Orleans is where M&A gathers every year, under the auspices of Tulane Law School, for a conference founded by Justice Andrew G. T. Moore II. In 2012, Peter Weinberg, who was co-head of global investment banking and a chief executive officer at Goldman Sachs and now runs an investment bank with Wasserstein's former partner Joe Perella, voiced the conviction of many: The next M&A boom is imminent, already overdue. There is no shortage of causes for pessimism, Weinberg admits, from Iran to Syria, from Europe to the fiscal challenges in the United States. "I think if you walked around New York or London or other financial centers around the world, you would find people very cautious about where the M&A business is going. I want to make the case for the exact opposite. I want to argue the case for optimism. We do have some conviction on this. We think that M&A activity is going to have a significant recovery over the next 12 to 24 months."[14]

Weinberg has an impressive list of the forces, for so long compressed, that will drive the next boom. US corporations have Scrooge McDuck–sized piles of cash, an estimated $2 trillion in dry powder. Apple alone has $100 billion in cash. Corporations now have nowhere else to go for growth but M&A. "Companies now are maxed out on productivity. Operating margins have increased very, very significantly over the years. What this tells you is there is really not much organic growth left, because you've squeezed the lemon as much as you can squeeze it." What's more, shareholders around the world are clamoring for growth, and there are vast new hunting grounds in a cheapening Europe and high growth rates in emerging markets.

Finally, CEOs are beginning to move toward a Gladwellian tipping point of confidence, the most powerful impetus, the sine qua non, of M&A. They see that existing home sales are rising, durable goods orders are strengthened, high-yield bond markets are seeing large inflows of cash, rail shipments are soaring, and small-business confidence is at last on the rise. Plenty of money, little room for growth from within, and intense pressure for profits from the shareholders are forces that will not remain dormant for long. "Shareholders are forcing companies to do acquisitions. Companies have the resources to do M&A. And they have the will to acquire," says Weinberg. "So: buying cheap in Europe, buying expensively in Asia, and buying to consolidate in the U.S.—that's my general theme."[15]

But when will it all start? That question has been echoing through the halls of law firms, investment banks, and boardrooms since the Great Recession. Weil Gotshal thinks it may never start again and in June 2013 fired 60 of its roughly 900 associates and cut the pay of 10 percent of its 334 partners. At the March 2013 Tulane conference, Mark Shafir was far less pessimistic. Citigroup's co-head of global M&A and head of global technology, media, and telecom banking said this: "Not yet." The value of M&A hit $2.8 trillion in 2011 and $2.7 trillion in 2012, still far below the 2007 record of between $4.4 and $4.6 trillion, depending on the metrics used to calculate the numbers. Yet Shafir agrees that all the pistons for M&A are poised to pump once more. And encouraging signs were seen in 2012: the Virgin Media deal for $24.1 billion, the Dell proposal at $20.7 billion, the US Airways–American Airlines merger at $13.1 billion, to name a few. And Warren Buffett has linked arms with 3G Capital to buy H. J. Heinz Company for $23 billion.

*   *   *

EZRA ZILKHA DEBATED THE QUESTION OF THE NEW M&A RICH WITH JIMMY GOLDSMITH at the Traveller's Club on the Champs Élysée one day in the late 1990s, not long before Jimmy's death. It was Jimmy's father's favorite club and an oddly appropriate place for them to meet. Both were luminaries in the world of late-twentieth-century mergers and acquisitions, and the club's headquarters is a storied creation of the Gilded Age, the great nineteenth-century era of M&A. The house is a *hotel particulier,* one of the private mansions that sprung up in Paris in the 1800s. Renowned for its dazzling interiors then and now, it started life as the love palace of a courtesan who rose from poverty to become one of the established divas of her day: an arriviste who made it into the ranks of the elect, like M&A itself.

The Marquise de Paiva, later the Countess von Donnersmark, was born Esther Lachman in the Moscow ghetto to Polish Jews, refugees from the latest pogrom. After a starter marriage to a local boy, she chose for her second husband a rich man with a fictitious marquisate, whom she quickly dispatched back to his native Portugal. For her second, she chose her lover, Count Henckel von Donnersmark, an even richer man with a genuine title. The countess, also known as "La Paiva" as well as "La Grande Horizontale," made great use of her husband's immense fortune to build and then expand her Parisian palace, where she gave some of the most decadent parties in the history of Europe. Napoleon III once asked to be shown around the place, with its risqué jewel-encrusted, bestatued bathing chambers and massive carved onyx staircase. Eventually, the count and his countess retreated to his other estates, allegedly to escape charges of spying, and she was never able to return to her beloved house. The bereaved Donnersmark was said to have kept the body of the love of his life in a large jar of embalming fluid, the nightly focus of his lachrymose devotions.

Amid all this splendor, Ezra Zilkha and Jimmy Goldsmith found that they agreed on the basic nature of the new world that had been brought on by the febrile corporate takeovers of the era. M&A has reshaped contemporary life—the weapons industry that supplies our wars, the candy companies, telecommunications firms, Internet businesses, the magazines and newspapers of our day, the media giants that produce the movies and television we watch, the mining companies, department stores, engine factories, commercial banks and investment banks, the cruise ships we sail aboard, the clothes we wear, the pharmaceuticals that save our lives—all of contemporary experience has been transformed and remains in thrall to a mercurial, little-known, rarely understood organism with a double-barreled name.

Fed by the democratization of capital—the ability of the undesirable to borrow as much as, if not more than, those traditionally favored by financial mandarins—this creature became the unstoppable force behind a social and cultural revolution that dragged to the tumbrels the global aristocracy that ruled untrammeled for generations. Women and people of color and of disparate sexual orientation, those without acceptable genealogical pedigrees and those educated outside privileged enclaves, all so long excluded from the repositories of wealth and control that was corporate Earth, broke their way into those silos of power that had proved so impenetrable across the generations.

But is it good, this M&A? Ezra Zilkha, the consummate courtly man, took the position that all that M&A has wrought has not been good, nor have those who played with the balance sheets of large and important companies, switching equity into debt, turned out to be the most *sympathiques* of fellow humans. A way of life had been ruined, for Ezra, a sense of place and decency gone: I am a banker by both birth and profession. I believe in solidity. The Milken culture turned shareholders from investors into speculators. Banks have become something other than banks. Law firms have turned into businesses. Making money has always been important, but it has become heroic. You and I are beneficiaries of all this, but I abhor that culture. Perhaps I am living in a world that does not exist, but I don't believe in that kind of roughness, that kind of vulgarity.

Jimmy, in contrast, maintained that the terms "good" and "bad" were inapposite. Like nature itself, M&A is possessed of a monumental indifference. It lives in a moral vacuum, utterly uninterested in the turmoil it wreaks, the jobs it may destroy, the debt with which it can marble both prey and predator, as well as the new enterprises it can catalyze. Jimmy applauded what M&A had brought to life, the vitality of upheaval, the thrill of the extreme. People are upset by vulgarity. But vulgarity is, to some degree, a sign of vigor. It means that new people coming from nowhere are making it. It's the old American dream: *Anybody* can become a millionaire. So if we want change, if we want vigor, we're going to have vulgarity. It's one of the things that irritates, but which is necessary.

If Jimmy's theory is valid, the time is ripe for another revolution. And it is coming. M&A was instrumental in opening up the world of business, power, and culture to those to whom all was barred, but the massive treasure they acquired, their golden parachutes and severance pay when their companies are taken over, the special and highly lucrative tax treatment of private-equity riches, the bonuses and benefits reaped by investment bankers, and the slightly more earthbound profits of law partners, all wrought by M&A, have re-created what mergers originally dismantled. The camps of "occupiers" on Wall Street and in other cities around the world, while admirable in so many ways, have since been dispersed with little impact on the new rich.

It is now well known for only the second time in the last century, 5 percent of the national income goes to those in the upper one one-hundredth of a percent of the income distribution, the almost 15,000 families with incomes of $9.5 million or more a year, according to an analysis of tax returns by the economists Emmanuel Saez at the University of California, Berkeley, and Thomas Piketty at the Paris School of Economics. "Such concentration at the very top occurred in 1915 and 1916, as the Gilded Age was ending, and again briefly in the 1920s, before the stock market crash," reported Louis Uchitelle in the *New York Times*. "Now it is back."[16]

Sir James argued that Zilkha should temper his revulsion at the new raw world with an acceptance of the cyclicality of the human condition. He cited the experience of a Jewish banking dynasty not unlike Ezra's own, one with which the Goldsmiths had been entwined for centuries, dating back to the days of the Judengasse. "Ezra," he said with one of his upward-gazing, brow-furrowed smiles, "don't forget that this has always been the case. Think of the Rothschilds. When they came to England, they, too, were upstarts."[17]

CHAPTER TWENTY
RETURN TO THE TEMPLE

M&A tipped over the contented cow that was corporate America and broke down the fences that enclosed its lush pastures. This powerful global creature has moved through several stages in its progress toward maturity. The St. Joe Minerals deal in 1981 was M&A just as it was beginning to crawl. TWA was M&A in early childhood, defenseless but stubborn. The deals of 1985 showed M&A just entering the full flower of adulthood, changing and growing by the minute. The Allied and Federated episodes revealed M&A in the midst of an intoxicated, self-absorbed, delusional, mendacious midlife crisis. Viacom's conquest of Paramount was M&A as the catalyst for an empire.

Many giants of M&A are now gone. Joe Flom, Morris Kramer, John Kluge, and Bruce Wasserstein are just a few of those who have recently died. The ones who remain from the early years are coming to the end of their careers. They have knee issues. They see audiologists. They endure landmark birthdays and the funerals of comrades. Many look back with nostalgia on the wild days of their youth when the business was also young and all was raw and new, manic Mondays when the week's hostile campaigns would launch themselves aloft, court rulings coming down within days of the next. Now, they say, there is nothing but routine. It is as if the savages, if you will, have taken over the farm to become the new incumbent bovine herbivores. Who will challenge the established order in the new era of M&A?

Look to shareholder activists and the Delaware courts. Some of the new crowd of shareholder activists are former M&A players. They include Don Drapkin of Skadden and Revlon fame, Nelson Pelz, and, in his own special way, Carl Icahn. Hedge fund managers are also found in this genus, notably the increasingly bold-faced Bill Ackman of Pershing Square and his $12 billion hedge fund. These investors do not take over companies. They buy into them and change their direction. They are the benevolent mirror image of the greenmailer of old, although no link to such a past is acceptable to Roy Katzovicz, the chief lawyer at Pershing Square: "I wouldn't want to be known as any derivative of a greenmailer, reflection or otherwise. We don't appropriate value for ourselves to the exclusion of other shareholders. Just the opposite. We incur transaction costs, reputation and regulatory risk, the fruits of which the blessed free-riding other shareholders enjoy."[1] Bill Ackman himself says, "Shareholder activists don't get no respect."[2]

It is irrefutable that investors like the young and aggressive team at Pershing Square do not buy large chunks of public companies so that they can hold their newly bought shares as hostages, extracting ransom money from companies eager to buy back the stock to get rid of potentially troublesome owners. Shareholder activists stress that they buy into companies to try to increase profits and sell their stock in the open markets when the share price rises accordingly, if all goes according to plan.

Shareholder activism is rising fast. No company is impregnable, no matter how large or how strong its performance. "Although 70 percent of activist campaigns target companies under $2 billion," says Citigroup's co-head of global mergers & acquisitions Mark Shafir, "recent trends highlight an increase in larger firms."[3] Sony, under pressure from hedge fund manager Daniel S. Loeb to sell its entertainment division; Apple, a $400 billion market cap company; Hewlett Packard at $93 billion; PepsiCo at $106 billion; Dell at $24 billion; Morgan Stanley at $38 billion; Hess at $22 billion; and Yahoo at $19 billion have all endured sharply aggressive shareholder activism, giants vulnerable to the giant killers. Even successful companies, with little it would seem for shareholder activists to complain about or to change, are now vulnerable to the giant killers. Although the average target underperformed other comparable corporations by 15 percent, Shafir reports, fully one-third of companies recently under attack were actually doing better than their peers in their industries. "As M&A activity increases," Shafir says, "so will M&A agitation."

Activists may not be as craven as their greenmailing collateral ancestors, but they are indisputably investors looking to make money, whether it comes quickly or over time. "If you believe that there are a lot of long-term investors," said Chancellor Leo Strine at the 2011 Tulane conference, "then you believe that Elizabeth Taylor had long marriages, because her typical marriage far exceeds the holding period of most institutional investors who own stock in American companies."[4] Carl Icahn, for one, has no patience with the term "shareholder activist." As he told Leslie Stahl on *60 Minutes* in 2008, "I don't say [shareholder activist]. The name is the same. An activist is the same as a raider. You call it by whatever name you want—a rose by any other name. . . . I make money. Nothin' wrong with that. That's what I want to do. That's what I'm here to do. That's what I enjoy."

* * *

THE JUDGE THOUGHT IT WAS TIME FOR HIS "STIFF-IN-THE-ROOM" STORY. AT CUYAHOGA
County Court of Common Pleas in 1998, Judge Timothy McGinty had
before him an array of investors led by Bill Ackman, and the object of their
desire, First Union, a real estate investment trust (REIT), whose management was visibly discombobulated by the young firebrands demanding volcanic change at the company. "I like to break up the tension with stories,"
Judge McGinty told *M&A Journal*'s Susan Pender in the course of her ex-
haustive analysis of the confrontation. "It releases the pressure," the judge
said, "and the parties will be either jointly amused or jointly irritated. Egos
come into play in these things, and I try to defuse them too."[5]

It seems that the young Mr. and Mrs. McGinty were on their honey-
moon in the late 1970s in Ireland. "My wife and I were driving down the
road to my aunt-in-law's house to stop in for tea and a shot—only they don't
call it a shot there, they call it whiskey. She lived in a stereotypically Irish
cottage right on the sea. We noticed a few people milling around her house.
We didn't know what was going on. When we went in, instead of having tea
on the table, they had a stiff on the table, packed in dry ice. I was introduced
to my distant—and dead—cousin-in-law. This seemed bad at first. I asked,
'When are we getting out of here?' and they told me, 'In the morning.' So
we smoked, and drank, and we sang, and by the end of the night, we were
having a good time, and I had gotten used to the stiff in the room." The
judge turned to the First Union people. "Things look bad, having Ackman
and his crew show up. But the stiff is here, and you've got to learn to have
your tea with it."

On the night of March 25, 1998, both houses of Congress agreed to
support President Bill Clinton's proposal in his 1999 budget to eliminate
the structure that had allowed so-called paired-share REITs to buy real
estate–intensive operating companies and to avoid corporate tax on that
income. For First Union and its suitors, this meant an instant loss of a structure worth some $200 million. "Was there any left to fight over?" Susan
Pender asks in her article. "The coveted structure had disappeared, literally overnight. [Bill Ackman's] Gotham [the predecessor to his present
Pershing Square hedge fund] had a $30 million investment in First Union,
representing 8.3 percent of the shares outstanding. It was mired in an expensive and no-holds-barred proxy fight with First Union management to
expand the board and install a majority of Gotham nominees. Should it
walk away? Could it?" Not Bill Ackman. "If we had blown out the stock,"
he told Pender, "it would have dropped to $5.00 per share [from $11.75]
immediately. But more importantly, we were carrying the ball for all the
shareholders. We take that responsibility seriously, and we're not quitters."

They certainly were not in this early saga, nor have they been ever
since. Bill Ackman, then 36 years old, fought for 18 months to take control

of the board of First Union, even after the obscure Cleveland real estate company turned valueless overnight. Ackman won the proxy fight in a landslide with support from 75 percent of the shares outstanding. It was always a fight between opposites, the stolid, God-citing James Mastandrea, First Union's chairman, president, and CEO, and the relentless, supremely confident young giant killer from Manhattan and his Gotham Partners. But it turned into more than just a conflict of cultures.

Reputations suffered, and millions were spent. Ackman and his fellow investors in First Union—including Apollo Real Estate Advisers, Black-acre Capital Group/Cerberus Partners, Franklin Mutual Advisers, and NorthStar Capital—were accused of a "calculated group effort—illegal under Section 13(d) of the Securities Exchange Act of 1934—to take over First Union without paying a premium for control using any and all means available."[6] Ackman, on the other hand, told Pender that the villains were Mastandrea and his counsel at Squire, Sanders & Dempsey. "This is a story about a company where the key protagonists, whether the Board of Trustees, the CEO or the company's counsel, operated under an agenda and in pursuit of interests that were not aligned with the shareholders."[7]

Susan Pender describes the miscalculations by the two adversaries as follows: "Mastandrea's strategy for shaking off Ackman in this dogfight was, to say the least, unpredictable. Mastandrea's behavior was at different times rude, obstreperous, illogical, and, as Judge McGinty found, 'not . . . designed to protect First Union's REIT status but rather management.' Who could foresee that a CEO of a public company would engage in such behavior? So it is understandable that Ackman may not have been totally prepared for battle in Mastandrea's Wonderland. However, once the battle was joined, it would appear that Ackman failed to pick up on and appreciate Mastandrea's confidence in himself borne out by past accomplishments. Even if Ackman didn't view Mastandrea as accomplished, the point is that Mastandrea did, unequivocally. So all Ackman's assumptions about First Union following in the footsteps of the other paired-shared REITs were irrelevant. Similarly, Mastandrea failed to appreciate Ackman's confidence and drive. Ackman is not a man to be pushed aside, threatened away, or bought off, approaches Mastandrea had used handily in the past but were totally ineffectual here. His batten-down-the-hatches, full-steam-ahead approach backfired on him this time."[8]

The 1997 fight for First Union was Ackman's breakout role, but it has largely been forgotten as he continues his tear through North American business. His new fund, Pershing Square, has bought stock and muscled its way into the boardrooms to fire up smoldering companies across the country and beyond. He single-handedly defrocked MBIA, "the largest of a handful of extraordinarily profitable companies that together guaranteed more than $2 trillion of debt issued by entities ranging from the

Cincinnati school system to a shell company in the Cayman Islands," as Christine Richards chronicles in her book, *Confidence Game*. Bill Ackman exposed the company's success "at insuring bonds on which it expected to pay no claims," as Richards puts it, as a sham: "[I]t wasn't the real insurer of the debt: Taxpayers were."[9] He has invested in Borders, Sears, McDonald's, General Growth Properties, Target, Canadian Pacific (Canada's second-largest railroad), and is now famously shorting stock at Herbalife, a large corporation that Ackman is convinced is nothing more than a 30-year-old pyramid scheme, which the company has vociferously denied.

J. C. Penney, the recent attempt to remake one of America's favorite, if faded, department stores, was classic Ackman. First, pinpoint a company with unlocked value. Second, buy a stake in the business, in this case fully 26 percent. Get a seat on the board of directors. Find the best person in the world to run the company and convince that person to leave his life and join yours. A central issue facing the company, Ackman said, was the fact that the CEO was 66 years old at the time. "We said, 'Look. We're going to help you with that." Ackman recruited Ron Johnson, a Harvard Business School graduate, who had spent 11 years remaking Target and had since moved to Apple, where he built what Ackman called "the most successful retail concept of all time"—Apple's 350 stores. "I went to see him and tried to convince him to leave Apple, the most valuable company in the world, where he had made 300 or 400 million on the stock personally, to go to Plano and go work for J. C. Penney," Ackman told the 2012 Tulane M&A conference. Steve Jobs himself asked Johnson, Ackman recalled, why he would "go work for a B-minus company with C people. A pretty straightforward guy, Steve Jobs," Ackman said.

Ackman knew that Johnson had his own not-so-hidden aspirations. "I knew that his dream was to be a CEO and become one of the great retailers of all time. And ultimately at Apple, he couldn't be CEO because he wasn't a technology guy." Johnson himself then had some convincing to do. "He went home and told his wife the deal he had made," Ackman said. "This is why you want to be married. She said, 'Okay. *Plano?* We're moving from Palo Alto to Plano. And you're going to make a dollar a year. And you're leaving Apple to go to—okay [*sigh*].'"

Ackman and Johnson had fervent hopes for the company. No more of the famous discounts and coupons and regular sales that the loyal customer base, incidentally, found so alluring. "They had 350 million sign changes last year," Ackman told the M&A gathering at Tulane, "because they were constantly changing their pricing and relabeling everything. They don't have to do that anymore, because they're marketing at the price. And they're actually treating the customer with respect, as opposed to misleading the customer. Only 0.2 percent—zero point two percent—of the goods J. C. Penney sold were at full retail last year. That was probably me running in to buy a pair of socks. It's been a very positive experience. I get along with all the other directors, and it's a great example, I think, of good governance and interaction. While the board was afraid of us in some sense on the way in, they could not be more friendly and complimentary about how the company is doing. It's a good story. It's early. Turnaround doesn't happen in a day. But Ron is on his way." Ron's way proved more difficult than even he and Ackman expected.

The Johnsons never did move to Plano. Ron commuted from Palo Alto. That was perhaps just the first of many ill-fated choices. On Tuesday, April 9, 2013, the entire experiment crashed. A week earlier, Bill told a conference that the turnaround had been "very close to a disaster." Johnson killed the recurrent sales at the store for which J. C. Penney was so well known and so well loved by its loyal fan base of bargain-hunting buyers. To recapture the customers who were abandoning the store en masse, Johnson reinstituted Ullman's practice of promotions, cuts in prices, and advertisements. He then turned to so-called pop-up stores, small outlets dotted throughout the main establishment. This landed the company in court fighting Macy's, which claims that J. C. Penney has violated Macy's contract with Martha Stewart. Revenue has tumbled by $4.3 billion, with no end yet in view; some 20,000 workers have been fired, the stock price has dropped by 18 percent, the board cut Johnson's compensation by 97 percent for 2012 to $1.9 million, and Ackman himself seemed to pull away from full-throated support for Johnson. At last, the board, now chaired by Thomas Engibous, stepped in after a 17-month whirlwind, fired Johnson, and reinstated the former CEO, Mike Ullman, now in his sixty-seventh year. Ackman later quit the board in disgust in 2013.

A final irony in the old adventures of the new J. C. Penney went viral in late May 2013. The company put a picture of a teapot designed by Michael Graves on a billboard in Culver City. Drivers along the road posted on social media their view that the item looked like the face of a certain deceased German dictator, with a curved black handle resembling his hair, the dark tip of the kettle lid calling to mind his nose and mustache, with the kettle spout reminiscent of an infamous wartime salute. It was quickly taken off company shelves. Then it reappeared. Sales exploded. It is known as the Hitler Teapot.

A few years after the First Union conquest, Gotham Partners ran into trouble, and Ackman agreed to wind down the fund and return as much money as possible to his investors. It was in the course of this fraught effort that Ackman and Icahn had their first encounter.

The toy airplanes emblazoned with the TWA logo and the toy railcars with the ACF insignia that first warned Ilan Reich that Icahn was on the prowl for both targets are still on display in Icahn's offices, now on the forty-seventh floor of the General Motors building. The old lion's collection of hunting trophies has burgeoned since we last saw him in the mid-1980s, when Steven Brill counted 14 framed annual reports, "each trumpeting a quick money triumph" along the halls of his offices on Sixth Avenue.[10] Icahn, now entering his late 70s, with a net worth of some $20 billion, which exceeds that of George Soros, fought 14 companies in the 15 months from January 2012 to April 2013. "Lucite so-called tombstones recount conquests involving many of the great companies of the twentieth century, from MBM to Morotola, Texaco to Nabisco."[11]

In 2003, when Bill was not yet famous, he called Icahn to offer to sell him stock in one of Gotham's investments known as Hallwood Realty as part of Bill's effort to recoup at least some of his investors' money. "His world was falling apart," Azam Ahmed recounted in his article in the *New York Times*. "Gotham Partners, the hedge fund he helped to found when he was in his 20s, had just blown up. The Securities and Exchange Commission and Eliot Spitzer, then attorney general of New York, were investigating him. His investors wanted their money back. So Mr. Ackman cold-called Mr. Icahn."[12] Carl agreed to buy the shares and offered what he called "schmuck's insurance." If Icahn sold the stock within three years, he would split any profits with Ackman above a 10 percent return. "In 2004," Ahmed wrote, "Hallwood merged with another company, for $137 a share, netting Mr. Icahn a tidy profit. After waiting a few days, Mr. Ackman called to compliment him and to ask about his share."[13] Carl claimed that a merger was not a sale and that he therefore owed Ackman nothing. Two New York courts sided with Ackman, and in 2011, when Carl's final appeal was denied, Bill got around $9 million from Carl, virtually double the original $4.5 million because of the accrued interest.

Their squabble poured onto the airwaves on CNBC's *Fast Money Halftime* on Friday, January 25, 2013, in a discussion that was meant to explore their respective hedge fund positions in Herbalife. Here is the inimitable Icahn:

> CARL ICAHN: Well, you know, listen. I really sort of have had it with this guy Ackman, you know? Why don't we go back over a little history with him. You know, I'm not going to get into talking about short positions as much as maybe you'd like. Hey, let's start with my history with this guy. I was minding my own business. In 2003 I get a call from this Ackman guy. I'm telling you, he's like the crybaby in the schoolyard. I went to a tough school in Queens. They used to beat up the little Jewish boys. He was like a little Jewish boy crying that the world was taking advantage of him. He's in my office talking about how I could help him, and it was like in the old song—"You will rue the day I ever met the guy." . . . I got involved with this Ackman guy, and it cost me money.
>
> SCOTT WAPNER: Well, it cost you money because a court said you reneged on the agreement you guys had, and a court repeatedly said that.

Here is a sample of Ackman's response:

> BILL ACKMAN: "We have a simple ten-page agreement." He said, "I'm not pay-
> ing." I said, "I will sue you." We got a summary judgment. He threatened
> to sue me. Why did he threaten to sue me? He was a bully. Okay? I was
> not in a good place in my business career. I was under investigation by
> Spitzer, winding down my fund. There was negative press about Gotham
> Partners. I was short MBIA. They were aggressively attacking me, and
> Carl Icahn thought this guy is roadkill on the hedge fund highway. He
> won't have the resources to sue me, so I won't pay him. The number of
> stories I have heard from bankers, lawyers, people he's worked with where
> he's done similar things to take advantage of someone. The unfortunate
> thing is I told Carl I would go to the end of the earth to make sure he
> paid my investors. Every penny he owed me with interest. . . . This is not
> an honest guy who keeps his word. This is a guy who takes advantage of
> little people.

The stiffs are in the room, as Judge McGinty might say, and they're not
going anywhere. They are likely to come into Chancellor Strine's courtroom as well, as their power and ambition grow ever more intense.

* * *

THE FRENCH AMBASSADOR KISSED EZRA ZILKHA ON BOTH CHEEKS, AND THE CEREMONY
at the consulate in New York was complete. Ezra was elevated from the
rank of *chevalier* to *officier* in the Légion d'honneur. Afterward, Ezra spoke
of his deep Francophilia: "I explained that Vercingetorix, Charlemagne,
Joan of Arc, the wisdom of Henry IV and Sully, the extraordinary life and
conquests of Napoleon, and historic figures like Poincaré and Clemenceau
had been part of my elementary education. Like all young Frenchmen of
the period," he said at the time, "I read history, and the first sentence in my
book read, 'My ancestors, the Gauls. . . .' That is how my original loyalty to
France was formed. I always say that I was born Iraqi, I became an American citizen, but in my heart I have always been French."

Afterward, Conrad Black came up to Ezra and asked why, in the litany
of famous Frenchman, Ezra had omitted Cardinal Richelieu. As king in
all but name, *l'Eminence rouge*, as he became known, had risen by courting
those who could confer favors. Once established at the pinnacle of power,
he forced the feudal aristocrats to bow before royal authority and is cred-
ited not only with transforming France into a centralized nation-state but
also with checking the advance of the Habsburgs across Europe. Bribes
and manipulation and diplomatic and court intrigue, power grabs, and vast

wealth: Was he not a great man as well? asked Black. "Yes," Ezra answered with reluctance, "but I never liked him."[14]

No stranger to power, intrigue, or aristocratic trimmings, Conrad Black, the former press magnate, owner of 500 titles across Canada, Britain, and the United States, gave up his Canadian citizenship in 2001 for a seat in the House of Lords as Baron Black of Crossharbour, or Lord Black for short. In April 2012, Lord Black wrote an essay excoriating an American judge. He began his essay in Canada's *National Post* with "This column is a warning."

He wrote his piece after serving 29 months of a six-and-a-half-year sentence at Coleman Federal Correctional Complex in Florida, incarcerated with a collection of Mafia chieftains, child molesters, drug offenders, and other inmates, ineligible as a foreigner for less rigorous imprisonment at a minimum-security prison. Once the ruler of a press empire that included London's *Telegraph,* the *Jerusalem Post,* and the *Chicago Sun-Times,* with houses in Palm Beach, New York, and London, he was accused of looting his company, Hollinger International, misappropriating funds, and enjoying massive so-called management fees paid to shell companies under his control that amounted to what was claimed to have been 95 percent of Hollinger's profits between 1997 and 2003. Former SEC chairman Richard Breedon's year-long report called all this "corporate kleptocracy." But Lord Black was undeterred by it all, including Vice Chancellor Leo Strine, who took him to task in Delaware's Chancery Court in 2004 for "repeatedly behaving in a manner inconsistent with the duty of loyalty he owed the company."[15]

Lord Black did not forget his encounter in Delaware. Herewith, excerpts from the baronial response:

A seriously irritating and dangerous Delaware corporate and commercial judge, Leo Strine, aspires to establish a personality cult without frontiers, even in Canada, where he has no automatic authority, a fact that should be a matter of profound and constant thanksgiving from St. John's to Victoria. As a public service to my native country, I must utter a Philippic against this improvident interloper.... Strine is, I am reliably told, conversationally and socially rather aggressive, and improbably, given his physical stature and Mr. Peepers likeness, is an ostentatious sports fan. He rules his court like a full-time martinet and constantly inflicts what he evidently considers to be his unfailingly rapier-like wit on all those to whom his judgments are too important to permit the groans that commend themselves. He will get to any plausible speaking event (including one in Toronto not long ago), if necessary by flapping his arms. He fancies himself a crusader for the little person, a holy terror against "hinky" boardroom and executive suite practices, a shoot-from-the-hip authority on almost anything, and a crack philologist, constantly adding funky new words to the language; what isn't "hinky" is apt to be "freakin" and so forth. A bright, energetic little man, seeking attention and trying to become a celebrity despite his rather dry and technical occupation, is not unprecedented and need not be exceptionable. . . . His throbbing little ego predominates, and he should have bells on his head like a medieval leper, to warn the unsuspecting, including all of Canada, of his approach.[16]

Lord Black seems all set for his next incarnation as a talk-show host in Canada. The show is to be produced by Moses Znaimer's ZoomerMedia and is to be called *The Zoomer—Television for Boomers with Zip.*[17]

Strine may be doing something right, as these things are often measured. He has not only angered a felon but annoyed a chief justice. In 2012, Strine ran afoul of Myron Steele, the seventh chief justice of the Delaware Supreme Court. At oral argument on September 12, 2012, in the case of *Auriga Capital Corp. v. Gatz Properties LLC,* Chief Justice Steele expressed deep annoyance at Chancellor Strine's penchant for skiing off piste. The details of the legal question before both courts are of less interest than the fact that this appears to be the first time the chancellor has been reprimanded for what might be called his penchant for unusual digressions.

In his decision, he indulged in a lengthy exploration of the legislative language on LLCs, citing several of his own rulings along the way. "Did the chancellor *have* to go there?" Chief Justice Steele asked of Steve Caponi of Blank Rome.[18] "Could this case not have been decided based on the language in the LLC agreement? Why did he go to this whole *diatribe,* for lack of a better word, about how ignorant people are who think other than he does about whether the default position is 'fiduciary duties apply or don't apply.' And then vacillate—*back and forth*—between the statutory analysis and an equitable analysis in what I find to be a *highly* confusing way of approaching it? Could he have stopped with the LLC language analysis and ended the case?"

As if such a public expression of annoyance in open court were not unusual enough, the high court justices, while affirming the chancellor's decision, criticized their lower court colleague in the text of their own opinion, calling his discussion "improvident and unnecessary" and, the ultimate rebuke, "without precedential value." It is reminiscent of the scene in Milos Forman's *Amadeus.* "My dear young man," Emperor Joseph II says to Mozart after the world premiere of *The Marriage of Figaro,* "don't take it too hard. Your work is ingenious. It's quality work. And there are simply too many notes, that's all. Just cut a few and it will be perfect." Undaunted, Mozart replies, "Which 'few' did you have in mind, Majesty?"

The public spat between the two leaders of Delaware's two courts involves two men who are the most senior referees of the M&A game, one of whom is approaching 70 years of age and the other nearing 50. Myron Steele's father was an army officer posted in Taunton, Massachusetts, when Steele was born, but the family moved to Morocco, Japan, New Orleans, and then Virginia. Steele graduated from the University of Virginia in 1967. His time in Morocco exposed him to French, which he studied for nine years, and he majored as an undergraduate in foreign affairs with a concentration in the Middle East. Then it was on to Virginia's law school, where he served as articles editor of the *Virginia Journal of International Law.*

Steele now lives in Dover, Delaware, as close to the English countryside and the English way of life he loves as one could possibly get. His wife, he once said, "teaches young ladies and gentlemen to ride English and boards jumpers and hunters." Steele has long loved fox hunting, duck and pheasant shoots, and his 104-acre estate known as Fox Den Farm. While he lives the life of a country gentleman, he has also been described by one friend as "peripatetic" and travels widely. He is a devoted Anglophile, reveres English common law, and travels regularly to England. "Under glass on his desk are photographs of Beefeaters, the Princess of Wales, and Churchill," Benjamin Wallace wrote in *Corporate Control Alert.* "On a table nearby lie two books: *The Guards* (of Buckingham Palace), and *Sporting Art of England 1700–1900.* Colnaghi prints of the Crimean War, bought in England, hang on the walls."

Nicknamed "Marn" for the way his name is pronounced in downstate Delaware, the chief justice, colleagues have said, is intolerant of unprepared lawyers but judges with patience and dispassion. "I've never seen him embarrass anyone in the courtroom," Nicholas Rodriguez, a Dover attorney, says. "He is if anything extremely critical of himself."[19] "With authority comes accountability. With authority comes responsibility," Steele has said more than once. Another friend says Steele's philosophical conservatism is tempered by a liberal attitude toward people. He likes to be with different kinds of people with different backgrounds, perhaps a recapitulation of his early years, and he is said to be as comfortable talking to a lawyer from Wall Street as he is to a person from the fire department or a fellow "gun" in a duck blind. Chief Justice Steele certainly has a sense of humor about himself, on display at a recent conference, when he responded to his introduction with a quip: "I'm sitting in the middle of the table, and therefore there is an inference that my views are moderate. Let me dispense with that one."

Tradition is paramount to the chief justice. He has been known to protest if the Civil War is referred to as anything but the "War between the States." With a sweeping set of changes on the table for shareholder voting in the late first decade of the new millennium, Steele sounded a note of caution, with typical erudition and elegance, which would seem to be one of the truths he lives by. "Whenever we talk about change in what has been fundamentally working well, I'm reminded of a comment that reportedly was made by Lord Salisbury. Now, those of you who like British history as much as I do will immediately recognize that Lord Salisbury was the last British prime minister to govern from the House of Lords, and was a Tory. In 1912, he made the following comment: 'Reform, sir? You speak to me of reform? Aren't things bad enough as they are?'" Steele was thus not perhaps the most receptive audience when Strine once mentioned during a break at the annual Tulane conference that, for him, visiting New Orleans was the equivalent of a "hormonal rush." There was a small strained silence as the senior judge of Delaware pondered that thought.

Chancellor Leo E. Strine Jr. was born in Baltimore in 1964, the son of teenage parents. In 1973, the family moved to Hockessin, outside Wilmington, where Leo's father got a job as a buyer for Lit Brothers, a Philadelphia department store. It was through Governor Thomas Carper, now a member of the US Senate, that Leo launched himself into public life. While a freshman at the University of Delaware, he volunteered for Carper's campaign for Congress, blowing up balloons and handing them out at football games. "In 1984, I did a lot of work for Senator Biden's re-election campaign as well as for Carper at the grunt level of getting out the vote and dropping literature. I can still do a political polling phone call pretty much from memory," he told David Marcus of *The Deal*.[20] Leo went to law school at the University of Pennsylvania and joined Skadden's Wilmington office. When Leo was 28 years old, the governor called for him, and Leo became Governor Carper's legal adviser and one of his top policy aides, responsibilities that would come back to haunt him when he was nominated to the Court of Chancery.

A memory that haunts him in a far more fundamental sense involves the death penalty. As Governor Carper's counsel, Strine had the unenviable task of giving the order by telephone to prison wardens to proceed with a scheduled execution. He had to do this about six times during his tenure, but one was notably gruesome. "It particularly bothered Strine," Susan Beck wrote for the *American Lawyer* in her recent profile of the new chancellor, "that the prisoner had to wait for many long minutes in the cold before Strine could tell the warden to proceed."[21] She quoted Strine as saying, "The case with the hanging—that still gets to me."

As chancellor, Strine also sits on the Delaware Board of Pardons, which voted in January 2012 to commute the death sentence of convicted murderer Robert Gattis to life in prison. The panel noted in its written explanation, Beck reports, that one member of the board announced that he believed it to be immoral and unethical to take another's life in the absence of self-defense. Strine told Beck that he was that man.

Delaware is home to more corporations than could physically fit within its boundaries. Delaware has been corporate America's favorite of all the 50 states since 1913, Governor Woodrow Wilson of New Jersey began taxing companies that were incorporated but not based in his state and decrying big business in general, spoiling paradise for corporations and sending companies fleeing to nearby Delaware. The corporate franchise tax, paid by the estimated 850,000 businesses that choose to incorporate in the state, is a fountain of youth and riches, accounting for some 20 to 25 cents of every tax dollar Delaware collects. Although there are perennial cries of anguish at a certain amount of drift toward other states of incorporation, Delaware remains the center of gravity for business and business law, partly because of its lawyers who specialize in such things and partly because of the two courts that referee American commerce and, increasingly, influence the practice of commercial law around the globe.

Oddly, the Delaware judiciary rests on an unconstitutional premise, understood by all but acknowledged by few. The judges on both the Chancery Court and the Supreme Court of Delaware must, by state law, be equally divided by political party and geographical location. If, therefore, you are not registered as either a Democrat or a Republican, of if you are not registered to vote at all, you cannot serve on the Delaware bench. This is a violation of the Fourteenth Amendment, which bans discrimination on the basis of location or political party. It is thus a complicated place, this small community of business people, judges, lawyers, and politicians. It is easy to poke fun at this Vatican City of M&A, but it does serious work, and it can exact its revenge on those who do not fit in.

Consider the case of one of the state's supreme court justices, who was the country's first and most eminent jurist in M&A. Justice Andrew G. T. Moore II did not always have two initials in the middle of his name or a Roman numeral at the end. He was born Emmet Assenheimer. He apparently abandoned that somewhere along his way. In mid-May 1994, a nine-member judicial nominating commission refused to submit the justice's chosen name to the governor for renomination. Justice Moore appealed the decision; the commission reconsidered the case but returned the same verdict. On May 25, Governor Thomas Carper announced that he would abide by the decision of his commission and would also deny Justice Moore's request that the commission's deliberations be made public.

No one denied then, or does to this day, Justice Moore's intellect, his diligence, or his dedication to the law. He decided a string of landmark cases in M&A the likes of which no one is ever likely to equal: *Revlon, Unocal, Ivanhoe Partners, Macmillan, Time/Warner,* the *Technicolor* case, and *QVC v. Paramount.* He chaired the annual conference at Tulane for years. He taught at Tulane's Institute of European Legal Studies in Paris and was an adjunct professor of law at Widener Law, the University of Iowa College of Law, and the Georgetown University Law Center. Despite all this, Justice Moore became the first sitting judge in Delaware in roughly 60 years to be denied reappointment to a second term. What went wrong?

One senior member of the Delaware bar explained it this way at the time: "There are a lot of lawyers who really do not like him because he has really gone out of his way to be unpleasant, rude, uncivil, and unfair."[22] Another equally respected Delaware lawyer agreed: "When you look at the case law for which he is responsible, he is a giant. But those of us who appear before him every day see him as intemperate, abusive of lawyers, irascible, and unpleasant. This is a very despised man."

Skadden's Jim Freund was one of the few voices of regret. "He has strong feelings about the issues," Jim said then, "but I never thought that was a disqualification. He calls them like he sees them. He is very lucid. He questions people strongly. He's a hard-hitting kind of guy. It's tough as a lawyer when you have fuzzy judges and fuzzy justice. That makes it hard to plan your next deal. But Justice Moore lets you know where you stand. I thought of him as one of the top judges in the country. This must be very painful for him—just terrible."[23] Governor Carper did not agree. In brief comments after the nominating commission's decision, he said it was Justice Moore's temperament, a "lack of civility," that caused his professional demise.

In 1998, Governor Carper nominated Leo Strine to the Court of Chancery. It was not pretty. Leo had made many enemies while wielding the governor's hatchet, and there were those who bore the scars from the wounds that hatchet inflicted. One Skadden partner led the charge against Leo's appointment, Ed Welch of the firm's Wilmington office. No one could understand why, until it was revealed that Welch had misunderstood a remark by Strine to be directed at Welch's own sister. All has now healed, friends of both men say, but not before the vote came in at 12 to 8, only one over the required minimum. It also required what Susan Beck called "some blatant horse trading" by the governor.[24] The confirmation hearing was held on the date that Strine's wife was expected to deliver their first child.

The investiture, held at the Court of Chancery in Wilmington, must have been a particular relief, surrounded as he was by people who both knew him and wished him well: Judge Walter Stapleton, a Third Circuit judge who had taken on Strine as a young clerk; Rod Ward from Skadden's Wilmington office, who, in an example of the smallness of the Delaware world, had interviewed Chief Justice Steele while Steele was a UVA law student; Stu Shapiro, who had worked with Strine when the latter was a young associate at Skadden; and Chief Justice Steele, then a vice chancellor. Steele noted that Leo had been described as a "wizard" and urged him to continue in that incarnation on the Court of Chancery. Rod Ward read from a report from the early 1990s to the Skadden partnership about Leo's first six months at the firm. The review was written by a partner known to be a tough grader. "Leo is lacking only one requirement for instant partnership," the report said. "He is severely lacking in the hirsute department." It was written by Stu Shapiro.[25]

Critics have argued that Strine is also lacking in the decorum department. They complain that he is what they call "unjudicial." His nickname is "The Owl." Sometimes it is "The Owl Unplugged" when his mind is racing and his mouth is open. Strine aficionados collect his sayings and aphorisms: "Bankers like to shackle themselves together. It's a fetishistic kind of thing they do." And then there is his joy in puns, including those made by others. At the Tulane conference of 2011, after Wachtell won a victory before then-chancellor William Chandler in a case known as *Airgas,* Strine asked a question of Wachtell partner David Katz:

> VICE CHANCELLOR STRINE: David, I heard a story out of school about you from Ted Mirvis [a Wachtell partner]. You coined a new term at the celebration party for the *Airgas* decision. Is it true now that an innovative defense is now referred to at Wachtell as "Airgasmic"? And that there are marketing materials portraying Wachtell as the leader historically in multiple orgasm? Airgasm. Same thing in a deal context. Is that true?
>
> DAVID KATZ: I'll let Ted comment on that on his panel.
>
> VICE CHANCELLOR STRINE: You mean maybe he's giving you this credit and maybe he should keep some for himself?

It can seem at times that Strine enjoys an idiosyncratic stream of consciousness when immersed in some of the less interesting duties of the job. At a scheduling conference in November 2012, for example, he is faced with the battle between fashion entrepreneurs Christopher Burch and Tory Burch, ex-spouses and ex-partners, and he finds himself overcome by a sense of absurdity.

> This is, like, a scheduling conference. That's all it is. It's just in a, you know, it's a grander room because of the things that hang on the wall. Otherwise, it's like a Hechinger test kitchen. The different colors—none that I would ever select, but were selected for us. I don't—I didn't see any reason to burden anyone's Hanukkah, New Year's, Christmas, Kwanzaa, Festivus with this preppy clothing dispute. I don't know—I guess I did this to myself, but somebody in the room started the other tradition of giving—where, for some reason, I get all the preppy clothier cases because I've had J. Crew. I've had—I think because I'm culturally steeped in it since I was nine years old and learned what was hard for a kid from Baltimore, duck shoes? What's a duck shoe? You know, and then you see all these freaks wearing this really ugly—I like L. L. Bean, but those duck shoes are ugly. I mean, there's no way around it. So I think for both sides, it might come as news, you know, there's really nothing all that new about bright clothing and all that kind of stuff. So the novelty of any of this may be something that I have to discover for myself, although I do think the juxtaposition of *Two Fat Guys* and *Talbot's* in Greenville is just a beautiful thing. . . .

You know, I've actually, totally unrelated to this case, I've been deep in it, in an autumnal Cheever phase. And so I've been reading all kinds of Cheever. So I'll have to just keep that up through the—through the case. Have you read Cheever lately? You know who he is? I mean, it's, you know, and *Mad Men* will be coming back at some point in time, so I think if you read Cheever, go see the new Virginia Woolf revival and watch *Mad Men*, we'll be all geared up and in the mood for this sort of drunken WASP fest. Are they WASPs? Are the Burches WASPs? Do we know?

> ROBERT ISEN [CHIEF LEGAL OFFICER; TORY BURCH]: I don't know how to answer that question.
>
> CHANCELLOR STRINE: Well, it's some sort of—it's not—I mean, it's nothing wrong—it's called White Anglo-Saxon Protestant. So you don't know.
>
> MR. ISEN: No . . . I mean, Tory Burch is Jewish, and Chris is not Jewish.
>
> CHANCELLOR STRINE: Okay. But not Jewish doesn't make you a WASP, because it could make you an equally excluded faith like Catholic, right? I mean, that's not a WASP. You know, a WASP is a WASP. So, you know—I think you're going to have to have interrogatories about who's a WASP. And I'll certainly be attacked as anti-WASP, probably, and then I love all WASPs. I'm bringing actually Rodman Ward Jr. in as my expert because I always used to tell Rod that he actually had a lineage chart in his basement which had all of the Du-Pont family trees on it. It was like some people have war rooms. He had that to determine how they were actually related to the DuPont family. So I think we might be able to have some unique experts in Delaware.

Down came a warning from Chief Justice Steele in front of hundreds of M&A experts gathered at the 25th conference in New Orleans in the spring of 2013:

I think all judges on all of our courts need to be very conscious of the fact that when they speak in hearings that result in nothing but a transcript that that transcript is widely circulated and can churn up conversations that are not helpful to the guidance function, not helpful to the future development of the law and are generally of no consequence It could be as bland a situation as discussions during a scheduling conference. But this information gets widely shared, and it causes people to have thoughts about the future and the law that are not well grounded in either fact or opportunity. So I would hope that our trial judges would remember where they are when they make their comments, what they're trying to accomplish, and not send signals that never will be manifested in a holding in the future. I'm a firm believer that when the Court of Chancery speaks, that is Delaware law until something happens that causes it to be reversed, in particular in the Court of Chancery, our chancellor and our vice chancellors need to be very conscious of the fact that when they open their mouths, they make the law when they're in the courtroom. So be—not necessarily reticent—that's too much for me to hope for—but at least be careful when you make comments in the context of scheduling conferences, conversations about pretrial motions on the whole, because you are making law as you speak and it is recorded.

In his interview with Susan Beck of the *American Lawyer,* Strine said, "I'm sure at times I'm going to say things that aren't the most diplomatic. I will always be mindful of the reputation of my state, but I'm going to be myself."

Strine has many interests. He was an avid soccer player in college. He watches *Parks and Recreation* and *The Iron Chef.* His cultural references are legion, from the length of Elizabeth Taylor's marriages to Gomer Pyle, from Herman Melville to English punk rock from the 1970s, which he first encountered on a trip to London with his parents, when his Anglophilia took hold. He is widely read—"I subscribe to the *Atlantic,* the *New Republic,* the *Sunday Times,* other things. I'm not unaware of the world." He can be self-deprecating as well, noting his "Shaq-like" physique or his former obsession with running that by the end wore down his body to the point where he says he looked drunk or in need of an ambulance. Like Rob Kindler, Strine uses humor in myriad ways, but fail to take Strine seriously as a jurist and a human being, and you do so at your peril. If to be irreverent, widely read, immersed in popular culture, rich in the experience of human beings whether privileged or "row house people," as he has described his parents, interested in plays and books and film and sport, in public policy and politics, aware of the depredations of strip mining, schooled in the causes of the financial crisis, aware of Delaware's need for reputable courts to protect its franchise and the prosperity of the state—if all this is "unjudicial," then one is tempted to say, "So be it."

As head of the most powerful business court in the land, and increasingly influential around the world, Chancellor Strine is the future of M&A, and he is determined to keep that interesting. On a panel in 2010, again at Tulane, he said, "We need to get past the point at which boards prudently take into account risk. We need to get them to do irrational deals." Why? "Those are the deals that make this conference fun." It may be, however, that Chancellor Strine, who turns 48 in 2013, has other plans for his future than a lifetime on the judiciary. In 2010, the state senate unanimously reappointed him to another term as vice chancellor. Will he stay on?

Strine himself has said that corporation law is not his passion. Public policy has his heart.[26] It is commonplace to note items in a person's office and extrapolate from there, but in Strine's case, it is revealing. He became known for two particular pictures in his chambers. One was of James Taylor, and the other was of LBJ. Who of the two leads the way to his future? "He is a conundrum to a lot of people who don't know him," says a close friend. There are many who assume his love of public policy and his admiration for the progenitor of the Great Society will lead him, someday, beyond Delaware.

Chancellor Strine is the same person whether as a panelist at a 500-person conference, at a small private dinner at an Italian restaurant in Oakland, or as a riveting and often discursive teacher of about 25 mostly foreign students on a Strinian journey through M&A at Berkeley, where he showed how his influence is extending to both future lawyers and jurists around the world. In the halls of the law school on the east coast of the San Francisco Bay, which celebrated its 100th year in 2012, Chancellor Strine was particularly taken by a large archival print of the original reading room at Boalt Hall, a handsome, manly sort of place with sturdy fluted columns and brass reading lamps that curve over each of the partitions of the long, shining, pale wood communal desks. The room is empty, quietly content. The caption to the photograph is an excerpt from an old text:

> Rules of Conduct in Boalt Hall 1924
>
> Men students of the first year class are reminded that they must study in the basement reading room and not in the main reading room. Study privilege in the attic is confined to third year students. Telephone, tobacco, newspapers, magazines and ink are furnished to members of the Law Association and are paid for out of the dues paid to the Law Association. The use of these articles is restricted to those persons who have paid their dues. No one may use the telephone for long distance calls.
>
> It is traditional that no man enters Boalt Hall without removing his hat.

The law school is no longer open only to young white men of privilege. No telephones or tobacco or ink are provided to dues-paying members of a law club. There are no hierarchical degrees of study privileges among the students. No man wears a hat unless it is worn backward with a sports logo on its brim. There is no longer any such thing as a separate market for long-distance telephone calls. It is the loss of the world of Boalt Hall in the 1920s for which one can justifiably mourn, the system of order and deference, of tradition and respect, of the law as a profession rather than a means to riches. It is the demise of this world that one can also celebrate, the end of exclusivity, snobbery, entitlement, and stagnation. And it is M&A that is largely responsible, for better or worse, for the upheaval.

Although in the first years of the second decade of the new millennium, there is an eerie hush over M&A, the future will come. There is a school of thought in Delaware that human ingenuity and greed will always generate new issues to address. The new questions and controversies, including the role of debt providers, how and when deals can be broken in the midst of financial crises—all these controversies may not seem as fundamental as those of the early years, but that is not a bad thing, revealing as it does progress and respect for the law. Chancellor Strine's view of his role and that of his court is straightforward: to try to decide cases effectively and efficiently, to give those involved a credible body of corporate and commercial law that encourages rational investment, and to hold those in power responsible for their use of other people's money. This is what offended Strine about Conrad Black.

Strine deliberately begins his opinion on the activities of Conrad Black with a pun on the defendant's surname, which must have irritated its target. "As Chancellor Allen has said," Strine wrote, "the most interesting corporate law cases involve the color gray." As always with Strine, however, the humor is the gateway to serious thought. In his Hollinger opinion, Strine shows that he writes with energy and precision and a sense of his own power and responsibility.

> In this opinion, I conclude that Black breached his fiduciary and contractual duties persistently and seriously. His conduct threatens grave injury to [Hollinger] International and its stockholders by depriving them of the benefits that might flow from the Strategic Process's search for a value-maximizing transaction. In the course of his improper dealings, Black acted functionally as both principal and agent for his holding companies, without restraint from the boards of those companies, which he dominated.[27]

He accuses the defendant of having betrayed his corporation and its stockholders, regardless of the rules that govern their relationship and permit him, legally at least, to take the actions he did. He bans Black from selling his *Telegraph* newspaper group without the support of the other shareholders. This ruling was the beginning of the end for Black's empire.

As the discussion leader on a panel examining M&A at Tulane in 2004, just after the ruling against Conrad Black, Rob Spatt of Simpson Thacher turned to his fellow panelist, then-vice chancellor Leo Strine, and asked about the decision. "So everybody agrees," Spatt said. "The case comes down to 'Bad Guy Does Bad Things, Gets Big Spanking?'" At the Hellfire Club all those years ago, Michelle, so ashamed, might have laughed as long and loud as did the bankers and lawyers of M&A at how Strine answered Spatt's question.

The vice chancellor paused and then said, "I'm not into spanking, Rob. Although I don't think there's anything *wrong* with it."

* * *

WHEN ILAN WOKE UP WITH A START IN THE COCKPIT OF HIS PLANE IN JUNE 2005, HE estimated that he had lost consciousness for about 20 seconds, long enough to start falling at a rate of 4,000 feet per minute over a small Hudson River town. He pulled the plane's parachute. "View across Haverstraw and the Hudson River while recovering from the dive," is the caption for one of five Google Earth photographs Ilan has on his website. The picture shows a panorama of densely populated cul-de-sacs and circles, dotted with the white roofs of the houses, trees, parking lots, shopping centers, churches, synagogues, and playing fields of a typical American town.

The Cirrus Airframe Parachute System worked well, but it was working too well. Ilan saw that his slowed descent had him heading straight for a set of six massive flat circles that he realized was a fuel tank farm. If he hit them, he would take with him most of the town of Haverstraw. "View over fuel tank farm just as plane stabilized from the parachute pull," the caption he wrote for the second picture, is only barely less frightening that the third picture, when the fuel tanks are close enough to hit with a pebble: "View over fuel tanks when it became clear that evasive action was necessary." He gunned the engine with the parachute fully open. "Plane gently veered right toward Hudson River tributary, avoiding descent into the fuel tank farm," according to an FAA report about the crash. He braced himself for the impact. "View just before crashing into the water." Thomas Hoving told *Fortune* magazine that Ilan's maneuver away from the fuel tank farm was "an extraordinary act of risk taking." The former director of the Metropolitan Museum of Art added, "This guy is an extraordinary hero to us fliers."[28] Yet more heroism was required.

As the plane began to sink into Bowline Pond, photographed by a rather shocked local resident, Ilan said, "So this is how it ends." He was surprised to hear himself say the sentence out loud. He was more surprised when, obeying some as-yet-unidentified Archimedean principle, the plane stopped sinking and popped fully to the surface. The door was jammed. He grabbed a life jacket and found the hammer. He broke the window. His back hurt. He cut his hands on the broken glass as he crawled out onto the wing. His leg was caught in the parachute lines. He worked himself free, and the plane began its second rapid descent, this time only a 30-foot drop to the bottom of the pond. He swam to shore. At Nyack Hospital, the doctor told him he had minor fracture of the spine, which he described as "no big deal." A brace would be all that was needed. He left the room but stuck his head back in with an afterthought: "Oh, by the way, did you know you have a brain tumor?"

The operation to remove the brain tumor was performed on August 2, 2005, at New York–Presbyterian Medical Center. It was a more difficult procedure than expected, as the growth had extended itself more deeply into the brain than was thought. It was not malignant, but it left Ilan paralyzed on his right side, with no sensation in his arm, torso, or leg. His shoulder, because he had no muscle movement, was left dislocated. He was helpless. He could do nothing for himself. Another maniacal pursuit of the unattainable began.

Ilan was determined to reclaim his life. "It took me 15 years to climb out of the pit. I was not going to spend 15 years in that pit again." He was so angry at his infantilized state that the nurses finally couldn't take it anymore and wheeled him to a wall and left him there. He had just enough strength to move the chair. From that moment on, he was obsessed—wheeling himself up and down the hospital corridors until he couldn't move his left arm anymore. He checked out of the hospital sooner than expected, walking out on his own, barely preventing himself from falling, a memory that he has found difficult to relate. His daughter Robin helped him practice lifting a glass of water, among other tasks mundane to the uninjured. He went to the Chelsea Piers and hit bucket after bucket of golf balls until his shoulder slotted back into place. He had to endure the removal of another benign tumor in 2006. The better part of a decade since the ill-fated plane trip, however, he walks with a barely perceptible limp, still with no feeling in his right foot. His famously white halo of hair is a bit thinner, but his intensity is undimmed. No one would guess what he has been through.

Ilan's search for a job in the law after he regained his license yielded nothing for six months. Still, he never gave up, and he found a position in a small law firm doing M&A work. Inamed, a maker of breast implants, was embroiled in liability suits and retained Ilan's firm—Olshan Grundman Frome Rosenzeig & Wolosky—to help it defend against a hostile takeover by a hedge fund. Quickly, Inamed found Ilan indispensable, and he joined the company as executive vice president and then co-CEO. The company in its proxy statement had to reveal his past, in large block letters, but that was to be expected. His fellow chief was accused of sexual harassment, and Ilan, admittedly perhaps a bit overeager to enforce a moral code, put him on leave. The board thought he acted hastily and asked him to step down. The job restored him in what he said was every respect: emotionally, psychologically, reputationally. And financially. His severance was $10 million. "By the time I got finished with Inamed, I think I was on par with, if not beyond, where my peers were at Wachtell Lipton. It was a measuring stick in my mind."[29]

With a fortune now safely in the bank, Ilan started anew once again. He bought an airplane and volunteered his time and his plane for Angel Flight, a charity that provides free air flights for patients and their families who need medical treatment and can't afford to travel to get it. With his typical intensity, he put 15 years of flight on his plane in 24 months, transporting people to their medical treatment as often as three times a week.

"When lawyers finish a deal," Reingold wrote in *Fortune*, "they often commission a bound leather book containing all the papers pertaining to the transaction. Now that Reich felt he had some closure, he decided to do the same. He consolidated all the correspondence around his case—his prison journals, the stories written about him, the materials on his readmission project, and even the psychiatric reports and the abstract doodle he drew while awaiting sentencing. He put the material into three bound volumes, with tabs separating sections and a gold-printed leather spine that reads: Ilan K. Reich: Selected Personal Documents, 1986–1995." The unvarnished history of the most shameful act of his life now sits on a shelf in his den, where his children are free to look at it. "You can't erase history," Reich says. "You have to live with it and deal with it."[30]

Ilan has a new vocation now. He is a venture capitalist. He looks for projects that have languished at universities for lack of funding and brings them to life. He has married again, a doctor named Ilene Fischer, whom he met online. He lives in a new glass tower in one of the most desirable neighborhoods of Lower Manhattan, close by Goldman's investment-banking factory of 15,000 people. He can see across the Hudson a building that houses another 8,000 financial workers. In the early 1980s, he remembers, the entire Goldman partnership could meet in one reasonably large room. He has no desire to be among them. He likes his own new life now. He recently invested $2 million of his own money and raised another $2 million from other investors in a portable, strap-on dialysis machine, an ironic choice, as he was once deemed toxic and removed from the circulatory system of M&A. Trials for the machine are set to begin in Europe. If it works, it will upend the lives of patients now strapped in place for five-hour stretches three times a week, as he once found himself after his operation.

Ilan Reich, after his times of troubles, set up a website, a portal to his life, his thoughts, his plane crash, his brain tumor, and "the home of 152 [MTV] videos from the early 1980s running a total of 10.1 hours." He includes on his site one of his favorite television moments, the *Saturday Night Live* skit that first aired during the 2005 Christmas season and often crops up in reruns. Darlene Love sings over a cartoon by Robert Smigel and his colleagues that is titled "Christmastime for the Jews." A series of claymation vignettes opens with an ostensibly Christian family performing all the rituals of the season and then moves into an outside world devoid of *goyim*, populated instead by Jews at last unfettered, joyously celebrating a moment as a majority. They eat in Chinatown. They have Barbra Streisand belting at full volume as they drive the empty streets. They get into fights in bars because they know that now at least they can win. They circumcise squirrels in the parks. The Gentiles "disappear one day each year and pass the eggnog 'round/But it's all right 'cause that's the night the Jews control the town." It's "Christmastime for the Jews."

It is in its way an anthem for M&A. Excluded for so long, denigrated for centuries even in the land of the free, Jews emerged from the shadows to lead the most dynamic and transformative force in law and business, even politics and culture. "Christmastime for the Jews" is also "The Song of Ilan."

Public disgrace, an abandoned suicide attempt, a trial, a conviction, a prison term, unemployment, ostracism, bankruptcy, divorce, loneliness, a plane crash, paralysis, two brain tumors: His three bound volumes of personal history seem hardly sufficient to hold all that was endured by this Icarus of M&A. During that first tumor surgery, Ilan's partially sedated brain fired off the same phrase in evenly spaced screams. It was both a cry of fear and a defiant assertion of renewal: "I'm going to crash! . . . I'm going to crash! . . . I'm going to crash!"

*   *   *

FIVE DAYS AFTER BOB CAMPEAU TOOK OVER FEDERATED DEPARTMENT STORES IN THE early spring of 1988, he went on what he turned into his very own triumphal tour of its most famous emporium, Bloomingdale's, at 59th Street and Lexington Avenue in Manhattan. The gala, entitled "Hooray for Hollywood!" was sponsored jointly by Revlon, *People* magazine and Bloomingdale's. The conceit was to link celebrity sponsors with their products, so Brooke Shields was there making sure that nothing got between her and her Calvins, and Ralph Lauren grinned amid his Chaps. Campeau, once the hungry urchin from the back of beyond, was in his element—*"The Stores!"* *"Times Square!" "The penthouse view! Park Avenue!"*—the limousines, the flashing paparazzi, and the stars, from Cher to Frank Gifford, from Fawn Hall to Judd Nelson, from Jacyln Smith to Lauren Hutton and Douglas Fairbanks Jr. Once, again, however, all of this was not, in fact, for him. It was an AIDS benefit. Never mind. Campeau and his wife Ilse blossomed in the hot lights, flushed by the attention Bob craved. Marvin Traub, who had started his career at Bloomingdale's in 1950 and had risen through the ranks to become its chief in 1978, the man who had once led the Queen and the Duke of Edinburgh through his pavilion during America's bicentennial in 1976, that night escorted the Campeaus on a royal progress through their newly conquered territory. Lee Traub, Marvin's wife, was heard to mutter darkly: "They don't belong here. It's our store."[31]

Later in the autumn of 1988, Bob and Ilse would at last have their very own moment, where they were the guests of honor, everyone knew it, and the intended guests actually accepted their invitations. They returned to the Temple of Dendur on September 8, 1988, two short years since the party for Allied at which the majority of the guests were investment bankers in masquerade. This time, Bob, recently named to *Chatelaine* magazine's list of Canada's ten sexiest men, immersed himself among the names of the day: Lawrence Tisch, Mortimer Zuckerman, Arthur Ochs Sulzberger, Anna Wintour, Beverly Sills, I. M. Pei, and S. I. Newhouse Jr. all stood in line to be received by Bob and Ilse, flanked by Marvin and Lee Traub. "There was Samuel Le Frak," the *New York Times* wrote in its account of the event, "talking real estate with Robert and Blaine Trump and Malcolm Forbes talking about spending the Fourth of July on Donald Trump's yacht and Mario Buatta almost knocking over a statue—'something B.C.,' he groaned."[32]

Much more was about to topple as well. By the time the holiday season came around in 1989, it could no longer be hidden: both Allied and Federated were starved for cash. In the fall of 1988, for example, Federated was predicting profits of $740 million. The actual number turned out to be a scary $372 million. Allied and Federated together had debts of $8.2 billion. Bloomingdale's, so recently a glittering set for Bob's walk-about, had descended into dust and disarray. "I walked into Bloomingdale's before Christmas," one former executive told *Fortune*'s Carol Loomis, "and I almost cried. It was dirty; it was schlocky; there were round tables in the aisles. It was criminal."[33]

By January 1990, Campeau's acquisitions tumbled into bankruptcy. There was no mystery surrounding what had happened. The businesses did not make enough money to pay the debts. The catastrophe roiled Campeau's lenders around the world, including Citibank, First Boston, Paine Webber, Prudential Insurance, Sumitomo and ten other Japanese banks, Equitable Life Assurance, Fidelity Investments, the Reichmann family's Olympia & York, and Edward J. DeBartolo Co. Thousands of employees, vendors, and suppliers suffered the agony of the innocents. The entire junk bond market slipped into a slump. Drexel went into bankruptcy and the era of the 1980s began to dissolve into the past. One executive at Paine Webber, Campeau's early ally, called Campeau a "financial Hitler."

In the fiscal year of 1986 and 1987, Robert Campeau had generated fully one-half of First Boston's profits. Even the unshockable Kim Fennebresque was aghast. He stumbled over his words as he remembered the scale of what was happening: "I heard it for the first time on a morning meeting, eight o'clock meeting in Bruce's office, because we needed to do it for that day—we had to execute the documents that morning. And Bruce said, 'It'll be fifty million.' And Campeau said, 'Fine.' And I thought, uh, I thought I'd heard a, uh, I thought I had a hearing impairment." Kim touches the corner of his left eye as if blinded by the riches. "In the end, when it was finally done, those fees amounted to about a hundred fifty million and eventually turned a decent year into a great year for First Boston, so you know, the BMW dealerships went nuts and the Mercedes dealerships went nuts and everyone was happy. All New York was happy because First Boston made a hundred fifty million dollars, and money got spent everywhere, and it hid a lot of problems. But we made a lot of money."[34]

The deals were the stuff of nightmare. Mike Rothfeld, part of the First Boston team at the time, had one that would not go away: "I remember I began to have dreams where I was the engineer on the space shuttle who was warning people about the O-rings and they weren't listening."[35] It is difficult to believe now that a stranger could wander into town, convince large established banks to lend him $3.6 billion to buy a company he had only just learned existed, and soon after that bruising contest, take out another $6.5 billion in loans to buy a much larger giant, turning himself into one of the most powerful retail owners in North America without knowing a thing about how to run a department store. Along the way, he is pushed ever further into the madness by advisers with very personal and lucrative agendas, all of which leads to a massive bankruptcy that sends shudders through the entire financial system. "Because we can be no more than what we aspire to be, we will always aspire to be more than the best of what we are": A kind of tongue-twisting tautology, Campeau's corporate credo said it all as it failed to say much of anything.

At one point in *Double or Nothing*, the Canadian docudrama on Campeau, Peter Solomon, then at Shearson Lehman and later vice chairman and co-head of investment banking at ill-fated Lehman Brothers, stares wearily into the camera. In *Barbarians at the Gate*, Solomon is described as "a boisterous bullying Lehman veteran," who to his fury gets frozen out of the RJR deal by Shearson Lehman's chief, Peter Cohen.[36] Here, looking back at the Campeau deals, he is grimly subdued. He likens B-a-a-a-b to the elephant that falls in love with the ant and takes her to a jungle motel. In the morning, she finds the elephant dead beside her. She realizes in horror that for one night of passion she must now spend the rest of her life digging an elephantine grave.

"Most of the raiders have, like old soldiers, faded away," Solomon says quietly. "They have disappeared. They have left a legacy of debris and unhappiness, and in some places, great wealth. In some places, they made, strangely enough, contributions by shaking up business establishments. But most of them have just faded away, and, for most of us, that's probably lucky."[37]

NOTES

CHAPTER 1: THE TEMPLE OF DENDUR

1. National Film Board of Canada and CTV Television Network, *Double or Nothing: The Rise and Fall of Robert Campeau,* dir. Paul Cowan, docudrama, 1992, at 7 min.
2. Ibid., at 21 min., 46 sec.
3. Interview with Samuel Butler (Cravath, Swaine & Moore), July 24, 2012.
4. John Rothchild, *Going for Broke* (New York: Simon & Schuster, 1991), 18.
5. Interview with Robert Kindler, June 21, 2012.
6. *Double or Nothing: The Rise and Fall of Robert Campeau,* at 47 min., 11 sec.

CHAPTER 2: WASPS, JEWS, AND M & A

1. Steven Brill, "Joseph Flom," *American Lawyer,* March 1989, 73.
2. Steven M. Davidoff, *Gods at War* (Hoboken, NJ: John Wiley & Sons, 2009), 1, 2.
3. Charles Francis Adams Jr. and Henry Adams, *Chapters of Erie* (Ithaca, NY: Cornell University Press, 1968), 3.
4. Ibid., 30.
5. Davidoff, *Gods at War,* 1, 2.
6. Interview with Stuart Shapiro (Shapiro Forman Allen & Sava), July 10, 2012.
7. Interview with Steven Brill, April 3, 2013.
8. Steven Brill, "Two Tough Lawyers in the Tender-Offer Game," *New York,* June 21, 1976, 52-53.
9. Interview with James Freund (Skadden, Arps, Slate, Meagher & Flom), August 2, 2012.
10. Brill, "Two Tough Lawyers," 57.
11. Malcolm Gladwell, *Outliers* (New York: Little, Brown, 2008), 156-158.
12. Ibid., 156.
13. Interview with Stuart Shapiro (Shapiro Forman Allen & Sava), June 29, 2012.
14. Brill, "Joseph Flom," 71, 73.
15. Interview with Associate Professor Justin Brashares (University of California, Berkeley; Department of Environmental Science, Policy and Management), October 10, 2012.
16. James B. Stewart, "Looking Back," *American Lawyer,* March 1989, 12.
17. Interview with Steven Brill, April 3, 2013.
18. Jeff Goodell, "The Supreme Court," *Wired,* March 1995.

19. "German Chanteuse Ute Lemper Proves You Don't Have to Be 50 to Take a Walk on the Weill Side," *People,* March 13, 1989.

CHAPTER THREE: THE HELLFIRE CLUB

1. Interview with Merrill Lynch former employee who requested anonymity, May 5, 2012.
2. Ibid.
3. Ibid.

CHAPTER 4: THE LAND OF THE SCREAMERS

1. Robert Safian, "High Times on the Fast Track," *American Lawyer,* March 1990, 75.
2. National Film Board of Canada and CTV Television Network, *Double or Nothing: The Rise and Fall of Robert Campeau,* dir. Paul Cowan, docudrama, 1992, at 29 min.
3. Safian, "High Times on the Fast Track," 78.
4. Interview with Ilan Reich, April 21, 2012.
5. "The 25 Most Intriguing People of 1981: A Liquor Baron Enlivens a Year of Corporate Merger Mania," *People,* December 28, 1981.
6. Edgar M. Bronfman, *Good Spirits: The Making of a Businessman* (New York: G. P. Putnam's Sons, 1998), 12.
7. Interviews with Ilan Reich, April 21, 2012; May 4, 2012.
8. Ibid.
9. Stephen Adler, "First Boston's M&A Prodigy," *American Lawyer,* January 1983, 69.
10. Ibid.
11. Interview with source who requested anonymity.
12. Lawrence Lederman, *Tombstones: A Lawyer's Tales from the Takeover Decades* (New York: Farrar, Straus & Giroux, 1992), 230.
13. Ibid.
14. Interview with Ilan Reich, April 21, 2012.
15. "The 25 Most Intriguing People of 1981."

CHAPTER 5: THE SIZE OF THEIR TOYS

1. "Separated at Birth," *Spy,* December 1987, 54.
2. Interview with Ilan Reich, May 4, 2012.
3. Mark Stevens, *King Icahn: The Biography of a Renegade Capitalist* (New York: Penguin Books, 1993), 11-15.
4. Ibid., 21.
5. Ibid., 22.
6. Steven Brill, "The Roaring Eighties," *American Lawyer,* May 1985, 11.
7. Stephen J. Adler, "Another Trophy for Icahn," *Corporate Control Alert* (editor: JoAnne Ganek), May 1985, 1, 7.
8. Ibid., 7.

CHAPTER 6: THE VISIT OF THE BRITISH COMPANY MAN

1. James Buchan, *Frozen Desire: The Meaning of Money* (New York: Farrar, Straus & Giroux, 1997), 232-234.
2. E-mail interview with R. K. O'Keeffe, November 30, 2012.

3. Connie Bruck, *The Predators' Ball: The Inside Story of Drexel Burnham and the Rise of the Junk Bond Raiders* (New York: Penguin Books, 1988), 14, 15.
4. Interview with Stuart Shapiro (Shapiro Forman Allen & Sava), June 29, 2012.
5. Interview with former Drexel banker, November 27, 2012.
6. Ibid.
7. Ibid.
8. Ibid.
9. Ibid.
10. Ibid.

CHAPTER 7: RUBBER PHOBIA

1. "Jimmy Goldsmith," *The Economist,* July 24, 1997.
2. Ivan Fallon, *Billionaire: The Life and Times of Sir James Goldsmith* (Boston: Little, Brown, 1991), 2.
3. Ibid., 63.
4. Ibid., 68.
5. Lady Annabel Goldsmith, *Annabel: An Unconventional Life* (London: Weidenfeld & Nicolson, 2005), 209, 210.
6. Ezra K. Zilkha, *From Baghdad to Boardrooms: My Family's Odyssey* (New York: privately printed, 1999), 1-2.
7. Interview with Ezra Zilkha, May 10, 2012.
8. Zilkha, *From Baghdad to Boardrooms,* 141-142.
9. Goldsmith, *Annabel,* 243, 244.
10. Zilkha, *From Baghdad to Boardrooms,* 141, 142.
11. Goldsmith, *Annabel,* 208.
12. Ibid., 211.

CHAPTER 8: THE GUNS OF AQABA

1. Ivan Fallon, *Billionaire: The Life and Times of Sir James Goldsmith* (Boston: Little, Brown, 1991), 2, 8–9.
2. John Weir Close, "Takeover Panel's Ruling in B.A.T Battle," *Corporate Control Alert,* October 1989, 1, 4.
3. Steven Prokesch, "Goldsmith Ends Bid for B.A.T," *New York Times,* April 24, 1990.
4. Benjamin Wallace, "A Household Name," *Corporate Control Alert* (editor: John Weir Close), April 1995, 6.
5. Ibid.
6. Ibid.
7. Moira Johnston, *Takeover* (New York: Arbor House, 1986), 23-27.

CHAPTER 9: ERECTILE DYSFUNCTION

1. Interview with Stuart Shapiro (Shapiro Forman Allen & Sava), June 29, 2012.
2. Malcolm Gladwell, "The Three Lessons of Joe Flom," in *Outliers* (New York: Little, Brown, 2008), 116.
3. Interview with James Freund (Skadden, Arps, Slate, Meagher & Flom), May 29, 2012.
4. Lincoln Kaplan, *Skadden: Power, Money, and the Rise of a Legal Empire* (New York: Farrar, Straus & Giroux, 1993), 33.
5. Interview with Stuart Shapiro, June 29, 2012.

6. Ibid.
7. Ibid.
8. Staff writers, "The 2013 AmLaw 100," *American Lawyer,* April 2013.

CHAPTER 10: A BONDIAN DEATH RAY

1. Interview with Stuart Shapiro (Shapiro Forman Allen & Sava), July 10, 2012.
2. *Moran v. Household,* Civil Action No. 7730, Court of Chancery, Plaintiffs' Pre-Trial Memorandum of Points and Authorities (September 17, 1984), 5, 6.
3. *Moran v. Household,* Defendants' Pre-Trial Memorandum (September 21, 1984), 8.
4. Moira Johnston, *Takeover* (New York: Arbor House, 1986), 271-274.
5. Interview with Ilan Reich, May 4, 2012.
6. Stephen J. Adler, "How to Lose the Bet-Your-Company Case," *American Lawyer,* January/February 1986, 29-30.
7. Ibid., 27.
8. Interview with Ilan Reich, May 4, 2012.
9. Interview with Joseph Flom (Skadden, Arps, Slate, Meagher & Flom), February 12, 2000.

CHAPTER 11: UP, UP, AND AWAY!

1. Aaron Bernstein, *Grounded: Frank Lorenzo and the Destruction of Eastern Airlines* (Washington, DC: Beard Books, 1999), 17.
2. Ibid., 12.
3. Pamela G. Hollie, "Continental without Its Chief," *New York Times,* August 11, 1981.
4. Ibid.; see also Bernstein, *Grounded,* 15.
5. Connie Bruck, "Kamikaze: How Texas Air's Frank Lorenzo Wrecked His Own Chance to Acquire TWA—and Carl Icahn Picked up the Pieces," *American Lawyer,* December 1985, 76, 77.
6. Moira Johnston, *Takeover* (New York: Arbor House, 1986), 230, 231.
7. Interview with James Freund (Skadden, Arps, Slate, Meagher & Flom), August 2, 2012.
8. Bruck, "Kamikaze," 78.
9. Elaine X. Grant, "TWA—Death of a Legend," *St. Louis Magazine,* October 2005.
10. Grant, "TWA"; see also Johnston, *Takeover,* 252.
11. Grant, "TWA."
12. James C. Freund, Stephen E. Jacobs, Richard D. Katcher, and David B. Chapnick, "Case Study of a Contest: TWA," in *Seventeenth Annual Institute on Securities Regulation, Practising Law Institute* (1986), 120-123.
13. Gay Jervey, "Dennis, the M&A Menace," *American Lawyer,* July/August 1986, 30.
14. Ibid.
15. *Unocal v. Mesa Petroleum,* 493 A.2d 946 (Del. 1985).
16. Ibid.
17. Freund et al., "Case Study of a Contest," 149, 150.
18. Bryan Miller, *"Restaurants," New York Times,* July 12, 1985.
19. Arnold H. Lubasch, "Shot by Shot, an Ex-Aide to Gotti Describes the Killing of Castellano," *New York Times,* March 4, 1992.
20. Jervey, "Dennis, the M&A Menace," 30.
21. "Briefs," *American Lawyer,* November 1979.

22. Jervey, "Dennis, the M&A Menace," 30.
23. Bruck, "Kamikaze," 76.
24. Ibid.
25. Jervey, "Dennis, the M&A Menace," 30, 31.
26. Mark Stevens, *King Icahn* (New York: Penguin Group, 1993), 181.
27. Johnston, *Takeover*, 286.
28. Jervey, "Dennis, the M&A Menace," 31.
29. Bruck, "Kamikaze," 77.
30. Ibid.
31. Stevens, *King Icahn*, 188.
32. Ibid., 193.
33. Bruck, "Kamikaze," 80.
34. Ibid.
35. Ibid.
36. Tony Kaye and Miriam Rozen, "Icahn's Words Come Back to Haunt Him," *American Lawyer*, March 1988, 21, 22.
37. Ibid.
38. Ibid.
39. Ibid.
40. Grant, "TWA."
41. Steven Brill, "The Roaring Eighties," *American Lawyer*, May 1985, 1, 10.
42. Grant, "TWA."

CHAPTER 12: THE BEGGAR'S PURSE

1. Jay Cheshes, "Caviar & Cocaine," *Town & Country*, November 2011, 131.
2. Interview with Stuart Shapiro (Shapiro Forman Allen & Sava), June 29, 2012.
3. Jill Abramson, "Skadden's Bid for Immortality: How Joe Flom & Co. Are Building an Institution," *American Lawyer*, March 1984, 39.
4. Steven Brill, "Flom Firm Takes Over as Top Money Maker in '78," *American Lawyer*, February 1979, 14, 15.
5. Peter Lattman, "Morris J. Kramer, Pioneer in Deal Law, Dies at 71," *New York Times*, April 19, 2013.
6. Cheshes, "Caviar & Cocaine," 131.
7. Ibid., 129.
8. Andrew Tobias, *Fire and Ice* (New York: Quill Edition, 1976), 204.
9. Connie Bruck, "How Drexel's Pawns Stormed Corporate America," *American Lawyer*, April 1988, 114-115.
10. Connie Bruck, *The Predators' Ball* (New York: Penguin Books, 1988), 204.
11. Interview with a senior M&A practitioner who requested anonymity, July 11, 2012.
12. Tobias, *Fire and Ice*, 13-15.
13. Ibid., 18.
14. Interview with Ezra Zilkha, May 10, 2012.
15. Ibid.
16. Ezra Zilkha, *From Baghdad to Boardrooms: My Family's Odyssey* (New York: privately printed, 1999), 217-218.
17. Ibid., 224.
18. Bruck, *Predators' Ball*, 194.
19. William D. Cohan, "Machiavelli and Mogul," *Vanity Fair*, January 2012.
20. Bruck, *Predators' Ball*, 222.

21. Interview with a senior M&A practitioner who requested anonymity, July 15, 2012.
22. Argument on Plaintiff's Motion for Preliminary Injunction, Delaware Court of Chancery, Superior Courtroom No. 30, Public Building, Wilmington, Delaware: Civil Action No. 8126, Before Justice Joseph T. Walsh (October 18, 1985), 48, 49.
23. Oral Argument, Delaware Supreme Court, Superior Courtroom No. 1, Public Building, Wilmington, Delaware: No. 353 & 354, Before Hon. John J. McNeilly, Hon. Andrew G. T. Moore II, Hon. Bernard Bailick (October 31, 1985), 56, 57.
24. Zilkha, *From Baghdad to Boardrooms,* 223.
25. Bruck, *Predators' Ball,* 219.
26. Zilkha, *From Baghdad to Boardrooms,* 223.
27. Ibid.
28. Interview with M&A specialist who requested anonymity.
29. *MacAndrews & Forbes Holdings, Inc. v. Revlon, Inc.,* 501 A.2d 1239 (Del. Ct. Ch. 1985).
30. Interview with Stuart Shapiro (Shapiro, Foreman Allen & Sava), June 29, 2012.
31. Oral Argument, Delaware Supreme Court, Superior Courtroom No. 1, Public Building, Wilmington, Delaware: No. 353 & 354, Before Hon. John J. McNeilly, Hon. Andrew G. T. Moore II, Hon. Bernard Bailick (October 31, 1985), 51, 52.
32. *Revlon, Inc. v. MacAndrews & Forbes Holdings, Inc.,* 506 A.2d 173 (Del. S. Ct. 1986).
33. Ibid.
34. Ibid.
35. Aaron Elstein, "Ron Perelman vs. Donald Drapkin," *Crain's New York Business,* January 23, 2011, http://www.crainsnewyork.com/article/20110123/FREE/301239973.
36. Susanne Craig, "Another Bitter Divorce for Perelman, *New York Times,* January 17, 2012.
37. David Blum, "Spoils Sport," *New York,* April 14, 1986, 68.
38. Ibid.
39. Elstein, "Ron Perelman vs. Donald Drapkin."
40. Ibid.
41. "Surprise Courtroom Star," *New York Post,* January 26, 2012.
42. Ibid.

CHAPTER 13: FOUL DUST

1. Donald P. Baker, "Va. Neighbors Say Kluges' Arrival Turned Way of Life Upside Down," *Washington Post,* June 5, 1988.
2. Ibid.
3. Interview with Ezra Zilkha, June 25, 2012.
4. Ibid.
5. Austen Chenoweth, "The Secret of Albemarle Farms," *Spy,* February 1989, 96.
6. Interview with Ezra Zilkha, June 25, 2012.
7. Interview with a lawyer who asked to remain anonymous, April 30, 2012.
8. William Shawcross, *Murdoch* (New York: Simon & Schuster, 1992), 205, 206.
9. Ibid., 206, 207.
10. D. M. Osborne, "Murdoch's Secret Weapon," *American Lawyer,* December 1993, 46-48.
11. Bruce Wasserstein, *Big Deal: Mergers and Acquisitions in the Digital Age* (New York: Warner Books, 1998), 438.
12. Chenoweth, "Secret of Albemarle Farms," 93.
13. Interview with Ezra Zilkha, June 25, 2012.
14. Eugenia Sheppard, "Metromedia Chairman Weds in St. Pat's Cathedral," *Palm Beach Daily News,* June 1, 1981, 2.
15. Ibid.

16. Michael Sheldon, "The Richest Brit in Virginia," *Telegraph,* December 15, 2003.

17. Sotheby's TV: Sotheby's Collection of Patricia Kluge & Albemarle House, Charlottesville, VA, June 8-9, 2010.

18. Ibid.

19. Interview with Ezra Zilkha, June 25, 2012.

20. Chenoweth, "Secret of Albemarle Farms," 96.

21. Lawrence Hardy, "Hawk Mystery Unfolds," *Daily Progress,* March 29, 1988, 1, 7.

22. Bryan D. McAllister, "British Defendants Win Trial by Jury," *Daily Progress,* May 10, 1988, A1, A12.

23. Jane Dunlap Norris, "Tapes Used as Lures, Jury Told," *Daily Progress,* May 28, 1988, A1, A13.

24. Jane Dunlap Norris, "Musgrave Displays British Gentility," *Daily Progress,* June 3, 1988, A1, A10.

25. Lawrence Hardy, "Center Visit Inspired Gift from Kluges," *Daily Progress,* April 16, 1988, B1.

26. "Kluges Given British Conservation Award," *Daily Progress,* May 14, 1988, C1.

27. Jane Dunlap Norris, "Three Guilty in Hawk Trial," *Daily Progress,* June 3, 1988, A1.

28. Jane Dunlap Norris, "Hawk Kill Defendants Fined, No Jail," and "Game Keepers Detained," *Daily Progress,* June 10, 1988, A1, A10; see also Staff and Wire Reports, "Hawk Kill Defendants Leave U.S. After Release," *Daily Progress,* June 11, 1988, A1, A11.

29. Chenoweth, "Secret of Albemarle Farms," 94.

CHAPTER 14: FAT MAN AND LITTLE BOY

1. National Film Board of Canada and CTV Television, *Double or Nothing: The Rise and Fall of Robert Campeau,* dir. Paul Cowan, docudrama, 1992, at 23 min.

2. Ibid., at 25 min., 10 sec.; 25 min., 54 sec.

3. Phil Patton, "The Man Who Bought Bloomingdale's," *New York Times,* July 17, 1988.

4. Interview with Stuart Shapiro (Shapiro Forman Allen & Sava), February 23, 2013.

5. Benjamin Wallace, "Who Says Masters of the Universe Can't Have Fun?" *Corporate Control Alert* (editor: John Weir Close), December 1994, 11.

6. Bryan Burrough and John Helyar, *Barbarians at the Gate* (New York: Harper Business, 1990), 385.

7. Wallace, "Who Says Masters of the Universe Can't Have Fun?" 11.

8. Ibid., 8.

9. Ibid., 11.

10. Carol J. Loomis, "The Biggest Looniest Deal Ever," *Fortune,* June 18, 1990; see also John Rothchild, *Going for Broke* (New York: Simon & Schuster, 1991), 63.

11. Rothchild, *Going for Broke,* 30.

12. Ibid., 38.

13. Loomis, "The Biggest Looniest Deal Ever."

14. Rothchild, *Going for Broke,* 67.

15. Ibid., 61.

16. Film Board of Canada and CTV Television, *Double or Nothing,* at 28 min., 55 sec.

17. Ibid., at 34 min., 15 sec.; 33 min., 19 sec.; 41 min., 34 sec.

18. Rothchild, *Going for Broke,* 80.

19. Film Board of Canada and CTV Television, *Double or Nothing,* at 19 min.; 21 min., 11 sec.; 36 min., 14 sec.; 44 min., 12 sec.

20. Rothchild, *Going for Broke,* 87.

21. Wallace, "Who Says Masters of the Universe Can't Have Fun?" 11.

22. Loomis, "Biggest Looniest Deal Ever."
23. Film Board of Canada and CTV Television, *Double or Nothing*, at 2 min., 56 sec.
24. Interview with James Freund (Skadden, Arps, Slate, Meagher & Flom), August 2, 2012.
25. Loomis, "Biggest Looniest Deal Ever."
26. Rothchild, *Going for Broke*, 176.
27. Loomis, "Biggest Looniest Deal Ever."
28. Film Board of Canada and CTV Television, *Double or Nothing*, at 38 min., 40 sec.

CHAPTER 15: A BIG BLOODY OUTCRY

1. Interview with Robert Kindler (Morgan Stanley), April 2, 2012.
2. Steven Brill, "What Recession? Why Cravath's Balance Sheet Looks as Good as Ever," *American Lawyer*, March 1983, 48.
3. Karen Dillon, "Kindler and Gordon: Cravath's Stand-Up Team," *American Lawyer*, November 1988.
4. Interview with Samuel Butler (Cravath, Swaine & Moore), July 24, 2012.
5. John Weir Close, "Lord Moneybags: The Life and Deals of James Hanson," *M&A Journal* 5, no. 7 (January 2005): 6.
6. Ibid.
7. Ibid.
8. Ibid.
9. Ibid., 7.
10. Ibid.
11. "Jimmy Goldsmith: Sir James Goldsmith, Tycoon, Politician and Cad, Died on July 19th Aged 64," *The Economist*, July 24, 1997.
12. Susan Stamberg, "Columbus, Ind.: A Midwestern Mecca of Architecture," *Weekend Edition*, NPR, July 31, 2012, at 3 min. 51 sec. to 4 min. 6 sec.
13. Jeffrey L. Cruikshank and David B. Sicilia, *The Engine That Could: Seventy-Five Years of Values-Drive Change at Cummins Engine Company* (Boston: Harvard Business School Press, 1997), 309.
14. Interview with Henry Schacht, September 1, 2011.
15. Cruikshank and Sicilia, *The Engine That Could*, 422-425.
16. Ibid.
17. Ibid.
18. Ibid.
19. Interview with Francis Barron (Cravath, Swaine & Moore), June 5, 2012.
20. John Weir Close, "Cummins Brings Potentially Hostile Shareholder to a Ten-Year Standstill," *Corporate Control Alert* (editor: Susan Pender), June 1990, 1.
21. *Cummins Engine Company, Inc. v. Industrial Equity (Pacific) Limited et al.*, Cause No. IP90 063C (US Dist. Ct., Southern District of Indiana, Indianapolis Division, Amended Complaint, February 4, 1990), at 8.
22. Close, "Cummins," 4-5.
23. Ibid., 5.
24. Ibid.
25. *Cummins*, Cause No. IP90 063C, 2-4.
26. Ibid., 8-10.
27. Ibid., 23.
28. Ibid., 24.
29. Ibid., 26.
30. Cruikshank and Sicilia, *The Engine That Could*, 433.

31. Interview with Francis Barron (Cravath, Swaine & Moore), June 5, 2012.
32. Close, "Cummins," 5-6.
33. Cruikshank and Sicilia, *The Engine That Could*, 434.
34. Close, "Cummins," 6.
35. Ibid.
36. Interview with Francis Barron, June 5, 2012.
37. Interview with Robert Kindler (Morgan Stanley), May 31, 2012.
38. John Weir Close, "M&A Enters a Brave New World Where Money Will Be Made the Old-Fashioned Way," *Corporate Control Alert* (editor: Susan Pender), January 1990, 1, 2.
39. Interview with Robert Kindler (Morgan Stanley), March 8, 2011.
40. James Buchan, *Frozen Desire: The Meaning of Money* (New York: Farrar, Straus & Giroux, 1997), 107, 108.
41. John Weir Close, "The UAL Debacle: Why the Banks Said No," *Corporate Control Alert* (editor: Susan G. Pender), November 1989, 1.
42. Ibid., 1-2.
43. John Weir Close, "United at Last," *Corporate Control Alert* (editor: John Weir Close), September 1994, 2.
44. Close, "M&A Enters a Brave New World," 2.
45. Interview with Stuart Shapiro (Shapiro, Foreman Allen & Sava), June 29, 2012.
46. Close, "M&A Enters a Brave New World," 1, 2.
47. John Weir Close, "M&A Deal Volume Hits a Plateau after Dizzying Two-Year Slide," *Corporate Control Alert* (editor: Martha Sellers Klein), July 1991, 2.
48. John Weir Close, "As U.S. Economy Improves and Financing Crunch Eases, M&A Activity Picks Up Speed," *Corporate Control Alert* (editor: Martha Sellers Klein), July 1993, 2.
49. Ibid., 4
50. Ibid., 2.

CHAPTER 16: ORION AND THE WOLVES

1. Sumner Redstone with Peter Knobler, *A Passion to Win* (New York: Simon & Schuster, 2001), 154.
2. Ibid., 153, 154.
3. Mark Lasswell, "The Lost Tycoons," *Spy*, May 1991, 71.
4. John Weir Close, "Will Orion's Restructuring Stop It from Reeling?" *Corporate Control Alert* (editor: Martha Sellers Klein), July 1992, 6.
5. Lasswell, "The Lost Tycoons," 70.
6. Close, "Will Orion's Restructuring Stop It from Reeling?" 6.
7. Ibid.
8. Ibid.
9. Ibid.
10. Lasswell, "The Lost Tycoons," 70.
11. Close, "Will Orion's Restructuring Stop It from Reeling?" 7.
12. Ibid.
13. Ibid.
14. Benjamin Wallace, "The Wisdom of Burton: With Vultures Circling, Macy's Fate Is in the Hands of One Man—Bankruptcy Judge Lifland, Who Has Presided over Some of the Largest Chapter 11 Cases of the Past 15 Years," *Corporate Control Alert* (editor: John Weir Close), May 1994, 8.
15. Ibid., 8, 11.
16. Close, "Will Orion's Restructuring Stop It from Reeling?" 7.

17. Ibid., 8.
18. Ibid.
19. Ibid.

CHAPTER 17: THE HEART OF HOLLYWOOD

1. John Weir Close, "Of Paramount's Importance," *Corporate Control Alert,* March 1994, 1.
2. Ibid., 30, 31.
3. *Paramount Communications Inc. v. QVC Network Inc.,* 637 A.2d 34 (Del. S. Ct. 1994), Addendum to Opinion.
4. Ibid.
5. Brenda Sapino Jeffreys, "Jamail Unfazed by Delaware Court's Blast," *Texas Lawyer,* February 14, 1994.
6. Sumner Redstone with Peter Knobler, *A Passion to Win* (New York: Simon & Schuster 2001), 245-247. See also John Weir Close, "Blockbuster Tearjerker," *Corporate Control Alert,* October 1994, 11.
7. Redstone, *A Passion to Win,* 41-47.
8. Ibid., 41, 42.
9. Ibid., 15-21.
10. Ibid., 232-237.
11. Ibid., 244-247.
12. Miriam Rozen, "Headstrong Client, Cowardly Counsel," *American Lawyer,* January/ February 1989, 159.
13. Karen Dillon, Helen O'Connor, and Miriam Rozen, "Macmillan's Auction: Blind in One Eye Only," *Corporate Control Alert* (editor: Susan G. Pender), November 1988, 1, 4-6.
14. Diana B. Henriques, *The White Sharks of Wall Street: Thomas Mellon Evans and the Original Corporate Raiders* (New York: Scribner 2000), 62.
15. Ibid., 67.
16. Ibid., 274, 288.
17. Ibid., 299, 300.
18. Ibid., 292.
19. Ibid., 294.
20. Diane Goldner and Helen O'Connor, "Change of Control? What Change of Control, Asks Macmillan Innocently," *Corporate Control Alert* (editor: Susan G. Pender), August 1988, 4, 5.
21. Ibid., 5.
22. *Robert M. Bass Group, Inc. v. Edward P. Evans et al., Defendants. In re Macmillan Shareholders Litigation,* 552 A.2d 1227 (Del. Court of Chancery, 1988). See also Goldner and O'Connor, "Change of Control?" 6.
23. William H. Meyers, "Megadealer for the Rothschilds," *New York Times,* December 4, 1988.
24. Interview with Stuart Shapiro (Shapiro Forman Allen & Sava), July 27, 2012.
25. Ibid.
26. Plaintiffs' Opening Brief in Support of Their Motion for a Preliminary Injunction, *Mills Acquisition Co. v. Macmillan, Inc.,* C.A. No. 10168 (October 5, 1988), at 29-31.
27. Ibid. at 32.
28. Memorandum in Opposition to Motion for Injunctive Relief, *Mills Acquisition Co. v. Macmillan, Inc.,* C.A. No. 10168 (October 7, 1988), at 9-11.

29. Reply Memorandum in Support of Motion for Preliminary Injunction, *Mills Acquisition Co. v. Macmillan, Inc.*, C.A. No. 10168 (October 9, 1988), at 1.

30. *Mills Acquisition Co. v. Macmillan, Inc.*, C.A. No. 10168, Memorandum Opinion (October 17, 1988), Jacobs, Vice Chancellor.

31. Ibid. at 42.

32. Ibid. at 45, 46.

33. Lawrence Lederman, *Tombstones* (New York: Farrar, Straus & Giroux, 1992), 313, 314.

34. Interview with Stuart Shapiro, July 27, 2012.

35. Lederman, *Tombstones*, 313, 314.

36. *Mills Acquisition Co. v. Macmillan, Inc.*, 559 A. 2d 1261 (1988), 1283; 1284.

37. Lederman, *Tombstones*, 314-316.

38. John Weir Close, "Paramount Wins Macmillan While Selling Itself: Has the Publishing House, Object of a Scandal-Ridden Sale in the 1980s, Finally Found a Home?" *Corporate Control Alert*, March 1994, 25.

39. Ibid.

40. Ibid., 26.

41. Ibid.

42. Geraldine Fabrikant, "Paramount to Acquire Macmillan," *New York Times*, November 11, 1993.

43. Close, "Paramount Wins Macmillan," 29.

44. Rozen, "Headstrong Client, Cowardly Counsel," 159.

45. Close, "Of Paramount's Importance," 10.

46. Carey Adina Karmel, "Simpson Thacher's G + W Connection," *American Lawyer*, June 1983, 10, 11.

47. Ibid.

48. Ibid.

49. Ibid.

50. Ibid.

51. Ibid.

52. Bryan Burrough, "The Siege of Paramount," *Vanity Fair*, February 1994.

53. Ibid.

54. Ibid.

55. Redstone, *A Passion to Win*, 180.

56. Ibid.

57. Ibid., 181-183.

58. Close, "Of Paramount's Importance," 11.

59. *QVC Network, Inc. v. Paramount Communications*, 635 A.2d 1245 (Court of Chancery; Jacobs, Vice Chancellor) (Decided: November 24, 1993; Revised: November 26, 1993, and December 7, 1993); *Paramount Communications Inc. v. QVC Network Inc.*, 637 A.2d 34 (Supreme Court of Delaware; Veasey, Chief Justice) (Decided by Order: December 9, 1993; Opinion: February 4, 1994).

60. Close, "Of Paramount's Importance," 8.

61. *QVC Network Inc. v Paramount Communications*.

62. Interview with M&A specialist who requested anonymity, January 18, 2013.

63. John Weir Close, "A Review of the Bidding," *Corporate Control Alert*, March 1994, 23-25.

64. Ibid.

65. Interview with M&A specialist who requested anonymity, January 18, 2013.

66. John Weir Close, "Redstone Almost Quit Paramount Fight, but Huizenga Won Him Over to 11th-Hour Deal," *Corporate Control Alert*, March 1994, 18-19.

67. Ibid.
68. Ibid.
69. Ibid.
70. Ibid.
71. Redstone, *A Passion to Win,* 230, 231.
72. Close, "Redstone Almost Quit Paramount Fight," 18-19.
73. John Weir Close, "The Financing Devices That Clinched Viacom's Victory," *Corporate Control Alert,* March 1994, 20.
74. Ibid.
75. Ibid.
76. Ibid.
77. Close, "A Review of the Bidding," 23-25.
78. Redstone, *A Passion to Win,* 243.
79. Amy Chozick, "The Man Who Would Be Redstone: For the Surrogate Son and Viacom Heir Apparent, a Test of Creative Prowess," *New York Times/Sunday Business,* September 23, 2012, 1.

CHAPTER 18: ICARUS FALLING

1. Interview with Elizabeth, a Merrill Lynch former employee, who asked that her surname be omitted, May 23, 2012.
2. Interview with Ken, a Merrill Lynch former employee, who asked that his surname be omitted, October 21, 2012.
3. Interview with Elizabeth, May 23, 2012.
4. John Weir Close, "The Second Reich," *Corporate Control Alert* (editor: John Weir Close), December 1995, 2.
5. Ibid., 3.
6. Ibid.
7. Steven Brill, "Redemption?" *American Lawyer,* March 1996, 6.
8. Close, "The Second Reich," 4.
9. Ibid.
10. Lawrence Lederman, *Tombstones* (New York: Farrar, Straus & Giroux, 1992), 240.
11. Ibid., 227.
12. Steven Brill, "Death of a Career," *American Lawyer,* December 1986, 29.
13. Ibid., 30.
14. Lederman, *Tombstones,* 243-245.
15. Brill, "Death of a Career," 32.
16. Lederman, *Tombstones,* 245.
17. Close, "The Second Reich," 3.
18. Robin Yeager, "Pleas for Leniency," *American Lawyer,* March 1987, 8.
19. Judge Robert Sweet, US District Court for the Southern District of New York, "Sentencing Statement for Ilan Reich," *American Lawyer,* March 1987, 8.
20. Lederman, *Tombstones,* 255.
21. Jennifer Reingold, "The Fall and Rise of Ilan Reich," *Fortune,* June 8, 2007.
22. Close, "The Second Reich," 5.
23. Ibid., 4.
24. John Weir Close, "The Mea Culpa," *Corporate Control Alert* (editor: John Weir Close), December 1997, 9.
25. Ibid., 7, 9.
26. Ibid., 4.

27. Ibid., 5.
28. Ibid.
29. Ibid., 6.
30. Close, "The Second Reich," 6.
31. Reingold, "Fall and Rise of Ilan Reich."
32. Interview with Robert Kindler (Morgan Stanley), April 1, 2012.
33. Emily Barker and Krysten Crawford, "Kindler's Calling," *American Lawyer,* April 1988, cover page.
34. Interview with Robert Kindler (Morgan Stanley), March 27, 2000.
35. Barker and Crawford, "Kindler's Calling," 54.
36. Ibid.
37. Ibid.
38. Interview with Robert Kindler (Morgan Stanley), June 21, 2012.
39. Ibid.
40. Eric Herman, "The Philadelphia Story," *Corporate Control Alert* (editor: John Weir Close), December 1996, 2.
41. Interview with Robert Kindler, June 21, 2012.
42. Herman, "The Philadelphia Story," 2.
43. Interview with Robert Kindler, June 21, 2012.
44. Herman, "The Philadelphia Story," 3.
45. Ibid., 2.
46. Ibid., 4.
47. Ibid., 4, 5.
48. Ibid., 5.
49. Ibid.
50. Barker and Crawford, "Kindler's Calling," 55.
51. Interview with Robert Kindler, June 21, 2012.
52. Ibid.
53. Barker and Crawford, "Kindler's Calling," 56.
54. Ibid.
55. Ibid.
56. Ibid., 57.
57. John Weir Close, "Despite Qualms, Dealmakers Plunge on after a Complicated Trillion Dollar Year," *M&A Journal* (editor: John Weir Close), February 1988, 1.
58. Ibid., 2.
59. Ibid.
60. Interview with Robert Kindler (then global head of M&A at JP Morgan), January 5, 2005.
61. John Weir Close, "Tulipomania?" *M&A Journal* (editor: John Weir Close), April 2006, 1, 2.

CHAPTER 19: BIRDS OF AMERICA

1. Frederick Townsend Martin, *Things I Remember* (London: Eveleigh Nash, 1913), 238, 239.
2. "Society Events of the Week," *New York Times,* January 17, 1897.
3. "Costumes of the Guests: History Ransacked to Provide Fancy Dress for Those Who Are to Be Present," *New York Times,* February 7, 1897.
4. "The Bradley Martin Ball: Preparations Nearly Completed for an Entertainment in Society Which Promises to Be Historic," *New York Times,* February 7, 1897.

5. "Echoes of the Ball: Society People Still Gossipping [*sic*] over Beautiful Surroundings and Pleasant Hours While Guests of the Bradley Martins," *New York Times,* February 12, 1897.

6. Ibid.

7. Jack Beatty, *Age of Betrayal: The Triumph of Money in America, 1865-1900* (New York: Vintage Books, 2008), 375.

8. "Why Police Close Streets: Police Protection for Bradley Martin's Was Such As Would Be Given to an East Side Clambake—President Roosevelt Says the Complaints Are Nonsense," *New York Times,* February 14, 1897.

9. Liz Smith, "An Affair to Remember," *New York,* April 7, 2003.

10. Andrew Ross Sorkin, *Too Big to Fail* (New York: Viking, 2009), 517.

11. Interview with a Lazard managing director who requested anonymity, January 23, 2013.

12. Peter Weinberg speech at the 24th Tulane Corporate Law Institute, March 8, 2012.

13. Ibid.

14. Ibid.

15. Ibid.

16. Louis Uchitelle, "The Richest of the Rich, Proud of a New Gilded Age," *New York Times,* July 15, 2007.

17. Ezra Zilkha, *From Baghdad to Boardrooms: My Family's Odyssey* (New York: privately printed, 1999), 226.

CHAPTER 20: RETURN TO THE TEMPLE

1. Interview with Roy J. Katzovicz, April 25, 2012.

2. William Ackman speech at the 24th Tulane Corporate Law Institute, March 8, 2012.

3. Mark Shafir speech at the 25th Tulane Corporate Law Institute, March 21, 2013.

4. Chancellor Leo Strine on a panel at the 23rd Tulane Corporate Law Institute, March 31, 2011.

5. Susan Pender, "War! When Diplomacy Fails: The Ugly Battle to the Death for the Last Paired-Share REIT," (editor: John Weir Close), *M&A Journal* 1, no. 8 (June 1999): 22.

6. Ibid., 2, 3.

7. Ibid., 3.

8. Ibid., 44.

9. Christine S. Richard, *Confidence Game: How Hedge Fund Manager Bill Ackman Called Wall Street's Bluff* (Hoboken, NJ: John Wiley & Sons, 2010), xi-xiii.

10. Steven Brill, "The Roaring Eighties," *American Lawyer,* May 1985, 11.

11. Steven Bertoni and Nathan Vardi, "Carl Icahn Unleashed: Wall Street's Richest Man Is on the Attack—Just Ask Michael Dell," *Forbes,* April 15, 2013.

12. Azam Ahmed, "Two Wall Street Titans, and a Seven-Year Tiff," *New York Times,* November 26, 2011.

13. Ibid.

14. Ezra Zilkha, *From Baghdad to Boardrooms: My Family's Odyssey* (New York: privately printed, 1999), 20.

15. *Hollinger International Inc. v. Conrad M. Black, et al.* C.A. No. 183-N (Del. Ct. Ch. 2004), 1.

16. Conrad Black, "Beware an Improvident Interloper," *National Post,* April 4, 2012.

17. Tristan Hopper, "Lord Have Mercy, Black Is Back: Conrad Black to Co-Host 'Magazine' Talk Show," *National Post,* January 28, 2012.

18. Oral Argument recording, Delaware Supreme Court, *Gatz Properties v. Auriga Capital,* September 19, 2012.
19. Benjamin Wallace, "Lord Myron," *Corporate Control Alert* (editor: John Weir Close), July 1994, 11.
20. David Marcus, "Leo Strine's Marvelous Adventures," *The Deal,* September 26, 2008.
21. Susan Beck, "Tell Us How You Really Feel, Leo," *American Lawyer,* March 2012.
22. John Weir Close, "Justice Denied," *Corporate Control Alert* (editor: John Weir Close), June 1994, 16.
23. Ibid.
24. Beck, "Tell Us How You Really Feel, Leo."
25. Interview with Stuart Shapiro (Shapiro Forman Allen & Sava), January 9, 2013.
26. Marcus, "Leo Strine's Marvelous Adventures."
27. *Hollinger v. Black* (Del. Ct. Ch. 2004), 4.
28. Jennifer Reingold, "Fall and Rise of Ilan Reich," *Fortune,* June 8, 2007.
29. Ibid.
30. Ibid.
31. John Rothchild, *Going for Broke* (New York: Simon & Schuster, 1991) 192, 193.
32. Georgia Dullea, "Poufs May Be Out, but Everybody Loves Campeau," *New York Times,* September 9, 1988.
33. Carol Loomis, "The Biggest Looniest Deal Ever," *Fortune,* June 18, 1990.
34. National Film Board of Canada and CTV Television Network, *Double or Nothing: The Rise and Fall of Robert Campeau,* dir. Paul Cowan, docudrama, 1992, at 56 min, 05 sec.
35. Ibid., 15 min, 39 sec.
36. Brian Burrough and John Helyar, *Barbarians at the Gate: The Fall of RJR Nabisco* (New York: Harper Business, 1990), 159.
37. National Film Board of Canada CTV Television Network, *Double or Nothing,* 28 min, 03 sec.

INDEX

Kramer Levin Naftalis & Frankel LLP,
      155–6, 159
Kravis, Henry, 103, 184–5, 190, 200–2
Krim, Arthur, 165–6, 169

labor unions, 69–71, 81, 84–9
Lachmann, Esther (La Païva), 258–9
Lambert, William, 136
Lawrence, Jeffrey, 239
Lazard Frères, 98, 102, 106, 112, 131–2,
      175–6, 189–91, 200, 202, 209, 233, 256
Lederman, Larry, 28–9, 184, 197, 299, 222,
      224, 226–7
Lehman Brothers, 53, 98, 102, 138, 164,
      203, 242–3, 285
Lemper, Ute, 12–13
Lenox Inc., 51
Lerner, Jonathan, 229
LeVan, David, 232, 237
Levin, Jerry, 243–4
Levine, Dennis, 98, 222–9
Levinson, Lawrence, 205
Levy, Jack, 164
Liedtke, J. Hugh, 175–9
Lifland, Judge Burton, 170–1, 173
Liman, Arthur, 98, 104–5, 106, 182, 204
Lipton, Marty, 94, 98, 105–6, 120, 175–6,
      232–3
   background of, 9
   and Flom, 8–9, 11
   and Household International, 61–7
   and poison pills, 49, 51–2, 61–3, 66, 110
   and Reich, 34, 223–5, 229
   and St. Joe Minerals, 22–30, 50, 261
Live and Let Die (film), 256–7
Loeb, Daniel S., 262
Loomis, Bill, 98, 106
Loomis, Carol J., 136–7, 284
Lord, Shirley, 123, 126
Lorenzo, Frank, 69–73, 80, 83–8
Lutolf, Franz, 176
Lynch, Gary, 219

MacAndrews & Forbes, 107, 112–15
Macioce, Thomas, 133, 135
MacKay, Charles, 161
Macmillan Inc., 176, 184–202, 206
Macy's, 2, 132, 138, 140–1, 154, 170, 266
Madoff, Bernie, 96, 170
Madonna, 20, 37, 167
Malone, John, 176, 182, 213, 215, 217

Manes, Donald, 199
Marcus, David, 272
Margin Call (film), 19
Mastandrea, James, 264
Maxwell, Robert, 184–5, 188, 190–1,
      193–202
Maxwell Communication Corporation
      PLC (MCC), 194–6, 200–1
May Department Stores, 136–8
McCurdy, Charles, 188
McEntire, Reba, 168
McFadden, Cynthia, 11
McGinty, Judge Timothy, 263–4, 268
MCI Communications, 231, 237–42
McNamara, Robert, 80
McNeilly, Justice John J., 106
Mehle, Aileen, 98
Meier, Bernie, 222
mergers and acquisitions (M&A)
   defined, 5–6
   future of, 256–68
   Tulane conference, 51, 61, 257–8, 262,
      265, 271–5, 277, 279
   See also specific firms and companies
Mermaids (film), 166, 172–3
Merrill Lynch, 16, 18–19, 132, 164, 177,
      219–20
Metromedia, 41, 119–22, 169–74
Meyers, William H., 190–1
Milken, Michael, 37–41, 95, 116, 121, 222,
      252, 259
Miller, Arjay, 80
Miller, Bryan, 79
Miller, Harvey, 70
Miller, J. Irwin, 149–50, 152–4
Miller, William I., 149, 152–4
Mirvis, Ted, 236, 275
Mitchell, Mike, 9, 63, 66, 109
Moore II, Justice Andrew G. T., 64, 77–8,
      106, 109–11, 180, 191, 193, 197–9,
      202–3, 210, 257, 273–4
Moore, Roger, 256
Moran, John, 62
Moran, Terry, 11
Moran v. Household, 66, 110
Morgan Stanley, 5, 102, 132, 151, 175, 206,
      230, 233, 240, 254–5, 262
Morosky, Bob, 137
Morris, Nichols, Arsht & Tunnell, 107,
      110, 194
Moscovitz, Harry, 144